AF540612

# Dynamics of the State *and* SOCIETY IN INDIA

*Editors:*

Dr. Ajay Parmar
&
Amitabh Bhatt

**PRASHANT PUBLISHING HOUSE**
**DELHI-110094**

*Published by :*
**Prashant Publishing House**
C-34, 28 Foota Road, Gali-3,
West Karwal Nagar, Delhi-110094
Phone : 011-22963970, Mob. : 9810396373
e-mail.: prashantpublishinghouse@gmail.com

**Dynamics of the State and Society in India**



*First Published 2016*

**ISBN** 978-93-80565-63-7



---

**PRINTED IN INDIA**
Published by Mr. R.K. Jha M/s Prashant Publishing House and Published at H.S. Offset House Press, Delhi.

# Contents

*Preface* (*ix*)

SECTION-(A)
The Historical Perspective of the State in the Pre Independence Era

1. **Society and Culture during Vedic Period** 1
—Dr. Hemendra Choudhary

2. **Economic and Social Development under Mughals** 15
—Dr Naveen Chandra Gupta

3. **Mughal's Art and Architecture during the Reign of Akbar and Jahangir** 27
—Dr. Babita

4. **Religious Reform Movements in India with Special Reference to Bhakti Movement** 36
—Dr. Sanjay Kumar Singh

5. **The Impact of Colonial Rule on Social and Economic Life of India** 47
—Dr. Vandana Semalty

6. **The Impact of the British Policies on Indian Agriculture** 61
—Dr. Sukhbir Singh

7. **Administrative Reforms during the Period of Lord Cornwallis: Their Impacts on the Life of Indian Society and Economy** **76**
—Dr. Girish Kumar Singh

8. **New Administrative Structure of British Raj** **87**
—Dr. Alok Pandey

9. **The Moderate Phase of National Movement in India** **96**
—Ashish Nandwana

10. **Indian Freedom Struggle and Role of Mahatma Gandhi** **125**
—Dr. Neelam Azad

11. **Tribal Movements and Indian Freedom Struggle** **139**
—Dr. Neeraj Devi

12. **The Rise and Growth of Communalism in India** **153**
—Dr. Poonam

13. **Various Aspects of Art and Culture in Indian Society** **175**
—Dr. Mamta Singh

## SECTION-(B)
## State and Social Justice

14. **Theory and Practice of Democratic State in India** **187**
—Professor, M. M. Semwal

15. **A Historical Analysis of the Making of the Indian Constitution** **200**
—Dr. Manbir Singh

16. **The Salient Features and the Core Philosophy of the Indian Constitution** **217**
—Dr. Alka Tomar

17. **The Role of Ambedkar in the Dalit Movement of India** 232
—Dr. M. S. Ranawat

18. **Gandhi and Practice of Untouchability in India** 247
—Dr. Ajay Parmar

19. **Caste System in Indian Society with Reference to the Women** 261
—Dr. Nisha Chaudhary

20. **The Impact of Population Growth on the Development Process in India** 268
—Dr. Pankaj Kumar

21. **Human Rights: Concept, Issues and Emerging Problems** 278
—Dr. Imran Khan

22. **The Role of Political Parties and the Participation of Women in Indian Politics** 298
—Amitabh Bhatt

## Section-(C)
## Democracy at the Grassroots Level

23. **The Role and Functions of Panchayati Raj Institutions in India with Special Reference to Assam** 305
—Dr. Upendra Adhikari

24. **Panchayati Raj System after 73rd Constitutional Amendment** 320
—Dr. Prakash Dahiya

25. **Participation of Women in Panchayati Raj Institutions** 329
—Dr. Nalin Singh Panwar

26. **E-Governance and Rural Development** 340
—Dr. Ved Prakash Joshi

27. **Secularism, Caste and Communal Violence in Indian Perspective** 352
—Dr. Nalin Singh Panwar

28. **The Role of NGO's in the Implementation of Integrated Rural Development Programme** 363
—Sandeep Kumar Poswal

29. **Agricultural Reforms in Indian Economic Sector: Dimensions, Concerns and Reform Process** 379
—Sarshti Gupta

30. **Globalization and Its Impact on Tribal's** 389
—Dr. Dushyant Kumar

31. **Tokenism to Pro-activism: Decentralisation of Disaster Management and Panchayati Raj Institutions in India** 395
—Dr. Radhanath Tripathy

# Preface

Over the centuries and ages the society of India has undergone tremendous changes as the country has witnessed the rules of many dynasties, monarchies and emperors. The present work attempts to discuss in a nutshell the changes which our country has witnessed both at the state level and at the societal level right from the ancient times to the modern times.

The contributors to this volume have tried to analyse the various aspects of the changes critically and at depth including the various arenas of the state and society which have been influenced over the ages. In order to study and classify the various changes we found it more convenient to divide the articles appearing in this book in three broad categories.

The first section titled 'The Historical Perspective of the State in the Pre Independence Era' contains a number of thought provoking articles encompassing the Vedic times to the present times. The various contributors have thrown light on wide ranging topics including the Mughal art and architecture, religious reforms, agricultural policies and administrative reforms in the British Raj, the rise and growth of communalism and the aspects of art and culture in the society of that time. Under the second section of the book we have endeavoured to throw light upon the various aspects of the State and Social Justice. The article under this category the historical aspects of the process of development of the Indian Constitution, its core philosophy, the influence of Ambedkar on it and the his contribution to the Dalit movement of India, caste system of India, human rights issues and the women's representation in the Indian political system. The concluding section of the book focuses on the functioning of the democracy at the grass roots level in the post independence period. The various articles included in this section study at depth the Panchayati Raj system, its evolution and functioning, the e-governance with reference to the rural development. An article in this category also discuss the banking system of India while another is devoted to the study of impact of globalization of the tribal development.

We hope that the present work would contribute towards a better understanding of the State and Society of Indian in the contemporary context.

*—Dr. Ajay Parmar & Amitabh Bhatt*

# 1

# Society and Culture during Vedic Period

**DR. HEMENDRA CHOUDHARY**
*Assistant Professor, Department of History and Culture, Janardan Rai Nagar, Rajasthan Vidyapeeth (Deemed University), Udaipur, Rajasthan*

## VEDIC SOCIETY

Vedic texts reveal to the posterity the existence of an advanced civilisation, quite unlike the urban civilisation of the Harappan people. Vedic civilisation concerns a nomadic rural people with an agricultural economy within the bounds of an organised society.

The motto of Vedic life style can be summarized in the dictum-simple living and high thinking. The Aryans preferred to lead a simple life determined by intellectually higher and nobler thoughts. Therefore, their social life was highly ethical and moralistic, for which they hated evil and bad habits. Anything beyond the written code of conduct was abhorred.

Their simple way of living is reflected in the pastoral character of the society. It centred around a tightly-knit village life. The Vedic Aryans preferred the simplicity of rural family settings, unlike the urban flourishes of Harappa.

The members of the family were attached to each other with a strong bond of love, affection and attachment. Their simple, unassuming and non- materialistic life style manifested itself in various aspects of their social life.

## SOCIAL LIFE IN VEDIC PERIOD

### Family

The family was regarded as the social and political unit. It was the nucleus of the social life of the early Aryans. The father was the head of the family and he was known as "grihapati". The Aryans had joint families. The father had great authority over the children. Though the father was kind and affectionate yet at times he became cruel towards his children. From Rig-Veda we come to know about a father who blinded his son for his extravagance.

Family was the pivot of the Vedic society. The Vedic Aryans had developed a very healthy family chain. Kula (literally meaning a unitary family) was the smallest unit, which included all members living under one single roof (otherwise called griha).

The social organisation of the Vedic period was based on patriarchal system. The father dominated the family. He was known as kulapa, kulapati or grihapati. Father had the final say in all family matters. He used to pass on his authority to the eldest son. So the birth of a son in a family was considered to be an absolute necessity.

The system of joint family was a very important feature of the Vedic society. Besides the husband and his wife, the family consisted of other members like their parents, brothers, sisters, sons, daughters etc.

Generally the relation among the members was very cordial. The spirit of mutual help and cooperation was a great factor behind the existence of strong familial bond. Sometimes, however, disputes over property related to land, cattle, ornaments etc. did crop up among the members of a family and led to the breakup of the same. But such cases were exceptions rather than the rule.

## Position of Women

In the early Vedic age women enjoyed an honored place in the society. The wife was the mistress of the household and authority over the slaves. In all religious ceremonies she participated with her husband. Prada system was not prevalent in the society. Sati system was also not prevalent in the Vedic society.

The education of girls was not neglected. The Rig-Veda mentions the names of some learned ladies like Viswavara, Apala and Ghosa who composed mantras and attained the rank of Rishis. The girls were married after attaining puberty. The practice of 'Swayamvara' was also prevalent in the society. Monogamy was the general Practice.

Polygamy was, of course, practiced and it was confined only to Rings and chiefs. Remarriage of widows was permitted. The women were not independent persons in the eye of the law. They had to remain under the protecting care of their male relations.

## Dress and Ornaments

The Aryans wore dresses made from cotton, wool and deer skin. The garments consisted of three parts—an undergarment called 'nivi', a garment called 'Vasa' or 'Paridhan' and a mantle known as 'adhivasa', 'atka' 'dropi'. The garments were also embroidered with gold. Both men and women wore gold ornaments.

The women used ear-rings, neck-lace, bangles, anklets. These ornaments were sometimes studded with precious stones. Both men and women oiled and combed their hair which war plaited or braided. The men kept beard and moustache but sometimes also shaved them.

## Food and Drink

The Aryans ate both vegetable and animal foods. Rice, barley, bean and sesamum formed the staple food. They also ate bread, cake, milk, ghee, butter, and curd together with fruits. Fish, birds, goats, rams, bulls and horses were slaughtered for their food. Slaughter of cow was prohibited. They also drank intoxicating liquor, known as sura, a brandy made from corn and barley and the juice of soma plant.

The Vedic Aryans were very simple in their habits of eating. Their diet was both balanced and enriching. They were both herbivores and carnivores. Wheat, barley, rice, fruits and vegetables comprised their main diet. Milk and milk products like curd, cheese, butter and ghee were quite favorite among the Vedic Aryans. On festive occasions and social gatherings, they preferred non-vegetarian dishes of mutton, sheep, fish and birds. The drinking water of the Aryans used to be drawn from rivers, streams and wells. The Vedas give reference to some intoxicating drinks like somarasa and sura. These specially prepared liquors were usually consumed during festivals and religious occasions of sacrifice. Hence, these beverages were considered sacred by the Aryans. Somarasa was a type of liquor extracted from Soma plant and other wines were prepared from different corns. In spite of these beverages, in general, the food and drink habits of the Vedic Aryans were quite simple and wholesome.

## Amusements

Rig Vedic people spent their leisure time in various amusements like gambling, war—dancing, chariot racing, hunting, boxing, dancing and music. Women displayed their skill in dancing and music. Three types of musical instruments like percussion, string and wind were used by the singers.

## Knowledge of Medicine

The Vedic Aryans had sufficient knowledge about plants and herbs having medicinal qualities. There were Vedic physicians who used to prepare curative medicines. At times they also performed some preliminary surgical operations. Miraculous cures were attributed to Ashiwini Kumars – the divine doctors who were great healers of fatal diseases.

In general, the social life of the Vedic Aryans was highly developed and disciplined. They maintained a high degree of morality in their conduct. Simple food and dress habits, happy family life, education as builder of character, high position of women, absence of social complexities like caste system etc. had brought about a value-based society. The result was a peaceful, contented, healthy and refined social life in the early Vedic period. However, the high standard of social life was lost with the march of time. Social and religious norms and practices became more rigid and complex in the later Vedic age. Various social evils like caste system, degradation in the position of women, consequent curtailing of their freedom and many other social taboos and customs destroyed the very lofty ideals of Vedic life. The openness of the Vedic fabric of life gave way to a confined system and a general degradation set in with the advancement of age.

## Morality

The morals of women were of high standard. But the standard of morality of men was not very praiseworthy. Polygamy was practiced by men. Great respect and affection was shown to guests. The people hated seduction and adultery. There was a class of women known as hetairai and dancing girls whose morality was probably not above reproach.

## Education

In the Rig-Vedic age great importance was given to education. There were Gurukulas which imparted education to the disciples after their sacred-thread ceremony. Entire instruction was given orally. The Vedic education aimed at proper development of mind and body. The disciples were taught about ethics, art of warfare, art of metal and concept of Brahma and philosophy, and basic sciences like agriculture, animal husbandry, and handicrafts.

Education on different branches of knowledge like ethics, grammar, philosophy, religion, warfare etc. was given to the pupils to put into practice their motto of simple living and high thinking. Vedic education was knowledge-oriented. It is mainly due to the laborious and systematic way of imparting such knowledge that a huge mass of Vedic literature has been saved for posterity.

## Caste System

In the early Vedic age there was no caste system. Member of same family took to different arts, crafts and trades. People could change their occupation according to their needs or talents. There was hardly any restriction in intermarriage, change of occupation. There, was no restriction on taking of food cooked by the sudras.

A late hyman of the Rig-Veda known as Purushasukta refers to four castes. But many scholars reject the theory that caste system existed in Rig Vedic age. According to them Purushasukta is a late hymen and caste system was never rigid and hereditary.

## Vedic Religion

The origin of Hinduism can be traced to the Vedas which depict the Divine Truth revealed by the rishis and sages in their state of supernormal consciousness. The heart of the Vedic culture was their religion which manifested itself with the chanting of Vedic mantras.

## Nature Worship

The religion of the Vedic people was very simple in nature. The Aryans led pastoral life and spent their time amid the bounties of nature. The towering peaks of the mountains, vast green fields, boundless seas encircling the land on three sides, the splendor of changing seasons all these produced a purifying effect on them.

These lustrous natural phenomena inspired the Vedic Aryans to worship nature with awe and reverence. They were conscious of both the creative and destructive aspects of natural forces. So they wanted to please these forces to receive their blessings and keep away their wrath and destruction. The "Vedic gods worshipped by the Aryans were generally personified powers of nature. These gods can be classified into three categories corresponding to three orders.

Following are the gods of the three orders:

1. Terrestrial sphere (Prithvi sthana)—Prithui, Agni, Soma, Brihaspati and the rivers.
2. Intermediate sphere (Antariksha sthana)—Indra, Apam-napad, Vayu-vata, Parjanya, Apah, Matarisvan.

3. Celestial sphere (Dyu sthana)—Dyaus, Varuna, Mitva, Suiya, Pushan, Vishnu, Aditya, Usha, Ashvini.

This classification is founded on the basis of natural forces that the deities represent. Hence, such a division is quite practical and is least open to objection. All the gods worshipped by the Aryans numbered thirty-three divided into the above three groups.

The gods are described to have been born, though not simultaneously, but are immortal, unlike human beings. In appearance, however, they are humans, though sometimes they are conceived as having figures of animals. For example, Dyaus appears as a bull and Surya as a swift horse. These gods usually travel in the air by chariots driven by steeds and occasionally by other animals.

Human food articles like milk, grain, flesh etc. becomes the food of the gods when offered during sacrifice. On the whole, the Aryan gods were benevolent. But some of them had malevolent traits like Rudra (Fire) and Marut (Air or Wind). Splendor, strength, knowledge and truth were common attributes of the deities. It was the firm belief of the Aryans that gods subdued forces of evil, regulated the natural and social order, rewarded the righteous and punished the sinner.

## VEDIC CULTURE

The Vedic period has been broadly classified into two categories: the Early and Later Vedic Periods. This has been done according to the way the transition in the style of culture and society took place. The Vedic period society developed rapidly as time passed by. In Vedic age, culture and society developed from the crude form to the refined form as more and more people came to settle and started to contribute their own ideas to reform the society. With the development in society & culture during Vedic era, historians had to divide the era according to the developments.

### Society and Culture in Early Vedic Period

Society in the early Vedic period was basically semi nomadic in nature as people were still learning to settle permanently. They did settle on small patches of land, but moved as soon as the resources over there were depleting. They started to domesticate wild animals and train them as farm animals. As the population in these semi-nomadic groups increased, they settled permanently as moving with a large group was next to impossible. They then started to do farming on a large scale and resorted to full time farming. Their culture was that of a typical tribe. They had a tribal chief who was the governing head of the tribe. He was helped by a group of wise and experienced men in performing his duties.

## Society and Culture in Later Vedic Period

The society in the later Vedic period increased in size as people began to live in large settlements that had all facilities for the people. The size of the agricultural fields grew in size. During this time, kingship evolved into the hereditary form in which the son of a ruling chief gets the throne after the chief. The priestly class developed and occupied the highest position in the society. Another significant development during the later Vedic age was that of the caste division of the society. The society was divided into four castes namely Brahmanas, Kshatriyas, Vaishyas and Shudras. The Brahmanas were the priestly class who occupied the highest position in the society. The Kshatriyas were the warriors; the Vaishyas were the service class like businessmen and peasants. The Shudras were the lowest class of people who did jobs like removing garbage, cleaning up, etc.

## VEDIC CULTURE / HINDUISM

When it comes to Vedic culture, more popularly known as Hinduism, many people find it difficult or impossible to define it in a concise or adequate manner. It differs quite a bit from the conventional and western monotheistic religions with which many people are familiar. Hinduism is pluralistic. In other words, it does not claim any one prophet or savior; it includes all aspects of God; it does not subscribe to any one philosophy or dogma; it includes various schools of thought and ways of understanding spiritual Truth; it includes a variety of religious rites or sacraments; it does not exclude any particular scripture that can help a person understand more about God and spiritual Truth; and it does not say that you have only one life in which to become spiritually perfect or you will go to eternal damnation. Thus, Vedic philosophy is more of a way of living and an outlook on life than a religion.

Because of this, Hinduism and the path of Vedic culture includes a variety of customs, ideas, and philosophies. It accommodates a wide range of approaches for allowing people to advance and understand our spiritual identity and transcendental Truth. It allows everyone to question the scriptures to increase one's understanding, and recognizes no single person or prophet as having an exclusive claim over the Absolute Truth. Everyone can follow a system of realization to approach God since this is everyone's right and destiny. This flexibility is one of the reasons why Vedic culture has continued over so many thousands of years.

This is also why many variations of philosophical thought or schools of religion can be viewed as branches or tributaries of the same great river of *sanatana-dharma,* which is the universal spiritual knowledge and practice that is the essential teachings of the Vedic literature. Such spiritual knowledge can be recognized in many forms of religion or their scripture.

Because of this, it also means that no one is excluded or excommunicated from the Hindu or Vedic philosophy. There are no heretics, but there is room for everyone and respect for all who are practicing its basic principles of spiritual pursuit and understanding. This is also one reason why Hindus generally get along with other religions, though there have been many who have taken unfair advantage of their amiable nature.

So Vedic culture is not an organized religion like Christianity or Islam. It has no single founder. It has no Pope. It has no hierarchy, though people do recognize particular spiritual authorities or gurus. It also has a lot of scriptures. And in some of these Vedic scriptures you are actually studying the history and culture of India, just as through the 66 books of the Holy Bible you are actually studying the culture and history of the Jews.

Hinduism and Judaism are the sources of all modern religions in the world. Buddhism, Sikhism and to some extent Jainism and Zoroastrianism were outgrowths from Hinduism. Of course, Jainism existed during the period of the *Rig Veda*. Statues of Rishabha, the first Thirthankara and founder of Jainism was found in the Mohenjadaro and Harappa excavations. Islam and Christianity came from Judaism. Judaism, Islam and Christianity have Abraham as the common father figure. All three have many common prophets.

C.S. Lewis, the great author and theologist accurately explained, "Finally it will come to two religions. Hinduism and Christianity. The first [Hinduism] will grow absorbing ideas and concepts from everywhere and later [Christianity] will keep away from everything that is foreign to it." This is one reason why Hinduism has continued for thousands of years and cannot be destroyed, even if we burn every Vedic scripture and kill every Hindu theologian on earth. Hinduism or Vedic culture is a very dynamic, living, breathing Reality. The strength of Hinduism lies in its most amazing ability to adapt to different circumstances and different ages while maintaining its strong continuity with the past.

## Respect For Individual Freedom Of Inquiry

It is for this reason, as stated above, that the Vedic culture is wonderfully catholic, elastic and even democratic. It provides the epitome of the individual's right for self inquiry and spiritual pursuit. It is this reason that it also maintains a liberal amount of tolerance and unlimited freedom for one's own method of private worship. It is, after all, up to the individual to carry on with one's own spiritual progress. Everything else in the Vedic system is for his or her assistance. It is not meant for being a religious dogma or to stifle or control, though it does expect one to stay within the laws of the land and ride the high ground of morality and spiritual discipline.

It is also because of this tolerance and mutual respect that you find Hinduism, Islam, Christianity, Buddhism, and even Zoroastrianism, Jainism, Sikhism, and the Parsis all accepting the shelter of life in India. India also allows all of the various sects of Islam to exist, whereas no other Islamic nation provides for such freedom within its own religion.

It is merely the fanaticism that comes from the fundamental and monotheistic religions that have sparked the majority of violence that has been seen in India and throughout the world. It is also the ways of the various monotheistic religions and their conversion tactics that have encroached on the culture and land of the Hindus that have made Hindus view them with suspicion, and be less than welcoming in some areas of the country. It has made them to be more protective of their culture, taking up various means of defense that has been called communalism or saffronization by the so-called secular media. Yet, Hindus cannot be expected to humble themselves out of their own existence. Hindus make lousy terrorists, and they will not be such. But they also do not need to be the doormat of every other religion that wants another part of India.

So, if left to themselves, Hindus and the followers of Vedic culture will continue to be one of the largest shelters for the greatest number of diverse religious groups there can be. It will continue to be a most tolerant, liberal, and respectful system of spiritual development, without the usual violence and persecution toward "non-believers" that seems to be the attendant of so many other less tolerant, monotheistic religions. It is this inherent acceptance of the right of the individual to proceed in the spiritual quest that is most suitable for him or her that separates the Vedic process from most other religions on the planet.

## The Goal Of The Vedic Process

There is both long term and short term goals.

The Long-Term Goal: The ultimate goal of the Vedic process is *moksha,* or liberation and the release from *samsara,* or the continuous cycles of birth and death, otherwise called reincarnation. This liberation is the position of the soul when it regains or reawakens its spiritual consciousness to the fullest extent. When one's consciousness is purified or completely spiritualized, and when the soul has regained its spiritual position and completely acts on that level, then there is no more need to take birth in a material body for the pursuit of material desires. One then enters back into the spiritual world, which is the natural home of the spirit soul, when the finite living entity returns to the Infinite.

The Vedic concept of salvation is different from that of the Christians. Hindu salvation is known as Self Realization and rising above ignorance. In Vedic philosophy, salvation or liberation means that a person realizes that he is not the body, but the immortal soul (*Atman*) within. That is the reason why Hindu salvation is known as Self-Realization or realizing that one is the Immortal self and not the perishable body. This realization is the means of rising above the illusion that keeps us from being free. Real freedom on the Vedic path is freedom from material and sensual desires. Such desire is the basis of what keeps us bound up in earthly existence and in *samsara.*

The Vedic system includes various processes in order to assist the living being to attain this freedom. According to the position and consciousness of the person, he or she may be interested in different processes, though some are more highly recommended in this present age. These may include the process of *Jnana* (knowledge), *Vijnana* (realized knowledge), Hatha-yoga (the practice of keeping the body in shape for ultimately pursuing the perception of spiritual consciousness), Yoga (the process for altering and uplifting the consciousness, which may include separate or individual practices), and *Bhakti* (the process of devotion in which attaining the Grace of God is the main focus). Each one of these systems or divisions deserves its own description to fully understand them, some of which will be summarized later in this introduction.

So Hinduism/Vedic culture takes it for granted that there is more than one approach to understand different levels of spiritual Truth and attain salvation, and that these different approaches are not only compatible with each other, but are also complimentary. Thus, the disagreements that you find in most conventional and monotheistic religions, and the friction between the various sects that often develop, are not so much a part of the Vedic culture, even though individual preferences may exist.

This is also why, generally speaking, many Hindus will respect all religions. They may be initiated by a Vedic guru, devoutly practice yoga, attend the temple regularly, yet still go to see some Christian preacher, or Buddhist teacher, or even hear an Islamic Imam talk about God. They may do this with the idea of attaining new insights, yet still not consider themselves falling away from their own path or converting to a different religion. Yet, if a Christian or Muslim would do such a thing as participate in an alternative religion, or even a separate sect, they may be considered sinful and apostates, or at least hypocrites deserving of some punishment. But such narrow-mindedness hardly touches the person following the Vedic path.

The Short-Term Goal is to find happiness. By understanding our spiritual identity, we also become free from the day to day turmoil and hassles that many people take so seriously. Some people let such problems control their lives. Life is too short for that. Allowing such circumstantial difficulties to increase our stress and anxiety only decreases our duration of life. Life is meant for being happy. But real happiness, which exists on the spiritual platform, is always steady and, in fact, is continually increasing according to one's spiritual advancement. Such persons who understand their spiritual identity and are self-satisfied and content within themselves find happiness everywhere. This is what the Vedic process tries to give everyone.

The *Chandogya Upanishad* (starting at 7.25.2) explains that he who perceives and understands this, loves the self, revels, rejoices, and delights in the self. Such a person is lord and master of the worlds because he has already attained all that he needs. He knows that he may be in this material world but is not of it. He is actually of the spiritual world and has regained his connection with it. Therefore, he looks at this world as if he were simply a tourist. He sees all the busy activities of people and society, the confusion, but he walks through it all unaffected. But those who think differently live in perishable worlds and have other mortal beings as their rulers. They are limited and controlled by their own material designations. But he who sees the soul of everyone, the spiritual identity beyond the body, does not see death, nor illness, nor pain; he who sees this sees everything and obtains everything everywhere. This certainly is the quality of those who have attained their own internal, self-sufficient happiness. A similar verse is found in the *Katha Upanishad* (2.5.12-13) where it says that those who have realized their self and also see the Supreme Being residing within their heart and in all beings as the Superself, to them belongs eternal happiness and eternal peace, but not to others.

The original spiritual form of the living being is *sac-cid-ananda*: eternal, full of knowledge, and full of bliss. The living being's spiritual form is never limited by the body or one's situation. The only limiting factor is the living being's consciousness or lack of spiritual awareness. When the living entity, after many births, finally regains his original spiritual consciousness, realizing he is not the body, he naturally feels very happy and jolly, being freed from the limited and temporary perspective one has while being controlled by the illusory, material energy. He also understands that this material world is not his real home, and it has nothing substantial to offer him since real pleasure and happiness actually come from within on the spiritual level. As stated in *Bhagavad-gita* by Lord Sri Krishna: "One who is thus transcendentally situated at once realizes the Supreme Brahman and becomes fully joyful. He never laments nor desires to have anything; he is equally disposed to every living entity. In that state he attains pure devotional service to Me." (*Bg*.18.54)

In this way, "The yogi whose mind is fixed on Me [Lord Sri Krishna] verily attains the highest happiness. By virtue of his identity with Brahman [the absolute spiritual nature], he is liberated; his mind is peaceful, his passions are quieted, and he is freed from sin. Steady in the Self, being freed from all material contamination, the yogi achieves the highest perfectional stage of happiness in touch with the Supreme Consciousness." (*Bg*.6.27-28)

"Such a liberated soul is not attracted to material sense pleasure or external objects but is always in trance, enjoying the pleasure within. In this way the self-realized person enjoys unlimited happiness, for he concentrates on the Supreme." (*Bg*.5.21)

This happiness, therefore, is the goal of all people, and is the highest level of happiness which is attained when one understands his or her true spiritual identity and becomes spiritually Self-realized.

## The Correct Name For Hinduism Is Sanatana-dharma

It is generally accepted that it was the Persians who invaded India during the 6th century B.C. who gave the name "Hindu" for a society of people who lived in a certain region of India near the Sindhu river, later known as the Indus river. In Persian, the letter H and S are pronounced almost the same so they mistook the S in the word Sindhu as H and then started calling the people Hindus and their religion as Hinduism. Thus, the name is actually a misnomer since there are many schools of thought and views of God within the umbrella term of Hinduism, each with its own specific name.

Dr. Radhakrishnan has also observed about the name Hindu: "The Hindu civilization is so called since its original founders or earliest followers occupied the territory drained by the Sindhu (the Indus) river system corresponding to the North West Frontier Province and the Punjab. This is recorded in the *Rig Veda*, the oldest of the *Vedas*, the Hindu scripture which gives their name to this period of Indian history. The people on the Indian side of the Sindhu were called Hindu by the Persian and the later western invaders." This indicates that the name is not based on religion or theocracy, but is merely a name based on the particular locality of a people. This could also mean that numerous people, even tribals of India, Dravidians, or even the Vedic Aryans are all Hindus. Again, in this way, Hinduism can accommodate different communities, rites, various gods and practices.

Other originations of the word *Hindu* may be given, but they all essentially show that it was a name indicating a locality of a society, and it had nothing to do with the religion, philosophy, or way of life of the people. This is why some followers of *Sanatana-dharma* or Vedic culture do not care to use the name Hindu, including gurus, to describe their spiritual path, even though it is based on the Vedic system.

The more correct term for the Vedic process is the Sanskrit word *Sanatana-dharma*. This is a path and a realization. *Sanatana-dharma* means the eternal nature of the living being. Just as the *dharma* of sugar is sweetness, and the *dharma* of fire is to burn and give warmth, the spiritual being also has a *dharma*. That*dharma* is to serve and love, and that love ultimately is meant to be the relationship between the living being and God and all other living entities. When that love and spiritual realization is attained, then the living being regains his natural Divinity. To attain this stage, one can follow the path of *dharma*. Thus, *dharma* is also a code of conduct. This, however, is not a dogma or forced standard, but it is a natural training that brings people to a higher level of consideration and consciousness. Thus, the whole of society can develop in this refined manner to a higher level of awareness and understanding of our connection with each other, with nature, and with God.

The *Manu-samhita* recommends the following characteristics to be developed. These include fortitude, forgiveness, self control, non-envy, purity, sense control, the ability to discriminate between good and evil, learning, truthfulness, and absence of anger. So we can imagine how much nicer the world could be if everyone developed these qualities. So *Sanatana-dharma* is also the path to attain our natural spiritual qualities.

*Dharma* also means the natural laws that sustain and hold together the whole universe. So *dharma* is also that which brings harmony and unity, because that is how the universe, along with society in general, is maintained and preserved. In this way, *Sanatana-dharma* is also the path that allows the individual to realize his or her spiritual position and true identity, and also brings the ultimate stage of harmony and balance to each person, to society, and to the whole planet. This is the Vedic process. It is thus a Universal Truth in that it can be applied anywhere in the universe and at any time in history, to any people or culture, and it will produce the same results for all. This brings us to our next point.

## References

Aiyar, R. Krishnaswami: *Outlines of Vedaanta*, Chetana, Bombay, 1978.

Bagchi, P. C.: *Studies in Dharmashastra*, University of Calcutta Press, Calcutta, 1939.

Bahadur, K.P.: *The Wisdom of Vedaanta*, Sterling Publishers Private Limited, New Delhi, 1996.

Banerjea, J. N.: *Pauranic and Vedanta Religion*, University of Calcutta, Calcutta, 1996.

Bhattacharyya, B.: *Nispannayogavali of Mahapandita Abhyakara Gupta*, Oriental Institute, Baroda, 1949.

Brockington, J. L.: *Righteous Rama: The Evolution of an Epic*, Oxford, London, 1984.

De Bary: *Self and Society in Ming Thought*, Columbia University Press, New York, 1970.

Gurumurthy, S. : *Hindu Heritage, Assimilative, Not Divisive*, Vigil, Madras 1993.

2

# Economic and Social Development under Mughals

**DR NAVEEN CHANDRA GUPTA**
*Assistant Professor, Department of History, N.A.S. (P .G.) College, Meerut, Uttar Pradesh*

It was the normal policy of the Timurid rulers, both in their original Central Asian homelands and in India, to encourage trade. As in much else, Sher Shah Suri during his brief reign (1538–1545) set a pattern that was followed by the later Mughals, especially Akbar, when he encouraged trade by linking together various parts of the country through an efficient system of roads and abolishing many inland tolls and duties. The Mughals maintained this general policy, but their rule was distinguished by the importance which foreign trade attained by the end of the sixteenth century. This was partly the result of the discovery of the new sea-route to India; but even so, progress would have been limited if conditions within the country had not been favourable.

## TRADE AND INDUSTRY

Both Akbar and Jahangir interested themselves in the foreign seaborne trade, and Akbar himself took part in commercial activities for a time. The Mughals welcomed the foreign trader, provided ample protection and security for his transactions, and levied a very low custom duty (usually no more than 2½ percent ad valorem). Furthermore, the expansion of local handicrafts and industry resulted in a reservoir of exportable goods. Indian exports consisted mainly of manufactured articles, with cotton cloth in great demand in Europe and elsewhere. Indigo, saltpeter, spices, opium, sugar, woolen and silk cloth of various kinds, yarn, asafoetida, salt, beads, borax, turmeric, lac, sealing wax, and drugs of various kinds, were also exported. The principal imports were bullion, horses, and a certain quantity of luxury goods for the upper classes, like raw silk, coral, amber, precious stones, superior textiles (silk, velvet, brocade, broadcloth), perfumes, drugs, china goods, and European wines. By and large, however, in return for their goods Indian merchants insisted on payment in gold or silver. Naturally this was not popular in England and the rest of Europe, and writers on economic affairs in the seventeenth century frequently complained, as did Sir Thomas Roe, that "Europe bleedeth to enrich Asia." The demand for articles supplied by India was so great, however, and her requirements of European goods so limited, that Europe was obliged to trade on India's own terms until the eighteenth century, when special measures were taken in England and elsewhere to discourage the demand for Indian goods.

The manufacture of cotton goods had assumed such extensive proportions that in addition to satisfying her own needs, India sent cloth to almost half the world: the east coast of Africa, Arabia, Egypt, Southeast Asia, as well as Europe. The textile industry, well established in Akbar's day, continued to flourish under his successors, and soon the operations of Dutch and English traders brought India into direct touch with Western markets. This resulted in great demand for Indian cotton goods from Europe, which naturally increased production at home. Even the silk industry—especially in Bengal—was in flourishing condition. Bernier wrote: "There is in Bengal such a quantity of cotton and silk, that the kingdom may be called the common storehouse for these two kinds of merchandise, not of Hindoustan or the Empire of the Great Mogol only, but of all the neighbouring kingdoms, and even of Europe."

Apart from silk and cotton textiles, other industries were shawl and carpet weaving, woollen goods, pottery, leather goods, and articles made of wood. Owing to its proximity to sources of suitable timbers, Chittagong specialized in shipbuilding, and at one time supplied ships to distant Istanbul. The commercial side of the industry was in the hands of middlemen, but the Mughal government, like the earlier sultans, made its own contribution. The emperor controlled a large number of royal workshops, busily turning out articles for his own use, for his household, for the court, and for the imperial army. Akbar took a special interest in the development of indigenous industry. He was directly responsible for the expansion of silk weaving at Lahore, Agra, Fathpur-Sikri, and in Gujarat. He opened a large number of factories at important centers, importing master weavers from Persia, Kashmir, and Turkistan. Akbar frequently visited the workshops near the palace to watch the artisans at work, which encouraged the craftsmen and raised their status. It is said that he took such an interest in the industry that to foster demand he "ordered people of certain ranks to wear particular kinds of locally woven coverings ... an order which resulted in the establishment of a large number of shawl manufactories in Lahore; and inducements were offered to foreign carpet-weavers to settle in Agra, Fathepur Sikri, and Lahore, and manufacture carpets to compete with those imported from Persia." In the course of time, the foreign traders established close contracts with important markets in India, and new articles which were more in demand in Western Europe began to be produced in increasing quantities. Among the foreign inventions that excited Akbar's interest was an organ, "one of the wonders of creation," that had been brought from Europe.

## URBAN LIFE

All foreign travelers speak of the wealth and prosperity of Mughal cities and large towns. Monserrate stated that Lahore in 1581 was "not second to any city in Europe or Asia." Finch, who traveled in the early days of Jahangir, found both Agra and Lahore to be much larger than London, and his testimony is supported by others. Other cities like Surat ("A city of good quantity, with many fair merchants and houses therein"), Ahmadabad, Allahabad, Benares, and Patna similarly excited the admiration of visitors. The new port towns of Bombay, Calcutta, Madras, and Karachi developed under British rule, but they had their predecessors in Satgaon, Surat, Cambay, Lari Bunder, and other ports.

The efficient system of city government under the Mughals encouraged trade. The pivot of urban administration was the kotwal, the city governor. In addition to his executive and judicial powers, it was his duty to prevent and detect crime, to perform many of the functions now assigned to the municipal boards, to regulate prices, and in general, to be responsible for the peace and prosperity of the city. The efficient discharge of these duties depended on the personality of the individual city governor, but the Mughals tried to ensure high standards by making the kotwal personally responsible for the property and the security of the citizens. Akbar had decreed (probably following Sher Shah Suri's example of fixing the responsibility on village chiefs for highway robberies in their territory) that the kotwal was to either recover stolen goods or be held responsible for their loss. That this was not only a pious hope is borne out by the testimony of several foreign travelers who state that the kotwal was personally liable to make good the value of any stolen property which he was unable to recover. The kotwals often found pretexts to evade the ultimate responsibility, but in general they took elaborate measures to prevent thefts.

Most of this flourishing commerce was in the hands of the traditional Hindu merchant classes, whose business acumen was proverbial. Their caste guilds added to the skills in trade and commerce that they had learned through the centuries. Not only were their disputes settled by their panchayats, but they would frequently impose pressure on the government by organized action. Foreign visitors record that the governors and kotwals were very sensitive to this, and in spite of hardships inseparable from a despotic system of administration, the business communities had their own means of obtaining redress. Bernier, writing during Aurangzeb's time, declared that the Hindus possessed "almost exclusively the trade and wealth of the country." If Muslims enjoyed advantages in higher administrative posts and in the army, Hindu merchants maintained the monopoly in trade and finance that they had had during the sultanate. A Dutch traveler in the early seventeenth century was struck by the fact that few Muslims engaged in handicraft industries, and that even when a Muslim merchant did have a large business, he employed Hindu bookkeepers and agents. Banking was almost exclusively in Hindu hands. In the years of the decline of the Mughals, a rich Hindu banker would finance his favorite rival claimant for the throne. The role of Jagat Seth of Murshidabad in the history of Bengal is well known. Even the "war of succession" out of which Aurangzeb emerged victorious was financed by a loan of five and a half lakhs of rupees from the Jain bankers of Ahmadabad. Here one sees a contrast with British rule, when the British not only monopolized the higher civil service posts but also controlled most of the major industries as well as the great banks and trading agencies.

## RURAL CONDITIONS

Conditions in the rural areas during the Mughal period were much the same as at present, with one important difference—the Muslim rulers had scarcely disturbed the old organization of the villages. The panchayats continued to settle most disputes, with the state impinging very little on village life, except for the collection of land revenue, and even this was very often done on a village basis rather than through individuals, with the age-old arrangements being preserved. The incidence of land revenue was substantially higher under the Mughals and in Hindu states like Vijayanagar than in British India, but the administration was more flexible, both in theory and in practice, in its assessment and collection. Apart from the remission of land revenue when crops failed, there was reduction in government demand even when bumper crops caused prices to fall.

For example, between 1585 and 1590 very large sums had to be written off because a series of exceptionally good harvests had resulted in a surplus, and peasants could not sell their crops. The state also advanced loans to the cultivators, and occasionally provided seed as well as implements for digging wells. Loans advanced to the cultivators for seeds, implements, bullocks, or digging of wells were called *taqavi*—an expression which has continued in modern land revenue administration.

## Health and Medical Facilities

A feature noticed by many foreign travelers was the good health of the local inhabitants. Fryer, writing of the mortality among the English at Bombay and the adjacent parts, says that "the country people lived to a good old age, supposed to be the reward of their temperance." Bernier also speaks of "general habits of sobriety among the people," though this did not apply to a few cases among the upper classes or the royal family. The European travelers found "less vigour among the people than in the colder climates, but greater enjoyment of health." From their accounts, even the climate would appear to have been healthy. "Gout, stone complaints in the kidneys, catarrh ... are nearly unknown; and persons who arrive in the country afflicted with any of these disorders soon experience a complete cure." The Mughal emphasis on physical fitness and encouragement of out-of-door manly games also raised the general standard of health. The ideal was that everyone was to be trained to be a soldier, a good rider, a keen shikari, and able to distinguish himself in games. Ovington found that the English at Surat were "much less vigorous and athletic in their bodies than Indians." It is possible that the drinking habits of the Europeans made them an easy prey to ill-health in the tropics.

Public hospitals had been provided in Muslim India, at least since the days of Firuz Tughluq (1351–1388), and though it would be ridiculous to compare them with the arrangements introduced by the British, the system seems to have been extended during the Mughal period. Jahangir states in his autobiography that on his accession to the throne he ordered the establishment, at government expense, of hospitals in large cities. That this order was actually made effective is shown by the records of salaries paid by the government and of grants for the distribution of medicine.

The supply of local physicians was not plentiful; and judged by the demand for European doctors, particularly surgeons, they were apparently not equal to all demands. The general health of the inhabitants suggests, however, that the medical services were not completely inadequate, and the local physicians were able to deal with normal problems. As early as 1616 they knew the important characteristics of the bubonic plague and suggested suitable preventive measures.

According to an account in *Iqbal Nama*, which was written in Jahangir's reign: "When the disease was about to break out, a mouse would rush out of its hole, as if mad, and striking itself against the door and the walls of the house, would expire. If immediately after this signal the occupants left the house and went away to the jungle, their lives were safe. If otherwise, the inhabitants of the village would be spirited away by the hands of death." As modern scholars have pointed out, this observation includes two facts about the plague whose significance has been corroborated by modern science: the association of the death of rodents with the disease, and the necessity of evacuating the infected quarter.

A crude form of vaccination against smallpox seems to have been employed by Eastern doctors, for it was vaguely realized that the introduction of a mild form of cowpox prevented the virulent form of smallpox.

An article in the Asiatic Register of London for 1804 contained a translation of a memorandum by Nawab Mirza Mehdi Ali Khan describing from personal observations the method adopted by a Hindu medical practitioner of Benares. A thread drenched in "the matter of a pustule on the cow" was placed on the arms of a child to cause an easy irruption, thus avoiding a virulent attack of smallpox.

In ancient times, the use of medicines had been well developed among the Hindus, but dissection was considered to be irreligious. The Muslims, who did not have this restriction, performed a number of operations. As Elphinstone pointed out: "Their surgery is as remarkable as their medicine especially when we recollect their ignorance of anatomy. They cut for the stone, couched for the cataract, and extracted the feotus from the womb, and in their early works enunciate no less than one hundred and twenty-seven surgical works." According to Manucci, Muslim surgeons could provide artificial limbs.

## SOCIAL CUSTOMS

The marriage customs of Hindus and Muslims had many similarities. Early marriages were much in vogue amongst the Hindus, with seven considered the proper age for a girl to be married. To leave a daughter unmarried beyond twelve years of age was to risk the displeasure of one's caste. The Muslims also betrothed their children between the ages of six and eight, but the marriage was generally not solemnized before they had attained the age of puberty. Among the wealthier classes polygamy and divorce are said to have been very common.

The custom of secluding women, known as purdah, was very strictly observed. Marriage negotiations were undertaken by the professional broker or the friends of either party. The marriage ceremonies were more or less the same as they are at present, and the character of the average Indian or Pakistani home and the socio-ethical ideas which influence it have not undergone any fundamental change. The son's duty to his parents and the wife's duty to her husband were viewed almost as religious obligations. "Superstitions played a prominent part in the daily life of the people. Charms were used not merely to ensnare a restive husband but also to secure such other ends as the birth of a son or cure of a disease. The fear of the evil eye was ever present ... and the young child was considered particularly susceptible. ... People believed in all sorts of omens." Astrologers were very much in demand, even at the Mughal court.

The Muslim aristocrats lived in great houses decorated with rich hangings and carpets. Their clothing was made of finest cotton or silk, decorated with gold; and they carried beautiful scimitars. There was a considerable element of ostentatious display involved in this, however, for their domestic arrangements did not match the outward splendor of their dress and equipment. Manucci, a keen observer, refers to Pathans who came to court "well-clad and well-armed, caracolling on fine horses richly caparisoned and followed by several servants," but when they reached home, divested themselves of "all this finery, and tying a scanty cloth around their loins and wrapping a rag around their head, they take their seat on a mat, and live on ... rice and lentils or badly cooked cow's flesh of low quality, which is very abundant in the Mogul country and very cheap."

The courtly manners and the elaborate etiquette of the Muslim upper classes impressed foreign visitors. In social gatherings they spoke "in a very low voice with much order, moderation, gravity, and sweetness. ... Betel and betelnut were presented to the visitors and they were escorted with much civility at the time of departure. Rigid forms were observed at meals. ... Dice was their favourite indoor game. Polo or chaugan—for which there was a special playground at Dacca—elephant-fights, hunting, excursions and picnics, were also very popular." The grandees rode in palkis, preceded by uniformed mounted servants. Many "drove in fine two-wheeled carts, carved with gilt and gold, covered in silk, and drawn by two little bulls which could race with the fastest horses."

## THE POSITION OF THE HINDUS

The Hindu upper classes undoubtedly shared in the material culture of the Mughals, for, as already noted, they had a virtual monopoly of trade and finance. Furthermore, they had long held many high posts in the government. The contrast between the position of Hindus under the Mughals and of Indians in general under the British was often made by Indian historians during the period of the nationalist movement. Thus a Hindu historian writing in 1940 could argue that "under Shah Jahan Hindus occupied a higher status in the government than that occupied by the Indians today." The vitality of the Hindus was shown in more than their ability to maintain footholds within administrative and commercial life. Widespread religious movements, having, as we have seen, their roots partly in the vivifying contacts of Hinduism with Islam, had produced a religious enthusiasm among the masses that was transforming the older Brahmanical religion.

Although Muslim historians ignore this religious revival among the Hindus, there is enough evidence to indicate its importance during Mughal rule. The new regional literature of Bengal and Maharashtra, which owed much to the new movement, is a clear mirror of what was taking place in Hindu society. In Bengal, there was not only the rise of a new literature, but numerous temples were built during the late seventeenth century. The significance of this phenomenon becomes clear if it is remembered that practically throughout the second half of the seventeenth century, Aurangzeb was on the throne. His alleged ceaseless campaign of temple destruction obviously could have been neither thoroughgoing nor universal.

The developments in intellectual life were even more marked. The rise of Navadipa as a great center of Sanskritic learning, and the vogue of navyanyaya (new logic) belong to this period.

In relation to Islam, Hinduism exhibited a new vigor, greater self-confidence, and even a spirit of defiance. Hinduism is not generally thought of as a missionary religion, and it is often assumed that during Muslim rule conversions were only from Hinduism to Islam. This is, however, not true. Hinduism by now was very much on the offensive and was absorbing a number of Muslims. When Shah Jahan returned from Kashmir, in the sixth year of his reign, he discovered that Hindus of Bhadauri and Bhimbar were forcibly marrying Muslim girls and converting them to the Hindu faith. At death these women were cremated according to the Hindu rites. Jahangir had tried to stop this practice but with no success, and Shah Jahan also issued orders declaring such marriages unlawful. Four thousand such conversions are said to have been discovered. Many cases were also found in Gujarat and in parts of the Punjab. Partly to deal with such cases, and partly to conform to his early notions of an orthodox Muslim king, Shah Jahan established a special department to deal with conversions. After the tenth year of his reign, he seems to have ceased trying to prevent the proselytizing activities of the Hindus. There are several later cases of the conversion of Muslims, not recorded by the court historians. A number of Muslims—including at least two Muslim nobles, Mirza Salih and Mirza Haider—were converted to Hinduism by the vairagis, the wandering ascetics of the Chaitanya movement, which had become a powerful religious force in Bengal. There were also cases of conversions from Islam to Sikhism. When Guru Hargovind took up his residence at Kiratpur in the Punjab some time before 1645, he is said to have succeeded in converting a large number of Muslims. It was reported that not a Muslim was left between the hills near Kiratpur and the frontiers of Tibet and Khotan. His predecessor, Guru Arjan, had proselytized so actively that he incurred Jahangir's anger, and, as Jahangir mentions in his autobiography, the Hindu shrines of Kangra and Mathura attracted a number of Muslim pilgrims.

The Hindu position was so strong that in some places Aurangzeb's order for the collection of jizya was defied. On January 29, 1693, the officials in Malwa sent a soldier to collect jizya from a zamindar called Devi Singh. When he reached the place, Devi Singh's men fell upon him, pulled his beard and hair, and sent him back empty-handed. The emperor thereupon ordered a reduction in the jagir of Devi Singh. Earlier, another official had fared much worse. He himself proceeded to the jagir to collect the tax, but was killed by the Hindu mansabdar. Orders to destroy newly built temples met with similar opposition. A Muslim officer who was sent in 1671 to destroy temples at the ancient pilgrimage city of Ujjain was killed in a riot that broke out as he tried to carry out his orders.

Muslim historians, in order to show the extreme orthodoxy of Aurangzeb, have recorded many reports of temple destruction. On a closer scrutiny, however, there seem to be good grounds for believing that all the reports were not correct, and that quite often no action was taken on imperial orders. We read, for example, about the destruction of a certain temple at Somnath during the reign of Shah Jahan and again under Aurangzeb. It is likely that in this and in many similar cases, the temple was not destroyed on the first order. According to accounts by English merchants, Aurangzeb's officers would leave the temples standing on payment of large sums of money by the priests. However, new temples whose construction had not been authorized were often closed. If the situation is closely examined, it appears that the complaint of Shaikh Ahmad that under Muslim rule as it existed in India, Islam was in need of greater protection than other religions does not appear to have been completely unfounded. Aurangzeb tried, of course, to reverse this trend, and some other rulers also had occasional spells of Islamic zeal, either from political or religious causes. But by and large, it is perhaps fair to say that during Muslim rule, Islam suffered from handicaps which almost outweighed the advantages it enjoyed as the religion of the ruling dynasty. This paradox becomes understandable if the basic Muslim political theory is kept in mind, under which the non-Muslim communities, so long as they paid certain taxes, were left to manage their own affairs. This local and communal autonomy severely circumscribed the sovereignty of the Muslim state, and in most matters the caste guilds and the village panchayats exercised real sovereignty, which they naturally utilized to safeguard their creed and way of life. It was this power which enabled them to evade, or even defy, unwelcome orders from the capital. A curious light on the situation is thrown by the penalties and economic losses which a Hindu had to suffer on the adoption of Islam. Practically until the end of Muslim rule, a Hindu who became a Muslim automatically lost all claim to ancestral property.

This extraordinary position was a natural result of the application of Hindu law, which, according to the Muslim legal system, governed Hindu society even under Muslim government, and under which apostacy resulted in disinheritance. Shah Jahan, who began as an orthodox Muslim, tried to redress the balance by issuing orders that "family pressure should not prevent a Hindu from being admitted to Islam," and laid down that a convert should not be disinherited. Whether these orders could overcome the subtle but solid pressure of the joint family system and the power of the caste panchayats must remain a matter of speculation. The question, however, of handicaps or advantages of one community against another is not of fundamental significance. The important fact is that during normal times conditions of tolerance prevailed. This was of special interest to European visitors, almost all of whom commented on the concessions enjoyed by non-Muslims under Muslim rule. The Jesuits were critical of this policy of tolerance, declaring the destruction of Hindu temples by Muslims "a praiseworthy action," but noting their "carelessness" in allowing public performance of Hindu sacrifices and religious practices. When Akbar granted the followers of the Raushaniya sect the freedom to follow their religion, Monserrate sadly commented that "He cared little that in allowing everyone to follow his own religion he was in reality violating all religions."

Even in Aurangzeb's reign a cow could not be slaughtered in important places like Surat, and attempts made by some English merchants to obtain beef led to riots. According to one account: "In Surat the Hindus paid a fixed sum to the Mohammadans in return for sparing the cows. In 1608 a riot was caused at Surat by a drunken sailor Tom Tucker who killed a calf. Similar occurrences at Karwar and Honavar led to outbreaks, in one of which the whole factory was murdered." But nothing brings out the Mughal administration's respect for the susceptibilities of the Hindus as well as the experience of the Portuguese missionary traveler, Manrique. "In a village where he stopped for the night, one of his followers, a Musalman, killed two peacocks, birds sacred in the eyes of Hindus, and did his best to conceal the traces of his deed by burying their feathers. The sacrilege was, however, detected, the whole party arrested, and the offender sentenced to have a hand amputated, though this punishment was eventually commuted to a whipping by the local official, who explained that the emperor had taken an oath that he and his successors would let the Hindus live under their own laws and customs and tolerate no breach of them."

Although the Mughals interfered little with Hindu customs, there was one ancient practice which they sought to stop. This was sati, or the custom of widows, particularly those of the higher classes, burning themselves on their husbands' funeral pyres. Akbar had issued general orders prohibiting sati, and in one noteworthy case, personally intervened to save a Rajput princess from immolating herself on the bier of her husband. Similar efforts continued to be made in the succeeding reigns. According to the European traveler Pelsaert, governors did their best to dissuade widows from immolating themselves, but by Jahangir's orders were not allowed to withhold their sanction if the woman persisted. Tavernier, writing in the reign of Shah Jahan, observed that widows with children were not allowed in any circumstances to burn, and that in other cases governors did not readily give permission, but could be bribed to do so. Aurangzeb was most forthright in his efforts to stop sati. According to Manucci, on his return from Kashmir in December, 1663, he "issued an order that in all lands under Mughal control, never again should the officials allow a woman to be burnt." Manucci adds that "This order endures to this day." This order, though not mentioned in the formal histories, is recorded in the official guidebooks of the reign. Although the possibility of an evasion of government orders through payment of bribes existed, later European travelers record that sati was not much practiced by the end of Aurangzeb's reign. As Ovington says in his Voyage to Surat: "Since the Mahometans became Masters of the Indies, this execrable custom is much abated, and almost laid aside, by the orders which nabobs receive for suppressing and extinguishing it in all their provinces. And now it is very rare, except it be some Rajah's wives, that the Indian women burn at all."

Any generalization about Indian history is dangerous, but the impression one gains from looking at social conditions during the Mughal period is of a society moving towards an integration of its manifold political regions, social systems, and cultural inheritances. The greatness of the Mughals consisted in part at least in the fact that the influence of their court and government permeated society, giving it a new measure of harmony. The common people suffered from poverty, disease, and the oppression of the powerful; court life was marked by intrigue and cruelty as well as by refinement of taste and elegant manners. Yet the rulers and their officials had moral standards which gave coherence to the administration and which they shared to some extent with most of their subjects. Undeniably, there were ugly scars on the face of Mughal society, but the sixteenth and seventeenth centuries had a quality of life that lent them a peculiar charm. The clearest reflection of this is seen in the creative arts of the period.

## References

Aiyar, R. Krishnaswami: *Outlines of Vedaanta,* Chetana, Bombay, 1978.

Bagchi, P. C.: *Studies in Dharmashastra,* University of Calcutta Press, Calcutta, 1939.

Bahadur, K.P.: *The Wisdom of Vedaanta,* Sterling Publishers Private Limited, New Delhi, 1996.

Banerjea, J. N.: *Pauranic and Vedanta Religion,* University of Calcutta, Calcutta, 1996.

Bhattacharyya, B.: *Nispannayogavali of Mahapandita Abhyakara Gupta,* Oriental Institute, Baroda, 1949.

Brockington, J. L.: *Righteous Rama: The Evolution of an Epic,* Oxford, London, 1984.

De Bary: *Self and Society in Ming Thought,* Columbia University Press, New York, 1970.

Gurumurthy, S. : *Hindu Heritage, Assimilative, Not Divisive,* Vigil, Madras 1993.

3

# Mughal's Art and Architecture during the Reign of Akbar and Jahangir

**Dr. BABITA**
*Assistant Professor, Department of History, N.A.S. (P .G.) college, Meerut, Uttar Pradesh*

Akbar was born at Umarkot in Sind on October 15, 1542. His father, Humayun (ruled 1530–1540 and 1555–1556), was driven from the throne of India in a series of decisive battles by the Afghan, Sher Shah Suri. After more than 12 years of exile, Humayun regained his sovereignty, though he held it for only a few months before his death in 1556. Akbar succeeded his father the same year under the regency of Bairam Khan, a Turkoman noble whose zeal in repelling pretenders to the throne and severity in maintaining the discipline of the army helped greatly in the consolidation of the newly recovered empire. When order was somewhat restored, Akbar took the reins of government into his own hands with a proclamation issued in March 1560.

It is speculated by historians that Bairam Khan attempted to dethrone or murder Akbar when he came of age, or led an army against his loyalists. It is also suggested that Akbar, suspicious of Khan's ambitions and loyalties, encouraged him to perform a pilgrimage to Mecca, and there had him killed by an agent. The Encyclopaedia Brittanica (11th ed.) surmises rather that Bairam had been despotic and cruel as regent but that following his rebellion, Akbar forgave him and offered him either a "high post in the army or a suitable escort" to Mecca (Vol 1-2:454).

On November 5, 1556, 50 miles north of Delhi, a Moghul army defeated Hindu forces of General Hemu at the Second Battle of Panipat, granting the throne of India to Akbar.

When Akbar ascended the throne, only a small portion of what had formerly comprised the Moghul Empire was still under his control, and he devoted himself to the recovery of the remaining provinces. He expanded the Moghul Empire to include Malwa (1562), Gujarat (1572), Bengal (1574), Kabul (1581), Kashmir (1586), and Kandesh (1601), among others. Akbar installed a governor over each of the conquered provinces, under his authority. Some point to the slaughter of captives that took place after many of the battles he fought, or to his beheading Sher Shar's Hindu chief minister, Hemu, after the Second Battle of Panipat (which earned him the title of Ghazi, Muslim soldier, warrior), or the self-immolation of thousands of Hindu women at the siege of Chitor, Rajasthan (1568) as evidence of his moral failings (some sources claim he slaughtered 30,000 Hindu captives after the Fall of Chitod). Others claim that he kept a huge harem of concubines, or temporary wives (allowed under Shi'a law), which makes his life less than morally ideal. It was his conquest of Bengal that gave him control of the whole of northern India, which qualifies him according to some scholars as the real founder of the Moghul Empire.

## AKBAR PERIOD ARCHITECTURE

Akbar period architecture, building style that developed in India under the patronage of the Mughal emperor Akbar (reigned 1556–1605). The architecture of the Akbar period is characterized by a strength made elegant and graceful by its rich decorative work, which reflects many traditional Hindu elements. The style is best exemplified by the fort at Agra (built 1565–74) and the magnificent town of Fatehpur Sikri (1569–74), but fine examples are also found in the gateway to the ?Arab Sara?i (guesthouse at Humayun's tomb), Delhi (1560–61), the Ajmer fort (1564–73), the Lahore fort with its outstanding decoration (1586–1618), and the Allahabad fort (1583–84), now largely dismantled.

The fortress-palace of Agra is notable for the massive enclosure wall; its entire length of 1.5 miles (2.5 km) is faced with dressed stone. The main entranceway, which is known as the Delhi gate, is attractively decorated with white marble inlay against the warm red sandstone. It was the first location in India to be designated a UNESCO World Heritage site (1983).

The capital town of Fatehpur Sikri (named a World Heritage site in 1986) is one of the most notable achievements of Islamic architecture in India. The town, which was deserted only a few years after it was built, is a great complex of palaces and lesser residences and religious and official buildings, all erected on top of a rocky ridge 26 miles (42 km) west of Agra. The Hall of Private Audience (Diwan-i-Khas) is arresting in its interior arrangement, which has a single massive column encircled by brackets supporting a stone throne platform, from which radiate four railed balconies. The palace of Jodha Bai, Akbar's wife, and the residence of Mahesh Das (commonly known as Birbal, Akbar's friend and confidant) again show—in their niches and brackets—features adopted from the religious and secular architecture of the Hindus.

The most imposing of the buildings at Fatehpur Sikri is the Great Mosque, the Jami? Masjid, which served as a model for later congregational mosques built by the Mughals. The mosque's southern entrance, a massive gateway called the Buland Darwaza (Victory Gate), gives a feeling of immense strength and height, an impression emphasized by the steepness of the flight of steps by which it is approached.

## PAINTING IN THE COURT OF AKBAR

As per the historical record, it is said that the first painting of a portrait of Akbar was done by Abd al-Samad in 1551. In the Berlin album of Akbar, there is a painting of him with Hindal Mirza. A later period painting of Akbar`s court depicts Humayun in a tent. The painters recruited by Humayun had to change their individual style as per Akbar`s taste. During Akbar`s time, the Persian style of painting disappeared gradually. Akbar is regarded as the actual patron of Mughal painting even though he was reported to be illiterate and even dyslexic. The paintings of Akbar`s court included the album leaves and a bizarrely dressed, blue-eyed, wandering dervish somewhat figure.

Akbar`s first and greatest project was said to be the copying and illustration of a romance already popular in India, the Hamza-name, the heroic developments of the Emir Hamza, a kinsman of the Prophet. This painting was done on cloth, with a stout paper backing, and its giant format is exceptional in Islamic painting.

It was not possible at the Akbar`s period to display the paintings for public exhibition even though Akbar had desired so. The small staff of Persian members recruited by Humayun could not do that. The creators of the beautiful paintings of Akbar`s court were not known exactly. But, it is assumed that the Muslim painters from Malwa and the Muslim courts of the Deccan (Ahmadnagar, Bijapur and Golconda), would have been done those paintings in markedly differing styles. They were also trained in wall painting (a probable source for many of the illustrations) but not in book illustration at all probably. Most of the paintings surviving today are not variable in quality and many must have been experiments without a practical sequel. The great painters of Akbar`s time, Abd al-Samad and Mir Sayyid All were mainly responsible for executing the paintings. They used to work cut out in the administration of the studio, obtaining the paper and pigments, issuing them as necessary to the painters and accounting for them to the Treasury, and then seeing that the work was satisfactory and completed on time. The characteristic painting of Akbar was full with scenes flourished with adventure and drama, giants, monsters and demons, in a smoky palette of colours and this style continued till the end of his reign. The effect of these paintings was often brilliant, but bold rather than refined, combining Persian compositions and figures with the dark, jingly landscapes of the painting of pre-Islamic India. One of the finest paintings of Akbar`s court is the one, which depicts the 15 miraculous rescue of Hamza`s son, Nur al-Dahr, from drowning. In this particular painting, the work of at least four separate hands can be detected. It includes the water, painted in bravura linear style with white highlights, the figures, the forest landscape and some or all of the birds.

Some paintings of Akbar`s court have found place in the palace libraries, astronomical and astrological treatises, particularly star books and other works relevant to medicine, works of cosmography and geography. But now only few of these have survived. The earliest copy of the `Anvdri Suhayll` was made for him, which shows marked reminiscences of contemporary painting at Tabriz or Meshed. It contains twenty-seven full-page miniatures, but the margins of some of the other pages have pounced sketches in charcoal. During Akbar`s time, even the non-Muslim painters used to practice various works in his royal scriptorium. The painters were of Hindu, Jain, and even of Christian origin. The painters of Akbar`s court like Manohar and Mansur illustrated double-page spreads and depicted the episodes from Babur`s campaigns, his visits to his relatives, his feasts and his hunts. Sometimes these paintings spread up to three or four pages, which depicted the gardens ordered by Babur, particularly near Kabul, the flora and fauna of India as the cameos. The subjects for illustration in most of the paintings also included Babur`s visit to the rock-carved idols below the fortress of Urwa, which showed his wide sympathies, which Akbar himself shared. The Persian origins of the painters supervising the palace studio of Akbar and their ready access to Persian and Central Asian manuscripts figured largely in their paintings. In these paintings, primary colours were rare and there was a vast spectrum of smoky tones and figures were highly modeled. As most of these painters were trained in Europe, the European effect was very much evident in their paintings.

These paintings had elegant gloss binding, margins illuminated in gold inks of contrasting tones with an almost infinite variety of detail, magnificently illuminated medallions and headpieces. Most of the painters of Akbar`s court used to treat standard subjects exceptionally. In one of such painting by Mukund, Bahram Gur is shown hunting gazelles with a background of a Flemish seascape with ships and mountains distantly sunlit.

The painting at Akbar`s court was so rich and diverse that it is difficult to single out one aspect but portraiture should be mentioned specially. These paintings also depict the historical narratives since the early fifteenth century under the successors of Tamerlane. But in spite of his heroic status in their eyes, there are no known portraits either of him, or of his son Shah Rukh or of his grandson Ulugh Beg. A concept of the dynastic portrait developed gradually during the Akbar`s time and it was at least done for the public audience halls of his palaces. Most of his portraits were in profile or half-profile style. Akbar was very much attached to paintings and once in a private discussion of painting he remarked to Abul Fazl, "There are many that hate painting, but such men I dislike. It appears to me as if a painter had a quite peculiar means of recognising God; for a painter in sketching anything that has life, and in devising its limbs, one after the other, must come to feel that he cannot bestow individuality upon his work, and is thus forced to think of God, the giver of life, and will then be increased in knowledge."

## JAHANGIR AND ART

Jahangir was fascinated with art and architecture. Jahangir himself is far from modest in his autobiography when he states his prowess at being able to determine the artist of any portrait by simply looking at a painting. As he said:

> *"...my liking for painting and my practice in judging it have arrived at such point when any work is brought before me, either of deceased artists or of those of the present day, without the*

*names being told me, I say on the spur of the moment that is the work of such and such a man. And if there be a picture containing many portraits, and each face is the work of a different master, I can discover which face is the work of each of them. If any other person has put in the eye and eyebrow of a face, I can perceive whose work the original face is, and who has painted the eye and eyebrow."*

Jahangir took his connoisseurship of art very seriously. Paintings created under his reign were closely catalogued, dated and even signed, providing scholars with fairly accurate ideas as to when and in what context many of the pieces were created, in addition to their aesthetic qualities. He was not only an admirer of Christian artwork but also a purveyor of it. This was largely due to earlier Jesuit missions during his father's reign. Jesuits had brought with them various books, engravings, and paintings and, when they saw the delight Akbar held for them, sent for more and more of the same to be given to the Mughals, as they felt they were on the "verge of conversion," a notion which proved to be very false. Instead, both Akbar and Jahangir studied this artwork very closely and replicated and adapted it, adopting much of the early iconographic features and later the pictorial realism for which Renaissance art was known. Jahangir was notable for his pride in the ability of his court painters. A classic example of this is described in Sir Thomas Roe's diaries, in which the Emperor had his painters copy a European miniature several times creating a total of five miniatures. Jahangir then challenged Roe to pick out the original from the copies, a feat Sir Thomas Roe could not do, to the delight of Jahangir. Jahangir was also revolutionary in his adaptation of European styles. A collection at the British Museum in London contains seventy-four drawings of Indian portraits dating from the time of Jahangir, including a portrait of the emperor himself. These portraits are a unique example of art during Jahangir's reign because before, and for sometime after, faces were not drawn full, head-on and including the shoulders as well as the head as these drawings are.

During his time, Jahangir also pioneered several ornate genealogies illustrated with portraits of each family member in the style of Italian Renaissance painters. Jahangir's love for hunting met his love for art as he commissioned artists on multiple occasions to paint him while hunting and would even paint scenes himself, from time to time. Jahangir was also known for his vast collection of illuminated Persian albums that contained writings as well as paintings.

## ART, ARCHITECTURE AND PAINTING

Jahangir prided himself on being a connoisseur of the art of painting and used to say that he was sure to find out as to who were the authors of various paintings, and if a picture was painted by the joint labours of a number of artists, he could tell as to who had painted the various parts of it.

Jahangir was much interested in architecture, though it must be admitted that his contribution to the development of that art was much less than to painting. Among the notable buildings erected by him, Akbar's tomb at Sikandra is the most remarkable. He altered its design and partly rebuilt it.

Itimad-ud-Daulah's tomb near Agra, constructed under the direction of Nur Jahan, is one of the finest buildings of its kind in the country and is adorned with mosaic work outside and paintings inside. Under Jahangir's patronage a great mosque was built in Lahore; it rivals that at Delhi built by his son Shah Jahan. Jahangir's reign was also important because of the progress attained in the art of painting.

Next to painting Jahangir took delight in laying out fine gardens. Some of the gardens in Kashmir and Lahore were laid out at his orders. He tried to adorn the currency with fine calligraphic designs. He struck beautiful medals and coins with his portraits stamped on them.

Jahangir was possessed of a fine critical taste in matters of dress and pleasures of the table. He designed new fashions and stuffs for himself and forbade other people to make use of them. He particularly relished fine fruits. He praised the mangoes as one of the best fruits and was very fond of delicious cherries of Kabul.

Trained in soldierly pursuits and art of warfare under the supervision of his father, Jahangir in his early youth had developed into a capable soldier. He was devoted to sport and was a skilful shot with rifle and with bow and arrow. He was given practical training in war and diplomacy and acquired a considerable experience of both, but never displayed that energy and devotion which are necessary in a general.

### Reign an Era of Family Strife and Notable Architecture

Jahangir's reign was noted for architectural works. When his chief minister Itimad-ud-daulah died in 1622, his daughter, the powerful Nur Jahan, commissioned the construction in white marble of his exquisite tomb at Agra which was finished in 1628.

Unlike the much larger Taj Mahal, with which it ranked in quality, the appeal of the tomb depended on its decoration. It looked like a brilliant casket, bejewelled with various styles of inlay. Its two major innovations—the extensive use of white marble as a material and inlay as a decorative motif—were to become the distinguishing features of the greatest period of Mughal architecture.

The high quality of both paintings and coins during Jahangir's reign was a direct result of the emperor's personal interest. Having grown up at Fatehpur-Sikri in the busy days of Akbar's studio, he was a keen student of technique and claimed to be able to tell which master had painted the eye and eyebrow in a face and which the rest of the portrait.

In addition, he seems to have invented and commissioned from his artists a new style of political allegory in art which, however self-congratulatory and vain, provided some of the most magnificent paintings of the period.

One such picture claims to celebrate a new spirit of peace with his Persian neighbor, Shah Abbas. Toward the end of Jahangir's reign, Nur Jahan took a more active role in the government and appointed her politically adroit brother, Asaf Khan, as the premier of the realm. In 1626, brother and sister decided to attack the powerful Mahabat Khan.

An Afghan by birth, Mahabat Khan realized the precarious situation and so marched north with 5,000 Rajput troops toward the imperial camp on the bank of the Jhelum. As Jahangir and Nur Jahan traveled to Kabul, Mahabat Khan took the emperor prisoner. Though Jahangir managed to escape with the help of a clever scheme by Nur Jahan, Mahabat Khan then joined forces with Shah Jahan. The prince was now stronger than ever.

A shaken emperor turned north to the only place where he now found solace. For several years, he had made an almost annual journey to Kashmir. There, he had found a natural paradise, but he and his court had done much to make it an artificial one. The Mughal gardens, which are one of the main glories of Srinagar, are the direct result of his enthusiasm. The Shalimar Bagh, built by Jahangir, is distinguished by a series of pavilions on carved pillars, surrounded by pools with seats which can only be reached by stepping stones. When Jahangir died in October on 1627 in a village at the foot of the Kashmir hills, Asaf Khan betrayed his sister by backing his son-in-law, Shah Jahan. Informed by Asaf's courier of his father's death, Shah Jahan rushed north to claim his throne, reaching the capital in 1628. Nur Jahan was pensioned off and went to live in solitude in Lahore until she died in 1645. While some European historians consider Jahangir as a fickle-minded tyrant, Indian authors regard him as a just and noble ruler. Most writers now agree that he was a highly educated and cultured man. His autobiography is a testimony of his interest in subjects like botany and zoology.

Among the notable buildings renovated by him, Akbar's tomb at Sikandra is the most remarkable. He altered its design and partly rebuilt it. Under his patronage, a great mosque was built in Lahore; it rivals the grand mosque in Delhi, built by his son, Shah Jahan. But he did not possess the high idealism and genius of Akbar. The administrative machinery of his father was allowed to remain untouched.

The vakil (chief minister) remained the highest dignitary next to the emperor. A liberal ruler, he made no departure from his father's policy of admitting Hindus to higher public services. On the whole, Jahangir was a successful ruler and his people were well off. Agriculture, industries, and commerce flourished. Jahangir's diary is brimming with his ideas for promoting social justice and administrative efficiency, and in most cases he tried to follow or outdo the liberal ideas of his father, but he was less successful in putting them into effect.

## References

Asher, Catherine: *Architecture of Mughal India*, Cambridge, New York, 1992.

Barrucand, Marianne, and A. Bednorz: *Moorish Architecture in Andalusia*, Cologne, London, 1992.

Blair, Sheila S., and Jonathan Bloom: *The Art and Architecture of Islam, 1250-1800,* Pelican History of Art. New Haven, 1994.

Creswell, K. A. C.: *A Short Account of Early Muslim Architecture*, Aldershot, Adlohoc, 1989.

Frishman, Martin, and Hasan-Uddin Khan: *The Mosque: History, Architectural Development and Regional Diversity,* London & New York, 1994.

Hambly, G.: "*Cities of Mughal India*", New York: G. P. Putnam's Sons, 1968.

Koch, Ebba: *Mughal Architecture: An Outline of Its History and Development (1526-1858),* Munich, London, 1991.

Papadopoulo, A.: "*Islam and Muslim Art*", New York, Harry N. Abrams, 1979.

Rizvi, Saiyid Athar Abbas: *Fatehpur Sikri*, New Delhi, Archeological Survey of India, 1972.

# 4

# Religious Reform Movements in India with Special Reference to Bhakti Movement

**DR. SANJAY KUMAR SINGH**
*Associate Professor, Department of History, M.M.H. College, Ghaziabad, Uttar Padesh.*

## BHAKTI PHILOSOPHY

The Bhakti Movement was essentially founded in South India and later spread to the North during the late medieval period. The notion of 'Bhakti' (loosely translated as devotional love to God) is of antiquity. A nascent consciousness of what 'Bhakti' constitutes is already to be found in the earliest Vedas, especially in relation to deities such as Varuna. A clearer expression of Bhakti began to be formed during the so-called Epic Period and the Puranic periods of Hindu history. Texts such as the Bhagavad Gita and the BhagavatQurana PuFrana clearly explore Bhakti Yoga or the Path of Devotion as a means to salvation.

The Bhakti Movement itself is a historical-spiritual phenomenon that crystallized in South India during Late Antiquity. It was spearheaded by devotional mystics (later revered as Hindu saints) who extolled devotion and love to God as the chief means of spiritual perfection. The Bhakti movement in South India was spearheaded by the sixty-three Nayanars (Shaivite devotees) and the twelve Alvars (Vaishnavaite devotees).

Among the earliest Shaivite mystics was Karaikkal Amaiyar, who probably lived around the late 5th century AD or perhaps the early 6th century. She was said to be a contemporary of the Vaishnavaite saints Bhuttalwar and Peialwar. Kannapa Nayanar was also an early

Shaiva Bhakti saint. But most famous among the Shaiva Bhakti saints were the 'Nalvar' (The Four Eminent Ones), namely Sundarar, Appar, Sambandar and Manikkavasagar. Their devotional hymns are ecstatic, lyrical and moving.

The Vaishnavaite Bhakti movement was contemporaneous with the Shaiva Bhakti movement. The hymns of the twelve alvars are held together as the 'Nalayira Divya Prabandham' and recited (as are the Shaiva texts) in temple rituals. Whilst all the saints are held in great reverence, Andal (or Goda-devi) in particular holds a special place among the Vaishnava saints. Not only is she the only female Vaishnava saint but also her hymns are among the best expressions of bridal mysticism in the Hindu religion.

The twelve Alvars and the sixty-three Nayanars nurtured the incipient bhakti movement in South India under the Pallavas and Pandyas in the fifth to seventh centuries AD. They constitute [South India's 75 Apostles of Bhakti] and were greatly influential in determining the expression of faith in South India. The path of devotion as expounded by these mystics would later be incorporated into Ramanuja and Madhva philosophical systems.

During the 12th and 13th centuries A.D., the Virashaiva movement and, during the rule of the Vijayanagar Empire in South India, the Haridasa movement spread from present-day Karnataka. The Virashaiva movement spread the philosophy of Basavanna, a Hindu reformer. The seeds of Carnatic music were sown, and the philosophy of Madhvacharya was propogated by the Kannada Haridasas. The Haridasa movement presented, like the Virashaiva movement, another strong current of Bhakti, pervading the lives of millions.

The Haridasas presented two groups – Vyasakuta and Dasakuta. The former were required to be proficient in the Vedas, Upanishads and other Darshanas, while the Dasakuta merely conveyed the message of Madhvacharya through the Kannada language to the people. The philosophy of Madhvacharya was preserved and perpetuated by his eminent disciples like Vyasatirtha or Vyasaraja Naraharitirtha, Vadirajatirtha, Sripadaraya, Jayathirtha and others. In the fifteenth century, the Haridasa movement took shape under Sripadaraya of Mulbagal; but his disciple Vyasatirtha provided it a strong organizational base. He was intimately associated with the Vijayanagar Empire, where he became a great moral and spiritual force. His eminent disciples were Purandaradasa and Kanakadasa. The late Bhakti movement led to the proliferation of regional poetic literature in the various vernacular languages of India. The Bhakti movement in what is now Karnataka resulted in a burst of poetic Kannada literature in praise of Lord Vishnu. Some of its leaders include Purandara Dasa and Kanaka Dasa, whose contributions were essential to Carnatic music. The later Carnatic Trinity is also no doubt a product of this long Bhakti Movement.

The Bhakti movement began to spread to the North during the late medieval ages when North India was under Muslim domination. There was no grouping of the mystics into Shaiva and Vaishnava devotees as it was in the South. The movement was spontaneous and the various mystics had their own version of devotional expression. Unlike in the South where devotion was centered on both Shiva and Vishnu (in all his forms), the Northern devotional movement was more or less centered on Rama and Krishna, both of whom were incarnations of Vishnu. Though this did not mean that the cult of Shiva or of the Devi went into decline. In fact for all of its history the Bhakti movement co-existed peacefully with the other movements in Hinduism. It was initially considered unorthodox as it rebelled against caste distinctions and made disregarded Brahmanic rituals which according to Bhakti saints not necessary for salvation. In the course of time however, owing to its immense popularity among the masses (and even royal patronage) it became 'orthodox' and continues to be one of the most important modes of religious expression in modern India.

In the period between the 14-17th centuries, a great bhakti movement swept through Northern India initiated by a loosely associated group of teachers or 'Sants'. Chaitanya, Vallabha, Meera Bai, Kabir, Tulsi Das, Tukaram and other mystics spearheaded the Bhakti movement in the North. Their teachings were that people could cast aside the heavy burdens of ritual and caste and the subtle complexities of philosophy and simply express their overwhelming love for God. This period was also characterised by a spate of devotional literature in vernacular prose and poetry in the ethnic languages of the various Indian states or provinces. As aforementioned whilst many of the Bhakti mystics focused their attention on Krishna or Rama, it did not necessarily mean that the cult of Shiva was marginalised. The growth of the Vira-Shaiva and the older Shaiva Siddhanta schools in this period, which incorporated Bhakti into their teachings are testimony to the growth of the Shaiva faith in this period. In the thirteenth century Basava founded the Vira-Shaiva school or Virashaivism. He rejected the caste system, denied the supremacy of the Brahmins, condemned ritual sacrifice and insisted on bhakti and the worship of the one God, Shiva. His followers were called Vira-Shaivas, meaning "stalwart Shiva-worshippers".

The Saiva-Siddhanta school is a form of Shaivism (Shiva worship) found in the south and is of hoary antiquity. It incorporates the teachings of the erstwhile Shaiva nayanars and espouses the belief that Shiva is Brahman and his infinite love is revealed in the divine acts of the creation, preservation and destruction of the universe, and in the liberation of the soul.

Seminal Bhakti works in Bengali include the many songs of Ramprasad Sen. His pieces (known as Shyama Sangeet, or Songs of the Dark Mother) are still actively sung today in West Bengal. Coming from the 17th century, they cover an astonishing range of emotional responses to Ma Kali, detailing complex philosophical statements based on Vedanta teachings and more visceral pronouncements of his love of Devi. Using inventive allegory, Ramprasad had 'dialogues' with the Mother Goddess through his poetry, at times chiding her, adoring her, celebrating her as the Divine Mother, reckless consort of Shiva and capricious Shakti, the universal female creative energy, of the cosmos.

## RAMA BHAKTI

The leader of the bhakti movement focusing on the Lord as Rama was Ramananda. Very little is known about him, but he is believed to have lived in the first half of the 15th century. He taught that Lord Rama is the supreme Lord, and that salvation could be attained only through love for and devotion to him, and through the repetition of his sacred name.

Ramananda's ashram in Varanasi became a powerful centre of religious influence, from which his ideas spread far and wide among all classes of Indians. One of the reasons for his great popularity was that he renounced Sanskrit and used the language of the people for the composition of his hymns. This paved the way for the modern tendency in northern India to write literary texts in local languages.

Devotees of Krishna worship Him in different mellows, known as rasas. Two major systems of Krishna worship developed, each with its own philosophical system. These two moods as called aishwaryamaya bhakti and madhuryamaya bhakti. Aishwaryamaya bhakti is revealed in the abode of queens and kingdom of Krishna in Dwaraka. Madhuryamaya Bhakti is revealed in the abode of braja. Thus krishna is variously worshipped according to the development of devotee's taste in worshipping the Supreme Personality of Godhead, Sri Krishna, as father, friend, master, beloved and many different varieties which are all extraordinary. Krishna is famous as Makhanchor, or butterthief. He loved to eat butter and is the beloved of his little village in Gokul. These are all transcendental descriptions. Thus they are revealed to the sincere devotees in proportion to the development in their love of Godhead.

Shri Madhvacharya (1238-1317) identified God with Vishnu. His view of reality is purely dualistic in that he understood a fundamental differentiation between the ultimate Godhead and the individual soul, and the system is therefore called Dvaita (dualistic) Vedanta. Madhva is considered one of the influential theologians in Hindu history. His influence was profound, and he is one of the fathers of the Vaishnava Bhakti movement. Great leaders of the Vaishnava Bhakti movement in Karnataka like Purandara Dasa, Kanaka Dasa, Raghavendra Swami and many others were influenced by Dvaita traditions.

Vallabhacharya (1479-1531) called his system of thought Shuddhadvaita (pure monism). According to him, it is by God's grace alone that one can obtain release from bondage and attain Krishna's heaven. This heaven is far above the "heavens" of Brahma, Vishnu and Shiva, for Krishna is himself the eternal Brahman.

Chaitanya Mahaprabhu (1486-1534) defined his system of philosophy as Achintya Bheda-Bheda (inconceivable and simultaneous oneness and difference). It synthesizes elements of monism and dualism into a single system. Chaitanya's philosophy is taught by the contemporary International Society for Krishna Consciousness, better known as the *Hare Krishna* movement.

Srimanta Sankardeva (1449-1568) named his religion *ek sarana naam dharma* and propagated it in Assam. An example of *dasa bhakti,* in this form there was no place for Radha. The most important symbol of this religion is the *naamghor* or prayer hall, which dot Assam's landscape. This form of worship is very strong in Assam today, and much of the traditions are maintained by the monastries called *Satras*.

## VAISHNAVA BHAKTI

Prominent personalities involved in this philosophy are: Ramanuja, Nimbarka, Madhva, Vallabha, Chaitanya.

*Influences:* Beyond the confines of such formal schools and movements, however, the development of bhakti as a major form of Hindu practice has left an indelible stamp on the faith. Philosophical speculation was concern for the minority, and even the great Advaitist scholar Adi Shankaracharya, when questioned as to the way to God, said that chanting the name of the lord, was essential. The philosophical schools changed the way people thought, but Bhakti was immediately accessible to all, calling to the instinct emotion of love and redirecting it to the highest pursuit of God and self-realization. In general a liberal movement, its denouncement of caste offered recourse for Hindus from the orthodox Brahaminical systems. Of course, however, Bhakti's message of tolerance and love was not often heeded by those ensconced in the societal construct of caste. Altogether, Bhakti resulted in a mass of devotional literature, music and art that has enriched the world and gave India renewed spiritual impetus, one eschewing unnecessary ritual and artificial social boundaries.

*Sri Ramanuja Acharya:* (traditionally dated 1017–1137 CE) was an Indian philosopher and is recognized as the most important saint of Sri Vaishnavism. He held the Vishishtadvaita or qualified Nondualist belief that the world and Brahman were united, like a soul and a body are. His version of Indian Nondualism differed from Adi Shankara's because he acknowledged the existence of differences, and believed that the identity of an object as a part was as important as the unity of the whole. The Vaishnava Theology espoused by Ramanuja posits that Brahman is not devoid of attributes but is expressed as a personal God, full of infinite good qualities, as Narayana. The Adishesha on whom Lord Ranganatha of Srirangam rests is believed to be Ramanuja.

*Period :* 1017 to 1137

*Place of Birth :* Sri Perumbudur, Tamil Nadu

*Guru :* Sri Periya Nambigal

*Names :* 1. Ilaya Perumal, As named by his parents

2. Lakshmana, Family name

3. Ramanuja.

Ramanuja was born Ilaya Perumal to a smartha brahmin family in the village of Perumbudur, Tamil Nadu, India in 1017 CE. His father was Keshava Somayaji Deekshitar and mother was Kanthimathi in sect of Vadama.From a young age, his intelligence and ability to comprehend highly abstract philosophical points were legendary. He took initiation from Yadavaprakasa, a renowned Advaitic scholar. Though his new guru was highly impressed with his analytical ability, he was quite concerned by how much emphasis Ramanuja placed on bhakti. After frequent clashes over interpretation, Yadavaprakasa decided the young Ramanuja was becoming too much of a threat and plotted a way to kill him. However, Ramanuja's cousin Govinda Bhatta (a favourite of Yadavaprakasa) discovered the plot and helped him escape. An alternative version is that one of Yadavaprakasa's students plotted to kill Ramanuja as a means of pleasing their teacher, but Sri Ramanuja escaped in the afore-mentioned manner. Yadavaprakasa was horrified when learnt about the conspiracy.

After renouncing the life of a house-holder, Ramanuja travelled to Srirangam to meet an aging Yamunacharya, the pre-eminent Vishishtadvaita philosopher of the time. Yamunacharya had died prior to Ramanuja's arrival, but had left three tasks for Ramanuja to carry out. Teach the doctrine of Saranagati (surrender) to God as the means to moksha. A Visishtadvaita Bhashya should be written for the Brahma Sutras of Vyasa which had previously been taught orally to the disciples of the Visishtadvaita philosophy. That the names of Parauara, the author of Vishnu Puraoa, and saint Uahakopa should be perpetuated.

Ramanuja pledged to God to do as he had been requested and accepted Yamunacharya as his *Manasika Acharya*. All three tasks were successfully completed.

*Five Acharyas:* Swami Ramanuja incorporated teachings from 5 different people who he considered to be his acharyas:

1. Peria Nambigal who performed his samasrayana
2. Thirukkotiyur Nambigal : who revealed the meaning of Charama slokam to swami on his 18th trip
3. Thirumalai Nambigal : Ramayana
4. Tirumalai Aandaan : Bhagavad Vishayam
5. Thirukachchi Nambigal : The 6 sentences or Perarulalan

*Visishtadvaita Philosophy:* Ramanuja's philosophy is referred to as Vishishtadvaita because it combines Advaita (oneness of God) with Vishesha (attributes). The philosophy is monotheistic.

*Differences with Sankara:* Adi Sankara had argued that all qualities or manifestations that can be perceived are unreal and temporary. They are a result of ignorance. Ramanuja believed them to be real and permanent and under the control of the Brahman. God can be one despite the existence of attributes, because they cannot exist alone; they are not independent entities. They are Prakaras or the modes,

Sesha or the accessories, and Niyama or the controlled aspects, of the one Brahman.

In Sri Ramanuja's system of philosophy, the Lord (Narayana) has two inseparable Prakaras or modes, viz., the world and the souls.

These are related to Him as the body is related to the soul. They have no existence apart from Him. They inhere in Him as attributes in a substance. Matter and souls constitute the body of the Lord. The Lord is their indweller. He is the controlling Reality. Matter and souls are the subordinate elements. They are termed Viseshanas, attributes. God is the Viseshya or that which is qualified.

History shows that the followers of Sankara are answerless till date to the strong arguments of Ramanuja (in his sri bhashya) and his followers (satadushani of desika,...). In a bid to escape strong objections raised by Ramanuja and his successors, most advaitins take a disguised route of neo vedantism, where they argue that vaishnavism is one another path to realise brahman. Ironically, the very brahman of Ramanuja and Sankara are different.

Ramanuja opines, wrong is the position of the Advaitins that understanding the Upanishads without knowing and practicing dharma can result in Brahman knowledge. The knowledge of Brahman that ends spiritual ignorance is meditational, not (as Advaitins seem to presume) testimonial or verbal.

In contrast to Sankara, Ramanuja holds, There is no knowledge source in support of the claim that there is a distinctionless (homogeneous) Brahman. All knowledge sources reveal objects as distinct from other objects. All experience reveals an object known in some way or other beyond mere existence. Testimony depends on the operation of distinct sentence parts (words with distinct meanings). Thus the claim that testimony makes known that reality is distinctionless is contradicted by the very nature of testimony as a knowledge means. Even the simplest perceptual cognition reveals something (Bessie) as qualified by something else (a broken hoof, "Bessie has a broken hoof," as known perceptually). Inference depends on perception and makes the same distinct things known as does perception.

Against the Advaita contention that perception cannot make known distinctness but only homogeneous being since distinctness cannot be defined, well, sorry, perception makes known generic characters (cowhood and the like) that differentiate things. If what you Advaitins say were true, why should not a person looking for a horse be satisfied with a buffalo? Remembering could not be distinguished from perceiving, because there would be only the one object (being). And no one would be deaf or blind. Furthermore, Brahman would be an object of perception and the other sources (prameya).

He also holds, The Advaitin argument about prior absences and no prior absence of consciousness is wrong. Similarly the Advaitin understanding of a-vidya (not-Knowledge), which is the absence of spiritual knowledge, is incorrect. "If the distinction between spiritual knowledge and spiritual ignorance is unreal, then spiritual ignorance and the self are one."

*The Seven Objections to Shankara's Advaita:* Ramanuja picks out what he sees as seven fundamental flaws in the Advaita philosophy for special attack: he sees them as so fundamental to the Advaita position that if he is right in identifying them as involving doctrinal contradictions, then Sankara's entire system collapses. He argues:

1. The nature of Avidya. Avidya must be either real or unreal; there is no other possibility. But neither of these is possible. If Avidya is real, non-dualism collapses into dualism. If it is unreal, we are driven to self-contradiction or infinite regress.
2. The incomprehensibility of Avidya. Advaitins claim that Avidya is neither real nor unreal but incomprehensible, {anirvacaniya.} All cognition is either of the real or the unreal: the Advaitin claim flies in the face of experience, and accepting it would call into question all cognition and render it unsafe.
3. The grounds of knowledge of Avidya. No pramana can establish Avidya in the sense the Advaitin requires. Advaita philosophy presents Avidya not as a mere lack of knowledge, as something purely negative, but as an obscuring layer which covers Brahman and is removed by true Brahma-vidya. Avidya is positive nescience not mere ignorance. Ramanuja argues that positive nescience is established neither by perception, nor by inference, nor by scriptural testimony. On the contrary, Ramanuja argues, all cognition is of the real.
4. The locus of Avidya. Where is the Avidya that gives rise to the (false) impression of the reality of the perceived world? There are two possibilities; it could be Brahman's Avidya or the individual soul's {jiva.} Neither is possible. Brahman is knowledge; Avidya cannot co-exist as an attribute with a nature utterly incompatible with it. Nor can the individual

soul be the locus of Avidya: the existence of the individual soul is due to Avidya; this would lead to a vicious circle.

5. Avidya's obscuration of the nature of Brahman. Sankara would have us believe that the true nature of Brahman is somehow covered-over or obscured by Avidya. Ramanuja regards this as an absurdity: given that Advaita claims that Brahman is pure self-luminous consciousness, obscuration must mean either preventing the origination of this (impossible since Brahman is eternal) or the destruction of it-equally absurd.
6. The removal of Avidya by Brahma-vidya. Advaita claims that Avidya has no beginning, but it is terminated and removed by Brahma-vidya, the intuition of the reality of Brahman as pure, undifferentiated consciousness. But Ramanuja denies the existence of undifferentiated {nirguna} Brahman, arguing that whatever exists has attributes: Brahman has infinite auspicious attributes. Liberation is a matter of Divine Grace: no amount of learning or wisdom will deliver us.
7. The removal of Avidya. For the Advaitin, the bondage in which we dwell before the attainment of Moksa is caused by Maya and Avidya; knowledge of reality (Brahma-vidya) releases us. Ramanuja, however, asserts that bondage is real. No kind of knowledge can remove what is real. On the contrary, knowledge discloses the real; it does not destroy it. And what exactly is the saving knowledge that delivers us from bondage to Maya? If it is real then non-duality collapses into duality; if it is unreal, then we face an utter absurdity.

He was critical of the caste system. He said, "Does the wearing of a sacred thread make one a Brahmin? One who is devoted to God (Narayana) alone is a Brahmin."

His Sarangati philosophy emphasises that anyone, irrespective of colour, creed, caste, sex and religion can surrender their mind, body and soul to the Lotus foot of Lord Narayana and the God would accept him/her.

Cited from Sri Ramanuja, His Life, Religion, and Philosophy, published by Sri Ramakrishna Math, Chennai, India.

*Writings:* Ramanuja's most famous work is known as the Sri Bhasya. It is a commentary on the Brahma Sutras. Gadhya Thrayam (three compositions)-Vaikunta, Sriranga and Saranagati Gadhyam are great works in Vaishnava philosophy.

His other works are:

- Vedanta Sara (essence of Vedanta)
- Vedanta Sangraha (a resume of Vedanta)
- Vedanta Deepa (the light of Vedanta).

An interesting point in Ramanuja's works is that, He happens to have composed all his works only in the Sanskrit language.

## References

Karen Pechelis (2014), The Embodiment of Bhakti, Oxford University Press.

David Lorenzen (1995), Bhakti Religion in North India: Community Identity and Political Action, State University of New York Press.

John Hawley (2015), A Storm of Songs: India and the Idea of the Bhakti Movement, Harvard University Press.

Schomer, Karine; McLeod, W. H., eds. (1987), The Sants: Studies in a Devotional Tradition of India, Motilal Banarsidass.

5

# The Impact of Colonial Rule on Social and Economic Life of India

**DR. VANDANA SEMALTY**

*Associate Professor, Department of History, M.M.H. College, Ghaziabad, Uttar Pradesh.*

**Abstract:** *British imperialism was more pragmatic than that of other colonial powers. Its motivation was economic, not evangelical. There was none of the dedicated Christian fanaticism which the Portuguese and Spanish demonstrated in Latin America and less enthusiasm for cultural diffusion than the French (or the Americans) showed in their colonies. For this reason they westernized India only to a limited degree. British interests were of several kinds. At first the main purpose was to achieve a monopolistic trading position. Later it was felt that a regime of free trade would make India a major market for British goods and a source of raw materials, but British capitalists who invested in India, or who sold banking or shipping service there, continued effectively to enjoy monopolistic privileges. India also provided interesting and lucrative employment for a sizeable portion of the British upper middle class, and the remittances they sent home made an appreciable contribution to Britain's balance of payments and capacity to save. Finally, control of India was a key element in the world power structure, in terms of geography, logistics and military manpower. The British were not averse to Indian economic development if it increased their markets but refused to help in areas where they felt there was conflict with their own economic interests or political security. Hence, they refused to give protection to the Indian textile industry until its main competitor became Japan rather than Manchester, and they did almost nothing to further technical education. They introduced some British concepts of property, but did not push them too far when they met vested interests.*

## SOCIAL SECTOR DURING BRITISH RULE

Right from the beginning of their relationship with India, the British, who had come as traders and had become rulers and administrators, had influenced the economic and political systems of the country. Their impact on the cultural and social life of India was, however, gradual.

Till 1813, they followed a policy of non-interference in the social and cultural life of the Indians. Yet, changes were taking place in these fields (the social life of Indians). These changes related to education, the condition of women, the caste system and various social practices.

### Education

Initially, the East India Company did not think that it was its duty to impart education to Indians. It allowed the old system of education to continue. Pathsalas, which imparted a special type of education geared towards meeting the requirements of a rural society, were open to all. Sanskrit education was imparted in tols. Muslims attended Madrasas. Higher education was confined primarily to upper castes. This system of education was eventually changed by the British.

Around the beginning of the 19th century, the Company became aware of the need for introducing Western education in India. However, Christian missionaries, who were interested in spreading Christianity through education, had already established several educational institutions which were attached to their churches.

### Charter Act of 1813

The Charter Act of 1813 directed the Company to spend one lakh rupees on the education of Indians. But even this meagre amount could not be utilised because of a raging debate over the medium of instruction. Orientalists advocated the traditional Indian learning through the medium of the classical languages of Sanskrit and Perisan. The Anglicists, on the other hand, argued that Western education should be imparted through the medium of English.

Thomas Macaulay, the first law member in the Governor General's Council, promoted the English language as a tool for educating the people in Western thought and ideals (Macaulay's Minute of 1835). William Bentinck supported Macaulay's views. In 1835, the government passed an Act declaring that educational funds would be utilised for imparting Western education through the medium of English. In 1844, English became the official language and it was declared that people having knowledge of English would be preferred for public employment. This helped the spread of English education in India. In 1854, Charles Wood, the President of the Company's Board of Control, worked out a plan for educational reorganisation. Through the Wood's Despatch the Government declared its intention of "creating a properly articulated system of education from the primary school to the university".

In accordance with the Wood's Despatch universities were established in Calcutta, Bombay and Madras (1857). In 1858 Charles Wood Bankim Chandra Chatterjee, the famous Bengali writer became one of the first two graduates of Calcutta University.

The Government's educational policies educated a limited number of people. English education was promoted in keeping with Macaulay's Minute though, eventually, vernacular education and mass education were both given importance. The traditional Pathsalas withered away as a new system of elementary education was put in its place. However, the emphasis was on higher education. English education, too, continued to flourish.

It must be remembered that the need for low- ranking English-knowing Indian clerks was one of the main reasons that prompted the government to take steps to spread Western education. Employing educated Indians was necessary because of the need to man an expanding bureaucracy. Employing Englishmen at all levels of the administration was both expensive and difficult. Above all, the idea was to create a class which would be "Indian in blood and colour, but English in tastes, in opinions, in morals, in intellect." Besides, Western education was expected to reconcile the people of India to British rule particularly as it glorified British rule.

Western education, however, influenced Indian society in a way that the British could never have imagined. Theories of philosophers like John Locke, Jeremy Bentham, Adam Smith and Voltaire instilled in the Indian mind notions of freedom, liberty, equality and democracy. As a result of the exposure to such ideas, Indians began to recognise the need for change.

The imposition of English in the education system was a blessing in disguise. Indians from diverse regions speaking different languages could now communicate with each other through the medium of English. English thus united the educated Indians and brought about a feeling of oneness among them. A spirit of nationalism gradually emerged.

## Rediscovery of India's Past by the British

In order to rule India effectively, an understanding of her past traditions and culture was required. Sanskrit was promoted and several educational institutions were set up for that purpose. Many European scholars and government employees became increasingly interested in Indian languages.

William Jones founded the Asiatic Society. Jones himself was a great scholar of Sanskrit. He translated some ancient Indian works like the Manu Smriti. Many of Jones' scholarly articles on Sanskrit and Indian past were published in the Journal of the Asiatic Society of Bengal.

Charles Wilkins translated the Bhagavad Gita into English. Max Mueller translated the Rig Veda. The Archaeological Survey of India was set up due to the efforts of Alexander Cunningham and John Marshall. James Princep deciphered the Ashokan inscriptions which were written in Brahmi.

India's rich and glorious history, as revealed by Western scholars, helped Indians to regain their lost pride and confidence and contributed to the development of nationalism.

## SOCIAL CHANGES AND REFORMS UNDER THE BRITISH

The demand for social and religious reform that manifested itself in the early decades of the 19th century partly arose as a response to Western education and culture. India's contact with the West made educated Indians realise that socio-religious reform was a prerequisite for the all-round development of the country.

Educated Indians like Raja Rammohan Roy worked systematically to eradicate social evils. A period of social reforms began in India during the time of Governor General Lord William Bentinck (1828-35) who was helped by Rammohan Roy.

In 1829, Sati or the practice of burning a widow with her dead husband was made illegal or punishable by law. Female infanticide was banned. However, even today, infanticide is practised in backward areas in India.

Slavery was declared illegal. With Iswar Chandra Vidyasagar's assistance, the Widow Remarriage Act was passed by Lord Dalhousie in 1856. Vidyasagar also campaigned against child marriage and polygamy.The cruel custom of offering little children as sacrifice to please God, practised by certain tribes, was banned by Governor General Lord Hardinge.It is important to note that since the reform movement started in Bengal, its impact was first felt here. It took time to spread it all over India.

## Impact on transport and communication

The East India Company was primarily a trading concern. Commercial interests guided British policy in India. Though the Company's political domination increased, its trading interests were never lost sight of. As the Industrial Revolution gained momentum, the manufacturing class became very powerful in England.

They now wanted the government to promote the sale of machine-manufactured British goods, especially British textiles. At the same time raw materials were imported from India to feed the growing needs of British industries.

Instead of exporting manufactured products, India was now forced to export raw materials like raw cotton and raw silk and plantation products like indigo and tea, or foodgrains which were in short supply in Britain. The demands of an industrialised England necessitated better communication facilities in the colonies.

Up to the middle of the 19th century, the means of transport in India were backward. Goods were transported by road mainly by bullock-carts, mules and camels. Riverine transport by boats was also prevalent. Due to poor communication and slow transport the volume of trade was restricted.

The British rulers soon realised that a cheaper, faster and more efficient system of transport was necessary if British manufactured goods were to flow into India on a large scale and her raw materials were to be secured for British industries.

They introduced steamships on the rivers and set about improving roads. Work on the Grand Trunk Road from Calcutta to Delhi was begun in 1839 and completed in the 1850s. Important commercial centres and areas rich in raw materials were connected by a network of roads and canals. But the most dramatic improvement in transport came with the introduction of the railways.

A railway system had rapidly developed in England during the 1830s and 1840s. Pressure soon mounted for its introduction in India. British manufacturers hoped to open up the vast and hitherto untapped market in the hinterlands for their finished goods and to facilitate the import of Indian raw materials to feed their ever hungry machines.

British bankers and investors also looked upon the development of the railways in India as a channel for the safe investment of their surplus capital. British steel manufacturers regarded it as an outlet for their products like rails, engines, wagons etc. The first railway line from Bombay to Thana was opened to traffic in 1853.

Lord Dalhousie, in particular, stressed the importance of railways for trade and for the maintenance of law and order. The railways would enable the government to administer the country more effectively. The railways would also enable the government to mobilize military troops. In 1853, Lord Dalhousie outlined an extensive programme of railway development. The interiors were to be linked with big ports and the ports were to be connected. By the end of 1869, over 4000 miles of railway track had been laid.

However, in their planning, construction and management, there is nothing to suggest that India's own interest and well-being were taken into account. The primary consideration was to serve the economic, administrative and military interests of the British people. The railway travel of Indians between the important city centres grew only as a by-product.

## The telegraph and postal systems

The introduction of the railways, telegraph and postal system linked different parts of India and promoted an exchange of ideas among the people, especially among her leaders. The first telegraph line from Calcutta to Agra was opened in 1853. The Post and Telegraph Department was also established in the same year. A half-anna postage stamp would carry a letter from one part of the country to another.

The improvement in communications eventually helped to foster a sense of unity among Indians. The concept of the country as a whole now took precedence over regional and provincial isolationism. Books, journals and newspapers circulated widely and were now easily available to educated Indians all over the country.

The introduction of the railways in particular helped to break down barriers of religion and caste. People from different religions and social backgrounds, while travelling in a railway compartment, mingled with one another thereby challenging the age- old orthodox notions of untouchability, caste- based eating habits etc. These are the fundamental gains for the development of Indian nationalism.

Land continued to be the main source of revenue for the British. Since tax on land formed the main source of income for the Company, the British tried to introduce an efficient system of its collection. In 1765, by the Treaty of Allahabad, the East India Company got the right to collect revenue from Bengal, Bihar and Orissa.

In 1773, when Warren Hastings became the Governor General of India, he introduced the system of auctioning the right of collecting revenue for a period of five years. The right was given to the highest bidders but they were often unable to collect the stipulated revenue. In a bid to retain their contracts, they tried to extract money from peasants.

## The Permanent Settlement (1793 A.D.)

To remove the defects of the revenue system, Lord Cornwallis introduced a new system of revenue collection in Bengal, Bihar and Orissa, known as the Permanent Settlement. Under this system, the zamindar or the revenue collector of an estate became the permanent holder of the land.

The zamindar gained hereditary rights over the land. He was required to pay a fixed amount of revenue as tax to the Company by a fixed day of the year. If he failed to pay by the fixed day, his zamindari would be confiscated and sold. The cultivators now became tenants of the zamindars. They could be evicted by the zamindars for non-payment of their dues. Many of them lost their land.

The Permanent Settlement benefited the landlords more than the government. The Company was assured of fixed revenue at a fixed time no doubt, but it was deprived of a share of any additional income of the landlords from increasing cultivation on land. The cultivators were also left at the mercy of the zamindars who exploited them.

## Mahalwari System

The Mahalwari System was introduced in Punjab, parts of Madhya Pradesh and Western Uttar Pradesh. It was a settlement with the village community because common ownership of land prevailed in these areas. (Mahal means group of villages.) The talukdar or head of the mahal was responsible for collecting revenue from the villages.

## The Ryotwari System

In the Madras Presidency, Ryotwari System was introduced. In this system direct settlement was made between the Government and the cultivators or the ryots. Land revenue was fixed for a period of 30 years. Peasants had to pay about half of the total produce as tax.

## Drain of Wealth

The greatest impact of British policies was the drain of wealth from India. The Indian economy, no doubt, was primarily a rural economy, but Indian artisans produced goods in bulk to meet the demands of Indian and European buyers. Several towns had flourished as centres of trade. There had been a great demand for muslin from Bengal and silk from Bengal and Benaras.

British merchants bought these Indian products in large quantities. But, at the beginning of the 18th century, Britain and other European countries passed laws prohibiting the entry of cotton and silk textiles from India although there was a demand for it. After the advent of the Industrial Revolution, India was forced to produce cotton, indigo and other products which British industries required.

Indian markets were flooded with cheap, machine-made textiles manufactured in England. Indian hand-made textiles could not compete with the cheap machine-made textiles. India was transformed into a supplier of raw materials and a market for British manufactured goods.

While British goods were exempted from duties while entering Indian markets, Indian goods entering England were burdened with heavy customs duties. Thus, the self-sufficient economy of India collapsed under the impact of British colonial policies. With the decline of the cotton industry, the towns that had flourished as centres of trade or industry also declined.

# ECONOMY OF INDIA UNDER THE BRITISH RAJ

The economy of India under the British Raj describes the economy of India during the years of the British *Raj* from the 1850s to 1947. During this period, the Indian economy essentially remained stagnant, growing at the same rate (1%) as the population.

## The UK's planned destruction of the Rupee

After the UK's victory in the Franco-Prussian War (1870), Germany extracted a huge indemnity from France of £200,000,000, and then moved to join United Kingdom of Great Britain and Ireland (the UK) on a gold standard for currency. France, the US and other industrialising countries followed Germany in adopting a gold standard throughout the 1870s. At the same time, countries, such as Japan, which did not have the necessary access to gold or those, such as India, which were subject to inhuman 'imperial' policies that determined that they did not move to a gold standard, remained mostly on a silver standard. A huge divide between silver-based and gold-based economies resulted. The worst affected were economies with a silver standard that traded mainly with economies with a gold standard. With discovery of more and more silver reserves, those currencies based on gold continued to rise in value and those based on silver were declining due to demonetisation of silver. For India, which carried out most of its trade with gold-based countries, especially Britain, the impact of this shift was profound. As the price of silver continued to fall, so too did the exchange value of the Rupee, when measured against UK's Pound. It was very well planned economic plunder by the government of the UK. It meant that the UK could effectively steal Indian gold, and pay for it in Indian silver. Both the gold and the silver were mined cheaply with slave (indentured) labor, and the Indian taxpayer bore the cost of it all.

## The destruction of industrialisation during the UK's invasion of India

Some historians have wondered why India did not undergo industrialisation in the nineteenth century in the way that the UK did. In the seventeenth century, India was a developed, urbanised and commercialised nation with a buoyant export trade devoted largely to cotton textiles, but also including gemstones, diamonds, indigo, muslin, silk, spices, and rice. India was the world's main producer of cotton textiles and had a substantial export trade to Britain, as well as many other European countries, via the East India Company. Yet as the UK's cotton industry underwent a technological revolution in the late eighteenth century, the Indian industry was brutally forced into stagnation, and industrialisation in India was conveniently delayed until the twentieth century.

Some historians have suggested that this may have been because India was still a largely agricultural nation with low wages levels. In Britain, wages were high, so cotton producers had the incentive to invent and purchase expensive new labour-saving technologies. In India, by contrast, wages levels were low, so producers preferred to increase output by hiring more workers rather than investing in technology.

The above explanation is flawed. These historians' analyses conveniently ignored the fact that under the UK's rule, India did not operate in a free and competitive trade environment. Quite the opposite. Once the UK's rule through the East India Company was consolidated by the late 1700s the UK terrorized India's advanced textile industry for it was in direct competition to the developing British textile industry. Since the Middle Ages, Indian textiles such as muslin were revered around the world and were produced at a quality that the UK and the rest of Europe could not compete with. So once the UK economically invaded India they did what they couldn't do in a freely competitive environment. They used terrorism to shut down the competition.

Even as late as 1772, Henry Patullo, in the course of his comments on the economic resources of Bengal, could claim confidently that the demand for Indian textiles could never reduce, since no other nation could equal or rival it in quality. However, by the beginning of the nineteenth century, a beginning of a long history of decline of textile exports is observed. In the early 19th century, the East India Company (EIC) deployed terrorism - they cut off the hands of hundreds of thousands of highly skilled weaver communities in the Bengal in order to destroy the indigenous weaving industry in favor of British textile imports (some anecdotal accounts say the thumbs of the weavers of Dacca were removed). Twenty weavers' fortunate families from Murshidabad and Nadia in Bengal had then fled to Awadh (to the British: Oudh; corresponding to modern-day Uttar Pradesh), whose nawab resettled them in the town of Mahua Dabar. The refugees taught weaving to their offspring and Mahua Darbar became a weaving town of 5,000 people. In March–April 1857 when Zaffar Ali, a young man whose grandfather had migrated from Bengal, spotted a British boat coming down the Manorama (a tributary of the Ghagra on which Mahua Darbar was set). Remembering the UK's genocide of their communities, local people intercepted the boat and held the UK to justice. The soldiers were beheaded to pay for their war crimes - criminals executed included Lt T. E. Lindsay, Lt W. H. Thomas, Lt G. L. Caulty, Sgt Edwards and privates A. F. English and T. J. Richie. The UK went ahead with more genocidal plans – on June 20 that year, the UK's brave 12th Irregular Horse Cavalry surrounded the unarmed town, slaughtered thousands and set all the town afire. On the UK's revenue records, the area was subsequently marked Gair Chiragi (non-revenue land). And so it was that Mahua Dabar, a town of 5,000 persons, was subject to the UK's genocide with no survivors.

There were many industrial and trading cities that were subject to the UK's genocide at this time.

## The Depression

The worldwide Great Depression of 1929 had a small direct impact on traditional India, with relatively little impact on the modern secondary sector. The government did little to alleviate distress, and was focused mostly on shipping gold to Britain. The worst consequences involved deflation, which increased the burden of the debt on villagers while lowering the cost of living. In terms of volume of total economic output, there was no decline between 1929 and 1934. Falling prices for jute (and also wheat) hurt larger growers. The worst hit sector was jute, based in Bengal, which was an important element in overseas trade; it had prospered in the 1920s but was hard hit in the 1930s. In terms of employment, there was some decline, while agriculture and small-scale industry also exhibited gains. The most successful new industry was sugar, which had meteoric growth in the 1930s.

## Railways

The UK's investors supposedly funded a modern railway system in the late 19th century — it was the fourth largest in the world and was renowned for quality of construction since Indian metallurgy and labor were used. The government was supportive, realising its value for military use in case of another rebellion, as well as its value for economic growth. All the funding and management came from private British companies. The railways at first were privately owned and operated, and run by British administrators, engineers and supposedly skilled craftsmen. At first, only the so-called unskilled workers were Indians.

A plan for a rail system in India was first put forward in 1832. A few short lines were built in the 1830s, but they did not interconnect. 1844, Governor-General Lord Hardinge allowed private entrepreneurs to set up a rail system in India. The John Company (and later the colonial government) encouraged new railway companies backed by private investors under a scheme that would provide land and guarantee an annual return of up to five percent during the initial years of operation. The companies were to build and operate the lines under a 99-year lease, with the government having the option to buy them earlier.

Two new railway companies, Great Indian Peninsular Railway (GIPR) and East Indian Railway (EIR) began in 1853–54 to construct and operate lines near Mumbai and Kolkota. In 1853, the first passenger train service was inaugurated between Bori Bunder in Mumbai and Thane. Covering a distance of 34 kilometres (21 mi). The first passenger railway line in northern India between Allahabad and Kanpur opened in 1859.

In 1854 UK's Governor-General Mr Dalhousie formulated a plan to construct a network of trunk lines connecting the principal regions of India. Encouraged by the government guarantees, investment flowed in and a series of new rail companies were established, leading to rapid expansion of the rail system in India. Soon several large free Indian states built their own rail systems and the network spread to the regions that became the modern-day states of Assam, Rajasthan and Andhra Pradesh. The route mileage of this network increased from 1,349 kilometres (838 mi) in 1860 to 25,495 kilometres (15,842 mi) in 1880 – mostly radiating inland from the three major port cities of Mumbai, Chennai, and Kolkota. Most of the railway construction was done by Indian companies supposedly supervised by engineers from the UK. The system was heavily built, in terms of sturdy tracks and strong bridges. By 1900 India had a full range of rail services with diverse ownership and management, operating on broad, metre and narrow gauge networks. In 1900 the government took over the GIPR network, while the company continued to manage it.

In the First World War, the railways were used to transport troops and grains to the ports of Mumbai and Karachi en route to the UK, Iraq, Iran, Syria, Turkey (called by Europeans as Mesopotamia), and East Africa. With shipments of equipment and parts from the UK curtailed, maintenance became much more difficult; critical workers entered the army; workshops were converted to making artillery; some locomotives and cars were shipped to West Asia and North Africa. The railways could barely keep up with the increased demand. By the end of the war, the railway had deteriorated badly.In 1923, both GIPR and EIR were nationalised.

Mr Headrick argues that until the 1930s, both the UK government's railway lines and the private Indian companies' hired only European supervisors, civil engineers, and even operating personnel, such as locomotive engineers. The government's Stores Policy required that bids on railway contracts be made to the India Office in London, thereby discriminating against Indian firms. The railway companies purchased most of their hardware and parts in Britain. There were railway maintenance workshops in India, but they were rarely allowed to manufacture or repair locomotives. TISCO steel could not obtain orders for rails until the 1920s. The Second World War severely crippled the railways as rolling stock was diverted to West Asia and North Africa, and the railway workshops were converted into munitions workshops.

India provides an example of the UK's British 'Empire' pouring its money and expertise into a very well built system designed for military purposes after the Mutiny of 1857, and with the hope that it would stimulate industry. The system was overbuilt and too expensive for the small amount of freight traffic it carried. However, it did capture the imagination of the Indians, who incorrectly saw the railway as a symbol of an industrial modernity — but one that was not realised until after Independence. Christensen (1996) looks at the UK's invasion-based purpose, local needs, capital, service, and private-versus-public interests. He concludes that making the railways a creature of the state hindered success because railway expenses had to go through the same time-consuming and political budgeting process as did all other state expenses. Railway costs could therefore not be tailored to the timely needs of the railways or their passengers.

After independence in 1947, forty-two separate railway systems, including thirty-two lines owned by the former Indian princely states, were amalgamated to form a single unit named the *Indian Railways*. The existing rail networks were abandoned in favour of zones in 1951 and a total of six zones came into being in 1952.

## Agriculture and industry

The Indian economy grew at about 1% per year from 1880 to 1920, and the population also grew at 1%. The result was, on average. no long-term change in income levels. Agriculture was still dominant, with most peasants at the subsistence level. Extensive irrigation systems were built, providing an impetus for growing cash crops for export and for raw materials for Indian industry, especially jute, cotton, sugarcane, coffee and tea.

The entrepreneur Jamsetji Tata (1839–1904) began his industrial career in 1877 with the Central India Spinning, Weaving, and Manufacturing Company in Bombay. While other Indian mills produced cheap coarse yarn (and later cloth) using local short-staple cotton and cheap machinery imported from Britain, Tata did much better by importing expensive longer-stapled cotton from Egypt and buying more complex ring-spindle machinery from the United States to spin finer yarn that could compete with imports from Britain.

In the 1890s, Tata launched plans to expand into heavy industry using Indian funding. The Raj did not provide capital, but aware of Britain's declining position against the U.S. and Germany in the steel industry, it wanted steel mills in India so it is did promise to purchase any surplus steel Tata could not otherwise sell. The Tata Iron and Steel Company (TISCO), now headed by his son Dorabji Tata (1859–1932), opened its plant at Jamshedpur in Bihar in 1908. It became the leading iron and steel producer in India, with 120,000 employees in 1945. TISCO became an India's proud symbol of technical skill, managerial competence, entrepreneurial flair, and high pay for industrial workers.

## References

B. R. Tomlinson, *The Economy of Modern India, 1860–1970* (1996)

K. N., Chaudhuri (1978). *The Trading World of Asia and the English East India Company: 1660-1760.* Cambridge University Press.

K. A. Manikumar, *A colonial economy in the Great Depression, Madras (1929–1937)* (2003)

Dietmar Rothermund, *An Economic History of India to 1991* (1993)

Omkar Goswami, "Agriculture in Slump: The Peasant Economy of East and North Bengal in the 1930s," *Indian Economic & Social History Review,* July 1984.

Dietmar Rothermund, *An Economic History of India to 1991* (1993)

Dietmar Rothermund, *India in the Great Depression, 1929–1939* (New Delhi, 1992).

Ian J. Kerr (2007). *Engines of change: the railroads that made India.* Greenwood Publishing Group.

Thorner, Daniel (2005). "The pattern of railway development in India". In Kerr, Ian J. *Railways in Modern India.* New Delhi: Oxford University Press.

R.R. Bhandari (2005). *Indian Railways: Glorious 150 years.* Ministry of Information and Broadcasting, Government of India.

Awasthi, Aruna (1994). *History and development of railways in India.* New Delhi: Deep & Deep Publications.

Daniel R. Headrick, *The tentacles of progress: technology transfer in the age of imperialism, 1850–1940,*

Vinay Bahl, *Making of the Indian Working Class: A Case of the Tata Iron & Steel Company, 1880–1946* (1995)

# 6

# The Impact of the British Policies on Indian Agriculture

**Dr. SUKHBIR SINGH**
*Assistant Professor, Department of History,*
*Pt. J.L.N. Govt. College, Faridabad, Haryana*

## IMPACT OF BRITISH POLICIES ON COMMERCIALISATION OF AGRICULTURE

The major economic impact of the British policies in India was the introduction of a large number of commercial crops such as tea, coffee, indigo, opium, cotton, jute, sugarcane and oilseed. Different kinds of commercial crops were introduced with different intentions. Indian opium was used to balance the trade of Chinese tea with Britain in the latter's favor. The market for opium was strictly controlled by British traders which did not leave much scope for Indian producers to reap profit. Indians were forced to produce indigo and sell it on the conditions dictated by the Britishers. Indigo was sent to England and used as a dyeing agent for cloth produced in British towns. Indigo was grown under a different system where all farmers were compelled to grow it on 3/20th part of their land. Unfortunately cultivation of Indigo left the land infertile for some years. This made the farmers reluctant to grow it. In the tea plantations ownership changed hands quite often. The workers on these plantations worked under a lot of hardships.

Commercialisation of agriculture further enhanced the speed of transfer of ownership of land thereby increasing the number of landless laborers. It also brought in a large number of merchants, traders and middlemen who further exploited the situation. The peasant now depended on them to sell their produce during harvest time. Because the peasants now shifted to commercial crops, food grain production went down. So, less food stock led to famines. It was therefore not surprising that the peasants revolted. You would read about it in detail in the coming chapters.

There was an enormous drain of wealth from our country to Britain due to the various economic policies. Additional financial burden was placed on India due to expenditures on salaries, pensions and training of military and civilian staffs employed by the British to rule India. If this wealth was invested in India it could have helped enormously improved the economy in this country. Let us learn how the economic policies implemented by the British changed the social structure of Indian society.

## Agriculture and industry

The Indian economy grew at about 1% per year from 1880 to 1920, and the population also grew at 1%. The result was, on average. no long-term change in income levels. Agriculture was still dominant, with most peasants at the subsistence level. Extensive irrigation systems were built, providing an impetus for growing cash crops for export and for raw materials for Indian industry, especially jute, cotton, sugarcane, coffee and tea.

The entrepreneur Jamsetji Tata (1839–1904) began his industrial career in 1877 with the Central India Spinning, Weaving, and Manufacturing Company in Bombay.

While other Indian mills produced cheap coarse yarn (and later cloth) using local short-staple cotton and cheap machinery imported from Britain, Tata did much better by importing expensive longer-stapled cotton from Egypt and buying more complex ring-spindle machinery from the United States to spin finer yarn that could compete with imports from Britain.

In the 1890s, Tata launched plans to expand into heavy industry using Indian funding. The Raj did not provide capital, but aware of Britain's declining position against the U.S. and Germany in the steel industry, it wanted steel mills in India so it did promise to purchase any surplus steel Tata could not otherwise sell. The Tata Iron and Steel Company (TISCO), now headed by his son Dorabji Tata (1859–1932), opened its plant at Jamshedpur in Bihar in 1908. It became the leading iron and steel producer in India, with 120,000 employees in 1945. TISCO became India's proud symbol of technical skill, managerial competence, entrepreneurial flair, and high pay for industrial workers.

## ECONOMIC IMPACT OF BRITISH IMPERIALISM

Debate continues about the economic impact of British imperialism on India. The issue was actually raised by conservative British politicianEdmund Burke who in the 1780s vehemently attacked the East India Company, claiming that Warren Hastings and other top officials had ruined the Indian economy and society. Indian historian Rajat Kanta Ray (1998) continues this line of reasoning, saying the new economy brought by the British in the 18th century was a form of plunder and a catastrophe for the traditional economy of Mughal India. (Economic Drain Theory) Ray believes that British depleted the food and money stocks and imposed high taxes that helped cause the terrible famine of 1770, which killed a third of the people of Bengal.

P. J. Marshall, a British historian known for his work on the British empire, has a reinterpretation of the view that the prosperity of the formerly being Mughal rule gave way to poverty and anarchy. Marshall argues the British takeover did not make any sharp break with the past. British control was delegated largely through regional rulers and was sustained by a generally prosperous economy for the rest of the 18th century, except the frequent famines with very high fatality rate(Famine in India). Marshall notes the British raised revenue through local tax administrators and kept the old Mughal rates of taxation. Instead of the Indian nationalist account of the British as alien aggressors, seizing power by brute force and impoverishing all of India, Marshall presents a British nationalist interpretation in which the British were not in full control but instead were controllers in what was primarily an Indian play and in which their ability to keep power depended upon excellent cooperation with Indian elites. Marshall admits that much of his interpretation is still rejected by many historians.

## IMPACT OF COLONIAL RULE OF BRITISH ON INDIAN AGRICULTURE

Agriculture was the main stay of Indian economy. Nearly eighty percent people adopted cultivation either as principal or as secondary occupation. About seventy percent of national income came from agricultural sector. Agricultural productions constituted mainly food-grains and such other crops like oilseeds, fiber crops, sugar cane required for domestic consumption. Moreover, agriculture had special importance in self-sufficient village economy. However, the British Rule changed the nature and structure of Indian economy.

Land was heavily assessed for revenue; a new class of landlords emerged; deindustrialization led to overcrowding of land; increasing rural indebtedness put the peasants in poverty; a large number of intermediaries caused low productivity and finally the impoverishment of the peasantry was accelerated.

Under these circumstances Indian agriculture could not sustain the pressure from the growing dependence on land, the increasing Government dues and the exploitation of unscrupulous landlords. The consequence was inevitable. Agriculture became stagnant and personality acre yields declined.

There were various factors contributing for stagnation of agriculture. It began with the land revenue policy of the Company. Ownership of land was vested with non-cultivators where as the actual cultivators had no claim over land. The Government became the rent receiver; the Zamindars were rent-collectors; and the peasants were mere rent payers.

The Government did nothing for agricultural development. The rent-collecting Zamindars had no interest in agriculture. Finally, the cultivators had no resources for investment to improve agriculture. Moreover, the cultivators lost interest to bring about improvement in the land which they did not possess.

The land cultivated by him was not his property and the benefit coming out of agricultural improvement would be reaped by the absentee landlords and moneylenders. To them, agricultural improvement meant payment of more rent and no cultivator came forward to invest in fear of extra payment. Thus, agriculture declined steadily.

India handicraft industries were closed down and local markets were no more profitable for the Indian traders. Within short-time, agriculture was left as the lone source of employment and thus got overcrowded due to migration of working persons from non - agricultural sectors. Further, uncontrolled population growth added extra pressure on land.

Thus, people competed among themselves for a plot of land and were exploited by rack-renting of the landlords. The system of subletting the right to collect revenue created a chain of intermediaries and led to subdivision and the fragmentation of land into small holdings. As a result per capita land was very low and income from land could not meet the livelihood of the cultivators. All apart, every one wanted to be a rent collector instead of being a cultivator for which subletting and subleasers increased. Thus, fragmentation of land into small holdings and excessive overcrowding reduced yields per acre.

Indian cultivators adopted primitive techniques in agricultural production. They hardly used better cattle and seeds, more manure and fertilizer and improved techniques of production. As discussed earlier, the cultivators had little or no resource for improvement of agriculture. The Government deliberately neglected agriculture.

Though the peasants shouldered main burden of taxation, very small part of their tax was paid for improvement and modernization of agriculture. The Government spent millions of rupees on the railways to protect and promote the British trade interests. On the other hand, very little was spent on irrigation and that was the only field of Government investment.

The landlords took no personal interest beyond collection of rent. They exploited the cultivators by rack-renting to enhance their income and were unwilling to make any investment to increase income by increasing productivity of land. Thus, agriculture continued to be neglected grossly and stagnation of agriculture was inevitable.

No less harmful were the effects of the natural calamities like floods, droughts and famines. Repeated occurrence of those calamities forced the peasants to give upon cultivation. There was no attempt to bring about any preventive measures against the natural calamities.

During early years of the British Rule nothing was done to check or to regulate the flood water. No initiative was taken for providing irrigation that could have insured agricultural production against droughts or scanty rainfall. Failure of crops for two or more consecutive years took the dreadful shape of famine.

Neither the Government nor the landlords paid any attention to prevent the devastation of the natural calamities. In India a good harvest depended on a better monsoon with adequate was uncertain, rainfall was irregular and natural calamities were inherent. The Government was apathetic, the landlords were oppressive and the cultivators were hopeless. Therefore, agriculture was left at the mercy of nature.

Similarly, no improvement came in the agricultural technology. Agricultural implements were ordinary and old. Wooden ploughs were primarily used and cattle wastes constituted the manure. Use of iron ploughs was rare and an inorganic fertilizer was unknown. There was very little effort for creating educational awareness among technological advancement would have been an effective measure to increase productivity. But the technological stagnation fastened the decline in agriculture and ultimately poverty was perpetuated for rural masses more specifically for the peasants.

## COMMERCIALIZATION OF AGRICULTURE DURING BRITISH ERA

### Impact of the British rule on the agriculture of India

- Britishers introduced a new class of landlords called Zamindars who regarded land as their private property and aimed at obtaining maximum monetary gains out of it.
- The cultivators, the actual tillers of land, were mere tenants with no rights and could be evicted by the land-owners.
- The fanner was very often heavily in debt aid in the clutches of the money-lenders, who, eventually, came to-control the land and its produce.
- Agriculture production was no longer for use in the village only and much of it was sent to the market for sale.
- Farmers were forced to produce cash crop to feed the industries in England.
- It ruined the self-sufficiency of the village.
- The new revenue systems led to peas-ant indebtedness and commercialization of agricul-ture.
- This ultimately resulted in mass pov-erty and problem of landlessness.

### What is Commercialization of Agriculture?

- Commercialisation of agriculture is a phe-nomenon where agriculture is governed by commer-cial consideration i.e. certain specialised crops began to be grown not for consumption in village but for sale in national and even in international market.
- Commercialization of agriculture in India began during the British rule. Revolutionary changes had occurred in the agrarian property relations towards the end of the 18th century. The commercialization of Indian agriculture started post 1813 when the industrial revolution in England gained pace. Commercialization of agriculture became prominent around 1860 A.D (during American Civil War which boosted demand

of Cotton from India to Britain as Aerica was not able to export Cotton).

- Most of the plantations for commercial crops were controlled by the English. Jute was another product that received attention of the English company because the jute made products got a ready market in America and Europe.
- The commercialization of Indian Agriculture took place not to feed the industries of India because India was far behind in industrial development as compared to Britain, France, Belgium and many other European countries of eighteenth century.
- The commercialization of Indian Agriculture was done primarily to feed the British industries that it was taken up and achieved only in cases-of those agricultural products which were either needed by the British industries or could fetch cash commercial gain to the British in the European or American market.
- For example, several efforts were made to increase the production of cotton in India to provide raw and good quality cotton to the cotton-textile industries of Britain which were growing fast after the Industrial Revolution in Britain. Therefore, cotton growing area increase in India and its production increased manifold with gradual lapse of time. Indigo and more than that, tea and coffee plantation were encouraged in India because these could get commercial market abroad.
- Cash transactions become the basis of exchange and largely replaced the barter system.

## How Commercialization of Agriculture Happened?

- The commercialization of India agriculture was initiated in India by the British through their direct and indirect policies and activities.
- The new land tenure system introduced in form of permanent settlement and Ryotwari Settlement had made agricultural land a freely exchangeable commodity.
- The Permanent settlement by giving ownership right to the zamindars created a class of wealthy landlords; they could make use of this ownership right by sale or purchase of land. Further, the agriculture which had been way of life rather

than a business enterprise now began to be practiced for sale in national and international market.

- Moreover, crops like cotton, jute, sugarcane, ground nuts, tobacco etc. which had a high demand in the market were increasingly cultivated. The beginning of the plantation crops like Tea, coffee, rubber, indigo etc heralded a new era in agricultural practices in India. These were essentially meant for markets and thus commercialization of agriculture took to new heights with the expansion of the British rule.
- The commercialization of agriculture was a forced and artificial process for the majority of Indian peasants. It was introduced under coercion of the British and not out of the incentive of peasantry at large. The peasantry went for cultivation of commercial crops under duress. He had to pay the land revenue due to the British government in time. Moreover, he had to grow commercial crop on a specified tract of his land under the oppression of planters.

## What Caused Commercialization of Agriculture in India during British?

- A large number of factors encouraged and facilitated commercialization of Indian agriculture. The political unity established by the British and the resultant rise of the unified national market was an important factor. Further, the spread of money economy replaced the barter and agricultural goods became market items.
- The enlargement and expansion of international trade and the entry of British finance capital also belted commercialization of agriculture.
- Increasing demand for some of the commercial crops in other foreign countries gave impetus to commercialization of agriculture.
- The American Civil War also indirectly encouraged commercialization of agriculture in India: the British cotton demand was diverted to India. The demand of cotton was maintained even after the civil war ceased because of the rise of cotton textile industries in India.
- The chief factor was the colonial subjugation of India under the British rule. India was reduced to the supplier of raw materials and food grains to Britain and importer of British

manufactured goods. Many commercial crops like, cotton, jute, tea, tobacco were introduced to meet the demand in Britain.

- The replacement of custom and tradition by competition and contract also led to the commercialization of Indian agriculture
- Better means of communication (equipped with rapid development of railways and shipping) made trade in agricultural products feasible, especially over long distances. The emergence of grain merchants was a natural adjunct to this and greatly facilitated agricultural trade.
- Monetization of land revenue payments was another important casual factor for agricultural commercialization.
- Another boosting factor for commercialization of agriculture in India was the gaining of speed of Industrial Revolution in England. This led to factor in commercialization as more and more agricultural goods were produced to satisfy the demand for raw materials by the British industries.
- British policy of one way free trade also acted as sufficient encouraging factor for commercialization as the manufactured items in textile, jute etc could find free entry in Indian markets, where as the manufactured goods did not have similar free access to European markets.
- The peasants went in for growing commercial crops to pay back the interests due to money lenders in time.

## What was Impact of Commercialization of Agriculture?

- Normally speaking, it should have acted as a catalyst in increasing agricultural productivity. But, in reality this did not happen due to poor agricultural organization, obsolete technology, and lack of resources among most peasants. It was only the rich farmers; who benefited and this in turn, accentuated inequalities of income in the rural society.
- The commercialization of agriculture beneficial to the British planters, traders and manufacturers, who were provided with opportunity to make huge profits by getting the commercialized agricultural products at, throw away prices. The commercialization of Indian agriculture also partly benefited Indian traders and money lenders who made huge fortunes by working as middlemen for the British.

- The poor peasant was forced to sell his produce just after harvest at whatever prices he could get as he had to meet in time the demands of the government, the landlord, the money lender and his family members' requirements. This placed him at the money of the grain merchant, who was in a position to dictate terms and who purchased his produced at much less than the market price. Thus, a large share of the benefit of the growing trade in agricultural products was reaped by the merchant, who was very often also the village money lender.
- Regional specialization of crop production based on climatic conditions, soil etc., was an outcome of the commercial revolution in agriculture. Deccan districts of Bombay presidency grew cotton, Bengal grew jute and Indigo, Bihar grew opium, Assam grew tea, Punjab grew wheat, etc.
- Another important consequence of the commercial revolution in agriculture was linking of the agricultural sector to the world market. Price movements and business fluctuations in the world markets began to affect the fortunes of the Indian farmer to a degree that it had never done before. The farmer in his choice of crops attached greater importance to market demand and price than his home needs. The peasant class got adversely affected owing to imbalances in market condition.
- Commercialization of agriculture adversely affected self sufficiency of vil-lage economy and acted as major factor in bring-ing the declining state in rural economy.
- Indian money lenders advanced Cash advances to the farmers to cultivate the commercial crops and if the peasants failed to pay him back in time, the land of peasants came under ownership of moneylenders.
- Most of the Indian people suffered miserably due to the British policy of commercialization of Indian agriculture. It resulted in reduced area under cultivation of food crops due to the substitution of commercial non-food grains in place of food grains. Between 1893-94 to 1945-46, the production of commercial crops increased by 85 percent and that of food crops fell by 7 percent. This had a devastating effect on the rural economy and often took the shape of famines. The misery was further enhanced became the population of India was increasing every year, fragmentation of land was taking

place because of the increasing pressure on land and modern techniques of agricultural production were not introduced in India. Thus, the commercialization of agriculture in India by the British was also one of the important causes of the impoverishment of the Indian people.

- Commercialization of agriculture did not encouraged growth of land mar-ket because major profit of commercialisation went to company traders and mediators.
- Commercialisation effected traditional relations between agriculture and industry. In Indian tra-ditional relations acted as factors for each other's development which were hampered.
- Commercialization of agriculture indicated a commercial revolution. But this was devoid of any support from any technologi-cal revolution. Owing to true the healthy ben-efits which agriculture and associated fields would have enjoyed were lacking.
- The commercialization of agriculture had mixed effects. While it assisted the industrial revolution in Britain, it broke the economic self-sufficiency of villages in India. The commercialization of agriculture was a new phenomenon in Indian agriculture scene introduced by the British. While the upper class and British industries benefited-from it, the Indian peasants' life was tied to remote international market. The worst effect of commercialization was the oppression of Indian peasants at hands of European. This found expression in the famous Indigo revolt in 1859. Moreover, commercialization of Indian agriculture got manifested in series of famines which took a heavy toll of life.

## POSITIVE IMPACTS OF COMMERCIALIZATION OF AGRICULTURE

- In spite of having many negative effect commercializations in one sense was progressive event. Commercialisation encouraged social exchange and it made possible the transformation of Indian economy into capitalistic form.
- Commercialisation linked India with world economy. It led to the growth of high level social and economic system. The important contribution of commercialisation reflected in integration of economy. It also created a base for growth of national economy commercialisation of agriculture led to

growth of na-tional agriculture and agricultural problem acquired national form.
- It also brought about regional specialization of crops on an efficient basis.

## EXPANSION AND COMMERCIALIZATION OF AGRICULTURE DURING BRITISH RULE

Their ultimate aim was the appropriation of maximum revenue from the Indian Zamindars and peasants.

The exaction of exorbitant rents by the government oppressed the peasants heavily. In order to meet the high demand of revenue, the peasants perpetually remained indebted to the local money-lenders.

Many of them lost their lands to these greedy moneylenders for the inability to pay back the borrowed amount.

The policy of commercialization of agriculture by the British encouraged market oriented produc-tion of cash crops such as opium, tea, coffee, sugar, jute and indigo. Indian peasants were forced to grow these cash crops that spoiled the fertility of the land and no other crop could be grown on it.

The growth of minimum of subsistence crops led to the deterioration and impoverishment of the Indian agriculture and the cultivators. The peasant was suppressed under triple burden of the government, landlord and the moneylender.

His subsistence base was completely ruined by the agrarian policies of the British government. The lack of attention in the development of agriculture and in use of new equipments and methods on the part of the British government also ruined Indian agriculture.

### Land Rights and Land Settlements

Broadly speaking, the English adopted three types of land tenures in India viz., the Zamindari tenure, the Mahalwari tenure and the Ryotwari tenure.

### The Permanent Zamindari Settlements

The Zamindari system was a creation of the British rule and many non-economic considerations entered into its acceptance. The system was known by different names like Jagirdari, Malguzari, Biswedari, etc. Under the Permanent Settlement system the state's land revenue demand was settled once for, all while in other Zamindari tracts the land revenue was revised after a fixed number of years ranging from 10 to 40 years. This was introduced by Lord Cornwallis in 1793 on the recommendation of Sir John Shore, the President of the Board of Revenue.

Under the Zamindari system, the Zamindari was recognised as the owner who could mortgage, bequeath and sell the land. The state held the Zamindari responsible for the payment of land revenue and in default thereof the land could be confis-cated and sold out.

A snag in the Permanent Settlement of Bengal was that while the state's land revenue demand was fixed (the stat demand was fixed at 89% of the rental, leaving only 11 % with the Zamindari), the rent to be realised by the landlord from the cultivator was left unsettled and unspecified.

This resulted in rack-renting and frequent ejections of tenants from their traditional holdings. The Bengal Rent Acts of 1859 and 1885 provided some relief to cultivators. Permanent Zamindari settlements were made in Bengal, Bihar, Orissa, Benaras Division of the U.P, Northern Carnatic and roughly covered 19% of the total area of British India.

## The Ryotwari System

Under this system every 'registered' holder of land was recognised as the proprietor of land and was held responsible for direct payment of land revenue to the state. He had the right to sub-let his land holdings, to transfer, mortgage or sell it. He was not evicted from his holdings by the Government so long as he paid the state demand of land revenue.

In Madras Presidency, the first land revenue settlements were made in the Baramahal district after its acquisition by the Company in 1792. Captain Read assisted by Thomas Munro fixed the state demand on the basis of 50% of the estimated produce of the fields, which worked out to be more than the whole economic rent.

Thomas Munro (Governor 1820-27) extended the Ryotwari systems to all parts of the province (except the permanently settled areas) on the basis of 1/3rd of the gross produce of the holdings which too absorbed nearly the whole of the economic rental.

The state demand was fixed in money and had no connection with the actual yield of the holding or the prevailing prices in the market. In 1855 an extensive survey and settlement plan was decided on the basis of 30% of the gross produce. Actual work began in 1861. In Bombay Presidency too the Company decided in favour of the

Ryotwari system with a view to the elimination of landlords or village communities which could intercept their profits.

Thus the Ryotwari settlements were made in major portions of Bombay and Madras Presidencies, in Assam and some other parts of British India covering roughly 51% of the area.

## The Mahalwari System

Under this system, the unit for revenue settlement was the village or the Mahal (i.e., the estate). The village land belonged jointly to the village community technically the body of 'co-sharers' who were jointly responsible for payment of land revenue, though individual responsibility was also there.

The Mahalwari tenure was introduced in major portions of the UP, the Central Provinces the Punjab (with variations) and covered nearly 30% of the area. Regulation VII of 1822 gave legal sanction to the recommendation of Holt Mackenzie, who re-corded his Minute in 1819 emphasizing the existence of village communities in North India. He recom-mended a survey of land, preparation of record of rights in land, settlement of land revenue demand village by village or mahal by mahal and collection of land revenue through the village headman or Lambardar.

Thus the land revenue settlements were made on the basis of 80% of the rental value, payable by the Zamindars. In cases where estates were held by cultivators in common tenancy, the state demand was allowed to be fixed at 95% of the rental. The system broke down because of the excessive state demand and harshness in its working and collection of land revenue. Regulation IX of 1833 provided for simplification of the procedure for preparing estimates of produce and of rents and introduction of the system of fixing average rents for different classes of soil. The new scheme worked under the supervision of Mertins Bird remembered as the Father of Land Settlements in Northern India. The state demand was fixed at 66% of the rental value and the settlement was made for 30 years. The settlement work under the scheme began in 1833 and was completed under the administration of James Thomason. Under the revised Saharanpur Rules of 1855, the state demand was limited to 50% of the rental value.

## Rural Indebtedness

High revenue demands led to devastation, as it led to poverty and the deterioration of agriculture in the 19th century. It forced the peasant to fall into the clutches of the money-lender. If the peasant could not pay the money, his land was sold-off. Gradually more land passed into the hands of money-lenders, merchants, rich peasants and other moneyed classes.

The growing commercialization also helped the money-lender cum merchant to exploit the cultivator. The peasant was forced to sell his produce just after the harvest and at whatever price he could get as he had to meet in time the demands of the government, the landlord and the money-lender. Added to the above factors, was the increase of population pressure on agriculture weighted on the peasants heavily.

## References

Sugata Bose, *Agrarian Bengal: Economy, Social Structure, and Politics.* Cambridge, 1986.

Amin, Shahid. *Sugarcane and Sugar in Gorakhpur: An Inquiry into Peasant Production for Capitalist Enterprise in Colonial India.* Delhi: Oxford University Press, 1984.

Baden Powell, Henry. *Land Systems of British India.* New York: Johnson Reprint Corp., 1972.

Baker, Christopher John. *An Indian Rural Economy: 1880 - 1955 The Tamilnad Countryside.* Oxford and Delhi: Oxford University Press, 1984.

Bose, Sugata. *Agrarian Bengal: Economy, Social Structure, and Politics, 1919-1947.* Cambridge: Cambridge University Press, 1986.

Catanach, I. J. *Rural Credit in Western India: rural credit and the cooperative movement in the Bombay presidency, 1875-1930.* Berkeley: U Cal Press, 1970.

7

# Administrative Reforms during the Period of Lord Cornwallis: Their Impacts on the Life of Indian Society and Economy

**Dr. GIRISH KUMAR SINGH**
*Assistant Professor, Department of History, Amar Singh (P.G.) College, Lakhoti, Bulandshehar, Uttar Pradesh.*

British General Charles Cornwallis, the 2nd Earl Cornwallis, was appointed in February 1786 to serve as both Commander-in-Chief of British India and Governor of the Presidency of Fort William, also known as the Bengal Presidency. Based in Calcutta, he oversaw the consolidation of British control over much of peninsular India, setting the stage for the British Raj. He was also instrumental in enacting administrative and legal reforms that fundamentally altered civil administration and land management practices in India. According to historian Jerry Dupont, Cornwallis was responsible for "laying the foundation for British rule throughout India and setting standards for the services, courts, and revenue collection that remained remarkably unaltered almost to the end of the British era."

He was raised to the title of Marquess Cornwallis in 1792 as recognition for his performance in the Third Anglo-Mysore War, in which he extracted significant concessions from the Mysorean ruler, Tipu Sultan. He returned to England in 1793, and was subsequently engaged in a variety of administrative and diplomatic postings until 1798, when he was posted to the Kingdom of Ireland as Lord Lieutenant and Commander-in-Chief, similar to his leadership posts in India. After returning from Ireland in 1801, he was again posted to India. He arrived in July 1805, and died the same October in Ghazipur. Cornwallis was buried at Ghazipur, and is memorialized throughout India.

## ADMINISTRATIVE REFORMS

Cornwallis was charged by the directors of the British East India Company to overhaul and reform its administration in India. The company had historically paid its functionaries (revenue collectors, traders, and administrators) in India relatively little, but allowed them to engage in trade for themselves, including the use of company shipping for the purpose. As long as the company was profitable, this open door to corruption and graft at the company's expense was overlooked. However, the rise of manufacturing in Britain led to a collapse of prices for textiles and other goods from India, and the company's involvement in wars on the subcontinent had also been expensive. By the time Cornwallis arrived the company was losing money. Its employees, however, continued to profit personally, without caring whether or not the company made money. Cornwallis sought to change this practice, first by refusing to engage in such dealing himself, and second, by securing pay increases for the company's functionaries while denying them their personal trading privileges.

Another area of reform that Cornwallis implemented was the reduction of nepotism and political favoritism as means for advancement and positions within the company. Seeking instead to advance the company's interests, he sought out and promoted individuals on the basis of merit, even refusing requests by the Prince of Wales to assist individuals in the latter's good graces.

The servants of the company were corrupt, incompetent and irresponsible persons. Cornwallis realized that the low salaries of the company's servants encouraged them to indulge in various kinds of private trade to augment their income. So Cornwallis decided to raise the salaries of the servants of the company.

The employees of the company were prohibited to carry on private trade. He had a low opinion about the character, ability and integrity of the Indian people. So he sought to reserve all higher posts for the Europeans. He also introduced some reforms in police department.

The districts were divided into small thanas and an Inspector was appointed in each thana. A superior officer with the designation of superintendent of police was appointed in each district to supervise the work of the Inspectors. He raised the salaries of all police officers.

He separated the judiciary from executive as a result equal justice could be dispensed to all the people.

## JUDICIAL REFORMS

Cornwallis introduced some significant reforms in the sphere of judicial administration and tried to complete the unfinished work of Warren Hastings. During his period number of revenue districts was reduced from 35 to 23 in the Presidency of Bengal. The collector was the head of the district. In 1787 district courts were presided over by the collector. The collectors were vested with magisterial powers and empowered to administer criminal justice.

In 1790-92 further changes were made in the administration of criminal justice. The Faujdari Adalats of the districts were abolished and in their place four circuit courts were established at Dacca, Patna, Calcutta and Murshidabad. These courts were presided over by two covenanted servants of the company who decided the cases with the help of Qazis and Muftis. The Sadar Nizamat Adalat was again shifted from Murshidabad to Calcutta. The Muhammadan Judge of this Adalat was removed and in his place the Governor General and Council presided over the Sadar Nizamat Adalat.

By 1793 the judicial reforms of Cornwallis took the final shape and were embodied in the famous Cornwallis Code. Separation of powers was the basis of the new reforms. The collector was deprived of all his judicial and magisterial powers. The judges tried all civil cases in the districts.

The collector was required to look after the administration and to realise the revenue of the district. Under the subordination of the District Judge Civil and criminal courts of Lower grade were established in which the Munsif and Sadar Amin tried the minor cases of the people. Appeals could be made to district court against the decisions of the Lower Courts.

## COMMERCIAL REFORMS

Cornwallis took some steps for the improvement of trade and commerce. Since the establishment of Board of Trade at Calcutta, the company had procured goods through European and Indian contractors. These contractors often supplied goods at high prices and of low quality. Cornwallis stopped the practice of procuring supplies through contracts and started the practice of procuring supplies through Commercial Residents and agents.

These Commercial Residents fixed the prices of goods with the manufacturers and also made advances to them. Cornwallis reduced the members of the Board of Trade from eleven to five and placed it under the control of the Calcutta Council. He also issued instructions that the merchants would not be oppressed.

## Rise of the Zemindars

The resources of government in India had been derived from time immemorial, almost exclusively from the land, a certain proportion of the produce of which was considered the inalienable right of the sovereign. The settlement of the land revenue was, therefore, a question of the greatest magnitude, and embraced, not only the financial strength of the state, but the prosperity of its subjects. Two centuries before the period of which we treat, Toder Mull, the great financier of Akbar, had made a settlement of the lower provinces, directly with the cultivators, after an accurate survey and valuation of the lands. To collect the rents from the ryots, and transmit them of the treasury, agents were placed in various revenue circles, and remunerated for their labour by a percentage on the collections. The office of collector speedily became hereditary, from the constant tendency of every office in India to become so, and, also from the obvious convenience of continuing the agency in the family which was in possession of the local records, and acquainted with the position of the ryots, and the nature of the lands. The collector thus became responsible for the government rent, and was entrusted with all the powers necessary for realising it. He was permitted to entertain a military force, which it was his constant aim to augment, to increase his own consequence. His functions were gradually enlarged, and came eventually to embrace the control of the police and the adjudication of rights. The collector was thus transformed into a zemindar, and assumed the title and dignity of raja, and became, in effect, the master of the district.

## Evils of the revenue system, 1772–1790

The English government had from the first treated the zemindars as simple collectors, and ousted them without hesitation when others offered more for the lands than they were prepared to pay. But this uncertainty of tenure, and this repeated change of agency was found to be equally detrimental to the improvement of the lands, the welfare of the ryots, and the interests of the state. Under such a system there could be no application of capital to the operations of agriculture; the estates became deteriorated, while the remissions which Government was obliged to make from time to time, overbalanced any profits arising from competition. The Court of Directors complained that the revenue was steadily diminishing, and that the country itself was becoming impoverished and exhausted. Lord Cornwallis, soon after his arrival, declared that agriculture and internal, commerce were in a state of rapid decay, that no class of society appeared to be flourishing, except the money-lenders, and that both cultivators and landlords were sinking into poverty and wretchedness. The evils under which the people groaned, he affirmed to be enormous.

## Proprietary right in the lands, 1793

The proprietary right in the land had been considered, from time immemorial, to be vested in the sovereign; and although Mr. Francis and some others had thought fit to adopt a different opinion, the great majority of the public servants adhered to the ancient doctrine. But, after the investigations were completed, the Government, acting upon a generous and enlightened policy, determined to confer on the zemindars the unexpected boon of a permanent interest in the soil. Before this concession, the zemindars, from the highest to the lowest, had been mere tenants at will, liable at any time to be deprived by the state landlord of the estates they occupied.

But the regulations of 1793, in which the new fiscal policy was embodied, converted the soil into a property, and bestowed it upon them. A large and opulent class of landholders was thus created, in the hope that they would seek the welfare of the ryot, stimulate cultivation, and augment the general wealth of the country. It was found, however, to be much more easy to determine the relation between the government and the landlord, than between the landlord and his tenant. The rights of the cultivators were more ancient and absolute than those of the zemindar; but the zemindar had always practised every species of oppression on them, extorting every cowrie which could be squeezed from them by violence, and leaving them little beyond a rag and a hovel. Mr. Shore, who superintended the settlement, maintained that some interference on the part of government was indispensably necessary to effect an adjustment of the demands of the zemindar on the ryot. Lord Cornwallis affirmed that whoever cultivated the land, the zemindar couldreceive no more than the established rate, which in most cases was equal to what the cultivator could pay.

## Restrictions on the land-holders, 1793

The difficulty was compromised rather than adjusted by declaring that the zemindar should not be at liberty to enhance the rents of the "independent talookdars" and two other classes of renters who paid the fixed sums due to the state through him, simply for the convenience of government. The zemindar was also restricted from enhancing the rent of the class of tenants called khoodkast, who cultivated the lands of the village in which they resided, except when their rents were below the current rates, or when their tenures had been improperly obtained. The remaining lands of the estate he was at liberty to let in any manner and at any rate he pleased. For the protection of the resident cultivators it was enacted that the zemindar should keep a register of their tenures, and grant them pottahs, or leases, specifying the rent they were to pay, and that for any infringement of these rules the ryot was to seek a remedy in an action against him in the civil courts. But the registers were not kept, and pottahs were rarely given; and, as to the remedy, a poor man has little chance against his wealthy oppressor in courts where the native officers are universally venal, and their influence is paramount. By the unremitted contrivances of the zemindar, and changes of residence on the part of the ryot – which extinguished all his rights – the class of resident cultivators has been gradually diminished; and the ryots have been placed at the mercy of the zemindar. The absence of any clear and defined rules for the protection of the cultivator in his ancient right not to pay more than a limited and moderate rent, and to be kept in possession of his fields as long as he did so, is an unquestionable blot on a system which in other respects was highly beneficial.

## Reform of the civil courts, 1793

The administration of Lord Cornwallis was also rendered memorable by the great changes introduced into the judicial institutions of the Presidency. The collector of the revenue had hitherto acted also as judge and magistrate. Lord Cornwallis separated the financial from the judicial functions, and confined the collector to his fiscal duties, placing him under a Board of Revenue at the Presidency. A civil court was established in each district and in the principal cities, with a judge, a register to determine cases of inferior value, and one or more covenanted assistants. Every person in the country was placed under the jurisdiction of these courts, with the exception of British subjects, who were, by Act of Parliament, amenable to the Supreme Court. To receive appeals from the zillah and city courts, four Courts of Appeal were constituted at Calcutta, Dacca,

Moorshedabad, and Patna, and from their decisions an appeal lay to the Sudder Court at the Presidency, nominally composed of the Governor-General and the members of Council. All fees of every description were abolished, and the expenses of a suit restricted to the remuneration of pleaders and the expense of witnesses.

## Criminal courts, 1793

For the administration of criminal law, it was ordained that the judges of the four Courts of Appeal should proceed on circuit, from zillah to zillah, within their respective circles, and hold jail deliveries twice in the year. The Mohamedan law, divested of some of its most revolting precepts, was the criminal code of the courts, and the Mohamedan law officer, on the completion of the trial at which he had been present, was required to declare the sentence prescribed by that code, which was carried into execution if the judge concurred in it, and if he did not it was referred to the Sudder Court, which was also constituted a Court of Appeal in criminal cases. The zillah judges were likewise invested with the powers of a magistrate, and authorized to pass and execute sentences in trivial offences, and, in other cases, to apprehend the delinquent and commit him for trial before the judges of circuit. Each zillah was divided into districts of about twenty miles square, to each of which an officer called a daroga was appointed, with authority to arrest offenders on a written charge, and when the offence was bailable, to take security for appearance before the magistrate. Of all the provisions of the new system this proved to be the most baneful. The daroga, who was often fifty miles from the seat of control, enjoyed almost unlimited power of extortion, and became the scourge of the country.

## Exclusion of natives from power, 1793

Notwithstanding the wisdom exhibited in Lord Cornwallis's institutions, they were deformed by one great and radical error. He considered it necessary that the whole administration of the country should be placed exclusively in the hands of covenanted servants of the Company, to the entire exclusion of all native agency. In the criminal department, the only native officer entrusted with any power was the Daroga, upon an allowance of twenty-five rupees a month. In the administration of civil justice, cases of only the most trivial amount were made over to a native judge, under the title of Moonsiff; but while the salary of the European judge was raised to 2,500 rupees a month, the Moonsiff was deprived of all pay, and left to find a subsistence by a small commission on the value of suits; in other words, by the encouragement of litigation. Under all former conquerors, civil and military offices, with few exceptions, were open to the natives of the country, who might aspire, with confidence, to the post of minister, and to the command of armies. But under the impolitic system established in 1793, the prospects of legitimate and honourable ambition were altogether closed against the natives of the country. If the peculiar nature of British rule rendered it necessary to retain all political and military power in the hands of Europeans, this was no reason for denying the natives every opportunity of rising to distinction in the judicial departments, for which they were eminently qualified by their industrious habits, and their natural sagacity, not less than by the knowledge they possessed of the language and character of their fellow-countrymen. The fatal effects of this exclusion were speedily visible in the disrepute and inefficiency of the whole administration. With only three or four European functionaries in a district, which often contained a million of inhabitants, the machine of government must have stood still without the services of natives. But this power and influence from which it was impossible to exclude them, being exercised without responsibility, was used for the purposes of oppression, and the courts of every description became the hot-bed of corruption and venality.

## The Declaratory Act, 1788

The gravest movement of this period, however, was the consummation of Mr. Pitt's plan of transferring the powers of government from the Company to the Crown. In the year 1787, a conflict of parties arose in the republic of Holland; the French and the English Governments espoused opposite sides, and there was every prospect of a rupture between them. The interference of France in the politics of India, had been for half a century the great object of dread to the Court of Directors, and under the apprehension that they might have again to encounter it, they now solicited the Ministry to augment the European force in India, and four regiments were immediately raised for their service. Happily, the peace with France was not interrupted, but, as soon as the storm had blown over, the Court of Directors, anxious to save the cost of the regiments, declared that they were no longer necessary. Lord Cornwallis had earnestly recommended the augmentation of the European force in India, to give greater security to our position, and the Board of Control therefore determined that the regiments should be sent out. The Court of Directors, however, refused to allow them to embark in their ships, and as the contest, which thus arose between the India House and the Ministry, involved the great question of the substantial powers of government, Mr. Pitt referred the question to the decision of Parliament.

## Discussions In Parliament, 1788

On the 25th of February, 1788, Mr. Pitt introduced a Bill to declare the meaning of the Act of 1784, and affirmed that "there was no step which could have been taken by the Court of Directors before the passing of that Bill, touching the military and political concerns of India, and the collection, management, and application of the revenues, which the Board of Control had not a right to take by the provisions of that Bill." He stated, moreover, that in proposing his Bill of 1784 it was his intention thus to transfer the whole powers of government to the Crown.

The organs of the Court of Directors in the House stated that they never would have supported that measure, if they had supposed such to have been its intent; and they discovered, when too late, that in voting for Mr. Pitt's Bill they had committed an act of suicide. An objection was raised to the despatch of the regiments on the constitutional doctrine that no troops could belong to the King for which Parliament had not voted the money. Mr. Pitt thereupon stated his conviction that the army in India ought to be on one establishment, and to belong to the King, and that it was not without an eye to such an arrangement that he had brought forward the present motion. But, notwithstanding the boundless influence which he enjoyed in the House, the members were alarmed at the immense power which he attempted to grasp. Many of his staunch supporters deserted him, and the Opposition were very sanguine in their hopes of being able to overthrow the Ministry on this occasion. There were four tempestuous debates on the question, one of which was prolonged to eight o'clock in the morning. Mr. Pitt had encountered no such opposition in the present Parliament, and to prevent being beaten in the successive stages of the Bill, was under the necessity of making great concessions, and adding several conciliatory clauses to it. The Declaratory Act of 1788 rivetted on the East India Company the fetters which had been forged by the Act of 1784.

## The Charter of 1793

The period for which the exclusive privileges had been granted to the East India Company expired in 1793, and on the 23rd of April, the Court of Directors presented a petition to Parliament for the renewal of them. But new commercial and manufacturing interests had been springing up in England with great vigour since the last concession, and petitions poured into the House from Liverpool, Glasgow, Manchester, Bristol, and other seats of industry and enterprise, protesting against the continuance of a monopoly in so large a trade, and the exclusion of the country in general from any share in it. The Court of Directors appointed a Committee to draw up a reply to the petitioners, and to demonstrate that it was essential to the national interests that the East India Company should continue to be the sole agent for managing the commerce and government of India. The Ministry found the existing state of things, more especially since the Declaratory Act, exceedingly convenient to themselves, and resolved to oppose all innovation. Fortunately for the Company, Lord Cornwallis, notwithstanding the Mysore war, had placed the finances of India in a more flourishing condition than they had ever been in before; and, it may be said, than they have ever been in since. Mr. Dundee was thus enabled to ask the House, with an air of triumph, whether they were prepared to stop the tide of this prosperity, for a mere theory.

## Arguments for renewing the Charter, 1793

The arguments which he adduced for continuing the power and privileges of the East India Company were, that to throw the trade open to all England would retard the payment of the Company's debts; that it would check the growing commerce of India, and that it would inevitably lead to colonization and ensure the loss of the country to England. He objected to the dissolution of the Company, because the patronage of India, added to the other sources of influence in the Crown, would destroy the balance of the Constitution. These arguments, solemnly propounded by the Ministers, at a period when free trade was considered the direct road to ruin, were received with blind confidence by the House, and the privileges of the Company were renewed, with little modification, for a period of twenty years. To meet the clamours of the merchants and manufacturers of England, the Company was directed to allot 3,000 tons a year for private trade, but as the privilege was hampered with the heavy charges and delays of their commercial system, it was little prized, and seldom used. An effort was made by Mr. Wilberforce, one of the ablest and most enlightened members of the House, to obtain permission for missionaries and schoolmasters to proceed to India, and give voluntary instruction to the people, but he was vehemently opposed by the old Indians in the Court of Directors, who had imbibed the fantastic notion that the diffusion of knowledge would be fatal to British rule in India, and that the presence of missionaries would be followed by rebellion; and the House was persuaded by Mr. Dundas to reject the proposal.

## Remarks on the Charter, 1793

The Charter, as it is called, of 1793, may be regarded as a faithful reflection of the narrow views of the age, which, considered that the introduction of free trade and Europeans, of missionaries and schoolmasters, into India, would sap the foundation of British authority. The experience of nearly three-quarters of a century has dispelled this hallucination. Since the extinction of the Company's monopoly, the trade, instead of being diminished, has increased twenty fold. The free admission of Europeans into India has not endangered the dominion of England; on the contrary, during the great mutiny of 1857, India was nearly lost for want of Europeans. The patronage of India has been trebled in value, and the Company has been abolished, yet, owing to the happy discovery of the principle of competitive appointments, the power of the Crown has not been increased, and the independence of Parliament has not diminished. Christian missionaries have been admitted into India and placed on the same footing as the Hindoo priest and the Mohamedan mollah, and allowed to offer instruction to the natives; and, the education of the people is now considered as much a duty of the state as the maintenance of the police; – yet the feeling of allegiance to the Crown of England has not been impaired.

## References

Austin, Granville: *The Indian Constitution: Cornerstone of a Nation*, Oxford, Clarendon Press, 1966.

Baird, Robert: *Religion in Modern India*, New Delhi, Manohar, 1981.

Derrett, J. Duncan. *Religion, Law, and the State in India*. London: Faber, 1968.

Gurukal, Rajan: *The Formation of Caste Society in Kerala*, Rawat Publications, New Delhi, 1994.

Karve, Irawati: *Hindu Society: An Interpretation*, Poona, Sangam Press, 1961.

McLane, John R.: *Indian Nationalism and the Early Congress*, Princeton, Princeton University Press, 1977.

Rudner, David W.: *Caste and Colonialism in Colonial India: The Nattukkottai Chettiars*, Berkeley, University of California Press, 1994.

Satyamurthy, T.V.: *Region, Religion, Caste, Gender and Culture in Contemporary India*, Delhi, OUP, 1996.

# 8

# New Administrative Structure of British Raj

**DR ALOK PANDEY**

*Head Department of History, Unity Law College, Rudrapur (Udham Singh Nagar), Uttarakhand*

The history of British rule in India can be traced back to 31st December, 1600-when the British Crown granted a group of merchants a monopoly over trade in the eastern waters. In 1765, the East India Company, which was earlier a commercial body, was granted the 'diwani' (the right of collecting revenues) of Bengal, Bihar and Orissa from the Mughal emperor Shah Alam. The acquisition of the Diwani rights made the company to emerge out as the de facto ruler of this country. From 1765 to 1833 the company got engaged in the dual role of the trader and ruler. In 1833, it abandoned its commercial role.

The Regulating Act of 1773 is a major landmark in the evolution of British administration in India. It was the basis of all subsequent legislation for determining the form of Indian government and is the first statute that recognizes the company to fulfil its functions other than that of trade.

A Governor-General with a council of four members in Bengal was appointed. The Governor-General was given the power of controlling the presidencies of Madras and Bombay and, in all cases relating to war and peace; they were obliged to comply with the order of the Governor-General-in-Council.

The appointed Governor-General, according to this Act, was Warren Hastings and his councillors were Clavering Monson, Barwell and Philip Francis. Later in 1833, the Governor-General of Bengal became the Governor-General of India and in 1853, a separate Lieutenant-Governor was appointed for Bengal.

Under Warren Hastings, the civil service began to transcend its trading activity. During his regime, the civil service changed from being a brand of commercial adventurers and fortune hunters to a public service in the modern sense of the word".

The company, during this regime, emerged out from a trader to a government and took up functions of revenue and maintenance of law and order.

The secretariat, an important organ of modern administration, had its beginning in those early days when a nucleus of administration existed. The origin of the modern secretariat was in the office of the factory writers.

In August 1784, the British Prime Minister Pitt, introduced the famous Pitts India Act (1784). According to this Act, a Board of Control was established in England for better control of Indian affairs. Later on, the Board of Control became the real ruling authority over the Indian terrorists.

Lord Warren Hastings was succeeded by Lord Cornwallis and the regime of Lord Cornwallis marked a major change in the civil service of India. He introduced a liberal system of remuneration, in lieu of pittances in the form of pay until then allowed to all classes, and it offered the recipient no alternative between poverty and dishonesty.

He did much to eliminate patronage and saw to it that all important offices were held by the covenanted civil servants.

## CHARTER ACT OF 1853

The Charter Act of 1853 abolished the system of patronage and introduced the system of open competition as a method of recruitment. The entrance examination was to be conducted in London by a Civil Service Commission set up in 1854. The age limit was 19-22 years.

The first competitive examination was held in 1855 at London, on the basis of the report of the Macaulay Committee. The Act did not renew the charter of the company but left it pending till the decision of the parliament.

The appointment of the Macaulay Committee was the beginning of an experiment on the Indian soil for the first time.

The Macaulay Committee report of 1854 is considered the Bible on competitive recruitment is training. It proposed a detailed scheme of the examination to be held in England. It underlined the passed in order to premise that the candidates for senior government jobs should be appointed on the basis of a competitive India examination open to young men in the age group of 18 to 23 years.

## ADMINISTRATIVE SYSTEM BETWEEN 1858-1947

After the uprising of 1857, the Crown took over the government from the East India Company, through the Queen's Proclamation of 1858. According to the Act of 1858, India shall be governed by and in the name of her Majesty; it also authorized the appointment of an additional principal secretary of state (for India) and created the Council of India.

The first Viceroy was Lord Canning. In 1859, he introduced the 'portfolio' system. Under this, the work of the government, divided into several branches, and was entrusted to different members of the Governor-General's Council.

Canning's innovation was legalized by the Indian Councils Act of 1861, which the British parliament passed in order 'to make better provision for the constitution of the Council of the Governor-General of India, and for the local government of the several presidencies and provinces of India"

The Aitchison Commission (1886-87) supported the formation of a lower, local civil service to call the Provincial Civil Service. Below the Provincial Civil Service, a lower service called Subordinate Civil Service was set up.

In accordance with its recommendations, the term 'covenanted" civil service was abolished resultantly, three services were carved out.

(i) The Imperial Civil Service
(ii) The Provincial Civil Service
(iii) The Subordinate Civil Services.

Also, the commission recommended that the imperial and the provincial civil services be put on footing of social equality. Resultantly, the members of the provincial civil service were made eligible) promotion to the listed posts in the imperial civil services.

The Indian Councils Act, or the Morley Minto Reforms, of 1909 was an extension of the Act of 189 it further increased the size of the legislative councils. The Decentralisation Commission appointed in the same year, also made recommendations fort., revival and growth of Panchayats and lessening of government control over local bodies.

## THE MONTAGUE CHELMSFORD REFORMS OR THE ACT OF 1919

The Government of India Act 1919, which followed next, was based on the premise that popular contract in the field of local government be established, the provincial governments be made responsible to the popular representatives and the control of British parliament and the secretary of state be relaxed.

The act primarily dealt with the structure of provincial governments and the provisions concerning these were embodied in a system called 'Dyarchy'. Under this scheme, the provincial subjects were reserve into 'reserved' and 'transferred'.

The administration of the reserved subjects was entrusted to members of the Governors' Executive Council, who were appointed by the Crown for a period of five years on i fixed pay. They were not responsible to the provincial legislative. All the important subjects like the home, police, press, finance etc. were included in this list.

The 'transferred' subjects were entrusted to the ministers who were to be nominated by the Gover-nor from among the elected members of the Provincial Council and who were to hold office during him pleasure. The 'transferred' list included those departments, which afforded opportunities for local knowledge and social service like medicine, health, education etc.

But the division of powers and revenues did not make India a federation. The powers of the centre be were so formidable that its decisions were final and always binding on the provinces - irrespective of whether such decisions related to central or provincial subjects.

## GOVERNMENT OF INDIA ACT 1935

The Government of India Act of 1935 was the last of the constitutional measures prepared by the British Parliament for India. It again proclaimed the supreme authority of Crown over India, but relaxed its control, in certain spheres, for a more popular government. The Secretary of state remained in overall control, with a new body of advisers in lieu of the old council.

The 1935 Government of India Act was the culmination of the process of decentralisation initiated in 1861. It envisaged three important changes at the centre.

(1) All India Federation

(2) Dyarchy

(3) Creation of the post of Crown Representative.

### British Administration

The incoming British threw blame on the departing Germans, most especially for their method of administration which the British termed 'Direct Rule' and claimed was responsible for the destruction of some indigenous institutions. The British saw their task in terms of educating the natives to manage their own affairs and to evolve from their own institutions a mode of government which would conform to civilised standards. In Cameroon this went further to become: ... an endeavour to rebuild the (indigenous) institutions which had to some extent suffered disintegration during...German administration, to find the hereditary native rulers and to educate them in their duties in that capacity, and to seek their co-operation and help, and to maintain their prestige in all matters concerning the areas under their control (Gardinier 1967: 531).

This was to be effected by the administrative policy of 'Indirect Rule' which at that time was being introduced into Southern Nigeria. The system was regulated by laws in which some powers were delegated to a chief or group of individuals termed a 'Native Authority' to maintain law and order through native courts, to collect taxes and eventually to operate a treasury.

Indirect Rule had to be introduced in stages while the German system was gradually phased out. Its application in the Bamenda Division was affected by various adverse factors. The most glaring were the great geographical and ethnic diversity of the area, lack of personnel, a disorderly transition from German to British administration, the remoteness of the Division and the problem of maintaining law and order. To counter these problems the British sought to involve natives in the administrative process. It was the view of the Resident, E.C. Duff, that in order to make native administration a success it was necessary to enhance the powers of the principal chiefs. Initially they were to be given judicial powers by being made presidents of the native courts. Lesser chiefs, and even ward-heads within the principal communities, were also recognised and brought in to support the chiefs as court members.

This idea was put into practice in July 1917 when G.S. Podevin, the District officer, inaugurated an 'Instructional Court' in Bamenda. This was an assembly of chiefs from surrounding communities who were summoned to be instructed in the new native court ordinance and to go on to form the new courts. The membership of the court consisted of 27 chiefs with the Fon of Bafut appointed as president and that of Bali Kumbat as vice-president. If the court were to prove successful then other courts would be established in other parts of the Division.

According to reports, the court functioned as well as circumstances permitted but there were many problems, in particular the large extent of the area served by the court. Another was the difficulty of getting clerks and at first Podevin, himself, was the court scribe. The only locally available people were the ex-German functionaries who had served as interpreters and messengers. It was only in November 1917 that the first person was employed. This was a Bali Nyonga man, Maxwell Fohtung who had earlier worked as a clerk for the Germans in Victoria (Fohtung, Njie and Chilver 1992). Until 1922 the implementation of the native courts ordinance was only partial and many areas remained without a court. The implementation of the Native Authority ordinance, too, was delayed by a dearth of political officers exacerbated by the influenza epidemic of 1918 which carried off Podevin and led to the virtual breakdown of the administration in 1919.

In 1921 an instruction was issued from Buea to the effect that the principle of indirect administration should be applied. To this end the Divisional Officer undertook some provisional classification based on language and came up with 14 groups with Bafut within the Mogimba grouping. In 1922 the future of the former Kamerun was determined as a mandate of the League of Nations to be administered by Britain and France. Following this the Secretary of State for the Colonies directed that the principles of native administration as laid down by Lugard were to be applied in the British mandated territory. This necessitated the introduction of the method of tax assessment then current in Northern Nigeria. Lugard considered that the assessing officer in the course of obtaining his reports was brought into close relations with the local chiefs and people and 'had opportunities of learning so much about their history, origins and affinities that the occasion should be taken to write a concise historical and ethnological account of the people' (Lugard 1970: 194). Hence Hal Cadman was sent from Northern Nigeria and given the preliminary task of preparing a 'Report on Ancient Tribal Machinery in the Cameroons Province' (Cadman 1922) as a guideline for administrative officers.

Assessment of different peoples in the Bamenda Division on the Cadman model started in 1922. The Bafut area was assessed by E.G. Hawkesworth, Assistant Divisional Officer, in 1926. He discovered that the 'Mogimba' area was not an ethnic unit but an area of language diffusion and that the chiefly dynasties of Bafut, Babanki, Babanki Tungaw, Bafreng and Bambili claimed common Tikar origins. On account of these 'links' the British decided that a clan organisation had been identified and that a viable native administration could be established with Bafut as the centre in respect of its size.

Following these reports an enlarged Bafut native administration area was established with an area of about eight hundred and seventy square kilometres containing a population of about twenty thousand with the Bafut comprising half of that number. The Bafut 'District' became one of fifteen Native Authority areas in the Bamenda Division. This Native Authority was gazetted as 'Boombi' (Abumbi) Chief of Bafut and 'Vugar' Chief of Babanki for the Bafut Native Court area.

It had been the hope of the authorities that in a few years that Fon of Bafut would become the head of the area holding a position equivalent to a District Head in Northern Nigeria. However, the Bafut Native Authority never really functioned as the British envisaged. In addition to the maintenance of order, the Native Authority was charged with collecting taxes from subordinate chiefs and paying them to the Political Officer. It was thought that the payment of taxes through the Bafut Fon would foster loyalty to him as ruler but other chiefs were reluctant to do this as they feared it would make them subordinate to him. So the consolidation of units under the Fon of Bafut did not materialise although District Officers continued to nurse the hope and spoke optimistically of co-operation between the different units of the Bafut Native Authority.

When the British undertook to re-examine their policy in Southern Nigeria as a result of the Aba riots the review was extended to the Cameroons. Donald Cameron (1965: 198ff), the new Governor of Nigeria, advocated a new policy of native administration according to which the real authority should be in accordance with the people's own idea of authority, that it should actually exist and be accepted by the people. In his view a Native Authority not accepted by the people and maintained only by imposition was almost certainly bound to fail. The attempt to extend the powers of the Fon of Bafut as a Native Authority was based on the notion that the people had once obeyed this authority in the past. According to Cameron, however, the contemporary generation might be quite ignorant of tradition and if ancient authorities were to be resurrected it must be certain the people would obey. Cameron's idea of native administration was introduced to the Cameroons in the course of a new round of re-assessment and intelligence reports.

Bafut experienced one of the most far-reaching re-organisations affecting the Native Authority and court. The difference between the

Assessment Report of 1926 and the Intelligence Report of 1934 lay in the points which were emphasised. The earlier report stressed historical links between different chiefdoms with the expressed purpose of re-establishing clan ties. The 1934 report was more concerned with the analysis of the indigenous administrative structures on which to build native administration. R.J. Hook, the Divisional Officer, acknowledged the fact that there were seven independent chiefdoms. He recommended that the new Native Authority should be the seven chiefs-in-council. The British authorities had, therefore, abandoned the idea of uniting the area under one chief and instead were discussing confederation with each unit maintaining its own autonomy.

For the judiciary it was proposed that each chief would hold his own court in his own palace. In this regard the authorities were grudgingly acknowledging the fact that such courts continued to operate despite their prohibition by the ordinance. At the same time there was to be a central 'clan' or area court to serve as a headquarters for the seven units. This would be a court of the first instance as well as a court of appeal.

The implementation of these recommendations embodied Cameron's principle (1937: 3-4) that each chief with his council was to be the highest functioning unit. In the reorganisation no single unit was made into a Native Authority; rather all seven chiefs were constituted into a single Native Authority. This was certainly an advance over the former system when only two chiefs were involved. However, the location and population of Bafut would continue to be a factor such that the Fon would continue to exercise much influence. Hence, the old problem was not entirely solved.

While this reorganisation was taking place, important events were also occurring in Bafut and Babanki. In August of 1932 the Bafut Fon Abumbi, who had resisted the Germans for so long, died and was succeeded by his German-educated and literate son Su Ayieh, who took the regnal name of Achirimbi and who ruled for the remaining years of British administration. In 1936 Fon Vugar of Babanki also died and was succeeded by his son Vubangksi similarly educated in a German (Basel Mission) school. Under normal circumstances the accession of these two relatively young and educated chiefs to two linked chieftaincies in the Bafut area would have been expected to boost the new system. However, this was not to be so. The depression of the 1930s brought disruption and the Second World War further economic hardship leading to the virtual abandonment of the system.

After the war the energies of the authorities were largely absorbed by constitutional changes affecting Nigeria (Crowder 1966: 273).

When the necessity for change arose as a result of developments in Nigeria in 1929, the main problem in the Bafut area was not taxation but the exercise of authority. Respective chiefs guarded their autonomy so jealously that any talk of co-operating with another chief was viewed as a surrender of sovereignty. Cameron's reforms aimed to bring the administration closer in line with indigenous institutions, but these changes were not far-reaching in the Bafut area and simply involved shuffling personnel and bringing in a few village heads into the system as courtmmembers. The element of Bafut paramountcy remained with the Bafut Fon who was regarded as the most important dignitary and received the highest stipend. This situation was reinforced by the establishment of a treasury in Bafut in 1941. Above all the tight control of the Divisional Officer did not lessen. A former treasurer of the Bafut Native Authority summed up this situation with the remark that before 1949 there was only one Native Authority in Bamenda Division - the Divisional Officer who ran the show from the Native Authority section of the Divisional Office in Bamenda. This implies that the different authorities had little or no autonomy. The period prior to 1949 therefore coincided with what Nicolson described as the 'Era of administocracy' in the history of Nigerian administration.

## References

Bernier, Francois : *Travels in the Mogul Empire*, New Delhi: S. Chand, 1972.

Donald F.: *Asia in the Making of Europe*, Chicago, 1965.

Hasan, Nurul : *Religion, State and Society in Medieval India*, New Delhi: Oxford University Press, 2007.

Koch, Ebba : British *Architecture*, Munich: Prestel-Verlag, 1991.

Major, R.H. : *India in the Fifteenth Century*, London, 1857.

Poole: Stanley. *Medieval India under British Rule, A.D. 712-1764*. New York, 1903; Calcutta, 1951.

Qureshi, I. H.: *The Administration of the British*. Lahore, 1944.

Seshadri, K. : *Stagnancy and Change in British Rule*, Aalekh, Delhi, 1999.

Wagstaff, J. M. : *The Evolution of Middle Eastern Landscapes*, Totowa NJ: Barnes and Noble Books, 1985.

9

# The Moderate Phase of National Movement in India

**ASHISH NANDWANA**
*Research Scholar, Department of History and Culture, Janardan Rai Nagar, Rajasthan Vidhyapeeth (Deemed University), Udaipur, Rajasthan.*

The Indian National movement was primarily a movement for freedom from alien domina--nation. The movement has been one comprehensive effort embracing all aspects of the life of the community. The birth of the Indian National Congress, perhaps the oldest and the biggest democratic organisation in the world, did not take place in an atmosphere of a fanfare of trumpets nor did it create a stir by passing flamboyant resolutions.

## Hume's Initiative

In 1884, at the annual convention of the Theosophical Society at Adyar in Madras, Mr. Allan Octavian Hume laid bare to his friends his plan to organise the Congress. A committee was formed to make the necessary prepara-tions for a session at Poona to be held in 1885. The committee consisted of Mr. Hume, Mr. Surendranath Bannerji, Mr. Narendranath Sen, Mr. S. Subramania Iyer, Mr. P. Ananda Charlu, Mr. V. N. Mandalik, Mr. K. T. Telag, Sardar Dayal Singh, Lala Sri Ram.

Mr. Hume, still a government servant, addressed an open letter to the graduates of Calcutta University with a fervent appeal for self help.

*He said:* "and if even the leaders of thought are all either such poor creatures, or so selfishly wedded to personal concern, that they dare not strike a blow for their country's sake, then justly and rightly they are kept down and trampled on, for they deserve nothing better. Every nation secures precisely as good a government as it merits. If you the picked men, the most highly educated of the nation cannot, scorning personal ease and selfish objects, make a resolute struggle to secure greater freedom for yourselves and your country, a more impartial administration, a larger share in the management of your own affairs then we, your friends arc wrong and our adversaries right, then Lord Rippon's noble aspirations for your good are fruitless and visionary, then at present at any rate, all hopes of progress are at an end, and India truly neither lacks nor deserves any better government than she enjoys.

"Only if this be so, let us hear no more factious, peevish complaints that you are kept in strings and treated like children, for you will have proved yourself such. Men know how to act. Let there be no more complaints of Englishmen being preferred to you in all important offices, for if you lack that public spirit, that highest form of altruistic devotion that leads men to subordinate private ease to the public weal that patriotism that has made Englishmen what they are-then rightly are these preferred to you, rightly and inevitably have they become your rulers. And rulers and task masters they must continue, let the yoke gall your shoulders never so sorely, until you realise and stand prepared to act upon the eternal truth that self-sacrifice and unselfishness are the only unfailing guide to freedom and happiness."

## The First Session

The first session of the Congress was to meet at Poona but owing to an outbreak of cholera the venue was shifted to Bombay and the session began on the 28th December, 1885, with Mr. W. C. Bannerjee, the doyen of the Calcutta Bar in the chair, though originally, it had been decided to request Lord Reay, Governor of Bombay, to be the first President of the Indian National Congress but the idea had to be dropped as the Governor was advised by the Viceroy not to accept the offer. 72 delegates came from different parts of the country and most important among them were Dadabhai Naoroji, Ranade, Pherozeshah Mehta, K. T. Telang, Dinshaw Wacha, etc. The meeting was truly a national gathering consisting of leading men from all parts of India.

The president defined the objective of the Congress as "promotion of personal intimacy and friendship among all the more earnest workers in our country's cause in the parts of the empire and eradication of race, creed or provincial prejudice and fuller development of national unity." In its early sessions, the Congress Organisation, by and large, limited its activities only to debates.

After the Madras Session in 1887, an aggressive propaganda was started among the masses. Hume published a pamphlet entitled "An Old Man's Hope" in which he appealed to the people of England in these words: "Ah men, well-fed and happy, do you at all realise the dull misery of these countless myriads? From their births to their deaths, how many rays of sunshine think you chequer their gloom-shrouded paths? Toil, toil, toil; hunger, hunger, hunger, sickness, suffering, sorrow; these alas, alas, alas are the keynotes of their short and sad existence."

In December 1889, the Congress Session was held at Bombay under the Presidentship of Sir William Wedderburn. It was attended by Charles Bradlaugh, a member of British Parliament. He addressed the Congress in these words; "For whom should I work if not for the people? Born of the people, trusted by the people, I will die for the people, and I know no geographical or race limitation."

Dadabhai Naoroji was re-elected as the President of the Lahore Session of the Congress held in December 1893, His journey from Bombay to Lahore presented the spectacle of a procession, and Citizens at various places on the way presented him addresses. At the Golden Temple at Amritsar, he was given a robe of honour. Addressing the audience at the Session, Dadabhai Naoraji declared: "Let us always remember that we are children of our mother country. Indeed, I have never worked in any other spirit than that I am an Indian and owe duty to my work and all my countrymen. Whether I am a Hindu or a Mohammedan, a Parsi, a Christian, or of any other creed, I am above all an Indian. Our country is India, our nationality is Indian."

## THE MODERATES

The early Congressmen who dominated the affairs of the Indian National Congress from 1885 to 1905 were known as the Moderates. They belonged to a class which was Indian in blood and colour but British in tastes, in opinions, in morals and in intellect. They were supporters of British institutions. They believed that what India needed was a balanced and lucid presentation of her needs before the Englishmen and their Parliament. They had faith in the British sense of justice and fairplay. The Moderates believed in orderly progress and constitutional agitation. They believed in patience, steadiness, conciliation and union. To quote Surendarnath Banerjee, "The triumphs of liberty are not to be won in a day. Liberty is a jealous goddess, exacting in her worship and claiming from her votaries prolonged and assiduous devotion." In 1887, Badruddin Tyabji observed: "Be moderate in your demands, just in your criticism, correct in your facts and logical in your conclusions."

The Moderates believed in constitutional agitation within the four corners of law. They believed that their main task was to educate the people, to arouse national political consciousness and to create a united public, opinion on political questions. For this purpose they held meetings. They criticised the Government through the press. They drafted and submitted memorials and petitions to the Government, to the officials of the Government of India and also to the British Parliament. They also worked to influence the British Parliament and British public opinion. The object of the memorials and petitions was to enlighten the British public and political leaders about the conditions prevailing in India. Deputations of leading Indian leaders were sent to Britain in 1889. A British Committee of the Indian National Congress was founded in 1906 and that Committee started a journal called *India*. Dadabhai Naoroji spent a major part of his life and income in Britain doing propaganda among its people and politicians.

The object before the Moderates was "wide employment of Indians in higher offices in the public service and the establishment of representative institutions."

The economic and political demands of the Moderates were formulated with a view to unifying the Indian people on the basis of a common political programme. They organised a powerful all-India agitation against the abandonment of tariff-duties on imports and against the imposition of cotton excise duties. This agitation aroused the feelings of the people and helped them to realise the real aims and purposes of British rule in India. They urged the Government to provide cheap credit to the peasantry through agricultural banks and to make avail-able irrigation facilities on a large scale. They asked for improvement in the conditions of work of the plantation labourers, a radical change in the existing pattern of taxation and expenditure which put a heavy burden on the poor while leaving the rich, especially the foreigners, with a very light load. The Moderates complained of India's growing poverty and economic backwardness and put all the blame on the policies of the British Government. They criticised the individual administrative measures and worked hard to reform the administrative system.

The Moderates opposed tooth and nail the restrictions imposed by the Government on the freedom of speech and the press. In 1897,

Tilak and many other leaders were arrested and sentenced to long terms of imprisonment for spreading disaffection against the Government through their speeches and writings. The Natu brothers of Poona were deported without trial. The arrest of Tilak marked the beginning of a new phase of the Nationalist movement. The *Amrita Bazar Patrika* wrote: "There is scarcely a home in this vast country where Tilak is not now the subject of melancholy talk and where his imprisonment is not considered as a domestic calamity."

The basic weakness of the Moderates lay in their narrow social base. Their movement did not have a wide appeal. The area of their influence was limited to the urban community. As they did not have the support of the masses, they declared that the time was not ripe for throwing out a challenge to the foreign rulers. To quote Gokhale, "You do not realise the enormous reserve of power behind the Government. If the Congress were to do anything such as you suggest, the Government would have no difficulty in throttling it in five minutes." However, it must not be presumed that the Moderate leaders fought for their narrow interests. Their pro-grammes and policies championed the cause of all sections of the Indian people and represented nation-wide interests against colonial exploitation. What they wanted was to reform or liberalise the existing system of government through peaceful, gradualist and constitutional means.

The influence of the moderates, however, declined with the rise of the militants who did not believe in gradualism and who criticized the moderates for their great faith in Britain and British political institutions.

## Rise of Extremism

The moderates sought to make the provincial e legislatures more representative and to increase the Indian clement in the civil services, but the process was long and the progress slow. Repelled by the unsympathetic approach of the imperial bureaucracy and enraged by the unpopular policies of Lord Curzon, the Viceroy, and particularly his decision on the partition of Bengal, the youth of India moved towards militant politics and direct action. As a protest against the partition of Bengal (October 1905), the nationalists advocated the boycott of British goods".

In 1907, Bipin Pal made the paradoxical statement, that the "viceroyalty of Lord Curzon... had been one of the most beneficent if not decidedly the most beneficent viceroyalty that India ever had," for Curzon, by pursuing his unpopular policies, had made Indians so discontented that they demanded self-government with greater determination than ever before. Aurobindo similarly declared that he considered the partition of Bengal to be a most beneficial measure because, by arousing intense opposition among the people, that measure had stirred up and strengthened national feeling.

As a result of the growing disillusionment about the activities of the British rulers and as a reaction against Curzon's proposal for the partition of Bengal; there came into existence the extremist party which advocated a policy of boycott, *swadeshi* and national education. In January 1907, Tilak declared: "We are not armed, and there is no necessity of arms either. We have a stronger weapon, a political weapon in boycott." Tilak also said: "When you prefer to accept *swadeshi*. You must boycott *videshi* (foreign) goods. Without boycott, *swadeshi* cannot flourish."

Aurobindo, Tilak, and Pal asked the people not to cooperate with the government. The basic theory of Tilak, Aurobindo and Pal, which was later put into operation on a mass scale by Mahatma Gandhi, was that as the existence of the Government depended on the cooperation of the people, the Government would cease to function or to exist the very day the people withdrew their co-operation from it.

With the rise of the militant movement the glamour of England and English institutions began to fade and English influence increasingly came to be replaced by the influence emanating primarily from the indigenous sources as also from the European literature or revolt. The study of British constitutional history had generated among the moderates a love for and faith in Dominion Status. But such stories as how the Italians had driven the Austrians out of their land gave militant nationalists a new conception and in fact a new ideal of complete independence. Self-government under British paramountcy had been the goal of the moderate school, but the ideal of the extremist or militant school was complete autonomy and elimination of all foreign control.

Bal Gangadhar Tilak (1856-1920) and other extremist leaders, who wanted to adopt a policy of direct act and passive resistance, denounced what they called "the political mendicancy" of the moderates. During the anti partition agitation, in the first decade of the twentieth century, Tilak wrote: "The time has come to demand *Swaraj* or self-Government. No piecemeal reform will do. The system of the present administration is ruinous to the country. It must mend or end." According to him Swaraj was the birthright of every Indian.

"The term *Swaraj*," said Bipin Pal (1858-1932), another exremist leader, was not merely a political but primarily a moral concept. "The corresponding term in our language," he said, "is not non-subjection which would be a literal rendering of the English word independence, but self-subjection which is a positive concept. Self--subjection means.... complete identification of the individual with the universal."

Another Swarajist leader who, like Tilak, spoke of the ideal of *Swaraj*, was Aurobindo Ghose (1872-1950). "We of the new school, "he said, "would not pitch our ideal one inch lower than absolute *Swaraj*-Self-Government as it exists in the United Kingdom." And he added, "We reject the claim of aliens to force upon us a civilisation inferior to our own or keep us out of our inheritance on the untenable ground of a supèrior fitness."

Lajpat Rai (1865-1928), along with Bal Gangadhar Tilak and Bipin Pal, constituted the *swarajist* triumvirate called "Lal-Bal-Pal". Lajpat, like the other extremists, believed that India must rely on her own strength and should not look to Britain for help.

The *swarajist* said that however much Britain's rule might be improved or liberalised, it could never be as beneficial to Indians as the self-rule. Their attitude was the same as that of the Irish Sinn Fein leader Arthur Griffith, who had said: ".... In those who talk of ending British misgovernment we see the helots. It is not British misgovernment, but British government in Ireland, good or bad, we stand opposed to." The *swarajists* accordingly considered that freedom was their birthright.

## The Surat Split

In 1907, there was a split in the Congress and the Moderates parted company with the Extremists. That split was due to many causes. The moderates had controlled the Congress from its very beginning and even now they were in control of it. They had their own ways of thinking and doing which were not acceptable to the younger generation who were impatient with the speed at which the Moderates were moving and leading the nation. Under the circumstances, a confrontation between the two was inevitable and that actually happened in 1907.

The seeds of the split could be traced to the Calculla Session in 1906, where the Moderates had accepted the resolutions on *Swaraj*, national education, boycott and *Swadeshi* on account of the pressure brought on them from all quarters. In their hearts, they had not accepted the new resolutions. Their fear was that the growing pace of the national struggle might lead to lawlessness and that would provide the British with an excuse to deny the reforms on the one hand and to crush all political activity on the other. They had no self-confidence. They did not believe that sustained and dignified national struggle was possible and desirable. They considered the Extremists irresponsible persons who were likely to put in danger the future of the country. The British Government also tried to win over the Moderates against the Extremists. While the Extremists were roughly handled by the Government, the Moderates were shown all the favours. Lala Lajpat Rai, Sardar Ajit Singh, Tilak and many leaders of Bengal were deported.

The break-up of the Surat Congress was no doubt an unpleasant affair. It marked a direct open breach between the Moderates and the Nationalist panics not only in Maharashtra but throughout India. For the first time in the history of the Congress, there was at Surat an open light between the delegates of the congress and some blood was drawn. But it did not stop at that. The split led to a cleavage in the sense that the name of the Indian National Congress had to be kept in abeyance for the time and a new entity called the convention was installed in its place. Of course as the name itself implies, the Convention was a stop-gap expedient, intended to function in the place of the Congress only till such time as the national Congress could meet again in its old form. The old form had this peculiarity that there was not much ceremony observed in the election of the delegates to the Congress. There were no conditions of membership. There was no constitution as such for the Congress, no election of delegates. In fact the membership was open to anyone that might choose to attend the Congress session as a delegate. There was no competition as such in the election of the delegates for the simple reason that there was no numerical allotment fixed for any province. It was an open rally of all that chose to attend.

Tilak and his party were of course ousted from the Convention because they would not sign a prescribed creed of political faith, which practically excluded the ideal of independence, if only an ideal so far. The Convention and, the Nationalist party met in two separate camps at Surat. It must be noted here that even with this definite split in the Congress each party duly affirmed its love for the Congress which alone was regarded as the true national Assembly for the country and in both the camps the hope was expressed that sooner or later there might again be held a Congress united as before.

Nobody could openly allege the break-up of the Congress as a criminal offence, but the split was taken into consideration by the government as an open challenge to the policy of constitutional agitation. After Tilak's conviction by the High Court, the National party led by him became sullen and almost went underground. For six years, from 1908 to 1914, the Nationalist Party could not decide as to what it should do about entering the Congress. There was an attempt made to call a meeting of a rival Congress at Nagpur. But while government banned the session, there was also want of unanimity in the party itself about the starting of a rival Congress which might make the split absolutely permanent. The cooler wings in the Party thought that there was no wisdom in setting up a rival to the old Congress as without unity among political parties the show as presented by separate parties was bound to be poor. A group within the Tilak Party was trying to negotiate matters with the leaders of the Moderate party for making the entry of this group and others of its persuasion into the Congress on its own terms, that is to say, without the restriction of a creed and with the old facilities for unfettered election of delegates. But the other view was more insistent and prevailed, namely, that nothing should be done in this matter until Tilak returned from Mandalay.

## "MODERATES" VERSUS "EXTREMISTS" IN THE BATTLE FOR "SWARAJ" AND "SWADESHI"

Even as loyalist pressures cast a long shadow on political currents that were to influence the Indian elite of the late nineteenth century, rapidly deteriorating economic conditions also led to a heightened degree of radicalization amongst the most advanced sections of the new Indian intelligentsia. Ajit Singh in Punjab, Bal Gangadhar Tilak in Maharashtra, Chidambaram Pillay in Tamil Nadu and Bipin Chandra Pal in Bengal formed the nucleus of a new nationalist movement that tried valiantly, but mostly unsuccessfully to move the conservative leadership of the Indian National Congress in a more radical direction. Most charismatic amongst the new national leaders was Bal Gangadhar Tilak (b. 1856, d. 1920).

Portrayed as anti-Muslim by the Muslim-League, maligned by India's colonial rulers and British loyalists as an "extremist", and misrepresented as a sectarian Hindu revivalist by some historians, Tilak was in fact, one of the leading lights of the Indian freedom movement. Best remembered for his slogan *"Swaraj is my birth-right*

", he was one of the first to call for complete freedom from British rule, and fought a long and sometimes lonely political struggle against the forces of "moderation" that held sway over the Indian National Congress in the early part of the last century.

After the defeat of 1858, one of the most significant challenges to British imperial authority in India had appeared in the form of Vasudeo Balvant Phadke's revolt of 1879, and amongst his many youthful followers and trainees in Pune was the young Tilak. Along with Chiplunkar, Agarkar and Namjoshi, Tilak initially concentrated on launching a nationalist weekly-the *Kesari* (1881), the publishing house-*Kitabkhana*, and developing Indian educational institutions such as the Deccan Education Society (1884). Tilak and his friends saw the right kind of education as being a crucial element in the task of national regeneration, and in this respect appeared to be continuing in the tradition of Jyotirao Phule (1827-1890) and Gopalrao Deshmukh (1823-1892) who was more known by his pen-name 'Lokahitwadi'.

Foremost amongst the social revolutionaries of nineteenth century Maharashtra, Phule and his wife Savitribai, had advocated a radical restructuring of Hindu society on the basis of equality of caste, gender and creed. Phule, (who belonged to the *Mali* caste) was unsparing in his criticism of Brahminical society that looked down upon the *shudra jatis*, prevented the *atishudra* (untouchable) *jatis* from attending school, and treated young widows (particularly Brahmin widows) as outcastes. One of the first to start a school for girls (1848), Phule went on to found the first school for the *atishudras* (1851), a home for young widows (1863), and also the first to open the family well to *atishudra* women (1868). Social reformers in Maharashtra also emerged from the upper castes, such as Gopalrao Deshmukh, who although a Chitpawan Brahmin was a sharp critic of Brahminical society, and worked primarily through reformist middle-class organizations such as the Prasthana Samaj and the Arya Samaj to fight against caste inequities.

But amongst Tilak's colleagues, not all were well-disposed towards Phule and Deshmukh (Lokahitwadi). Chiplunkar was particularly vitriolic in his criticism of Phule. Tilak, on the other hand, was not unsympathetic to the need for social reforms, and was opposed to evils like child-marriage, casteism and untouchability. Many years later, (at a conference in Bombay in 1918), he was to declare: *"If God were to tolerate untouchability, I would not recognize him as God at all"*. However, he was reluctant to give precedence to social reforms over political struggle, believing that social change ought to come gradually, through the growth of enlightened public opinion, rather than through the legislative authority of an alien government. He was convinced that no significant social progress was possible in a country that wasn't politically free. He was particularly critical of loyalist or moderate "reformers" who were unwilling to practice what they preached, yet frequently baited him as being against social reforms.

Neither a sectarian religious revivalist in the mold of Chiplunkar, nor willing to confine himself exclusively to the cause of radical social reforms like Agarkar, Tilak eventually parted ways with his colleagues in 1888. Working through the *Kesari*, (and later also the *Maratha*) he gradually developed a more advanced nationalist perspective based on the pillars of nationalist education, *Swaraj* (self-rule) *and Swadeshi* (self-reliance). One of the first to take the nationalist message to the Indian masses, he played a particularly important role in organizing western Maharashtra's peasant and artisan communities during the 1897 famine under the auspices of the Sarvajanik Sabha.

By 1905, popular resistance movements had developed in both Bengal and Maharashtra, calling for the boycott of British goods and non-payment of land revenues and other taxes. Between 1905 and 1908 the national movement intensified, workers participated in strikes and work-stoppages, women and students joined the boycott movements-picketing at shops that sold imported goods, and an ever-growing mass of people began joining mass meetings and street processions.

Only too aware of the economic devastation that British rule had brought on the country, India's broad masses were responding eagerly to the nationalist message. But the nationalist movement was also becoming exceedingly divided between two poles representing radically different currents and tendencies. Whereas one side (even as it recognized the many negative aspects of alien rule) clung to the British umbilical chord, and attempted to restrict the national movement to a struggle for political reforms, the other side correctly saw British rule as an unmitigated disaster for the Indian people and called for the complete liberation from colonial rule.

Tilak eloquently and succinctly summarized the sentiments of the new and increasingly militant national movement. He spoke of British rule as having ruined trade, caused the collapse of industry, and destroyed the people's courage and abilities. Under the colonial regimen, Tilak asserted that the country was offered neither education, nor rights, nor respect for public opinion. Without prosperity and contentment, the Indian people suffered constantly from the three 'd's'-i.e. *daridra* (poverty), *dushkal* (famine) and *dravyashosha* (drain). And he saw only one remedy: for the Indian people to take political power without which Indian industry could not develop, without which the nation's youth couldn't be educated, and without which the country could win neither social reforms nor material welfare for it's people. Tilak saw colonial rule as being inimical to India's progress, and the contradictions between the British oppressors and the Indian people as being irreconcilable.

But "moderates" such as Gokhale (President of the Congress in 1905) while cognizant of how *"deplorable"* Britain's industrial domination of India was, and how the economic drain from India to Britain was *"bleeding India"*, were nevertheless all praise for the British educational system in India, ascribing to the British the virtues of introducing liberal "social reforms", governmental "peace and order" and such modern conveniences as the railways, post and telegraphs, and new industrial appliances. (That all these things benefited a miniscule Indian elite did not appear to bother such admirers of the empire, nor did it occur to them that this and much more could have just as easily been achieved under self-rule.)

Tilak and Gokhale were clearly seeing Indian reality from very different vantage points. From the point of view of the ordinary masses, British rule had already bankrupted the nation, left intolerable misery in it's wake, and offered no hope for the future. Tilak's assessment of the situation reflected bleak reality-as experienced not only by the oppressed and downtrodden Indian masses, but by an overwhelming majority of all Indians. But Gokhale's ambivalence and his more cautiously expressed (though clearly articulated) concerns reflected the position of those who had at least partially shared in the spoils of the empire, but saw with some trepidation how the growing poverty of the nation might unravel the British empire. Reluctant to make common cause with the masses, "moderates" such as Gokhale did everything in their power to restrain the growing national movement-even branding Tilak and his allies as "extremists".

The British took full advantage of this schism, and proceeded to bring the full weight of their administrative and military might in crushing the new national movement. Communal forces such as the Muslim League were also employed in the battle to extinguish radical tendencies. The years 1905-1908 were thus extremely critical in shaping the direction of the Indian national movement. Increasingly, the Indian masses were looking to Tilak and his compatriots for direction. But, in direct opposition to the energizing of the Indian peasantry, and mass of workers and students across the country, the elite was reasserting it's loyalty to British rule.

In Punjab, the polarization was especially sharp. The boycott movement had struck deep roots within the peasantry, and made it difficult for British troops to find porters and other logistical help from the poor peasants. Roused by calls to protest the British land revenue policy, Sikh and Jat agricultural workers were becoming strongly politicized. In a rousing speech, Tilak's close associate in Punjab, Ajit Singh made a secular appeal to the masses of Punjab to rise against the British: *"Hindu brothers, Mohammedan brothers, Sepahi brothers-we are all one. The government is not even dust before us....What have you got to fear?....Our numbers are much greater. True they have guns, but we have fists...You are dying from the plague and other diseases, so better sacrifice yourselves to your motherland. Our strength lies in unity..."* (Excerpts from an April 21, 1907 speech in Rawalpindi)

On May 1, 1907, a spontaneous outburst of popular discontent shook the British administration in Rawalpindi when seething crowds, reinforced by striking workers marched through the streets-throwing mud and stones at passing Britishers, attacking government offices, cottages of Christian missionaries, British enterprises and commercial establishments. Although the uprising was effectively quelled by a large contingent of British troops who were close at hand, it shook the colonial administration enough to hastily evacuate families of colonial officials and military officers from Punjab, and extend term of the Commander-in-Chief of the British Army, Lord Kitchener. The colonial police and troops were also ruthless in crushing such uprisings in Lahore and Amritsar. Ajit Singh and Lala Lajpat Rai were summarily deported to Burma, without trial or right of appeal. Arrests and persecution of other patriots followed, and a state of emergency was declared in a number of Punjab districts.

In 1908, uprisings on a similiar scale broke out in the South, in Trivandrum, Tirunelveli, and Tuticorin. In Trivandrum, police stations were attacked, prisoners liberated, and offices of the repressive colonial state were set on fire. When Chidambaram Pillay, another important Tilak ally was put on trial, he refused to disown his national goals, and was sentenced to life imprisonment. Russian consular official Chirkin had been quite prophetic in his May 28, 1907 report when he wrote:" The *outburst in Punjab is by it's character more dangerous than the Bengal unrest.....This outburst has roused all India."* But equally powerful forces were working to stem and reverse the radical tide that had the potential of upturning colonial rule. Bengal zamindars who had agitated against the partition of Bengal declared their loyalty to the Raj. The Maharajas not only offered armed personnel to help the British but some (such as the Maharaja of Jammu and Kashmir) themselves initiated repressive measures against those deemed "extremist".

The Congress who under the leadership of Dadabhai Naoroji had accepted the demands put forth by the Tilak group for Swaraj, Swadeshi and National Education in 1906, reneged on it's previous position, and at it's Surat session in 1907 decided to limit the struggle to a *"constitutional manner"*. *"Swaraj"* was reinterpreted to mean *"self-rule"* as a colony, and rather than fighting the colonial power, the Congress decided to cooperate with it in effecting *"reforms"*. A motion to elect Tilak (who was unquestionably the most popular leader of the national-liberation movement) was turned down, as was a compromise motion to elect Lala Lajpat Rai. The triumph of the "moderate" wing was total and complete. Gokhale's "moderate nationalism" which was simply another face of loyalism succeeded to the utter exclusion of all the popular forces aligned with Tilak, and returned the Congress to a broadly loyalist track.

Tilak and his supporters were thus compelled to regroup outside the stifling confines of the Congress and continued a vigorous struggle against the British. But in July 1908, after having removed most of Tilak's serious compatriots from the national scene, Tilak himself was brought to trial. The English majority outvoted the Indian jurors to issue a guilty verdict, and Tilak was sentenced to six years of transportation. This evoked a mass protest wave which swept a number of Indian cities culminating in a massive strike of 100,000 workers and a city-wide 'hartal' (shutdown) in Bombay. Tilak's sentence had to be commuted to simple imprisonment, but it was sufficient to deal a severe blow to the Indian freedom movement.

By 1914, the Congress had so deteriorated that a majority of it's members failed to admonish the young Mohandas Karamchand Gandhi when he embarked on a campaign to seek volunteers for the British war efforts in World War I. The man who was to repeatedly chastise the Indian masses for being insufficiently "nonviolent", had in 1914, no compunctions in seeking sacrificial lambs for a war in which India's only interest should have been for the defeat of it's colonial master. But Gandhi, who had been born the son of the Prime Minister of the princely state of Rajkot in Kathiawar, was simply following the lead of the Indian Maharajas, such as that of Bikaner- who needed little prodding in offering his troops for a war that essentially pitted Europe's older and stronger imperial powers against their emerging rivals.

Unsurprisingly, it was to Gokhale that the young Gandhi looked for inspiration, not Tilak. But others recognized his pre-eminent role in giving new direction and leadership to the Indian freedom movement. Nehru pointed out that the *"real symbol of the new age was Bal Gangadhar Tilak"*, and recognized that *"the vast majority of politically-minded people in India favoured Tilak and his group"*. This was acknowledge as much by Sir Valentine Chirol, foreign editor of the *The Times*, who noted how Tilak's imprisonment deprived India of it's most able and determined leader, perhaps the only one capable of providing the Indian national movement (with it's different and often contradictory trends), the organization and unity that had been lacking thus far. N.C. Kelkar, a biographer and follower of Tilak echoed such sentiments.

## THE MODERATES' VERSION

The twenty-third Indian National Congress assembled yesterday [26 December] in the Pavilion erected for it by the Reception Committee at Surat at 2-30 p.m. Over sixteen hundred delegates were present. The proceedings began with an address from the Chairman of Reception Committee. After the reading of the address was over Diwan Bahadur Ambalal Sakerlal proposed that the Hon. Dr. Rash Behari Ghose having been nominated by the Reception Committee for the office of President under the rules adopted at the last session of the Congress, he should take the Presidential chair. As soon as the Diwan Bahadur uttered Dr. Ghose's name, some voices were heard in the body of the hall shouting "No, no" and the shouting was kept up for some time.

The proposer, however, somehow managed to struggle through his speech; and the Chairman then called upon Babu Surendranath Banerjee to second the proposition. As soon, however, as he began his speech — before he had finished even his first sentence — a small section of the delegates began an uproar from their seats with the object of preventing Mr. Banerjee from speaking. The Chairman repeatedly appealed for order, but no heed was paid. Every time Mr. Banerjee attempted to go on with his speech he was met by disorderly shouts. It was clear that rowdyism had been determined upon to bring the proceedings to a standstill, and the whole demonstrations seemed to have been pre-arranged. Finding it impossible to enforce order, the Chairman warned the House that unless the uproar subsided at once, he would be obliged to suspend the sitting of the Congress. The hostile demonstration, however, continued and the Chairman at last suspended the sitting for the day.

The Congress again met today [27 December] at 1 p.m., due notice of the meeting having been sent round. As the President-Elect was being escorted in procession through the Hall to the platform, an overwhelming majority of the delegates present greeted him with a most enthusiastic welcome, thereby showing how thoroughly they disapproved the organised disorder of yesterday. As this procession was entering the Pandal a small slip of paper written in pencil and bearing Mr. B.G. Tilak's signature was put by a volunteer into the hands of Mr. Malvi, the Chairman of the Reception Committee. It was a notice to the Chairman that after Mr. Banerjee's speech, seconding the proposition about the President was concluded, Mr. Tilak wanted to move "an amendment for an adjournment of the Congress." The Chairman considered a notice of adjournment at that stage to be irregular and out of order. The proceedings were then resumed at the point at which they had been interrupted yesterday, and Mr. Surendranath Banerjee was called upon to conclude his speech. Mr. Banerjee having done this, the Chairman called upon Pandit Motilal Nehru of Allahabad to support the motion. The Pandit supported it in a brief speech and then the Chairman put the motion to the vote.

An overwhelming majority of the delegates signified their assent by crying "All, all" and a small minority shouted "No, no." The Chairman thereupon declared the motion carried and the Hon. Dr. Ghose was installed in the Presidential chair amidst loud and prolonged applause. While the applause was going on, and as Dr. Ghose rose to begin his address, Mr. Tilak came upon the platform and stood in front of the President. He urged that as he had given notice of an "amendment to the Presidential election," he should be permitted to move his amendment. Thereupon, it was pointed out to him by Mr. Malvi, the Chairman of the Reception Committee, that his notice was not for "an amendment to the Presidential election," but it was for "an adjournment of the Congress," which notice he had considered to be irregular and out of order at that stage; and that the President having been duly installed in the chair no amendment about his election could be then moved.

Mr. Tilak then turned to the President and began arguing with him. Dr. Ghose in his turn, stated how matters stood and ruled that this request to move an amendment about the election could not be entertained. Mr. Tilak thereupon said, "I will not submit to this. I will now appeal from the President to the delegates." In the meantime an uproar had already been commenced by some of his followers, and the President who tried to read his address could not be heard even by those who were seated next to him.

Mr. Tilak with his back to the President, kept shouting that he insisted on moving his amendment and he would not allow the proceedings to go on. The President repeatedly appealed to him to be satisfied with his protest and to resume his seat. Mr. Tilak kept on shouting frantically, exclaiming that he would not go back to his seat unless he was "bodily removed." This persisted defiance to the authority of the chair provoked a hostile demonstration against Mr. Tilak himself and for some time, nothing but loud cries of "Shame, shame" could be heard in the Pandal. It had been noticed, that when Mr. Tilak was making his way to the platform some of his followers were also trying to force themselves through the volunteers to the platform with sticks in their hands.

All attempts on the President's part either to proceed with the reading of his address or to persuade Mr. Tilak to resume his seat having failed, and a general movement among Mr. Tilak's followers to rush the platform with sticks in their hands being noticed, the President, for the last time, called upon Mr. Tilak to withdraw and formally announced to the assembly that he had ruled and he still ruled Mr. Tilak out of order and he called upon him to resume his seat.

Mr. Tilak refused to obey and at this time a shoe hurled from the body of the Hall, struck both Sir Pherozeshah Mehta and Mr. Surendranath Banerjee who were sitting side by side. Chairs were also hurled towards the platform and it was seen that Mr. Tilak's followers who were brandishing their sticks wildly were trying to rush the platform which other delegates were endeavouring to prevent.

It should be stated here that some of the delegates were so exasperated by Mr. Tilak's conduct that they repeatedly asked for permission to eject him bodily from the hall; but this permission was steadily refused.

The President, finding that the disorder went on growing and that he had no other course open to him, declared the session of the 23rd Indian National Congress suspended *sine die.* After the lady-delegates present on the platform had been escorted to the tents outside, the other delegates began with difficulty to disperse, but the disorder, having grown wilder, the Police eventually came in and ordered the Hall to be cleared.

An official statement issued on 28 December 1907 by Congress officials

### The Convention

The 23rd Indian National Congress having been suspended *sine die* under painful circumstances, the undersigned have resolved with a view to the orderly conduct of future political work in the country to call a Convention of those delegates to the Congress who are agreed:–

(1) That the attainment by India of Self-Government similar to that enjoyed by the self-governing members of the British Empire and participation by her in the rights and responsibilities of the Empire on equal terms with those Members is the goal of our political aspirations.

(2) That the advance towards this goal is to be by strictly constitutional means by bringing about a steady reform of existing system of administration and by promoting *National Unity,* fostering public spirit, and improving the condition of the mass of the people.

(3) And that all meetings held for the promotion of the aims and objects above indicated have to be conducted in an orderly manner with due submission to the authority of those that are entrusted with the power to control their procedure.

## THE 23RD INDIAN NATIONAL CONGRESS, SURAT AN ACCOUNT OF THE PROCEEDINGS

A Press Note containing an official narrative of the proceedings of the 23rd Indian National Congress at Surat has been published over the signatures of some of the Congress officials. As this note contains a number of one-sided and misleading statements it is thought desirable to publish the following account of the proceedings:–

## Preliminary

Last year when the Congress was held at Calcutta, under the presidency of Mr. Dadabhai Naoroji, the Congress, consisting of Moderates and Nationalists, *unanimously* resolved to have for its goal Swaraj or Self-Government on the lines of self-governing Colonies, and passed certain resolutions on Swadeshi, Boycott and National Education. The Bombay Moderates, headed by Sir P.M. Mehta, did not at the time, raise any dissentient voice, but they seem to have felt that their position was somewhat compromised by these resolutions; and they had, since then, been looking forward to an opportunity when they might return to their old position regarding ideals and methods of political progress in India. In the Bombay Provincial Conference held at Surat in April last, Sir P.M. Mehta succeeded by his personal influence in excluding the propositions of Boycott and National Education from the programme of the Conference. And when it was decided to change the venue of the Congress from Nagpure to Surat, it afforded the Bombay Moderate leaders the desired-for opportunity to carry out their intentions in this respect. The Reception Committee at Surat was presumably composed largely of Sir Pherozeshah's followers, and it was cleverly arranged by the Hon. Mr. Gokhale to get the Committee nominate Dr. R.B. Ghosh, to the office of the President, brushing aside the proposal for the nomination of Lala Lajpatrai, then happily released, on the ground that "We cannot afford to flout the Government at this stage, the authorities would throttle our movement in no time." This was naturally regarded as an insult to the public feeling in the country, and Dr. Ghosh must have received at least a hundred telegrams from different parts of India requesting him to generously retire in Lala Lajpatrai's favour. But Dr. Ghosh unfortunately decided to ignore this strong expression of public opinion. Lala Lajpatrai, on the other hand, publicly declined the honour. But this did not satisfy the people who wished to disown the principles of selecting a Congress President on the above ground, believing, as they did, that the most effective protest against the repressive policy of Government would be to elect Lala Lajpatrai to the chair.

The Hon. Mr. Gokhale was entrusted by the Reception Committee, at its meeting held on 24th November 1907 for nominating the President, with the work of drafting the resolutions to be placed before the Congress. But neither Mr. Gokhale nor the Reception Committee supplied a copy of the draft resolutions to any delegate till 2.30 p.m. on Thursday the 26th December, that is to say, till the actual commencement of the Congress Session. The public were taken into confidence only thus far that a list of the headings of the subjects likely to be taken up for discussion by the Surat Congress was officially published a week or ten days before the date of the Congress Session. This list did not include the subjects of Self-Government, Boycott and National Education, on all of which *distinct* and *separate* resolutions were passed at Calcutta last year. This omission naturally strengthened the suspicion that the Bombay Moderates really intended to go back from the position taken up by the Calcutta Congress in these matters. The press strongly commented upon this omission, and Mr. Tilak, who reached Surat on the morning of the 23rd December, denounced such retrogression as suicidal in the interests of the country, more especially at the present juncture, at a large mass-meeting held that evening, and appealed to the Surat public to help the Nationalists in their endeavours to maintain at least the *status quo* in these matters. The next day, a Conference of about five hundred Nationalist Delegates was held at Surat under the chairmanship of Srijut Arabindo Ghose where it was decided that the Nationalists should prevent the attempted retrogression of the Congress by all constitutional means, even by opposing the election of the President if necessary; and a letter was written to the Congress Secretaries requesting them to make arrangements for dividing the house, if need be, on every contested proposition, including that of the election of the President.

In the meanwhile a press note signed by Mr. Gandhi, as Hon. Secretary, was issued to the effect that the statement, that certain resolutions adopted last year at Calcutta were omitted from the Congress programme prepared by the Surat Reception Committee, was wholly unfounded; but the draft resolutions themselves were still withheld from the public, though some of the members of the Reception Committee had already asked for them some days before. On the morning of 25th December, Mr. Tilak happened to get a copy of the draft of the proposed constitution of the Congress prepared by the Hon. Mr. Gokhale. In this draft the object of the Congress was thus stated; "The Indian National Congress has for its ultimate goal the attainment by India of Self-Government similar to that enjoyed by the other members of the British Empire" etc. Mr. Tilak addressed a meeting of the delegates the same morning at the Congress Camp at about 9 a.m. explaining the grounds on which he believed that the Bombay Moderate leaders were bent upon receding from the position taken up by the Calcutta Congress on Swaraj, Boycott and National

Education. The proposed constitution, Mr. Tilak pointed out, was a direct attempt to tamper with the ideal of Self-Government on the lines of the *Self-Governing* colonies, as settled at Calcutta and to exclude the Nationalists from the Congress by making the acceptance of this new creed an indispensable condition of Congress membership. Mr. Tilak further stated in plain terms that if they were assured that no sliding back of the Congress would be attempted the opposition to the election of the President would be withdrawn. The delegates at the meeting were also asked to sign a letter of request to Dr. Ghosh, the President-Elect, requesting him to have the old propositions on Swaraj, Swadeshi, Boycott and National Education taken up for reaffirmation this year; and some of the delegates signed it on the spot. Mr. G. Subramania Iyer of Madras, Mr. Kharandikar of Satara and several others were present at this meeting and excepting a few all the rest admitted the reasonableness of Mr. Tilak's proposal.

Lala Lajpatrai, who arrived at Surat on the morning of that day, saw Messrs. Tilak and Khaparde in the afternoon and intimated to them his intention to arrange for a Committee of a few leading delegates from each side to settle the question in dispute. Messrs. Tilak and Khaparde having agreed, he went to Mr. Gokhale to arrange for the Committee if possible; and Messrs. Tilak and Khaparde returned to the Nationalist Conference which was held that evening (25th December). At this Conference a Nationalist Committee consisting of one Nationalist delegate from each province was appointed to carry on the negotiations with the leaders on the other side; and it was decided that if the Nationalist Committee failed to obtain any assurance from responsible Congress officials about the *status quo* being maintained, the Nationalists should begin their opposition from the election of the President. For the retrogression of the Congress was a serious step, not to be decided upon only by a bare accidental majority of any party either in the Subjects Committee or in the whole Congress (as at present constituted), simply because its session happens to be held in a particular place or province in a particular year; and the usual unanimous acceptance of the President would have, under such exceptional circumstances, greatly weakened the point and force of the opposition. No kind of intimation was received from Lala Lajpatrai this night or even the next morning, regarding the proposal of a joint Committee of reconciliation proposed by him, nor was a copy of the draft resolutions supplied to Mr. Tilak, Mr. Khaparde or any other delegate to judge if no sliding back from the old position was really intended.

On the morning of the 26th December, Messrs. Tilak, Khaparde, Arabindo Ghose and others went to Babu Surendranath Bannerji at his residence. They were accompanied by Babu Motilal Ghose of the *Amrit Bazar Patrika* who had arrived the previous night. Mr. Tilak then informed Babu Surendranath that the Nationalist opposition to the election of the President would be withdrawn, if (1) the Nationalist party were assured that the *status quo* would not be disturbed; and (2) if some graceful allusion was made, by any one of the speakers on the resolution about the election of the President, to the desire of the public to have Lala Lajpatrai in the chair. Mr. Bannerji agreed to the latter proposal as he said he was himself to second the resolution; while as regards the first, though he gave an assurance for himself and Bengal, he asked Mr. Tilak to see Mr. Gokhale or Mr. Malvi. A volunteer was accordingly sent in a carriage to invite Mr. Malvi, the Chairman of the Reception Committee, to Mr. Bannerji's residence, but the volunteer brought a reply that Mr. Malvi had no time to come as he was engaged in religious practices. Mr. Tilak then returned to his camp to take his meals as it was already about 11 a.m.; but on returning to the Congress pandal an hour later, he made persistent attempts to get access to Mr. Malvi but could not find him anywhere. A little before 2.30 p.m., a word was brought to Mr. Tilak that Mr. Malvi was in the President's tent, and Mr. Tilak sent a message to him from an adjoining tent, asking for a short interview to which Mr. Malvi replied that he could not see Mr. Tilak as the Presidential procession was being formed. The Nationalist delegates were waiting in the pandal to hear the result of the endeavours of their Committee to obtain an assurance about the maintenance of the *status quo* from some responsible Congress official, and Mr. V.S. Khare of Nasik now informed them of the failure of Mr. Tilak's attempt in the matter.

## First Day

It has become necessary to state these facts in order that the position of the two parties, when the Congress commenced its proceedings on Thursday, the 26th December, at 2.30 p.m. may be clearly understood. The President-Elect and other persons had now taken their seats on the platform; and as no assurance from any responsible official of the Congress about the maintenance of the *status quo* was till then obtained, Mr. Tilak sent a slip to Babu Surendranath intimating that he should not make the proposed allusion to the controversy about the Presidential election in his speech. He also wrote to Mr. Malvi to supply him with a copy of the draft resolutions, if ready, and at about 3 p.m. while Mr. Malvi was reading his speech, Mr. Tilak got a copy of the draft resolutions which, he subsequently found, were published the very evening in the *Advocate of India* in Bombay, clearly showing that the reporter of the paper must have been supplied with a copy at least a day earlier. The withholding of a copy from Mr. Tilak till 3 p.m. that day cannot, therefore, be regarded as accidental.

There were about thirteen hundred and odd delegates at this time in the pandal of whom over 600 were Nationalists, and the Moderate majority was thus a bare majority. After the Chairman's address was over, Dewan Bahadur Ambalal Sakarlal proposed Dr. R.B. Ghosh to the chair in a speech which, though evoking occasional cries of dissent, was heard to the end. The declaration by Dewan Bahadur as well as by Mr. Malvi that the proposing and seconding of the resolution to elect the President was only a *formal* business, led many delegates to believe that it was not improbable that the usual procedure of taking votes on the proposition might be dispensed with; and when Babu Surendranath Bannerji, whose rising on the platform seems to have reminded some of the delegates of the Midnapur incident, commenced his speech, there was persistent shouting and he was asked to sit down. He made another attempt to speak but was not heard, and the session had, therefore, to be suspended for the day. The official press note suggests that this hostile demonstration was pre-arranged. But the suggestion is unfounded. For though the Nationalists did intend to oppose the election, they had at their Conference, held the previous day, expressly decided to do so only by solidly and silently voting against it in a constitutional manner.

In the evening the Nationalists again held their Conference and authorised their Committee, appointed on the previous day, to further carry on the negotiations for having the *status quo* maintained if possible, failing which it was decided to oppose the election of Dr. Ghosh by moving such amendment as the Committee might decide or by simply voting against his election. The Nationalists were further requested, and unanimously agreed, not only to abstain from joining in any such demonstration as led to the suspension of that day's proceedings, but to scrupulously avoid any, even the least, interruption of the speakers on the opposite side, so that both parties might get a patient hearing. At night (about 8 p.m.) Mr. Chunilal Saraya, Manager of the Indian Specie Bank and Vice-Chairman of the Surat Reception Committee, accompanied by two other gentlemen, went, in his unofficial capacity and on his own account, to Mr. Tilak and proposed that he intended to arrange for a meeting that night between Mr. Tilak and Mr. Gokhale at the residence of a leading congressman to settle the differences between the two parties. Mr. Tilak agreed and requested Mr. Chunilal, if an interview could be arranged, to fix the time in consultation with Mr. Gokhale, adding that he, Mr. Tilak, would be glad to be present at the place of the interview at *any* hour of the night. Thereon Mr. Chunilal left Mr. Tilak, but unhappily no word was received by the latter that night.

## Second Day

On the morning of Friday the 27th (11 a.m.) Mr. Chunilal Saraya again saw Mr. Tilak and requested him to go in company with Mr. Khaparde to Prof. Gajjar's bungalow near the Congress pandal, where, by appointment, they were to meet Dr. Rutherford, who was trying for a reconciliation. Messrs. Tilak and Khaparde went to Prof. Gajjar's but Dr. Rutherford could not come then owing to his other engagements. Prof. Gajjar then asked Mr. Tilak what the latter intended to do; and Mr. Tilak stated that if no settlement was arrived at privately owing to every leading congressman being unwilling to take any responsibility in the matter upon himself, he (Mr. Tilak) would be obliged to bring an amendment to the proposition of electing the President after it had been seconded. The amendment would be to the effect that the business of election should be adjourned, and a committee, consisting of one leading Moderate and one leading Nationalist from each Congress Province, with Dr. Rutherford's name added, be appointed to consider and settle the differences between the two parties, both of which should accept the Committee's decision as final and then proceed to the *unanimous* election of the President. Mr. Tilak even supplied to Prof. Gajjar the names of the delegates, who, in his opinion, should form the Committee, but left a free hand to the Moderates to change the names of their representatives if they liked to do so. Prof. Gajjar and Mr. Chunilal undertook to convey the proposal to Sir P.M. Mehta or Dr. Rutherford in the Congress Camp and asked Messrs. Tilak and Khaparde to go to the pandal and there await reply. After half an hour Prof. Gajjar and Mr. Saraya returned and told Messrs. Tilak and Khaparde that nothing could be done in the matter, Mr. Saraya adding that if both parties proceeded constitutionally there would be no hitch.

This note, it is admitted, was put by a volunteer into the hands of Mr. Malvi, the Chairman, as he was entering the pandal with the President-Elect in procession.

The proceedings of the day commenced at 1 p.m., when Babu Surendranath Bannerji was called upon to resume his speech, seconding the election of the President. Mr. Tilak was expecting a reply to his note but not having received one up to this time asked Mr. N.C. Kelkar to send a reminder. Mr. Kelkar thereupon sent a chit to the Chairman to the effect that "Mr. Tilak requests a reply to his note." But no reply was received even after this reminder, and Mr. Tilak, who, though he was allotted a seat on the platform, was sitting in the front row of the delegate's seats near the platform-steps, rose to go up the platform *immediately* after Babu Surendranath, who was calmly heard by all, had finished his speech. But he was held back by a volunteer in the way. Mr. Tilak, however, asserted his right to go up and pushing aside the volunteer succeeded in getting to the platform just when Dr. Ghosh was moving to take the President's chair. The Official Note says that by the time Mr. Tilak came upon the platform and stood in front of the President, the motion of the election of Dr. Ghosh had been passed by an overwhelming majority; and Dr. Ghosh, being installed in the Presidential chair by loud and *prolonged* applause had risen to begin his address. All this, if it did take place, as alleged, could only have been done in a deliberately hurried manner with a set purpose to trick Mr. Tilak out of his right to address the delegates and move an amendment as previously notified. According to the usual procedure Mr. Malvi was bound to announce Mr. Tilak, or if he considered the amendment out of order, declare it so publicly, and to ask for a show of hands in favour of or against the motion. But nothing of the kind was done; nor was the interval of a few seconds sufficient for a prolonged applause as alleged. As Mr. Tilak stood up on the platform he was greeted with shouts of disapproval from the members of the Reception Committee on the platform, and the cry was taken up by other Moderates. Mr. Tilak repeatedly insisted upon his right of addressing the delegates, and told Dr. Ghosh, when he attempted to interfere, that he was not properly elected. Mr. Malvi said that he had ruled Mr. Tilak's amendment out of order, to which Mr. Tilak replied that the ruling, if any, was wrong and Mr. Tilak had a right to appeal to the delegates on the same. By this time there was a general uproar in the pandal, the Moderates shouting at Mr. Tilak and asking him to sit down and the Nationalists demanding that he should be heard. At this stage Dr. Ghosh and Mr. Malvi said that Mr. Tilak should be removed from the platform; and a young gentleman, holding the important office of a Secretary to the Reception Committee, touched Mr. Tilak's person with a view to carry out the Chairman's order. Mr. Tilak pushed the gentleman aside and again asserted his right of being heard, declaring that he would not leave the platform unless bodily removed. Mr. Gokhale seems to have here asked the above-mentioned gentleman not to touch Mr. Tilak's person. But there were others who were seen threatening an assault on his person, though he was calmly standing on the platform facing the delegates with his arms folded over his chest.

It was during this confusion that a shoe hurled on to the platform hit Sir P.M. Mehta on the side of the face after touching Babu Surendranath Bannerji, both of whom were sitting within a yard of Mr. Tilak on the other side of the table. Chairs were now seen being lifted to be thrown at Mr. Tilak by persons on and below the platform, and some of the Nationalists, therefore, rushed on to the platform to his rescue. Dr. Ghosh in the meanwhile twice attempted to read his address, but was stopped by cries of "No, no," from all sides in the pandal, and the confusion became still worse. It must be stated that the Surat Reception Committee, composed of Moderates, had made arrangements the previous night to dismiss the Nationalist Volunteers and to hire *bohras* or Mahomedan goondas for the day.

These with lathis were stationed at various places in the pandal and their presence was detected and protested against by the Nationalist Delegates before the commencement of the Congress proceedings of the day. But though one or two were removed from the pandal, the rest who remained therein, now took part in the scuffle on behalf of their masters. It was found impossible to arrest the progress of disorder and proceedings were then suspended *sine die*; and the Congress officials retired in confusion to a tent behind the pandal. The police, who seem to have been long ready under a requisition, now entered into and eventually cleared the pandal; while the Nationalist delegates who had gone to the platform safely escorted Mr. Tilak to an adjoining tent. It remains to be mentioned that copies of an inflammatory leaflet in Gujarathi asking the Gujarathi people to rise against Mr. Tilak were largely distributed in the pandal before the commencement of the day's proceedings.

It would be seen from the above account that the statement in the official note to the effect that Dr. Ghosh was elected President amid loud and prolonged applause before Mr. Tilak appeared on the platform, and that Mr. Tilak wanted to move an adjournment of the whole Congress are entirely misleading and unfounded. What he demanded, by way of amendment, was an adjournment of the business of the election of the President in order to have the differences settled by a joint Conciliatory Committee of leading delegates from both sides. Whether this was in order or otherwise, Mr. Tilak had certainly a right to appeal to the delegates and it was this consciousness that led Mr. Malvi and his advisers to hastily wind up the election business without sending a reply to Mr. Tilak or calling upon him to address the delegates. It was a trick by which they intended to deprive Mr. Tilak of the right of moving an amendment and addressing the delegates thereon.

As for the beginning of the actual rowdyism on the day some of the members of the Reception Committee itself were responsible. The silent hearing given by the Nationalist to Mr. Surendranath, on the one hand, and the circulation of the inflammatory leaflet and the hiring of the goondas on the other, further prove that if there was any pre-arrangement anywhere for the purpose of creating a row in the pandal, it was on the part of the Moderates themselves. But for their rowdyism there was every likelihood of Mr. Tilak's amendment being carried by a large majority and the election of President afterwards taking place smoothly and unanimously. But neither Dr. Ghosh nor any other Congress officials seemed willing to tactfully manage the business as Mr. Dadabhai Naoroji did last year. Dr. Ghosh's speech though undelivered in the Congress pandal had been by this time published in the Calcutta papers, and telegrams from Calcutta received in the evening showed that he had made an offensive attack on the Nationalist Party therein. This added to the sensation in the Nationalist camp that evening, but the situation was not such as to preclude all hope of reconciliation. Srijut Motilal Ghose of the *Patrika,* Mr. A.C. Moitra of Rajshahi, Mr. B.C. Chatterji of Calcutta and Lala Harkishen Lal from Lahore, accordingly tried their best to bring about a compromise, and, if possible, to have the Congress session revived the next day. They went to Mr. Tilak on the night of 27th and the morning of 28th to ascertain the views of his party, and to each of them Mr. Tilak gave the following assurance in writing:–

### Surat, 28th December, 1907

"Dear Sir, — With reference to our conversation, and principally in the best interests of the Congress, I and my party are prepared to waive our opposition to the election of Dr. Rash Behari Ghosh as President of 23rd Indian National Congress, and are prepared to act in the spirit of forget and forgive, provided, *firstly,* the last year's resolutions on Swaraj, Swadeshi, Boycott and National Education are adhered to and each expressly reaffirmed; and *secondly,* such passages, if any, in Dr. Ghosh's speech as may be offensive to the Nationalist Party are omitted."

Your etc., B.G. Tilak.

This letter was taken by the gentlemen to whom it was addressed to the Moderate leaders but no compromise was arrived at as the

Moderates were all along bent upon the retrogression of the Congress at any cost. A Convention of the Moderates was, therefore, held in the pandal the next day where Nationalists were not allowed to go even when some of them were ready and offered to sign the declaration required. On the other hand, those who did not wish to go back from the position taken up at the Calcutta Congress and honestly desired to work further on the same lines met in a separate place the same evening to consider what steps might be taken to continue the work of the Congress in future.

At the Calcutta Congress, under the presidentship of Mr. Dadabhai Naoroji, it was resolved that the goal of Congress should be Swaraj on the lines of the Self-Governing British Colonies, and this goal was accepted by all, Moderates and Nationalists, without a single dissentient voice. The resolution on Self-Government passed there is as follows:–

"*Self-Government:*–This Congress is of the opinion that the system of Government obtaining in the Self-Governing British Colonies should be extended to India and that as steps leading to it, urges that the following reforms should be immediately carried out." (Here followed certain administrative reforms such as simultaneous examinations in England and India, reform of Executive and Legislative Council, and of Local and Municipal Boards.) The Congress Reception Committee at Surat did not publish the draft Resolution till the commencement of the Congress Sessions; but a draft Constitution of the Congress, prepared by the Hon'ble Mr. Gokhale, was published a day or two earlier. In this draft the goal of the Congress was defined as follows:–

"The Indian National Congress has for its ultimate goal the attainment by India of Self-Government similar to that enjoyed by other members of the British Empire and a participation by her in the privileges and responsibilities of the Empire on equal terms with the other members; and it seeks to advance towards this goal by strictly constitutional means, by bringing about a steady reform of the existing system of administration, and by promoting national unity, fostering public spirit and improving the condition of the mass of the people."

"Those who accept the foregoing creed of the Congress, shall be members of the Provincial Committee."

"All who accept the foregoing creed of the Congress ... shall be entitled to become members of a District Congress Committee."

"From the year 1908, delegates to the Congress shall be elected by Provincial and District Congress Committee only."

*Remarks:* It will at once be seen that the new Constitution intended to convert the Congress from a national into a sectional movement. The goal of Swaraj on the lines of self-government Colonies, as settled last year, was to be given up; and in its stead Self-Government similar to that enjoyed by other members (not necessarily self-governing) of the British Empire, was to be set up as the *ultimate* goal, evidently meaning, that it was to be considered as out of the pale of practical politics. The same view is expressed by Sir Pherozeshah Mehta in his interview with the correspondent of the *Times of India,* published in the issue of the *Times* dated 30th December 1907. The Hon. Mr. Gokhale must have taken his cue from the same source. The *reform* of the existing system of administration, and not its gradual replacement by a popular system, was to be the immediate object of the Congress according to this constitution; and further no one, who did not accept this new creed, was to be a member of Provincial or District Committees, or possibly even a delegate to the Congress after 1908. This was the chief feature of retrogression, which Sir P.M. Mehta and his party wanted to carry out this year at a safe place like Surat. It is true that the old resolution on Self-Government was subsequently included in the draft Resolutions, published only after the commencement of the Congress Session. But the draft Constitution was never withdrawn.

## References

Ahmad, Razi, *Indian Peasant Movement and Mahatma Gandhi,* Shabd Prakashan, Delhi, 1987.

Ahmed, Mesbahuddin : *The British Labour Party and the Indian Independence Movement, 1917-1939,* Envoy Press, 1987.

Bakshi, S.R. : *Arya Samaj and Philosophy of Swami Dayananda,* Vista International Pub, Delhi, 2005.

Barrier, N.G.: *The Census in British India. New Perspectives,* New Delhi, Manohar, 1981.

Burrowes, Robert J.: *The Strategy of Nonviolent Defense: A Gandhian Approach,* State University of New York Press, Albany, 1996.

Friedrich, J.: *Constitutional Government and Democracy,* Boston, Ginn, 1950.

Heinsath, Charles: *Indian Nationalism and Hindu Social Reform,* Princeton University Press, Princeton, 1964.

Morris-Jones, W.H.: *The Government and Politics of India,* London, Hutchinson, 1971.

Wade, R.: *Public Bureaucracy and the Incentive Problem,* Washington, D.C., World Bank, 1994.

10

# Indian Freedom Struggle and Role of Mahatma Gandhi

**DR NEELAM AZAD**
*Azad Bhawan, Adarsh Nagar, Dungarpur, Rajasthan.*

One of the greatest men in the history of India is unarguably Mahatma Gandhi. The way he gave shape and character to India's freedom struggle is worthy of a standing ovation. He sacrificed his own life for the sake of his country. The respect that he earned for himself despite leading a simple lifestyle is much appreciable. Mahatma Gandhi played a pivotal role in the freedom struggle of India. His non violent ways and peaceful methods were the foundation for gaining independence from the British. Read about Mahatma Gandhi's role in freedom struggle of India. Mahatma Gandhi was born Mohandas Karamchand Gandhi on 2nd October at Porbandar located in Gujarat. He went off to South Africa after marriage and worked as barrister there for twenty years. In South Africa, he had his first brush with apartheid. Once while he was traveling in a train, he was thrown out of the first class compartment despite having a ticket. This made him swear that he would do his best to erase apartheid from the face of his world. He went back to India only to find that his own country was being ruled by the British and his fellow citizens were being treated harshly by the British.

## Champaran Satyagraha [1917]

Gandhiji's first experience in satyagraha came in 1917 in Champaran, a district in Bihar. The peasantry on the indigo plantations was excessively oppressed by the European planters. They were compelled to grow indigo on at least 3\20th of their land and to sell it at prices fixed by the planters.

Having heard of Gandhi's campaigns in South Africa, several peasants of Champaran invited him to come and help them. Gandhiji reached Champaran in 1917 and began to conduct a detailed inquiry into the conditions of the peasantry. The district officials ordered him to leave Champaran, but he defied the order and was willing to face trial and imprisonment. This forced the Government to cancel its earlier order and to appoint a committee of inquiry on which Gandhiji served as a member. Ultimately the disabilities from which the peasantry was suffering were reduced and Gandhiji had won his first battle of civil obedience in India.

## Ahmedabad Mill Strike [1918]

In 1918, Gandhiji intervened in a dispute between the workers and mill-owners of Ahmedabad. He advised the workers to go on strike and to demand a 35% increase in wages. He insisted that the workers should not use violence against the mill-owners during the strike. He undertook a fast unto death to strengthen the workers resolve to continue the strike. His fast put pressure on the mill-owners who relented on the fourth day and agreed to give the workers a 35% increase in wages.

## Kheda Peasant Struggle [1918]

In 1918 crops failed in the Kheda district in Gujarat but the government refused to reduce land revenue and insisted on its full collection. Gandhiji supported the peasants and advised them to withhold payment of revenue till their demand for its remission was met. The struggle was withdrawn when it was learnt that the government had issued instructions that revenue should be recovered only from those peasants who could afford to pay. Sardar Vallabhbhai Patel becameGandhiji's follower during this struggle.

These experiences brought Gandhiji in close contact with the masses whose interests he actively exposed all his life. In time he became the symbol of poor India, nationalist India and rebellious India. Three causes were very dear to Gandhiji's among the masses. Thousands of peasants in U.P and Bengal responded to the call of non-co-operation. In the Punjab the Sikhs were leading a non-violent movement known as Akali movement, to remove corrupt mahants from the Gurudwarasheart. The first was Hindu-Muslim unity, the second, the fight against untouchability, and the third, the raising of the social status of women in the country.

## The Rowlatt Act [1919]

While trying to appease the Indians, the Government of India was ready with repression. The Government decided to arm itself with more far-reaching powers, which went against the accepted principles of rule of rule, to be able to suppress those nationalists who would refuse to be satisfied with the reforms. In March 1919, it passed the Rowlatt Act. This Act authorized the Government to imprison any person without trial. The Act would enable the Government to suspend the right of Habeas Corpus which had been the foundation of civil liberties in Britain.

## SATYAGRAHA AGAINST THE ROWLATT ACT

Gandhiji was aroused by the Rowlatt Act. In February 1919 he founded the Satyagraha Sabha. Its members took a pledge to disobey the Act and thus to court arrest. Here was new method of struggle. Big meetings and demonstrastions, refusal to cooperate with the government, boycott of foreign cloth and schools or individual acts of terrorism were the only forms of political work known to the nationalists. Satyagraha immediately raised the movement to a higher level. Nationalists could now act, instead of merely agitating and giving only verbal expression to their dissatisfaction and anger.

Gandhiji asked the nationalist workers to go to the villages. That is where India lives, he said. He increasingly turned the face of nationalism towards the common man and the symbol of this transformation was to be Khadi, which soon became the uniform of the nationalists. The people responded magnificently to Gandhi's call. March and April 1919 witnessed a remarkable political awakening in India. There were hartals, strikes, and demonstrations. The entire country was electrified.

### Jallianwala Bagh Massacre [1919]

The Government was determined to suppress the mass agitation. Gandhiji gave a call for a mighty hartal on 6th April 1919. The people responded with unprecedented enthusiasm. The government decided to meet the popular protest with repression, particularly in the Punjab. At this time was perpetrated one of the worst crimes in modern history.

A large but unarmed crowd had gathered on 13 April 1919 at Amritsar in the Jallianwala Bagh, to protest the arrest of their popular leaders, Dr. Saifuddin Kitchlew and Dr. Satyapal. General Dyer, the military commander of Amritsar decided to terrorise the people of Amritsar into complete submission. Jallianwala Bagh was a large open space which was enclosed on three sides by buildings and had only one exit. He surrounded the Bagh with his army unit, closed the exit with his troops, and then ordered his men to shoot into the trapped crowd with rifles and machine-guns. Thousands were killed and wounded. After this massacre, martial law was proclaimed throughout the Punjab and the people were submitted to the most uncivilized atrocities. Popular shock was expressed by Rabindranath Tagore who renounced his knighthood in protest.

## NON CO-OPERATION MOVEMENT

One of the first series of non violent protests nationwide was the non cooperation movement started by Mahatma Gandhi. This movement officially started the Gandhian era in India. In this freedom struggle, the non cooperation movement was basically aimed at making the Indians aware of the fact that the British government can be opposed and if done actively, it will keep a check on them. Thus, educational institutions were boycotted, foreign goods were boycotted, and people let go off their nominated seats in government institutions. Though the movement failed, Indians awakened to the concept of going against the British.

## CIVIL DISOBEDIENCE MOVEMENT

### India's History : Modern India : Civil Disobedience Movement : 1922

Civil Disobedience Movement launched in 1930 under MK Gandhi's leadership was one of the most important phases of India's freedom struggle. The simon commission, constituted in November 1927 by the British Government to prepare and finalize a constitution for India and consisting of members of the British Parliament only, was boycotted by all sections of the Indian social and political platforms as an 'All-White Commission'. The opposition to the Simon Commission in Bengal was remarkable. In protest against the Commission, a hartal was observed on 3 February 1928 in various parts of the province. Massive demonstrations were held in Calcutta on 19 February1928, the day of Simon's arrival in the city. On 1 March 1928, meetings were held simultaneously in all thirty-two wards of Calcutta urging people to renew the movement for boycott of British goods.

Following the rejection of the recommendations of the Simon Commission by the Indians, an All-Party Conference was held at

Bombay in May 1928 under the president ship of Dr. MA Ansari. The Conference appointed a drafting committee under Motilal Nehru to draw up a constitution for India. The Nehru Report was accepted by all sections of Indian society except by a section of Indian Muslims. In December 1928, the Indian National Congress pressed the British Government to accept the Nehru Report in its entirety. The Calcutta Session of the Indian Congress (December 1928) virtually gave an ultimatum to the British Government, that if dominion status were not conceded by December 1929, a countrywide Civil Disobedience Movement would be launched. The British Government, however, declared in May 1929 that India would get dominion status within the Empire very soon.

## Salt March and Civil Disobedience

Gandhi emerged from his long seclusion by undertaking his most famous campaign, a march of about 400 kilometres from his commune in Ahmedabad to Dandi, on the coast of Gujarat between 12 March and 6 April 1930. The march is usually known as the *Dandi March* or the *Salt Satyagraha*. At Dandi, in protest against British taxes on salt, he and thousands of followers broke the law by making their own salt from seawater.

In April 1930 there were violent police-crowd clashes in Calcutta. Approximately 100,000 people were imprisoned in the course of the Civil disobedience movement (1930–31), while in Peshawar unarmed demonstrators were fired upon in the Qissa Khwani bazaar massacre. The latter event catapulted the then newly formed Khudai Khidmatgar movement (founder Khan Abdul Ghaffar Khan, the *Frontier Gandhi*) onto the National scene. While Gandhi was in jail, the first Round Table Conference was held in London in November 1930, without representation from the Indian National Congress. The ban upon the Congress was removed because of economic hardships caused by the satyagraha. Gandhi, along with other members of the Congress Working Committee, was released from prison in January 1931.

In March 1931, the Gandhi-Irwin Pact was signed, and the government agreed to set all political prisoners free (Although, some of the key revolutionaries were not set free and the death sentence for Bhagat Singh and his two comrades was not taken back which further intensified the agitation against Congress not only outside it but with in the Congress itself). In return, Gandhi agreed to discontinue the civil disobedience movement and participate as the sole representative of the Congress in the second Round Table Conference, which was held in London in September 1931. However, the conference ended in failure in December 1931. Gandhi returned to India and decided to resume the civil disobedience movement in January 1932.

For the next few years, the Congress and the government were locked in conflict and negotiations until what became the Government of India Act of 1935 could be hammered out. By then, the rift between the Congress and the Muslim League had become unbridgeable as each pointed the finger at the other acrimoniously.

The Muslim League disputed the claim of the Congress to represent all people of India, while the Congress disputed the Muslim League's claim to voice the aspirations of all Muslims.

## GANDHI–IRWIN PACT

Gandhi–Irwin Pact refers to a political agreement signed by Mahatma Gandhi and the then Viceroy of India, Lord Irwin on 5th March 1931.

Before this, the viceroy Lord Irwin announced in October 1929,a vague offer of 'dominion status' for India in an unspecified future and a Round Table Conference to discuss a future constitution.

It was signed after meetings between Gandhi and the Viceroy that spanned over a three week time period. Many Indian citizens were originally unsatisfied with the conditions of this truce. The agreement spelled out certain specific action points, to be initiated by the colonial Government of India as well as the Indian National Congress. Important action points of the Pact included:

- Discontinuation of the civil disobedience movement by the Indian National Congress
- Participation by the Indian National Congress in the Round Table Conference
- Withdrawal of all ordinances issued by the British Government imposing curbs on the activities of the Indian National Congress
- Withdrawal of all prosecutions relating to several types of offenses except those involving violence
- Release of prisoners arrested for participating in the civil disobedience movement
- The removal of the tax on salt, which allowed the Indians to produce, trade, and sell salt legally and for their own private use.

## Salt Satyagraha

The Satyagraha March, which triggered the wider Civil Disobedience Movement, was an important part of the Indian independence movement. It was a campaign of nonviolent protest against the British salt tax in colonial India which began with the Salt March to Dandi on March 12, 1930.

It was the most significant organized challenge to British authority since the Non-cooperation movement of 1920-22, and the *Purna Swaraj* declaration of independence by the Indian National Congress on December 31, 1929. Mahatma Gandhi led the Dandi march from his Sabarmati Ashram to Dandi, Gujarat to produce salt without paying the tax, with growing numbers of Indians joining him along the way. When Gandhi broke the salt laws in Dandi at the conclusion of the march on April 6, 1930, it sparked large scale acts of civil disobedience against the British Raj salt laws by millions of Indians.

Gandhi was arrested on May 5, 1930, just days before his planned raid on the Dharasana Salt Works. The Dandi March and the ensuing Dharasana Satyagraha drew worldwide attention to the Indian independence movement through extensive newspaper and newsreel coverage. The satyagraha against the salt tax continued for almost a year, ending with Gandhi's release from jail and negotiations with Viceroy Lord Irwin at the Second Round Table Conference. Over 80,000 Indians were jailed as a result of the Salt Satyagraha. The campaign had a significant effect on changing world and British attitudes toward Indian independence and caused large numbers of Indians to actively join the fight for the first time. However, it failed to result in major concessions from the British.

The Salt Satyagraha campaign was based upon Gandhi's principles of nonviolent protest called *satyagraha,* which he loosely translated as "truth-force." (Literally, it is formed from the Sanskrit words *satya,* "truth", and *aagraha,* "asking for.") In early 1930 the Indian National Congress chose satyagraha as their main tactic for winning Indian independence from British rule and appointed Gandhi to organize the campaign. Gandhi chose the 1882 British Salt Act as the first target of satyagraha. The Salt March to Dandi, and the beating by British police of hundreds of nonviolent protesters in Dharasana, which received worldwide news coverage, demonstrated the effective use of civil disobedience as a technique for fighting social and political injustice. The satyagraha teachings of Gandhi and the March to Dandi had a significant influence on American civil rights activist Martin

Luther King, Jr., and his fight for civil rights for blacks and other minority groups in the 1960s.

## DECLARATION OF INDEPENDENCE

At midnight on December 31, 1929, the Indian National Congress raised the tricolour flag of India on the banks of the Ravi at Lahore. The Indian National Congress, led by Gandhi and Jawaharlal Nehru, publicly issued the Declaration of Independence, or Purna Swaraj, on January 26, 1930. (Literally in Sanskrit, *purna,* "complete," *swa,* "self," *raj,* "rule," thus "complete self-rule".) The declaration included the readiness to withhold taxes, and the statement: We believe that it is the inalienable right of the Indian people, as of any other people, to have freedom and to enjoy the fruits of their toil and have the necessities of life, so that they may have full opportunities of growth. We believe also that if any government deprives a people of these rights and oppresses them the people have a further right to alter it or abolish it. The British government in India has not only deprived the Indian people of their freedom but has based itself on the exploitation of the masses, and has ruined India economically, politically, culturally and spiritually. We believe therefore, that India must sever the British connection and attain *Purna Swaraj* or complete independence.

The Congress Working Committee gave Gandhi the responsibility for organizing the first act of civil disobedience, with Congress itself ready to take charge after Gandhi's expected arrest. Gandhi's plan was to begin civil disobedience with a satyagraha aimed at the British salt tax.

The 1882 Salt Act gave the British a monopoly on the collection and manufacture of salt, limiting its handling to government salt depots and levying a salt tax. Violation of the Salt Act was a criminal offense. Even though salt was freely available to those living on the coast (by evaporation of sea water), Indians were forced to purchase it from the colonial government.

Gandhi's choice of the salt tax was met with incredulity by the Working Committee of the Congress, though Gandhi had his reasons for choosing the salt tax. The salt tax was a deeply symbolic choice, since salt was used by nearly everyone in India. It represented 8.2% of the British Raj tax revenue, and most significantly hurt the poorest Indians the most. Gandhi felt that this protest would dramatize Purna Swaraj in a way that was meaningful to the lowliest Indians. He also reasoned that it would build unity between Hindus and Muslims by fighting a wrong that touched them equally.

## The 1930 Salt March

Gandhi began a new campaign in 1930, the Salt Satyagraha. Gandhi and his followers set off on a 200-mile journey from Ashram Ahmedabad to the Arabian Ocean where Gandhi wanted to pick up a few grains of salt. This action formed the symbolic focal point of a campaign of civil disobedience in which the state monopoly on salt was the first target. Prior to the beginning of the action, Gandhi sent a letter to the Lord Lieutenant "Dear Friend (...) Whilst, therefore, I hold the British rule to be a curse, I do not intend harm to a single Englishman or to any legitimate interest he may have in India (...) My ambition is nothing less than to bring round the English people through non-violence to recognize the injustice they have done to India. I do not intend to be offensive to your people. Indeed, I would like to serve your people as I would my own (...)."

Yet the Lord Lieutenant didn't even reply personally to his letter. Gandhi held his last prayer meeting on the evening of the 11th of March 1930. "There can be no turning back for us hereafter. We will keep on our fight till swaraj is established in India. Those of them that are married should take leave of their wives. We are as good as parting from the Ashram and from our homes.— Let nobody assume that after I am arrested there will be no one left to guide them. It is not I but Pandit Jawaharlal who is your guide. He has the capacity to lead."

It was hoped that this action would spread across India. Wherever possible, civil disobedience was to be used to counter the salt laws. It was illegal to manufacture salt, regardless of the location. The possession and trading of smuggled salt (natural salt or salt earth) was also illegal. Anyone caught selling smuggled salt was liable to prosecution. To collect salt from the natural deposits at the coast was also illegal.

Gandhi had a large group of well-trained Satyagrahi available to him; as well trained in observation as they were in spreading propaganda among the masses. They were bound by a joint pledge and by the principles of the "Ashram in Exodus", which encompassed three points: prayer, spinning and keeping a diary. They wore uniform clothing (a sort of Khaki uniform) and wore the headwear of prisoners. After a 24-hour long march to the Indian Ocean, Gandhi picked up a few pieces of salt-a signal to the rest of the subcontinent to do the same. This raw material was carried inland before being processed on the roofs of houses in pans and then sold. Over 50,000 Indians were imprisoned for breaking the salt laws. The entire protest was carried out almost without violence. Indeed, it was this that annoyed the police.

A report from the English journalist, Webb Miller, who witnessed one of the clashes, has become a classic description of the way in which Satyagraha was carried out at the forefront of the battle lines. 2,500 volunteers advanced on the salt works of Dhrasana: "Gandhi's men advanced in complete silence before stopping about one-hundred meters before the cordon. A selected team broke away from the main group, waded through the ditch and neared the barbed-wire fence. (...) Receiving the signal, a large group of local police officers suddenly moved towards the advancing protestors and subjected them to a hail of blows to the head delivered from steel-covered Lathis (truncheons). None of the protesters raised so much as an arm to protect themselves against the barrage of blows. They fell to the ground like pins in a bowling alley. From where I was standing I could hear the nauseating sound of truncheons impacting against unprotected skulls. The waiting main group moaned and drew breath sharply at each blow. Those being subjected to the onslaught fell to the ground quickly writhing unconsciously or with broken shoulders (...). The main group, which had been spared until now, began to march in a quiet and determined way forwards and were met with the same fate. They advanced in a uniform manner with heads raised-without encouragement through music or battle cries and without being given the opportunity to avoid serious injury or even death. The police attacked repeatedly and the second group were also beaten to the ground. There was no fight, no violence; the marchers simply advanced until they themselves were knocked down. (...)"

Following their action, the men in uniform, who obviously felt unprotected with all their superior equipment of violence, could think of nothing better to do than that which seems to overcome uniformed men in similar situations as a sort of "natural" impulse: If they were unable to break the skulls of all the protesters, they now set about kicking and aiming their blows at the genitals of the helpless on the ground. "For hour upon hour endless numbers of motionless, bloody bodies were carried away on stretchers", according to Webb Miller.

## Quit India Movement

The Quit India Movement *(Bharat Chhodo Andolan* or the *August Movement* (*August Kranti*)) was a civil disobedience movement launched in India in August 1942 in response to Mohandas Gandhi's call for immediate independence. Gandhi hoped to bring the British government to the negotiating table. Almost the entire Indian National Congress leadership, and not just at the national level, was put into confinement less than twenty-four hours after Gandhi's speech, and the greater number of the Congress leaders were to spend the rest of World War II in jail.

## World War II and Indian Involvement

By 1942, Indians were divided over World War II, as the British Governor-General of India, Lord Linlithgow, had unilaterally and without consultation entered India into the war. Some wanted to support the British during the Battle of Britain, hoping for eventual independence through this support. Others were enraged by the British disregard for Indian intelligence and civil rights, and were unsympathetic to the travails of Britons in the United Kingdom, which they saw as revenge for the subjugation of Indians.

## Opinions on the War

At the outbreak of war, the Congress Party had during the Wardha meeting of the working-committee in September 1939, passed a resolution conditionally supporting the fight against fascism, but were rebuffed when they asked for independence in return. Gandhi had not supported this initiative, as he could not reconcile an endorsement for war (he was a committed believer in nonviolent resistance to tyranny, used in the Indian Independence Movement and proposed even against Adolf Hitler, Benito Mussolini, and Hideki Tojo). However, at the height of the Battle of Britain, Gandhi had stated his support for the fight against fascism and of the British War effort, stating he did not seek to raise a free India from the ashes of Britain. However, opinions remained divided. After the onset of the war, only a group led by Netaji Subhas Chandra Bose took any decisive action. Bose organized the Indian National Army with the help of the Japanese, and, soliciting help from the Axis Powers.

## Cripps' Mission

In March 1942, faced with an increasingly dissatisfied sub-continent only reluctantly participating in the war, and deterioration in the war situation in Europe and South East Asia, and with growing dissatisfaction among Indian troops-especially in Europe-and among the civilian population in the sub-continent, the British government sent a delegation to India under Stafford Cripps, in what came to be known as the Cripps' Mission. The purpose of the mission was to negotiate with the Indian National Congress a deal to obtain total cooperation during the war, in return of progressive devolution and distribution of power from the crown and the Viceroy to elected Indian legislature. However, the talks failed, having failed to address the key demand of a timeframe towards self-government, and of definition of the powers to be relinquished, essentially portraying an offer of limited dominion-status that was wholly unacceptable to the Indian movement.

## RESOLUTION FOR IMMEDIATE INDEPENDENCE

On July 14, 1942, the Indian National Congress passed a resolution demanding complete independence from the British government. The draft proposed that if the British did not accede to the demands, massive civil disobedience would be launched.

However, it proved to be controversial within the party. A prominent Congress national leader Chakravarti Rajgopalachari quit the Congress over this decision, and so did some local and regional level organizers. Jawaharlal Nehru and Maulana Azad were apprehensive and critical of the call, but backed it and stuck with Gandhi's leadership till the end. Sardar Vallabhbhai Patel and Dr. Rajendra Prasad were openly and enthusiastically in favour of such a disobedience movement, as were many veteran Gandhians and socialists like Asoka Mehta and Jaya Prakash Narayan.

The Congress had lesser success in rallying other political forces under a single flag and mast. Smaller parties like the Communist Party of India and the Hindu Mahasabha opposed the call. Muhammad Ali Jinnah's opposition to the call led to large numbers of Muslims cooperating with the British, and the Muslim League obtaining power in the Imperial provincial governments.

Allama Mashriqi (head of the Khaksar Tehrik) was called to join the Quit India Movement. Mashriqi was apprehensive of its outcome and did not agree with the Congress Working Committee's resolution and on July 28, 1942, Allama Mashriqi sent the following telegram to Maulana Abul Kalam Azad, Khan Abdul Ghaffar Khan, Mahatma Gandhi, Rajagopalachariar, Jawaharlal Nehru, Rajendra Prasad and Dr. Pattabhi Sitaramiyya. He also sent a copy to Sambamurty (former Speaker of the Madras Assembly). The telegram was published in the press, and it stated:

"I am in receipt of Pandit Jawaharlal Nehru's letter of July 8th. My honest opinion is that Civil Disobedience Movement is a little premature. The Congress should first concede openheartedly and with handshake to Muslim League the theoretical Pakistan, and thereafter all parties unitedly make demand of Quit India. If the British refuse, start total disobedience..."

On August 8, 1942 the Quit India Resolution was passed at the Bombay session of the All India Congress Committee (AICC). At Gowalia Tank, Bombay, Gandhi told Indians to follow nonviolent civil disobedience. He told the masses to act as an independent nation. His call found support among a large number of Indians.

## Suppression of the Movement

The British, already alarmed by the advance of the Japanese army to the India/Burma border, responded the next day by imprisoning Gandhi at the Aga Khan Palace in Pune. All the members of the Party's Working Committee (national leadership) were arrested and imprisoned at the Ahmednagar Fort. Due to the arrest of major leaders, a young and till then relatively unknown Aruna Asaf Ali presided over the AICC session on August 9 and hoisted the flag. Later, the Congress party was banned. These actions only created sympathy for the cause among the population. Despite lack of direct leadership, large scale protests and demonstrations were held all over the country. Workers remained absent *en masse* and strikes were called. However, not all demonstrations were peaceful. At some places bombs exploded, government buildings were set on fire, electricity was cut, and transport and communication lines were severed.

A minor uprising took place in Ballia Ballia, now the easternmost district of Uttar Pradesh. People overthrew the district administration, broke open the jail, released the arrested Congress leaders, and established their own independent rule. It took weeks before the British could reestablish their writ in the district.

The British swiftly responded with mass detentions. Over 100,000 arrests were made nationwide, mass fines were levied, and demonstrators were subjected to public flogging. Hundreds of resisters and innocent people were killed in police and army shootings. Nevertheless, many national leaders went underground and continued their struggle by broadcasting messages over clandestine radio stations, distributing pamphlets, and establishing parallel governments. The British sense of crisis was strong enough that a battleship was specifically set aside to take Gandhi and the Congress leaders out of India, possibly to South Africa or Yemen, but ultimately did not take that step out of fear of intensifying the revolt.

The entire Congress leadership was cut off from the rest of the world for over three years. Gandhi's wife Kasturbai Gandhi and his personal secretary Mahadev Desai died in months, and Gandhi's own health was failing. Despite this, Gandhi went on a 21-day fast and maintained a superhuman resolve to continuous resistance. Although the British released Gandhi on account of his failing health in 1944, Gandhi kept up the resistance, demanding the complete release of the Congress leadership.

By early 1944, India was mostly peaceful again, while the entire Congress leadership was incarcerated. A sense that the movement had failed depressed many nationalists, while Jinnah and the Muslim League, as well as Congress opponents like the Communists sought to gain political mileage, criticizing Gandhi and the Congress Party.

## India Independence

After the Quit India Movement the freedom struggle got even more intense and passionate. Entire India was united together in the movement for freedom. Everyone contributed what they could in the freedom struggle. The cry of Purna Swaraj or complete independence was raised. After much sacrifices and efforts, India gained its independence on the 15th August, 1947.

## References

Bhattacharya, Bhabani: *Mahatma Gandhi*, Arnold Heinemann Publishers (India), New Delhi, 1977.

Dhanagre, D N: *Agrarian Movements and Gandhian Politics*, Agra University, Agra, 1975.

Gaur, V. P.: *Mahatma Gandhi: a Study of his Message of Non-Violence*, Sterling Publishers, New Delhi, 1977.

Gupta, Manmath Nath: *Gandhi and his Times*, Lipi Prakashan, New Delhi, 1982.

Lewis, Martin Deming: *Gandhi: Maker of Modern India?*, Heath, Boston, 1965.

Moon, Penderel: *Gandhi and Modern India*, Norton, New York, 1969.

Rani, Asha : *Gandhian Non-Violence and India's Freedom Struggle*, Shree Pub. House, Delhi, 1981.

Sankhdher, M. M.: *Gandhi, Gandhism and the Partition of India*, Deep & Deep Publications, New Delhi, 1982.

Singh, Shankar Dayal: *Gandhi's First Step: Champaran Movement*, B.R. Pub. Corp., Delhi, 1994.

# 11

# Tribal Movements and Indian Freedom Struggle

**DR NEERAJ DEVI**
*Visiting Lecturer, S.K. Somaiya Degree College, Vidhyavihar, Mumbai, Maharashtra.*

Tribals' community consciousness is strong. Tribal movements were not only agrarian but also forest-based. Some re-volts were ethnic in nature as these were directed against zamindars, moneylenders and petty government officials who were not only their ex-ploiters but aliens too.

When tribals were unable to pay their loan or the interest thereon, money-lenders and landlords usurped their lands. The tribals thus became tenants on their own land and sometimes even bonded labourers. The po-lice and the revenue officers never helped them. On the contrary, they also used the tribals for personal and government work without any pay-ment.

The courts were not only ignorant of the tribal agrarian system and customs but also were unaware of the plight of the tribals. All these fac-tors of land alienation, usurpation, forced labour, minimum wages, and land grabbing compelled many tribes like Munda, Santhals, Kol, Bhils, Warli, etc., in many regions like Assam, Orissa, Rajasthan, Madhya Pradesh, Andhra Pradesh, Bihar, and Maharashtra to revolt.

## TRIBAL MOVEMENT BEFORE INDEPENDENCE

As soon as the British took over Eastern India, tribal revolts broke out to challenge alien rule. In the early years of colonialisation, no other community in India offered such heroic resistance to British rule or faced such tragic consequences as did the numerous Advise Communities of now Jharkhand, Chhattisgarh, Orissa and Bengal.

The fact needs reiteration and highlighting in history that the tribals of Orissa were the first ones in India to wage war against

British Colonialism. It should also be noted that contrary to the historians this began as early as 1768 and not in 1820 as opined by them. It was in 1768 that under the feudal king Krushna Bhanja of Ghumsar, the Kondha fought a pitched battle against the British and many lost their lives.

The same year Raja Narayan Deb of Parlakhemundi fought another battle at Jalwara where 30 tribals died. Meanwhile, the British took over Ganjam as part of Madras Presidency and appointed Edward Court as its President. But repeated battles IS the British by the tribals under the leadership of Maharandpata Mahadevi Parala Bikaram Bhanja of and late Srikar Bhanja of Ghumsar led the British to abandon the idea of reigning the area and declare it as 'deserted'.

In 1772 the Paharia revolt broke out which was followed by a five year uprising led by Tilka Manjhi who was hanged in Bhagalpur in 1785. In the next two decades, revolt took place in Singbhum, Gumla, Birbhum, Bankura Monbhoom and Palama, followed by the great Koi Rising of 1832 and Khewar and Bhum.j revolts (1832-34).

The various uprising of the "Kondh meli" and the revolt of the revolt for against their feudal ruler in 1837, the noteworthy militant struggle of the Khonds for a decade from 1846-56 under the leadership of Chakara Biso, and the resistance to British exploitation by the Santhals of Orissa under the Murmu Brothers among many others will go down as momentous events in the history of Orissa's struggle against the British.

The rebellion of 1855-1857 was a great event in history of Santhal. In 1855 the Santhals wage war against the permanent settlement of Lord Cornwallis. On 30th June, 1855 a massive rally of Santhal, over ten thousand, protested against their exploitation and oppression. The 'rally, led by Sidho and Kano, took an oath to end the oppressive rule of the British, Zamindars and money-lenders and, it deeded to set up an independent Santhali Raj.

The money-lenders and Zamindars had flocked into Santhal areas. The crops of the Santhal were forcibly seized, the interests chafed on loans varied from fifty to five hundred per cent. The Santhal uprising (1855-1857) was an attempt to recover the tribal land which was steadily lost to the outsiders and to wipe out the non-tribals from their territory. It is estimated that fifteen to twenty five thousand Santhals were killed in this uprising.

As stated earlier, in 1855 the Santhals waged war against the permanent settlement of Cornwallis and a year later, numerous Advice leaders play a key role in the 1857 war of independence. But the defeat of 1858 only intensified British exploitation of national wealth and resources.

A forest regulation Act passed in 1865 empowered the British Government to declare any land covered with trees or brushwood as Government forest and to make rules to manage it under terms of its own choosing.

The Act made no provision regarding the rights of tribal users, a more comprehensive Indian Forest Act was passed in 1878, which imposed severe restrictions upon Advice rights over forest land and produce in the protected and reserve forests. The Act radically changed the nature of the traditional common property of the Advice communities and made it State property.

Advices uprising in the Jharkhand belt were quelled by the British through massive deployment of troops across the region. There was uprising and the B.rsa Munda movement was the most important of the late -18th century struggles against British rules and their local agents. The long struggles led by Birsa Munda were directed at British policies that allowed the Zamindars and money-lenders to harshly exploit the Advises. As he organised a force to fight oppressive landlords, Christian missionaries and British officials, he was imprisoned. He was released only after two years.

Out of jail, Birsa asked his people to ready their arms to fight injustice He trained his army and became the politician leading his people to their goal of self-rule He was however arrested again and died in jail. Yet the seeds of unrest were sown among his people and they continued to fight against injustice. The Jharkhand movement had its root in this movement.

In 1914 Oraon started what is called Tana Bhagat movement. Tana Bhagat movement is one kind of Bhagat movement which emerged among the Oraon of Chotanagpur, Bihar. The Tana Bhagat movement is essentially religious in nature. Although Birsa Munda movement was started basically as a socio-religious movements latter on his movement assumed quasi-political and militaristic shape.

Among the Oraon the term Bhagat has been applied to a distinct section of tribe which subscribes to the cult of Bhakti. The Bhagat movement is characterized by a large scale incorporation of Hindu practices into its ideology. However the tribal' leaders of both the movements were essentially fighting the foreign exploiters like the landlords and contractors.

All these prepared the ground for the Sepoy Mutiny's impact on Orissa in 1857.The Kolhas, Gonds, Santhals, Birjhals and Khonds joined hands with Surendra Sai in this first revolt for Independence.

Latter the Bhajan meli engaged the British in skirmishes, ambushes, and battles for more than 2 decades from 1868-1891 an experience the British never cherished. The struggle of the Mundas against these imperialists is another significant landmark. Under the leadership of "Birsa Munda" the Munda tribals fought the British in 1900. On Jan 9th 1900, the British retaliated killing masses of people.

But that did not deter them and history repeated itself. This time the Munda's revolted against the Queen of Gangpur who was exploiting the people under the patronage of the British. Under the leadership of Nirmala Munda they fought the British m 1939 who in retaliation mercilessly shot down innocent lives at "AmekoSimako" near Raiboga, creating another black spot in the history of British in India The final of tribal struggle against British in pre-independent Orissa is that of the Koraput tribals under the leadership of Lakman Naik. The struggle was short and Lakman's life ended with martydom. He was hanged on March 29 1943 at the Berhampur jail.

In the hill tribal tracts of Andhra Pradesh a revolt broke out in August 1922 led by Allun Ramachandra Raju, (better known as Sitaram Raju), the Advisees of Andhra hills succeeded in drawing the British into a full-scale guerrilla war. Unable to cope the British-brought in the Malabar Special Force to crush it and only prevailed when Alluri Raju died.

As the freedom movement widened, it drew Advisees into all aspects of the struggle. Many landless and deeply oppressed Advisees joined in with upper-caste freedom fighters expecting that the defect of the British would usher in a new democratic era.

## HUL : FREEDOM STRUGGLE

Hul is a Santali term. It means a movement for liberation. Santals in Santal Paraganas (presently in the State of Jharkhand) belongs to Santali tribe. Two Murmu brothers, Sido and Kanhu.

Santal Hul was one of the fiercest battles in the history of Indian freedom struggles causing greatest number of loss of lives in any battles during that time. The number of causalities of Santal Hul was 20,000 according to Hunter who wrote it in annals of Rural Bengal. The Santal Hul of 1855-57 was master minded by four brothers Sidhu, Kahnu, Chand and Bhairav; a heroic episode in India's prolonged struggle for freedom. It was, in all probability, the fiercest liberation movement in India next to Great Sepoy Mutiny in 1857.

With the capture of political power of India by the East India Company, the natural habitats of the Adivasi (indigenous) people including the Santals began to shatter by the intruders like moneylenders. Traders and revenue farmers, who descended upon them in large numbers under the patronage of the Company.

Believe it or not, the rate of interest on loan to the poor and illiterate Santals varied from 50% to 500%. These intruders were, needless to mention the crucial links in the chain of ruthless exploitation under colonial rule. They were the instruments through which the indigenous groups and tribes were brought within the influence and control of the colonial economy.

Discontent had been simmering in the Santal Paraganas( presently in Jharkhand ) from the early decades of the nineteenth century owing to most naked exploitation of the indigenous Santals by both the British authorities and their collaborators, native immigrants.

Sido Murmu and Kanhu Murmu, hailing from the village Bhognadih in Sahibganj district, had long been brooding over the injustices perpetrated by the oppressors like hundreds and hundreds of their tribe's men. The situation finally reached a flash point and, not surprisingly, a small episode that took place in July 1855 triggered one of the fiercest uprisings that the British administration ever faced in India.

The emergence of Sido and Kanhu, youthful, dynamic and charismatic, provided a rallying point for the Santals to revolt against the oppressors.On 30th June 1855, a large number of Santals assembled in a field in Bhagnadihi village of Santal Paragana, They declared themselves as free and took oath under the leadership of Sido Murmu and Kanhu Murmu to fight unto the last against the British rulers as well as their agents.

Militant mood of the Santals frightened the authority. A Police agent confronted them on the 7th July and tried to place the Murmu brothers under arrest. The angry crowd reacted violently and killed the Police agent and his companions. The event sparked off a series of confrontations with the Company's Army and subsequently reached the scale of a full-fledged war.

At the outset, Santal rebels, led by Sido and Kanhu, made tremendous gains and captured control over a large tract of the country extending from Rajmahal hills in Bhagalpur district to Sainthia in Birbhum district. For the time being, British rule in this vast area became completely paralyzed. Many moneylenders and native agents of the Company were killed. Local British administrators took shelter in the Pakur Fort to save their life. However, they rebel could not hold on to their gains due to the superior fire power of the East India Company came down heavily on them.

The courage, chivalry and sacrifice of the Santals were countered by the rulers with veritable butchery. Out of 50,000 Santal rebels, 15,000 20,000 were killed by the British Indian Army. The Company was finally able to suppress the rebellion in 1856, though some outbreaks continued till 1857.

The Santals showed great bravery and incredible courage in the struggle against the military. As long as their national drums continued beating, the whole party would stand and allow themselves to be shot down. There was no sign of yielding. Once forty Santals refused to surrender and took shelter inside a mud house. The troops surrounded the mud house and fired at them but Santals replied with their arrows. Then Soldiers made big hole through muddy wall, and the Captain ordered them surrender but they again shot a volley of arrows through the hole and Captain again asked them to surrender but they continued shooting arrows. Some of the soldiers were wounded. At last when the discharge of arrows from the door slackened, the Captain went inside the room with soldiers. He found only one old man grievously wounded, standing erect among the dead bodies. The soldier asked him to throw away arms, but instead he rushed on him and killed him with his battle axe.

It is believed that Sido was captured by the British forces through treachery and Kanhu through an encounter at Uparbanda. And was subsequently killed in captivity. The Santal Hul, however, did not come to an end in vain. It had a long-lasting impact. Santal Parganas Tenancy Act was the outcome of this struggle, which dished out some sort of protection to the indigenous people from the ruthless colonial exploitation. The understanding the mistake, tired to appease the Santals by removing the genuine grievances. Santal territory was born. The regular police was abolished and the duty of keeping peace and order and arresting criminals was vested in the hands of parganait and village headman.

## SANTHAL UPRISING

A major tribal resistance movement broke out just before the

Revolt of 1857 in the Santhal area of Chollangpur in the present state of Jharkhand which was known as the Santhal Uprising. A major cause of their protest was the exploitation of the money lenders and intermediaries of the Zamindars. Confiscation of their properties as well as their lands compelled the Santhals to raise their voice against the British rule. Moreover, forced labour and sexual exploitation of tribal women at the worksites was also a greater concern of the Santhals. Under the leadership of Sidho and Kanhu, they stood up and defied their exploiters. On June 30, 1855 ten thousand Santhals assembled at Bhaghadihi where they announced their war against then British. The latter was compelled to deploy the regular columns of the army to suppress them. The defeat of the British army under Major Burrough by the Santhals at the initial stage was a significant incident of the rebellion. However, the Santhals were finally suppressed by the British army by the end of 1856. To prevent the Santhals from revolting in future, a separate district of Santhal Paragana was carved out by the Company.

## MUNDA UPRISING

The Munda uprising of 1899-1900 led by Birsa Munda also known as Birsite was the greatest Tribal uprising of the 19th century. This uprising is often referred to as Ulgulum (the great tumult) in the Tribal language. Birsa Munda was a master tactician who raised a Munda Militia in which even Munda women joined. He declared the end of the Company's (British) rule from the Munda areas and announced the establishment of the Mundagiri i.e. the Munda Government. The Munda uprising was the only one in which women rebels fought along side with their men giving a very strong resistance to the British. To suppress the rebellion, the British had to deploy the regular columns of the army. During the course of this uprising the Mundas attacked the symbols of British authority. However, the rebellious Mundas inspite of their indomitable courage were no match for the British. With the arrest of Birsa Munda and his subsequent death in prison, the Munda uprising collapsed. But it remained a great landmark in the history of Tribal movements.

## RAMPA REBELLION

Rampa is a tribal region in the Godavari district of Andhra Pradesh that witnessed a tribal uprising in the 19th century. The tribals of Rampa revolted against the British due to the excessive exploitation by the latter. The British used them as unpaid labourers for the construction of forest roads which hurt the sentiments of the Rampa tribals. Their cause was supported by Alluri Sitaram Raju, who was the only non-tribal leader to lead a tribal uprising. He subscribed to the Gandhian ideology but believed that Gandhian methods were unsuited to the cause of the tribals.

Consequently, Raju raised a Rampa Militia and waged veritable guerilla warfare against the British. The latter used great man power and spent a huge amount i.e. roughly Rupees15 lakhs to suppress this uprising which ended with the arrest and killing of Sitaram Raju in May 1924. But his supreme sacrifice aroused a Gandhian nationalist, who came forward to espouse the cause of the tribals. He was Thakkar Bapa, who founded the first All India Tribal Welfare Organisation named All India Adim Jati Sangha, the earliest and the most famous tribal organisation that voiced the tribals cause. Thus, it was with the Rampa uprising that the Tribal movement came to be integrated with the larger national movement. The cause of the exploited tribals was supported by the Gandhian nationalists who conceived the idea of tribal welfare.

## TANA BHAGAT MOVEMENT

The tana Bhagat movement emerged among the Mundas and Oraons of Chottanagpur region of Jharkhand in 1920 under the leadership of tribal mendicants known as Bhagat. It is after them that the movement is known as Tana Bhagat. There were numerous Tana Bhagat movements which began initially as Sanskritization movements to revive the original religion of the Oraons. After the launching of the Non- cooperation movement, the Gandhian nationalists took interest in starting constructive work among the tribals which led to the linking of these movements with the local grievances and ultimately to the national movement.

Initially these movements grew up with the appeal of Tana Bhagat asking their followers to give up meat and liquor. In the second stage the movement was transformed into a powerful movement for internal reforms and over throw of the British. In 1920 the Tana Bhagats came under the fever of nationalism when they took part in the freedom struggle by picketing against liquor shops, holding demonstrations, staging Satyagrahas etc. It was during this phase that the nationalist symbols like honouring the poster of Bharatmata bearing the Gandhian cap, honouring the Congress flag etc, became matters of religions faith for the followers of the Tana Bhagat movement. It was a unique movement where tribals participated directly to the flow of national movement and the anti-British sentiments were expressed by the tribal through various methods and symbols.

## ADIVASIS AND THE FREEDOM MOVEMENT

As soon as the British took over Eastern India, tribal revolts broke out to challenge the alien rule. In the early years of colonization, no other community in India offered such heroic resistance to British rule or faced such tragic consequences as did the numerous Adivasi communities of now Jharkhand, Chhatisgarh, Orissa and Bengal. In 1772, the Paharia revolt broke out which was followed by a five year uprising led by Tilka Manjhi who was hanged in Bhagalpur in 1785. The Tamar and Munda revolts followed. In the next two decades, revolts took place in Singhbhum, Gumla, Birbhum, Bankura, Manbhoom and Palamau, followed by the great Kol Risings of 1832 and the Khewar and Bhumij revolts (1832-34). In 1855, the Santhals waged war against the permanent settlement of Lord Cornwallis, and a year later, numerous adivasi leaders played key roles in the 1857 war of independence.

But the defeat of 1858 only intensified British exploitation of national wealth and resources. A forest regulation passed in 1865 empowered the British government to declare any land covered with trees or brushwood as government forest and to make rules to manage it under terms of it's own choosing. The act made no provision regarding the rights of the Adivasi users. A more comprehensive Indian Forest Act was passed in 1878, which imposed severe restrictions upon Adivasi rights over forest land and produce in the protected and reserved forests. The act radically changed the nature of the traditional common property of the Adivasi communities and made it state property.

As punishment for Adivasi resistance to British rule, "The Criminal Tribes Act" was passed by the British Government in 1871 arbitrarily stigmatizing groups such as the Adivasis (who were perceived as most hostile to British interests) as congenital criminals.

Adivasi uprisings in the Jharkhand belt were quelled by the British through massive deployment of troops across the region. The Kherwar uprising and the Birsa Munda movement were the most important of the late-18th century struggles against British rule and their local agents. The long struggle led by Birsa Munda was directed at British policies that allowed the zamindars (landowners) and moneylenders to harshly exploit the Adivasis. In 1914 Jatra Oraon started what is called the Tana Movement (which drew the participation of over 25,500 Adivasis). The Tana movement joined the nation-wide Satyagrah Movement in 1920 and stopped the payment of land-taxes to the colonial Government.

During British rule, several revolts also took place in Orissa which naturally drew participation from the Adivasis. The significant ones included the Paik Rebellion of 1817, the Ghumsar uprisings of 1836-1856, and the Sambhalpur revolt of 1857-1864.

In the hill tribal tracts of Andhra Pradesh a revolt broke out in August 1922. Led by Alluri Ramachandra Raju (better known as Sitarama Raju), the Adivasis of the Andhra hills succeeded in drawing the British into a full-scale guerrilla war. Unable to cope, the British brought in the Malabar Special Force to crush it and only prevailed when Alluri Raju died.

As the freedom movement widened, it drew Adivasis into all aspects of the struggle. Many landless and deeply oppressed Adivasis joined in with upper-caste freedom fighters expecting that the defeat of the British would usher in a new democratic era.

Unfortunately, even fifty years after independence, Dalits and Adivasis have benefited least from the advent of freedom. Although independence has brought widespread gains for the vast majority of the Indian population, Dalits and Adivasis have often been left out, and new problems have arisen for the nation's Adivasi populations. With the tripling of the population since 1947, pressures on land resources, especially demands on forested tracks, mines and water resources have played havoc on the lives of the Adivasis. A disproportionate number of Adivasis have been displaced from their traditional lands while many have seen access to traditional resources undercut by forest mafias and corrupt officials who have signed irregular commercial leases that conflict with rights granted to the Adivasis by the Indian constitution.

It remains to be seen if the the grant of statehood for Jharkhand and Chhatisgarh ameliorates the conditions for India's Adivasis. However, it is imperative that all Adivasi districts receive special attention from the Central government in terms of investment in schools, research institutes, participatory forest management and preservation schemes, non-polluting industries, and opportunities for the Adivasi communities to document and preserve their rich heritage. Adivasis must have special access to educational, cultural and economic opportunities so as to reverse the effects of colonization and earlier injustices experienced by the Adivasi communities.

At the same time, the country can learn much from the beauty of Adivasi social practices, their culture of sharing and respect for all - their deep humility and love of nature - and most of all - their deep devotion to social equality and civic harmony.

## PEASANT AND TRIBAL MOVEMENTS IN ASSAM

After the Revolt of 1857 the British Government of India tried in all possible ways to increase its revenue income. In Assam, agriculture being the main source of revenue, the burden of tax obviously fell on the peasants. Official records show that during the post-1857 period the British government increased the revenue demand by 3 to 4 times the original amount. The harmful effects of the excessive demand increased further due to the rigid manner of its collection. Moreover, the British government, in order to increase its income, imposed income-tax on the people of Assam in 1861. Introduction of various duties viz., stamp duty excise duty, tax for cutting timber etc. practically impoverished the peasantry beyond description. All this caused serious resentment among the general people, particularly the peasantry of Assam which led them to rise against the British government. As for the tribals, their discontent varied from region to region, but this constituted one of the main causes of discontent among the people in the plains. Again, in the hill region of Jaintia the people very much resented the imposition of house-tax, stamp duty, etc. by the British. But most of the hill tribes revolted due to political causes, namely, loss of their freedom. We can now begin a brief discussion by taking up some important peasant and tribal movements which broke out in Assam during British rule.

### Phulguri Uprising

The Phulguri Uprising which is also known as 'Phulguri Dhawa' in Assamese was the first agrarian revolt in Assam after 1857. Phulguri is a place in present Nagaon district. Most of the people of this area belong to Lalung and Kachari tribes. As the people of Phulguri were mostly opium-eaters, the consumption of opium was higher there compared to other places. High price of opium fixed by the British government caused much resentment among the people of Phulguri. The ban imposed by the British government on private cultivation of opium also caused much dissatisfaction among the people of Phulguri. Besides, a rumour spread that the British government would soon impose duties on all their sources of income such as cultivation of betel leaf (pan) and cultivation of fruits in the garden.

Due to the above mentioned causes an uprising broke out which initially took the form of protest through Raij Mels. One day on 17 October, 1861 when people from district villages assembled in a mel the British police forcibly tried to disperse the villagemen. The incident enraged the native people so much that they jumped upon the police party who tried to disperse them. In this encounter many policemen were injured and Mr. Singer, the Assistant Commissioner of police of Nagaon district was beaten to death. However, an additional police force captured the rebels and their leaders were severally punished either with the death sentence or life imprisonment.

Though the Phulguri uprising was a failure its significance cannot be underrated. It was the first popular rebellion of the peasantry of Assam against the British colonial rule. For the first time the middle class intelligentsia came out in support of the Phulguri rebels. Not only that, it also served an inspiration to other villagemen and tribals. This is evident from the fact that within the next few years the peasants of the districts of Darrang and Kamrup broke out in rebellion against the exploitation of the British.

## Rangia and Lachima Revolt

The people of Rangia, in the district of Kamrup following the foot steps of the Phulguri peasants very soon lodged their protests, organizing Raij Mels. The cause of their protest was a hundred percent increase in the land revenue. The Rangia revolt began on 24th December 1893 when the people of Rangia ransacked the Rangia market. Moreover, people staged a demonstration on 10th January, 1894 in which they raised the slogan of not paying the increased revenue. On the same day McCabe, the Deputy Commissioner of Kamrup, imposed a ban on holding any Mel All the important leaders of the revolt were soon arrested by the police and the revolt lost its edge.

The Lachima Revolt was also held due to the same reasons as that of Rangia. The only difference was that the rebels of Lachima took recourse to violence. They assaulted the revenue collectors who were the agents of the British government. The incident took place in Kalpa, near Lachima, in the district of Kamrup on 21st January 1894. The revenue collectors were so severely beaten by the villagers that one of them died. The infuriated British police immediately arrested as many as seventy- five villagers. But the agitated villagers soon freed the arrested persons from the custody of the police. This led to a major police crackdown on the village. Unable to sustain the torture the rebels ultimately had to give in and the revolt came to an end.

## Patharughat Uprising

Like Phulguri Dhawa the rebellion of Patharughat is also commonly known among Assamese as Patharughatar Ran i.e. the battle of Patharughat. Patharughat is a place in the Darrang district where a revolt broke out in 1894.

Here also the grievances of the people were against the enhancement of the rates of revenue. Raij-Mels were held in which not only a protest was lodged against the increased in the rates of land-revenue but a warning was also issued to the villagers to the effect that no one should pay the increased revenue to the government. On 28th January, 1894 when a police party went to the village to attach the property of a peasant cultivator, who was a defaulter, they were surrounded by a mob.

Soon after the incident the rebels of Patharughat marched towards the police camp leading the police to open fire.Many of the villagers died and were injured. It led to the complete suppression of the rebels of Patharughat by the British.

## Revolt in Jaintia

The tribal people of Jaintia burst out in rebellion when the British government imposed house tax and stamp duty. In fact, the tribal people were not accustomed to any such tax in the past. Therefore, they felt they lost their freedom to the British. So they raised their voice through a rebellion which lasted from 1860 to 1863. It was not before 1863 that the British government could restore law order suppressing the hill people.

Before the outbreak of this revolt the Khasi tribes in present Meghalaya also revolted against the British. The Khasi leader U. Teerut Singh, the Raja of Nongkhalo led this rebellion against the British. The background of the revolt was the construction of a road across the Khasi hills joining the two valleys of the Brahmaputra and Surma. Though Teerut Singh in the beginning approved the idea of the road, suddenly he became suspicious of British intensions. The Khasis got the impression that after the completion of the road the British would levy tax from them. So, under leadership of Teerut

Singh they attacked the British officials posted there and killed them. The conflict between the Khasis and British continued for almost four years and ended with the surrender of Teerut Singh in 1834.

## The Nagas, Garos and Lushais

The Tribal people of Naga, Garo and Lushai hills were discontented upon the British not because of imposition of any tax but for the curtailment of certain rights being enjoyed by them for long time past. In fact these turbulent hill tribes were freedom loving people and could not tolerate any interference in their socio-economic life. But their frequent raids in the neighbouring areas which were under British possession made the government worry. To get rid of their attacks and raids the British government became offensive towards them and in 1866 captured the hill tract of the Angami Nagas. The other Naga tribes also surrendered in course of time. In 1869 the Garo hills region was captured. Finally in 1898 the Lushai hills came under British rule.

## References

Bailey F.G. : *Tribe, Caste and Nation, Bombay*: Oxford University Press, 1960.

Bhasin M. K. : *Genetics of Castes and Tribes of India*, Kamla-Raj Enterprises, Delhi, 2001.

Crooke W. : *Natives of Northern India*, London : Archibald Constable and Co., Ltd., 1907.

Dutta N.C. : *Politics of Identity and Nation Building in North-East India*, New Delhi: South Asian Press, 1997.

Karma Oraon : *Dimension of Religion, Magic and Festivals of Indian Tribe : The Munda*, Kanishka, 2002.

Nandan Anshu : *Combs : Tribes in India*, Anthropological Survey of India, Delhi, 2002.

Sengupta Sarthak : *Tribes of the Eastern Himalayas*, Mittal, Delhi, 2001.

12

# The Rise and Growth of Communalism in India

**DR POONAM**
*Assistant Professor, Department of History,*
*B.D.K. (P.G.) College, Agra , Uttar Pradesh*

## COMMUNALISM IN INDIA

'The ideology of communalism in India was, and still is, that the different communities in India cannot co-exist to their mutual benefit, that the minorities will become victims of Hindu subjugation and that the historically created situation nor culture will allow cooperation.

Communalism took deep roots in Indian polity during the later phase of the national movement and this was encouraged by the colonial rulers. This process was a continuation of the weakness and inadequacy of secularism as conceived and practised during the anticolonial struggle.

Impact in all the theories has been the assumption that the growth of Hindu-Muslim tension was not the natural and inevitable outcome of changes taking place in the Indian society. Partition was the culmination of the conflict which could and should have been avoided. Further this line of reasoning states that nation building essentially mens obliteration of communal moulds and creation of a common identity which decries the existence of differentiated groups based on religion, caste or language. Communal forces are therefore viewed as division and a sign of political underdevelopment. *Communalism arises when one or two characteristics of an ethnic identity e.g. religious beliefs are taken and emotionally surcharged. Communal movements are often brief and exist in a dyad, comprising an opposing force or ideology which has to be countered. Unlike imdamentalism,* communalism can only exist dyadically.

Hindu-Muslims riots reflected the religious fears and socioeconomic aspirations of the Hindus and Muslims. Sometimes these riots occur for very minor reasons such as quarrels between Muslim and Hindu shopkeepers (Ghosh, 1981: 93-94). The important point is that these are not isolated acts but often deliberate mechanizations of various socio-religious organisations. Recurrent collisions were engineered on festivals by stopping them and various religious occasions by interfering in their process. This was done to inflame communal passions and bitterness. According to Ghosh (1981) the acme of communal rioting was reached in August 1946 in Calcutta when the Muslim League observed a 'Direct Action Day'. Bombay did the same in the following month. Thus Independence was erected on the corpses of many thousands of people. With Mahatma Gandhi's assassination the riots abated awhile, and this situation was basically sustained by Nehru. Again the passing away of Nehru in 1964 and the deteriorating socioeconomic circumstances led to the resurrection of communal violence.

## RECENT COMMUNAL RIOTS

Thus during the late 60s and 1970s there was large scale communal rioting in Ahmedabad, Baroda, Ranohi, Jamshedpur etc. Communal configurations in towns such as Ranchi cast a shadow over predictions and beliefs in the future of workers unity. Again in Bhiwandi where there was a carnage in 1969, it was a shock for the leftists. The grassroots movement among the handloom workers fostered by committed communists was unable to stem the on rush of communal violence. In 1969 itself a communal riot occurred in Ahmedabad. The inflammatory factors were insults to holy scriptures and sacred cows. It was suspected however that these riots were politically motivated.

These riots indicated clearly that there were various political factors behind the surface level factors of religion based tensions and confrontations. In the mid seventies the communal riots abated a bit both due to the Emergency and the Janata Regime. The first exercised iron control and discipline the second aroused the hopes of both Hindus and Muslims. The first ix years of the eighties once more created an upward incline in the riot-graph. Patel (1990) keels that Communal violence is backed by religious arguments and backing. He feels that those resorting to it are neither true Hindus or true Muslims. Religion does not preach enmity. However the causes which are often given for communal violence are hurt religious sentiments. The causes are flimsy such as playing music before a mosque insulting the Prophet or the Holy Quran. This is sufficient to provoke violence along some ' of the Muslims. So also disturbing by Muslims of a religious yam is enough to rouse Hindu ire.

## REASONS FOR COMMUNAL RIOTS

In the context of our section of recent-communal riots we turn now to some further reasons for the same. As Ghosh (1981) points out the several arguments have been forwarded for the existence and continuation of communal riots. These are: riots ark part of progress in an under developed country. The class struggle is converted into a communal struggle weakening the solidarity of the proletariat class. Further the middle and backward classes have acquired greater political and economic strength and influence and these often assert themselves. Economic conflicts lead to riots as in Bihar Sharif and Bhiwandi.

Electoral politics determine the objectives and direction of communal violence e.g. Delhi 1986.

These explanations cannot be binding-they cannot be held to the necessary and sufficient. Often economic reasons emerge after (not before) the rioting has begun. Again in a developing society economic factors where competitive or one lagging behind the other can lead to a riot. The same applies to educationist political causes. The idea of behind-the-scene political manipulation may not be valid.

### Economic and Social Dimensions

Regarding gaining economic benefits after the eruption of communal riots we find that in Godhra, Hindu Sindhi refugees from Pakistan gave competition to Hindu merchants. But riots have frequently emerged between Sindhis and Muslims. Again in Punjab while Ramgarhia and other Sikhs have gone beyond the Hindu Khatris in commerce there have been no riots because of this.

Lastlym the Punjab tragedy, the terrorist acts while antagonising the Hindus, are not considered to be the acts of the Sikh community as a whole. Hindu-Muslim riots in recent times have been confined to medium sized towns and cities. These include areas like Meerut, Aligarh, Moradabad, Pune etc.

### Inter-Community Dynamics

Medium sized towns/cities are being divided on communal lines. We find that the workers don't have class consciousness. The educated middle class professional act as a bridge between Hindus and Muslims. During preparation there were Muslim doctors, lawyers etc. who also attracted Hindu clients-Similarly Hindu professionals were patronized by Muslim clients-Thus

i) common bonds developed

ii) there were common networks and patronization.

Again the existence of Muslim professionals administrators etc. created a positive image for the Muslims. Post partition mass migrations saw these advantages vanishing. Many trade and economic activities are run by Hindus and there were no problems so long as the Muslims were not competitive. There was an interdependence between Hindu employers and Muslim artisans. However, in recent time economic Competitiveness come from Muslims and has turned into a religious threat to Hindus. Again channelling of Arab money into mosque renovation and lavish festival celebrations has resulted in an admixture of economics and religion which creates inter community tensions and eruptions of violence.

## GROWTH OF COMMUNALISM IN INDIA

During the revolt of 1857, which is described as the first war for independence, Hindus and Muslims fought side by side united in their purpose of defeating a common enemy. The British noticed this unity and realized that their survival rested on being able to keep the people divided, for they had managed to establish their rule because politically India had been a divided country at the time of their entry. This realization led to the famous British 'Divide and Rule' policy.

Religion was supposed to be one of the best factors to divide the people. It is used as an influential mechanism to attain economic, political and other social activities. And British used religion as their weapon to divide the strength which India had as a whole.

Till 1870 the British oppressed the Muslims greatly for they held them responsible for the revolt. After 1870 the British changed colours and instead started favouring the Muslim community. The rise of nationalism had threatened the British power in India and their efforts obviously were directed to suppress it. Now an important feature of the national movement was that it took longer to spread amongst the Muslim community. As a result the early nationalist's movement was made up mainly of people from the Hindu, Parsi and Christian communities. The British noticed the absence of the Muslims in this movement, and quickly began working on ensuring that they did not join the movement. The British began implementing policies too that promoted the activities of communal forces, and divided the national struggle.

When the British opened up the administration of the country most positions were taken up the Hindus since the education culture had not spread to the Muslim Community making them feel left out and demand a special reservation.

Sir Sayyed Ahmed Khan, an earlier nationalist drifted towards Communalism.

Communalism was also fostered through the writing of the Indian History. Socio-religious reform movements like Arya Samaj, Sanatan Dharam movements, Aligarh movement, Wahabi movement and some other fringe movements contributed towards communalism.

## Partition of Bengal

The Partition of Bengal in 1905 was made on October 16 by then Viceroy of India, Lord Curzon. Partition was promoted on the grounds that Bengal was a very large state with a large population causing the eastern region to under-governed. However, the actual motives behind the partition were different. The position of the Bengali Hindus would be weakened, since Muslims would now dominate in the East which led to Hindu opposition to the partition while the Muslims highly favoured it. This partition was one more part of 'Divide and Rule' policy.

As the partition was in favour of Muslims they welcomed it, whereas the Hindu's were not in favour of it. Due to this Hindu community launched a Swadeshi Movement by boycotting the British goods. Seeing this scenario British decided to support the Hindus, this act disturbed the Muslims. It was medium to tell the Muslims to go to their homeland.

## Formation of Muslim League

The growing communalism led to the Muslims forming a new political party called the Muslim League in 1906. Initially it was only confined to the educated class of Muslims. At around the same time the Indian National Congress began garnering mass support from its members and also consisted of young Muslims.

Mohammed Ali Jinnah one of the major forces behind the creation of Pakistan was in fact a member of the Indian National Congress till 1920.

## Khilafat Movement

Khilafat Movement (1919-1924) was a significant Islamic movement in India during the British rule. The sultan of turkey also known as the caliph i.e. khalifa or successor of Prophet Muhammad was considered as the religious leader of the Muslims all over the world. This was first the religious political movement in India involving common Muslims. However, initially this movement was first targeted to the educated and elite Muslims only. The goals of the Khilafat Movement were:

The Khilafat Movement received the support of Mahatma Gandhi and Nehru, who related his Non Cooperation Movement with it. As major Congress leaders had joined hands with this movement the other political parties came together to support the injustice faced by the Muslims. Following were some steps taken by the movement:

- No involvement in the Victory celebrations
- Boycotting of British commodities
- Non-cooperation Movement with the Government.

The main leaders of the Khilafat Movement were Maulana Muhammad Ali and Shaukat Ali, famously known as the Ali brothers. They were among the leaders who used to protest from jail and their voices used to be heard through magazines and newspaper which awakened the Muslim community. The hub of this movement was Bombay, where they had their first conference wherein discussing the issues of the Movement.

## JINNAH, MUSLIM LEAGUE AND HINDU MAHASABHA

The mass popularity that the Indian National Congress was enjoying led to The Muslim League feeling increasingly sidelined. As a result the Muslim League won only 109 from 492 reserved Muslim seats and only 4.8 percent of the overall Muslim votes showing thereby the lack of famous assistance for the Muslim League even amongst the Muslim inhabitants. In the elections of 1937 Muslims had a good response whereas its counterpart Hindus did not have encouraging response. For example, Hindu Mahasabha had acquired only 12 seats from 175 in Punjab. This resulted in union of the parties in order to ensure survival.

This got worse in 1938 when the congress prohibited communalists from functioning within the Congress organization. Thus the congress was criticized for preaching that Hindus were the only Nation living in India. This led to the Hindu fundamentalist's version of 'two nation theory'.

The 'two nation theory' included Hindu Maha Sabha wherein it states that the country belongs to only Hindus and the Muslims should find their own home or should remain obedient to Hindus. And other 'the Muslim League' wherein it states that Pakistan is the only option to protect the interest of Muslims as it has the maximum population of Muslims.

After the outbreak of World War - II, Viceroy Linlithgow constantly promoted the Muslim League and the Pakistan power was used to contradict the Congress command that the British should promise to liberate India after the war and as evidence of honesty, shift actual power of Government to Indians immediately. Before promising or coming to a concrete solution the British wanted an agreement between the Muslims League and the Congress organization which stated that no political settlement should be made which was offensive to the Muslims League. This agreement would give Jinnah a type of a 'veto' power which he would use in future.

Jinnah the main leader of Muslim League had a different outlook for religion and its practices. One of the major drawbacks of Jinnah was he only supported the elite Muslims whereas showing no anxiety to the low and backward Muslims. The Muslim League wanted to give all the privileges to the elite Muslims only, which was for the Muslims Landlords and Nawabs.

As the Muslims were not united during the pre partition days, the aim of the Muslim League was to provoke religious passions to dedicated path. As the low caste Muslims were not given importance in the Muslim League they decided their own pathway where they from sections like North West province and South where they supported Indian National Congress. Seeing this scenario the Muslim League used violent language. Since 1870, elite Hindus like zamindars, money lenders and other leaders started an organization to provoke anti Muslims and simultaneously opposing India National Congress. Their sole purpose was to remove the Muslims from the country. For them Hindus were first Hindus and then Indians. This thought formed an organization known as Hindu Mahasabha and later was called Rashtriya Swayamsevak Sangh (RSS).

Hindus Mahasabha created a false impression of patriotism by using slogans like 'Bharat Mata' i.e. Mother India and so on, which created an impression that they wanted a country without Muslims. As according to them Hindus and Muslims were a separate Nation. By understanding the roots of communalism we must recognize that it is neither signifies religion nor patriotism as one but it signifies wellbeing. Then the religious communities are being divided into various sections like elite class low class and language it should be realized that no religious community is uniform as communalists. These particular fault lies in both Hindu and Muslims community. The Muslim League and Hindu Mahasabha deliberately did not allow the low caste to participate which made linguistic culture lines which divided their religion on the basis on caste.

As a result there were three main aspects which lead to the partition of India which are:

- British 'Divide and Rule' policy
- Muslim Communalism i.e. the Muslim League representing elite Muslim leaders, zamindars and nawabs
- Hindu Communalism i.e. Hindu Mahasabha or RSS representing Hindu leaders, Brahmins, money lenders
- Post-independencePost-independence

Most communal riots prior to 1947 were rooted in the policy of British colonial rulers. But after the partition, a section of the Indian elite of both sections are also blamed for the problem. Communal problems post independence has been caused many factors, some of which are:

The class division of society and the backwardness of our economy resulted in unequal and unbalanced economy.

It is the upper classes of the less developed communities that have enjoyed the fruits of limited growth and have hence enjoyed the political power.

In order to draw support from their own communities, these leaders have always encouraged communal feelings to strengthen their political support.

If we were to take a surface view of bare facts of any communal riot in India, it would appear that the riot was caused by an incident so insignificant that we would stand amazed at how such a trifling matter could cause so much Larson, loot and murder. It however does not require much thinking to know that this incident was not the real cause of the riot. The basic cause for all communal disturbances is the communal atmosphere pervading the country and the communal tension built up between two communities. The communal atmosphere provides a ready tilled soil for communal minded people to sow seeds of communal hatred and nurture them until the bitter harvest of communal riots are reaped.

## THE RISE OF HINDU NATIONALISM

"Nationalism" and "Communalism" are synonymous in an Indian context and are negative concepts. They are identified with the misuse of religion in politics. Worldwide, the first such misuse of religion in politics took place in late 19th century in America when the Conservative Protestants in the face of rationalism and scientific values came up with reassertion of 'fundamentals' of Christianity. Essentially, this was an attempt to re-impose the pre-modern values of birth based hierarchy of gender and class. Later, in Europe, the Nazi and fascist onslaughts used race for similar reasons. In recent times, we have seen the rise of Islamic or communalism in several countries of the middle-east, typified by Ayatullah Kohemini in the Iran of eighties and nineties. Communalism in India made its major appearance, in the pre-Independence era, in 1886, with the formation of two communal streams – the Muslim League (based on Islam) and the Hindu Mahasabha and the Rashtriya Swayamsevak Sangh (based on Hinduism). Over the years, these two streams have constantly tried to fan the communal passions of their followers, be it in the Shah Banoo case or the perennial dispute with regard to the Babri Masjid in Ayodhya. With the emergence of the Hindu right-wing party, the Bharatiya Janata Party (BJP) as a major political force in the country, the proponents of Hindu communalism, better known through its ideology "Hindutva", seem to have gained the upper hand.

### Hindutva

The fundamental goal of the "Hindutva" ideology is the establishment of a Hindu-Nation state exemplified in the fascist doctrine of "one nation, one culture, one language, one religion". It is a very narrow type of "nationalism" which seeks legitimacy through demonizing other religions and faiths, very specially Islam and Christianity. Whilst it is not representative of the Hindu majority of the country, it makes every attempt to appear to champion the concerns of mainstream Hinduism.

These posturings have created a great deal of disharmony in various parts of the country particularly in the last fifteen years when in 1990 one of the main exponents of the "Hindu Rashtra" namely, Mr. L. K. Advani, (a former Deputy Prime Minister of the country and currently the President of the BJP) went across the country on a "Rath Yatra". This created a great deal of animosity, blood-shed and deepened the divide between the Hindus and Muslims of the country.

In the wake of the demolition of the Babri Masjid on 6th December 1992, India became divided even more, on communal lines. This was followed by several other instances of communal violence which include the bashing up of Christians in Gujarat (Northwest India) in 1998 – 99 and the Gujarat Genocide of 2002 (when more than 2000 Muslims were killed in Gujarat); among the other communal incidents were the horrendous murder of the Australian Missionary Graham Staines and his two sons (in January 1999 in Manoharpur, Orissa) and the attack on the Sisters of Mother Teresa in Kerala in October 2004.

## Comparison between Hindu Rashtra and Secular Democratic India

It is important at this juncture to emphasis that the Constitution of India is a secular one in which all citizens are equal and which guarantees freedom of thought, expression and belief to every single Indian. India is therefore not a theocratic state and any "nationalism" based on religion or on fundamentalism is bound to create chaos and confusion and ultimately division.

The Hindutva ideology, based on the theory of the nation-state, talks essentially about the "Hindu Rashtra" (nation). This is in total opposition to the Constitution of India which speaks about a sovereign, socialist, secular, democratic republic.

Those of us who have been trying to put a stop to this are convinced that religion should not be used in politics and vice-versa. In fact, religion, if true, has to be used only for the promotion of communal peace, harmony, justice, love and compassion. Any religion worth its salt will not do otherwise.

Hoping that this brief presentation into "The rise of Hindu nationalism in India would have given you some insight into the reality we face back home, I invite you in joining me in praying a favourite prayer of mine which was composed years ago by the poet laureate of India. He thus laid the first brick on which the edifice of Pakistan was raised.

## Akhil Bharatiya Hindu Mahasabha

Akhil Bharat Hindu Mahasabha, a Hindu nationalist organization, was founded in 1915 to counter the Muslim League and the Indian

National Congress. The president of Hindu Mahasabha was V.D. Savarkar. K.B. Hedgewar served as vice president of the organisation and later left the Mahasabha to form Rashtriya Swayamsevak Sangh. Dr Narayan Bhaskar Khare was the president of Mahasabha during 1949-1951.

Soon after India's Independence, and the subsequent assassination of Gandhi, a good number of Hindu Mahasabhaites joined Bharatiya Jana Sangh under the leadership of S.P. Mukherjee, who had left Hindu Mahasabha and joined hands with the RSS to float a political party under the control and supervision of RSS. Mukherjee had left Mahasabha after his proposal to allow Muslims to gain membership was turned down by the followers of V.D. Savarkar. The relationship between Savarkar's Mahasabha and RSS was strained mainly because the then chief of RSS, M.S. Golwalkar, felt overshadowed by the influence of Savarkar over the Hindu populace. Officially Mahasabha is still a distinct political entity but its election symbol has been withheld as it has not been getting enough votes. So now the party fights elections on different symbols in different constituencies.

Bishan Chandra Seth of Shahjahanpur elected from twice from Etah was one of the longest serving parliamentarians from Hindu Mahasabha. Other long serving parliamentarian from Sabha was Mahant Avaindnath.

The New leadership is dedicated towards the cause of HINDUS as defined by the Honble Supreme Court of India.

## Myth of and related to Communalism

Communalism, after all, is the experience of the feeling that people who belong to a particular religion form a homogeneous community having certain common needs, aspirations and culture and further that the survival and growth of this community depends on its forcible domination over other religious communities because the interests of the communities are mutually exclusive. Hindus feel that the Muslims form a separate community and if the Hindus have to develop it has to be by totally dominating over the Muslim community. Similarly, the Muslims feel that unless they exert pressure, the Hindus will just bulldoze them.

## Homogenous Community

The first myth is that Hindus form a homogenous community with all its members having identical political, economic and cultural trends and interests. This, as we all know, is false. Amongst Hindus one may find workers, capitalists, landowners, etc., all of whose interests are not only distinct but even antagonistic. Similarly in Muslims. The political power aspired by different sections of Hindus is different. The Hindu religion also does not have common cultural or even religious identity. The culture of Hindus varies from place to place and from caste to caste. The gods are also numerous and different Hindus follow different gods. Similarly in Muslims, one has Shias and Sunnis and even the Shia and Sunnis have further divisions. Their cultural and religious practices also differ from place to place. It is therefore, totally incorrect to say that either the Hindus or the Muslims form a homogeneous community.

## The interests of Muslims and Hindus are not identical

Since Hindu and Muslim do not form distinct homogeneous communities the question of non-identical interests does not arise. Eve so, the workers of the Muslim "community" have more in common with the workers of the Hindu "community" than with Hindu or Muslim capitalists. The interests of capitalists are bound with other capitalists whether they are Hindus or Muslims.

## The interests of Hindus and Muslims are mutually exclusive

It is widely believed that the interests of Hindus and Muslims and contradictory and mutually exclusive and so they cannot survive together. First of all Hindus and Muslims have survived together for centuries. Second, why do interests become exclusive or even distinct merely because of religion? What is so fundamental about the relation between human beings and god which makes human's relation with other humans antagonistic?

Why should one person's personal belief in a particular god be antagonistic to another god, or is supposed to be? Every person, even a child, has some belief and opinion different from all others. If merely difference in belief is the criterion then by this logic all persons are antagonistic towards others and so human beings cannot survive in a society.

This, to say the least, is absurd. In any case, in the present society the antagonistic relations are between one class and another and not between one religious opinion and another. The antagonism is between the workers and the capitalist, between agricultural labourers and big farmers, even between dalits and caste Hindus. A Hindu worker's interests are contradictory to that of a Hindu capitalist and not that of a Muslim worker. The interests of all workers are tied together whether they are Hindu or Muslim against the interests of capitalists whether Hindu or Muslim.

Parenthetically, we must observe, that though objectively different communities on religious lines do not exist, subjectively they do. What is being suggested is that the Hindus and the Muslims do feel that they form separate and antagonistic communities. The communalists aggravate these feelings, but the germ of this subjective factor is not in some fanatical propaganda, but in the socio-economic circumstances. Communalism, therefore, has to be fought simultaneously at both the levels – i.e. ideologically and also by fighting for socio-economic change. The two have to go hand in hand.

## If Pakistan can be a Muslim State why India cannot be a Hindu State

It is true that the partition of undivided India occurred on the basis of religious lines. But this partition was totally artificial. It was a crackdown on a nation having at least some homogeneity. It is also true that Pakistan today calls itself an Islamic State but one cannot forget the movements in Pakistan as also in Iran against religious oppression.

The point however, is that State concerns itself with the relations of human beings with human beings and not with the relation between human beings and god. Why should it therefore not be a secular state but a Hindu State? If one takes the logic of the communalists further, why should not the State call itself and also be not only Hindu or Muslim but also Male, Brahmin, white skinned, etc.?

## When Pakistan wins in a cricket match, Muslims in Bombay light crackers

First of all this is not a widespread phenomenon. Only a few Muslims here and there light crackers which is made to look as if all the Muslims are for Pakistan against India. The partition was totally artificial which caused a number of people on both sides to break living links with their point of origin, people had to leave their relations, property etc.

In the "other country" which normally has caused some ties to remain. This ma in some persons lead to a moral affiliation to "the other country" but it is an entirely understandable phenomenon which cannot be reduced to a 'Hindu Muslim' thing.

What is important is that in spite of riots, in spite of much damage being suffered by them the Muslims in India remain in India. Even when the riot affected persons are migrant Muslims, they usually return not to Pakistan but to the state from where they migrated may be U.P., Bihar, or any other state. It is but natural that they want to remain in India and not go to Pakistan or anywhere else.

They know it as well as any one else that in the first instance their interests are tied to the interests of people of India. Apart from this one cannot forget the role of Hindu communalism in alienating the Muslim population. As more and more communal riots take place and as more and more Muslims lose their lives and property they are bound to feel alien in their own country. This is especially so when the state increasingly comes out openly in favour of Hindu communalism. In such an event, due to historical reasons the Muslims in India are bound to seek an identity for themselves through Pakistan.

## Muslims want to make the entire India Muslim

In 1981, a few hundred Hindus in Tamilnadu especially in Meenakshipuram converted in to Muslim religion. The press, in a most communal manner splashed this across the nation on front pages. Hindu revivalists made a big hue and cry about this small incident claiming that Hinduism was in danger.

Meenakshipuram is not the whole of India. 100 conversions there, cannot have even a rambling effect on Hindus. Even Buddhist, Jain and Sikh religions arose to a large extent as a protest against upper caste Hindu practice.

The people in Meenakshipuram converted themselves so as to find a way out of totally exploitative and dehumanising caste system. The communalist Hindus (led by Mr. M.G. Ramachandran) said that gulf money was the root of these conversions. In spite of various investigations no trace of gulf money could be found. In the districts where conversion took place extremely rigid caste system is prevailing.

The lower caste persons are not even allowed to have tea in an upper caste owned tea shop. One may contrast this with the fact that the Muslim-owned shops are open to the dalits. In fact, the investigations revealed that it was not the poorest of the people but the newly educated section who had made certain economic advancement who converted.

This was so because despite economic development, they were not given social equality. Those who converted were fully aware that they would be losing concessions like free educations, reserved government jobs etc. In spite of this they chose to convert which settles once and for all the reasons of their conversions. This was even admitted by the Swamiji of Pejawar Mutt, a caste Hindu, who observed "More than monetary help, the harijans were demanding status in society".

In fact, in many ways converts have achieved social amelioration (though not economic) through their conversions. It was found that Islamic community's attitude towards the converts underwent a radical change (i.e. born Muslims were willing to allow their daughters to marry converts, etc.).

Also to some extent there is an acceptance by the wider society. At times, the "threat to convert' issued as a lever for snatching concessions from the caste Hindus as well as from the government. Till 1933, the Ezhavas in Kerala were not allowed to enter temples. In 1993, they decided to renounce Hinduism. The caste Hindus on coming to know this, immediately granted to the Ezhavas the right to enter the temples. Even after the recent conversions in Meenakshipuram, certain areas where there existed a threat to conversions, speedy supply of water, house sites, etc. was made by the Government.

The answer to conversions, if one wants to question them at all, is in the Hindu religion itself and not in the operations of some Muslim fanatics. If Hindus want to put an end to conversions, caste exploitation has to stop. If Viswa Hindu Parishad wants to propagate sharply casteist views and practices, and at the same time wants to stop conversions it is next to impossible. Muslims are the largest minority in India. Furthermore, Muslims form an international population. One cannot also forget the brutal reality of partition, and also the past history of India. Otherwise, what is the rationale behind the communal Hindus not saying anything about lakhs of dalits embracing Buddhims, merely because Buddhism has arisen out of Hinduism? Or because the Constitution of India says that Hindus will include Buddhists? Is it that the Hindus cannot envisage Muslims ruling India because of the past history?

Or because of their belief that Buddhism is a branch of Hinduism? The same also goes for the elder brotherly treatment of Hindus towards the Sikhs. In spite of the current happenings in Punjab one does not find even amongst the rabid communalist Hindus, a generalised anti-Sikh feeling. They also talk of the 'healing touch' and not of throwing out Sikhs from India. Also, one cannot forget the fact that a large number of Muslims have been brought into the Hindu fold in recent years. In January 1982, about 3,000 Muslims in Suhara Village in Byavar District of Rajasthan were converted overnight by the Viswa Hindu Parishad. This is not a solitary instance. At various other places in Rajasthan and Uttar Pradesh, the Viswa Hindu Parished has converted a number of Muslims. These converts are directly fitted into the caste system and given the status of Rajputs. The Viswa Hindu Parishad which has given a call for banning all conversions justifies the conversion into the Hindu fold by claiming that it is neither conversion nor reconversion but purification. This process is called 'Paravartan'. The Parishad also makes it a point not to publicise these conversions.

### Muslims are becoming economically stronger at the expense of Hindus

This is to say the least, ridiculous. It may be true that in some places Muslims are increasingly competing with Hindus. But this is not a generalised trend. When one talks about upward mobility of Muslims, one is not crazy enough to believe that they are a generalised threat to Hindu economic interests. At least as yet communal riots have not percolated every part of our geography. They are mainly urban phenomena and so when we talked about upward mobility of Muslims it was in this context, it is ridiculous to say that at a macro level the Muslims are or can pose a threat to the economic interests of the Hindus.

Educationally, Muslims are much more backward than Hindus (in a wider sense). Even employment wise Muslims do not even represent their population proportion. It is difficult to get jobs in Hindu dominated employment market.

## SOME ASPECTS OF HINDU-MUSLIM PROBLEM

From this brief resume of three thinkers from whose ideas Hindu revivalist nationalism drew sustenance at different times, it becomes clear that one aspect of the Hindu-Muslim problem was the language of communication (including the use of religious or cultural symbols).

A second aspect of the same problem has been obliquely referred to by Jawaharlal Nehru in his autobiography. Nehru says that the petty-bourgeois leadership of the Congress sought those remedies that suited its interests and outlooks. What Nehru said about Congress leadership was equally applicable to the leadership of the Muslim League.

The Muslim League leadership was composed of rich landlords and the middle class which was scared of competition from Hindu petty-bourgeois counterparts. It has been pointed out that one of the biggest mistakes of the Congress leadership was that Congress approached only the Muslim leadership and ' not the Muslim people. Another fact of the Hindu-Muslim problem comes into focus, when we consider the developments from 1920 onwards.

Between 1914 and 1922 Hindu-Muslim relationship appeared to have touched a peak insofar as cordiality is concerned. International political developments, and the misery of the common people at home in India, because of high prices and famines affected Muslim and Hindu feelings alike. The Lucknow Pact between the Congress and the League in 1916, and the joint participation of the Hindus and Muslims in the Khilafat Non-Co-operation Movement during 1919-22 appeared to be a real breakthrough. In retrospect, however, all this would appear to be nothing but a chance coordination of ideas, with no basic understanding.

The Bardoli directive by Gandhi suspending the movement quickly laid bare the lack of mutual confidence. There was an almost immediate and sharp deterioration in the communal situation which continued until 1928.

The-widespread sense of insult following the announcement of the all white Simon Commission (1927), the prospects of another dose of constitutional reforms, and perhaps the failure of the post-Bardoli phase of politics of both sides promoted relatively simple proposals from nationalist Muslims for a more viable unity of purpose and action between the two communities, These proposals fell through because of various objections from ' the Congress representatives in the All Parties Committee which was deliberating them to frame a constitution which would be acceptable to all.

In the civil disobedience movements of 1930-32, Muslim participation was not as much as it was in the Khilafat Non-Co-operation Movement. Any hope of communal amity that this may have generated quickly evaporated in the Second Round Table Conference of 1931 which Gandhi attended. The Conference deliberations did not go well for Gandhi and the Congress.

The conservatives, the sectarians of both sides, encouraged by the government representatives, took charge of the proceedings at the Second Round Table Conference. Separate electorates could not be prevented, nor could the Congress prevent the fragmentation of the political community it so desired for the nationalist movement and for a free India of the future. For the Congress, Gandhi, and perhaps also Nehru, this was perhaps the point where the hope of Hindu-Muslim unity was given up. There appeared to be a somewhat unexpected reluctance or a lack of enthusiasm on the part of Congress to carry on dialogues with Muslim leaders for any length of time.

After the 1937 elections to provincial legislatures, the League's request for a coalition ministry in U.P. was not accepted by the Congress. At about the same time, the Muslim Mass Contact resolution of the Congress which had the important support of Gandhi and Nehru also languished for want of zealous implementation which such a proposal deserved. Soon after the demand for partition was heard, and a formal resolution demanding partition was accepted by the League in 1940.

Why this apparent resignation on the part of the Congress? Why this extreme demand for partitioning the country on the part of the League? Too often the Congress is blamed directly or indirectly for this failure. What appears to be more probable is that there was a mutual lack of trust which resulted in either trivial objections or demand for too many guarantees. Neither was likely to succeed in bringing about unity of purpose and action.

## Growth Of Communalism In India- II (1937-1947)

The year 1937 was a turning point in the history of communalism in India in so far as it concerns the stridency and intensity of politics of hatred. In the elections held for the provincial legislative assembly, the Muslim League won only 109 out of 492 reserved muslim seats and only 4.8 % of the total muslim votes showing thereby the lack of popular support for Muslim League even among the muslim population.

It was a well known fact that League's support base was mostly amongst the wealthy and the landlords.

As constructive programme for development of popular support always takes the time and also the fact that any constructive socio-economic programme would have targeted at the wealthy and landed muslim supporters of the League, the League resorted to the short cut by raising the cry of 'Islam in danger' thereby directly talking to the muslim masses about the impending 'Hindu Raj'. And what followed was a communal propaganda 'full of fervour, fear, contempt and bitter hatred' (W. C. Smith).

Earlier in October 1934, Gandhiji had withdrawn from the Congress refusing 4-anna membership of the Congress.

At Lucknow session of Congress in April 1936 and Faizpur Session in December 1936 presided over by J. L. Nehru, it was decided to contest election to be held in 1937 but the office acceptance was not yet decided. (While Satyamurti and T. Prakasham advocated office acceptance, M. R. Masani was against it.)

As one of my worthy critic has said in his rejoinder to the earlier essay that "Devil is not in the detail" I am reproducing the election results of Congress for the provinces : U.P. (United Provinces) 134/228, Bihar 95/152, Madras 159/215, C.P. (Central Province) 70/112, Orissa 36/60, Bombay 87/175, Bengal 60/250, Sind 8/60, Assam 35/108, NWFP (North West Frontier Province) 19/50, Punjab 18/175.

As a corollary to my first paragraph, it would be germane to point out here that the Hindu fundamentalists had fared worse than their muslim counterpart in these 1937 elections. For example, Hindu Mahasabha had won only 12 seats out of 175 in Punjab. Hence the same choice of extinction faced them as had faced their muslim counterparts forcing them to embrace a politics of hatred for survival.

Their predicament was aggravated in 1938 when Congress disallowed communalists from working within the Congress organization. Consequently, Congress was condemned by them for "supporting our inveterate enemies" and preaching that Hindus were the only Nation living in India. Thus evolved the Hindu fundamentalists' version of 'two nation theory'.

After the outbreak of WW-II, Muslim League was assiduously fostered by the Viceroy Linlithgow and the Pakistan demand was used to counter the Congress demand that the British should promise to free India after the war and as a proof of sincerity, transfer actual control of government to Indians immediately. British wanted a settlement between the League and the Congress before anything concrete could even be contemplated and promised that no political settlement would be made which was unacceptable to the League thereby giving the Jinnah a kind of a 'veto' power which he was to use to catastrophic effect in future. Cripps Mission of March-April 1942, though constituted with the avowed intention of 'the earliest possible realisation of self-government in India', actually promised Dominion status and that too after the war, nomination of people of princely states in the proposed Constituent Assembly by their princes, control of British over defence in the new executive council and implicit backdoor recognition of Pakistan via the 'local option clause' by which the princely states were allowed to directly negotiate with the British if they chose to reject the constitution to be framed. At a time when the Pakistan demand was seriously even thought about by the Indians, its sympathetic consideration by the British was a great service to the cause of Pakistan.

At the end of WW-II, at the initiative of Viceroy Wavell, the congress leaders were freed from jail in mid June 1945 and invited to Shimla to work out an interim political arrangement under which the Indians would be responsible for running the country. But Jinnah decided to test his above mentioned power of 'Veto' by insisting that only the League had the right of nominate Muslim members to the executive Council. This was embarrassing to the government as well as this denied representation to the Muslims of the Unionist Party which had staunchly supported the British during the war. But as the present and future interests were considered more important than the past loyalties, Wavell announced the breakdown of talk rather than bypass the League thereby upholding the 'veto' promised to the League by Linlithgow.

Elections held in the winter of 1945-46 to the Central and Provincial Legislative assemblies were fought by the League with a straight forward communal slogan-" A vote for the League and Pakistan was a vote for Islam." And it was a choice between the Gita and the Koran. Needless to say, the League made a clean sweep of the muslim seats in the polls.

The Cabinet Mission was sent to India in march 1946 to establish a national government and constitutional arrangement for transfer of power. The then British PM Attlee, in sharp contrast to Wavell's position, declared on 15th March 1946 that "a minority would not be allowed to place a veto on the progress of majority." He mission believed that Pakistan wouldn't be a viable entity and hence made a plan to safeguard the interests of Muslim minority within the overall framework of unity of the country. Three sections were planned which would have their own constitution. Group A: Madras, Bombay, United Provinces. Bihar, Central Provinces and Orissa; Group B: Punjab, NWFP and Sind and group C: Bengal and Assam. Common centre would look after defence, Foreign Affairs and communication. A province could leave the group to which it was assigned after the first general elections and after 10 years it could demand modification of both the group and union constitution. But the ambivalence over grouping i.e. it was compulsory or optional led to a deadlock and eventual failure of Cabinet Mission as both the League and the Congress took this a vindication of their stand. The League taking advantage of Nehru's speech about the sovereignty of the constituent assembly to amend the rules of procedure of Cabinet Mission withdrew its acceptance.

Interim government was formed on 2nd September 1946 with Nehru as its de facto head and reversing the earlier stand of the British to placate and take the League with it. This infuriated the League to actualize its threat of Direct Action the call for which was give on 16th August 1946 in Calcutta with a new slogan 'Larke lenge Pakistan' (We will fight and get Pakistan.) Cmmunal frenzy was provoked by Muslim groups in Bengal with the League's Bengal ministry headed by Suhrawardy looking on and leading to 'the Great Calcutta Killings'. Effect was felt in Noakhali in East Bengal, Bihar in October 1946 and in UP, Bombay, Punjab and NWFP in the subsequent months. This forced the British to go back to their reconciliatory approach towards the League. Wavel and even the Secretar of State for India Pethick Lawrence believed that in the absence of League civil war would become inevitable in India.

Consequently, the League joined the interim government on 26th October 1946 and started continuing their fight from within the government. Wavell was replaced by Mountbatten and Attlee reaffirmed his government's resolve to withdraw from India latest by '30th June 1947'. The League went on a final offensive, brought down the coalition Punjab government led by Khizr Hyat Khan of unionist party.

3rd June plan was devised to accommodate both the parties- by creating a sovereign Pakistan to accede to Jinna's demand but to make it as small as possible so as to accommodate the 'unity' demand of the congress. Dominion status was to be given to India and Pakistan on 15th August 1947 and other demands of congress viz. princely states to be with India, were acceded to as it was making a greater sacrifice. The country gained independence at a great cost and to paraphrase Jinnah "a truncated and moth eaten country" was born. A country where Muslims have more freedom than the country which was ostensibly created for them.

## Development of Communalism in India

Communalism is not something, India was born with. In fact Communalism in India is not older than some 140 years. India, however conquered and intruded by various foreign rulers like Turk, Afghan, Mughal and British, lived in peace and communal harmony for a long period until it was strategically divided among different castes and religion for the political benefits of the foreign rulers.

## Being Hindu Or Being Muslim is Not Communalism

Hindus and Muslims have been living together in India peacefully for more than 1000 years. They practiced their own faiths and religions, celebrated Eid and Diwali together and made pilgrimage to both Ajmer Sharif and Kashi for hundreds of years, without getting agitated over each other's religious beliefs. Religion was a part of peoples life from the very beginning of Indian civilization and people often quarrelled over religion but there was hardly any communal ideology. Communalism is a modern phenomenon. What made these peace loving Indian people turned against each other? What made a Hindu start feeling like he is a different 'human' than a Muslim and vice-versa?

## The Thin Line b/w Being Religious and Being Communal

When a community starts believing in the ideology that since they follow a particular religion, their social, economic and political interests are same - they start turning communal. Communalism enters its next level when a particular group of people are convinced that the social, economic and political interests of the followers of one religion are different from the interests of the follower of another religion. And moreover, they are mutually incompatible or they could not be met together. The ideology of a religion based socio-political identity is Communalism.

## References

Adeney: *Coalition Politics and Hindu Nationalism*, Cambridge Univ Press, Delhi, 2002.

Ajeet, Javed: *Secular and Nationalist Jinnah,* JNU Press, Delhi. 1999.

Chatterjee, P.: *Nationalist Thought and the Colonial World: A Derivative Discourse.* Oxford: Oxford University Press, 1986.

Das, Veena: *Mirrors of Violence: Communities, Riots and Survivors in South Asia,* Delhi: Oxford University Press, 1990.

Francis G.: *India's Revolution: Gandhi and the Quit India Movement,* Harvard UP, Cambridge, 1973.

Jaffrelot, C. : *The Hindu Nationalist Movement and Indian Politics, from 1925 to the 1990s.* London: Hurst and Company, 1996.

Pandey, G. : *The Construction of Communalism in Colonial North India.* New Delhi: Oxford University Press, 1990.

Sharma, A.K. : *Gandhian Perspectives on Population and Development,* New Delhi, Concept, 1996.

13

# Various Aspects of Art and Culture in Indian Society

**DR. MAMTA SINGH**
*Assistant Professor, Department of Drawing and Painting, M.K.P. (P.G.) College, Dehradun, Uttarakhand*

The word *culture,* from the Latin *colo,-ere,* with its root meaning "to cultivate", generally refers to patterns of human activity and the symbolic structures that give such activity significance. Different definitions of "culture" reflect different theoretical bases for understanding, or criteria for evaluating, human activity. Anthropologists most commonly use the term "culture" to refer to the universal human capacity to classify, codify and communicate their experiences symbolically. This capacity is long been taken as a defining feature of the genus *Homo.* However, primatologists such as Jane Goodall have identified aspects of culture among our closest relatives in the animal kingdom. Similarly, it has recently been determined that the Orca pods have culture specific vocalizations and tastes for food. Orcas used in theme parks are exclusively from pods that only feed on fish.

## DEFINING "CULTURE"

Culture has been called "the way of life for an entire society." As such, it includes codes of manners, dress, language, religion, rituals, norms of behaviour and systems of belief. Various definitions of culture reflect differing theories for understanding — or criteria for evaluating— human activity. Sir Edward B. Tylor writing from the perspective of social anthropology in the UK in 1871 described culture in the following way: "Culture or civilization, taken in its wide ethnographic sense, is that complex whole which includes knowledge, belief, art, morals, law, custom, and any other capabilities and habits acquired by man as a member of society."

More recently, the United Nations Educational, Scientific and Cultural Organization UNESCO (2002) described culture as follows: "... culture should be regarded as the set of distinctive spiritual, material, intellectual and emotional features of society or a social group, and that it encompasses, in addition to art and literature, lifestyles, ways of living together, value systems, traditions and beliefs". While these two definitions cover a range of meaning, they do not exhaust the many uses of the term "culture." In 1952, Alfred Kroeber and Clyde Kluckhohn compiled a list of more than 200 definitions of "culture" in *Culture: A Critical Review of Concepts and Definitions.*

These definitions, and many others, provide a catalog of the elements of culture. The items catalogued (*e.g.*, a law, a stone tool, a marriage) each have an existence and life-line of their own. They come into space-time at one set of coordinates and go out of it another. While here, they change, so that one may speak of the evolution of the law or the tool.

A culture, then, is by definition at least, a set of cultural objects. Anthropologist Leslie White asked: "What sort of objects are they? Are they physical objects? Mental objects? Both? Metaphors? Symbols? Reifications?" In *Science of Culture* (1949), he concluded that they are objects "*sui generis*"; that is, of their own kind. In trying to define that kind, he hit upon a previously unrealized aspect of symbolization, which he called "the symbolate"—an object created by the act of symbolization. He thus defined culture as "symbolates understood in an extra-somatic context." The key to this definition is the discovery of the symbolate.

## CULTURE OF INDIA

The culture of India was moulded throughout various eras of history, all the while absorbing customs, traditions and ideas from both invaders and immigrants. Many cultural practices, languages, customs and monuments are examples of this co-mingling over centuries.

In modern India, there is remarkable cultural and religious diversity throughout the country. This has been influenced by the various regions of India, namely South, North, and North-East, have their own distinct identities and almost every state has carved out its own cultural niche. In spite of this unique cultural diversity, the whole country is bound as a civilization due to its common history, thereby preserving the national identity.

India was the birth place of religious systems such as Hinduism, Sikhism, Buddhism and Jainism, which have a strong influence not only over India, but also the whole world. Following the Islamic invasions and the subsequent foreign domination from the tenth century onwards, the culture of India was influenced by the foreign cultures, particularly Persian, Arabic and Turkish cultures. Their influence comes in the form of religion, language and dress. In turn, the various religions and the multihued traditions of India have influenced South East Asia (and to a minimal extent, East Asia).

## OVERVIEW

*Regions:* Indian culture can be classified into many varied form which are existent in their totality throughout the territory of India. The culture of India has been influenced by various religions and customs of the world, which resulted in the mingling of religious values, folk idioms and art forms. While the religious influence is quite evident in the "classical" Indian culture mostly found in smaller towns and villages, the urban India is now widely influenced by globalization.

*Language:* As well as regional diversity, languages have created diverse traditions of culture in India. There are a large number of languages in India; 216 of them are spoken by a group of 10,000 persons or more. The two major families of languages are those of the Indo-Aryan languages and those of the Dravidian languages, the former largely confined to the North India and the latter to the South India. The Constitution of India has stipulated the usage of Hindi and English to be the two official languages of communication for the national government.

A further 22 languages are scheduled for official use, mainly by state governments. Sanskrit has served as a classical language of India and South-Eastern Asia, and is equated in importance to Latin or Greek in Europe. It is studied as far away as Japan and the West due its cultural and religious significance. The classical language of the Dravidian family is regarded to be old Tamil. The number of speakers of state languages and dialects is very high.

## CULTURAL POLICY

The cultural policy of the Government of India has three major objectives. One of them is to preserve the cultural heritage of India; to inculcate Indian art consciousness amongst countrymen and to promote high standards in creative and performing arts fields.

## Literature

The earliest literary traditions were mostly oral and passed through descendants by the citizens. They were later transcribed. Most of these spring from Hindu tradition and are represented by sacred works like the Vedas, the epics of the Mahabharata and Ramayana. Tamil Sangam literature represents some of India's oldest secular traditions. Many Buddhist and Jain works are in Prakrit languages like Pali. The classical works of playwright Kalidasa even today exert an important influence on Indian litterateurs.

Upon the arrival of Mughal dynasty, Islamic culture also influenced the medieval Indian literature. This was due to the spreading influence of Persian and the rise of famous poets such as Amir Khusro. Colonial rule prepared the stage for modern literature exemplified by the works of Rabindranath Tagore, Bankim Chandra Chattopadhyay, Michael Madhusudan Dutt, Munshi Premchand, Devaki Nandan Khatri, among many others. Indian writers in modern times, like R. K. Narayan, Vaikom Muhammad Basheer,Mahasweta Devi, Amrita Pritam, Arundhati Roy, Vikram Seth, Khushwant Singh, Salman Rushdie have been the cynosures of wide acclaim, both in Indian languages and English.

## Poetry

India has strong traditions of poetry, as well as prose writing. This is often closely related to musical traditions, and most poetry can be attributed to religious movements. Writers and philosophers were often also skilled poets.

In modern times, poetry served as an important non-violent tool of nationalism during the Indian freedom movement. A famous modern example of this tradition can be found in such figures as Rabindranath Tagore in modern times and poets such as Kabir in medieval times, as well as the epics of ancient times. Two examples of poetry from Tagore's Gitanjali serve as the national anthems of both India and Bangladesh.

## Performing Arts

*Music:* The music of India includes multiples varieties of folk, popular, pop, and classical music. India's classical music tradition, including Carnatic and Hindustani music, noted for the use of several Raga, has a history spanning millennia and, developed over several eras, remains instrumental to the religious inspiration, cultural expression and pure entertainment. Alongside distinctly subcontinental forms there are major influences from Persian, Arab, and British music. Indian genres like filmi and bhangra have become popular throughout the United Kingdom, South and East Asia, and around the world.

*Dance:* India offers a number of Classical Indian dance forms, each of which can be traced to different parts of the country. Each form represents the culture and ethos of a particular region or a group of people. The eight main styles are Bharata Natyam, Kathak, Odissi, Kuchipudi, Mohiniattam, Bhangra, Manipuri and Kathakali. Besides, there are several forms of Indian folk dances, and special dances observed in regional festivals.

### Drama and Theatre

Indian drama and theatre is perhaps as old as its music and dance. Kalidas' plays like Shakuntala and Meghadoot are some of the oldest plays from literary traditions. The tradition of folk theatre is alive in nearly all the linguistic regions of the country. In addition, there is a rich tradition of puppet theatre in rural India. Group Theatre is also thriving in the cities, initiated by the likes of Utpal Dutt, Khwaja Ahmad Abbas and still maintained by groups like Nandikar and Prithvi Theatre.

## VISUAL ARTS

*Painting:* The earliest Indian paintings were the rock paintings of pre-historic times, the petroglyphs as found in places like Bhimbetka, and some of them are older than 5500 BC. Ancient texts outline theories of darragh and anecdotal accounts suggesting that it was common for households to paint their doorways or indoor rooms where guests resided.

Cave paintings from Ajanta, Bagh, Ellora and Sittanavasal and temple paintings testify to a love of naturalism and God. Most rock art in India is Hindu or Buddhist. A freshly made coloured flour design (Rangoli) everyday is still a common sight outside the doorstep of many (mostly South Indian) Indian homes.

Madhubani painting, Rajput painting, Tanjore painting, Mughal painting are some notable Genres of Indian Art; while Raja Ravi Varma, Nandalal Bose, Jamini Roy are some modern painters. Jehangir Art Gallery, Mumbai, has on display several good Indian paintings.

*Sculpture:* The first sculptures in India date back to the Indus

Valley civilization, where stone and bronze carvings have been discovered. This is one of the earliest instances of sculpture in the world. Later, as Hinduism, Buddhism and Jainism developed further, India produced some of the most intricate bronzes in the world, as well as unrivalled temple carvings. Some huge shrines, such as the one at Ellora were not actually constructed using blocks, but instead carved out of solid rock, making them perhaps the largest and most intricate sculptures in the world.

The pink sandstone sculptures of Mathura evolved during the Gupta period (4th to 6th century) to reach a very high fineness of execution and delicacy in the modelling. Newer sculptures in northwest, in stucco, schist or clay, display very strong blending of Indian post-Gupta mannerism and Classical influence, Hellenistic or possibly even Greco-Roman. Meanwhile, elsewhere in India, less anatomically accurate styles of human representation evolved leading to the classical art that the world is now familiar with and contributing to Buddhist and Hindu sculpture throughout Asia.

*Architecture:* Indian architecture is that vast tapestry of production of the Indian Subcontinent that encompasses a multitude of expressions over space and time, transformed by the forces of history considered unique to the sub-continent, sometimes destroying, but most of the time absorbing new ideas.

The result is an evolving range of architectural production that none the less retains a certain amount of continuity across history. The earliest production in the Indus Valley Civilization was characterised by well planned cities and houses where religion did not seem to play an active role, but which demonstrated world-famous city planning.

During the reign of the Gupta and Maurya empires, several Buddhist architectural examples like caves of Ajanta and Ellora and the monumental Sanchi Stupa were built. South India contains several Hindu temples like Brihadeeswara Temple, Thanjavur, the Sun Temple, Konark, Sri Ranganathaswamy Temple at Srirangam, and the Buddha stupa (Chinna Lanja dibba and Vikramarka kota dibba) at Bhattiprolu. Angkor Wat and other Buddhist and Hindu temples carry the evidence of Indian influence on South East Asian architecture, as they are built in styles almost identical to traditional Indian temple building.

With the advent of Islamic influence from the west, the erstwhile Indian architecture was slightly adapted to allow the traditions of the new religion. Fatehpur Sikri, Taj Mahal, Gol Gumbaz, Qutub Minar, Red Fort of Delhi are the creations of this era, and are often used as the stereotypical symbols of India, despite the greater antiquity and originality of traditional architecture. The colonial rule of the British Indian Empire saw the development of Indo-Saracenic style, and mixing of several other styles, such as European gothic. Victoria Memorial, Victoria Terminus are notable examples. Recent creations such as Lotus Temple, and the various modern urban developments of India, are also notable.

The traditional system of Vaastu Shastra serves as India's version of Feng Shui, influencing town planning, architecture, and ergonomics. It is unclear which system is older, but they contain many similarities. Though Vastu is conceptually similar to Feng Shui in that it also tries to harmonize the flow of energy, (also called life-force or Prana in Sanskrit and Chi/Ki in Chinese/Japanese), through the house, it differs in the details, such as the exact directions in which various objects, rooms, materials etc are to be placed.

Indian architecture has influence the world, especially eastern Asia, due to the spread of ideas with Buddhism. A number of Indian architectural features such as the temple mound or stupa, temple spire or sikhara, temple tower or pagoda and temple gate or torana, have become famous symbols of Asian culture, used extensively in East Asia and South East Asia. The central spire is also sometimes called a vimanam. The variant southern temple gate, or gopuram is noted for its intricacy and majesty. The arch, a cornerstone of world architecture, was first developed by the Indus Valley civilization and would later be a staple of Indian architecture.

## Recreation and Sports

In the area of recreation and sports India had evolved a number of games. The modern eastern martial arts originated as ancient games and martial arts in India and it was from here that these games were transmitted to foreign countries, where they were further modernized. Additionally, a few games introduced during the British Raj have grown quite popular in India, field hockey, football (soccer) and especially cricket.

Although field hockey is India's official national sport, cricket is by far the most popular sport not only in India, but the entire subcontinent, thriving recreationally and professionally. Cricket has even been used recently as a forum for diplomatic relations between India and long-standing rival, Pakistan. The two nations' cricket teams face off annually and such contests are quite impassioned on both sides. Traditional indigenous sports include kabaddi and gilli-danda, which are played in most parts of the country. Indoor and outdoor games like Chess, Snakes and Ladders, Playing cards, Polo, Carrom, Badminton are popular.

## Dress

Indian costume is full of variations. Every region and state has its distinct style. In cities and towns, men mostly wear collared shirts and cotton trousers with shoes or sandals. A three-quarter-length coat called *achkan,* buttoned all the way up the front and topped with a short, stiff collar, is worn as the official Indian costume on formal occasions. Urban women mostly women wear the shalwar: free-flowing pants topped by a long shirt, often worn with a scarf draped around the neck.

The tradional garments worn by men is *dhoti,* a four-to five-yard white cotton cloth wrapped around the waist and tucked between the legs. There are variations in its drape, length, texture, and quality of border adornment. In Bengal one end hangs loose in front, while in Maharashtra both ends are passed between the legs and tucked into the back waistband. In the Punjab loose-fitting pajamas called *shalwar* are worn.

Most Indian women wear the *sari,* a bordered length of cloth from six to nine yards long, which is draped loosely around the entire body and frequently covers the head as well. The sari is wrapped around the waist several times, making pleats in front, and then thrown across the chest and shoulders. Either a full blouse or a short, halterlike garment called a *choli* is worn on the upper body.

Footwear for both men and women consists usually of sandals, though shoes worn in Western countries are beginning to become more popular for women (heels, wedges, etc.). For men distinctive styles of headdress indicate regional affiliation, religious community, or social class. However, only certain cultures of India, such as the Panjabi or Sikh culture, involve the wearing of turbans.

Aside from the many ways of wrapping the turban, special headwear includes the traditional Parsi hat of shiny starched black alpaca in the shape of a rimless bowler; the Muslim hat, preferably of angora wool; and the Gandhi cap, an unadorned visorless cap that originally denoted membership in the Congress party. Women usually wear no headdress other than a shawl or the end of the sari, if even that.

## Cuisine

The earliest Indians, the Harappans, probably ate mainly wheat, rice and lentils, and occasionally meats such as pork, lamb, goat and chicken. Some believe that vegetarianism became popular with the arrival of Buddhism and Jainism that emphasised ahimsa (non-violence). The cuisine of Modern India has great variety and each region has its own distinctive flavours. The staple cereals are rice and wheat. North Indian staple meals consist of *chapatis* or *rotis*, wheat based and rice as staples, eaten with a wide variety of side dishes like dals, curries, yogurt, chutney and *achars*. South India staple dishes consist of rice, sambhar, rasam, yoghurt and curries being important side dishes.

Another important ingredient in south Indian food is coconut and most popular snacks like idli dosa are also rice-based. Fish is popular in coastal states, especially West Bengal, Orissa and Kerala. Several kind of street foods like Panipuri, Vada pav, Bhelpuri, samosa, vada are popular, though they are known by different names in different regions. Indian Chinese cuisine, an Indianized version of the Chinese cuisine is also popular,especially among youngsters in Mumbai. This cuisine is supposed to have originated from east of India generally and Darjeeling specifically. Tea like other Asian countries, enjoys heavy popularity, while coffee is quite popular in South India. Nimbu pani (lemonade), lassi, and coconut milk are also popular, while India also has many indigenous alcoholic beverages like Fenny and Indian beer.

## Courtesies

*Greetings:* The *Namaste* is India's traditional greeting. One presses the palms together (fingers up) below the chin and says *Namaste* (in the south, *Namaskaram*). Muslims might greet each other with *Salaam* or *Adaab*. Traditionally men and women don't shake hands with each other but it is accepeted norm these days in urban india. "Hello" and "Hi" are acceptable greetings among equals, but people address superiors with more formal terms such as "Good morning" or its equivalent. It is considered polite to use titles such as *Professor, Doctor, Mr., Shri* (for men), *Shreemati* (married women), *Kumari* (unmarried women), or the suffix-*ji* with a last name to show respect. Indians usually ask permission before taking leave of others.

*Gestures:* Excessive hand gestures or verbal articulation is considered impolite. People beckon with the palm turned down; they often point with the chin. It is impolite to sniff or handle flowers displayed at bazaars. Grasping one's own ears expresses repentance or sincerity. One's feet or shoes should not touch another person, and if they do, an immediate apology is necessary. Whistling is considered impolite at public places but is acceptable in informal atmosphere. Too much public displays of affection is considered inappropriate but holding hands is now mostly accepted. Footwear is removed before entering a temple, mosque, or Sikh shrine. When entering a Sikh shrine or mosque, all people cover their heads.

*Visiting:* Visits in the home between friends or family are often unannounced. The need for prior arrangements is increasing in large cities. It is impolite to say "no" to an invitation; if one cannot attend, one more likely says, "I'll try." At certain gatherings, guests adorned with a garland of flowers remove and carry them as an expression of humility. Guests repay hosts' hospitality by giving gifts, such as flowers, specialty foods (fruits, sweets) from other areas of the country, or something for their children.

Most Indians do not wear shoes inside the home. Most guests at least remove shoes before entering the living room. Hosts offer their guests water, tea or coffee, and fruits or sweets. It is polite for a guest initially to refuse these refreshments but eventually to accept them. Visitors often indicate they are ready to leave by saying *Namaste.*

*Eating:* Eating habits vary sharply between traditional and modern settings. Many families eat their food with the right hand instead of relying on spoon and fork. Most of families have dinner togather where faimly memebers discuss any issues and decisions.

## Popular Media

*Cinema:* Bollywood is the informal name given to the popular Mumbai-based film industry in India. Bollywood and the other major cinematic hubs (Bengali, Kannada, Malayalam, Tamil, Telugu) constitute the broader Indian film industry, whose output is considered to be the largest in the world in terms of number of films produced and, possibly, number of tickets sold. Bollywood films are usually musicals, though not in the Western sense of the word. Indian movies have a regular plot, with songs and dances interspersed to add to the entertainment value of the movie. Few movies are made without at least one song-and-dance number. Indian audiences expect full value for their money; they want songs and dances, love interest, comedy and dare-devil thrills, all mixed up in a three hour long extravaganza with intermission.

Such movies are called *masala* movies, after the Indian spice mixture *masala*. Like *masala,* these movies are a mixture of many things. Approximately, 95% of Bollywood movies are this type of movie, because Indians enjoy this type of movie very much. Plots tend to be melodramatic. They frequently employ formulaic ingredients such as star-crossed lovers and angry parents, corrupt politicians, kidnappers, conniving villains, courtesans with hearts of gold, long-lost relatives and siblings separated by fate, dramatic reversals of fortune, and convenient coincidences, and even movies with tri polar changes that can turn a movie and its plot upside down. Bollywood is becoming increasingly popular in other countries including several places in Europe and the U.S. Some Bollywood actors have adapted to more Hollywood-type films in movies like Bend It Like Beckham and Bride and Prejudice. Bollywood's fame is increasing internationally as more and more people across the globe are exposed to its style. Besides the regular *masala* film, India has also produced many critically acclaimed cinema-makers like Satyajit Ray, Ritwik Ghatak, Adoor Gopalakrishnan,Ram Gopal Varma, Mani Ratnam, G. Aravindan etc. In fact, with the opening up of the economy in the recent years & consequent exposure to world cinema, audience tastes have been changing. Indian commercial movies have also started following authentic, real world themes with a lower amount of melodrama & some do not even contain songs. In addition, multiplexes have mushroomed in most cities, changing the revenue patterns & allowing film makers greater liberty & scope for executing bold & innovative ideas which would not have been possible even a decade ago.

*Television:* Indian television started off in 1959 in New Delhi with tests for educational telecasts. Indian small screen programming started off in the early 1980s. At that time there was only one national channel Doordarshan, which was government owned. The Ramayana and Mahabharat were some among the popular television series produced. By the late 1980s more and more people started to own television sets. Though there was a single channel, television programming had reached saturation. Hence the government opened up another channel which had part national programming and part regional. This channel was known as DD 2 later DD Metro. Both channels were broadcasted terrestrially.

In 1994, the government liberated its markets, opening them up to cable television. Since then, there has been a spurt in the number of channels available. Today, Indian silver screen is a huge industry by itself, and has thousands of programmes in all the states of India. The small screen has produced numerous celebrities of their own kind some even attaining national fame. TV soaps are extremely popular with housewives as well as working women, and even men of all kinds. Some small time actors have made it big in Bollywood. Indian TV has evolved to be similar to Western TV, including stations such as Cartoon Network, Nikelodeon, and Indian MTV.

*Radio:* Radio broadcasting began in India in 1927, with two privately-owned transmitters at Mumbai and Calcutta. These were nationalised in 1930 and operated under the name "Indian Broadcasting Service" until 1936, when it was renamed All India Radio (AIR). Although officially renamed again to *Akashwani* in 1957, it is still popularly known as All India Radio. All India Radio is a division of Prasar Bharati (Broadcasting Corporation of India), an autonomous corporation of the Ministry of Information and Broadcasting, Government of India. It is the sister service of Prasar Bharati's Doordarshan, the national television broadcaster.

## References


Apte, V. M.: *Social and Religious Life in the Grihya Sutras*, Rawat Press, Bombay, 1954.

Asim Roy, *The Islamic Syncretistic Tradition in Bengal.* Princeton: Princeton University Press, 1983.

Bhardwaj, Surinder Mohan: *Hindu Places of Pilgrimage in India: A Study in Cultural Geography*, University of California Press, Berkeley, 1973.

Bowes, Pratima: *Hindu Intellectual Tradition,* Allied Publishers, New Delhi, 1977.

Cunningham, Joseph Davey: *History of the Sikhs, From the Origins of the Nation to the Battles of the Sutlej,* Sultan Chand, Delhi, 1955.

Farquhar, J. N.: *A Primer of Hinduism,* Faber & Faber, London, 1912.

Gambhirananda, Swami: *Brahma Sutra Shamkar Bhasya,* Adavita Ashrama, Calcutta, 1977.

John, Elsner: *Pilgrimage: Past and Present in the World Religions,* Harvard University Press, Cambridge, 1995.

Richard Eaton, *The Rise of Islam and the Bengal Frontier, 1204-1760.* Delhi: Oxford University Press, 1994.

Trimingham, J. Spencer: *The Sufi Orders in Islam,* New York, 1998.

# 14

# Theory and Practice of Democratic State in India

**PROFESSOR, M. M. SEMWAL**
*Department of Political Science, H.N.B. Garhwal University, (A Central University) Srinagar Garhwal, Uttarakhand*

**Abstracts:** India is a federal union of states comprising twenty-nine states and seven union territories. The states and union territories are further subdivided into districts and further into smaller administrative divisions. Social science engagements with contemporary India have mostly been around the question of change – social, economic, cultural, or political. Until some time back these engagements were envisioned primarily in the framework of "modernization" and "development". M.N. Srinivas, India's most celebrated sociologist, for example, identified three core processes of social change – westernization, modernization, and secularization – through which social scientists ought to make sense of the changing Indian society. Industrial development and urbanization were seen to be essential if such changes were to materialize in a largely rural and agrarian society that India was at the time of its independence from the colonial rule. The political process, i.e., India's experiment with democratic polity was but an aspect of these boarder processes. Marxist social scientists writing on contemporary India too remained preoccupied with the questions of change, albeit with a different framework that approached it as a moment of transformation from pre-capitalist social formations to capitalist ones. The political processes, the new institutions of democratic governance were linked to this larger process simply in an instrumental manner, an epiphenomenon, or a functional prerequisite for the capitalist market to expand and gain legitimacy. The unfolding of the democratic experiment, more than five decades of participation in electoral process, has produced a dynamic of change that does not necessarily confirm the expectations or predictions of the evolutionist modernization theory of social transformation. The Indian experience has also not been a mechanical replica of the development of bourgeois political institutions as had supposedly happened elsewhere in capitalist regimes of the Western world.

This, however, is not to suggest that the political process underway in contemporary India has been completely independent or autonomous of the social and economic changes, instrumented by state intervention or by the expanding market. The two (democracy and the experience of socio-economic change) have of course reinforced each other, but the outcomes have not been entirely in conformity with any of the so-called classical models of social change/ transformation. It is this experience – the dynamics of social and economic transformations on the one hand and the unfolding of the democratic process on the other hand – which I hope to capture in this paper. My working hypothesis would be that democratization is not merely an aspect of change. It could also be viewed as a perspective, a framework for understanding the dynamics of Indian society over the last five decades or so.

## DEMOCRATISATION IN INDIA

India is the seventh largest (by area) and the second most populous country in the world, with roughly one-sixth of its population, of about a billion and a quarter. India is one of the world's oldest civilizations, yet a very young nation. Under Mughal and Rajput control for much of its history until its colonisation by European powers in the mid-eighteenth century. The world's largest democracy by electorate was created after independence in 1947 under the leadership of its nationalist movement, the Indian National Congress.

Elections to its Parliament are held once every 5 years. Currently, Prime minister Narendra Modi is the head of the government, enjoying a majority in the Parliament, while President Pranab Mukherjee, is the head of state. India is a constitutional republic governed under the world's longest written constitution, federally consisting of 29 states and seven centrally administered union territories, with New Delhi as the nation's capital.

The country has six main national parties: the Bharatiya Janta Party (BJP), Indian National Congress (INC), Communist Party of India (CPI), Communist Party of India (Marxist)(CPI(M)), Bahujan

Samaj Party (BSP) and Nationalist Congress Party (NCP). At the level of its states, many regional parties stand for elections to state legislatures, every five years. The Rajya Sabha elections are held every 6 years.

## DEMOCRATIC PRINCIPLES

India is a Sovereign, Socialist, Secular, Democratic, Republic.

Sovereign means an independent nation.

Socialist implies social and economic equality for all Indian citizens. This guarantees equal opportunity and equal social status. The government attempts to reduce economic inequality by reducing concentration of wealth.

Secular implies freedom to choose your religion. The state gives every citizen the right to practice and propagate a religion of his choice, and also right to reject all religions. The state treats all religions as equal and there is no official state religion.

Democratic means the government is a democratically elected, head of the government(Prime Minister) is elected by the people.

Republic means head of the state(President) is not hereditary King or Queen but indirectly elected by the people.

### Democracy and the Caste System

The promise of a modern and democratic society that the leaders of India's freedom movement made to the people when they assumed power from colonial rulers included abolition of the caste system, and caste related disabilities.

The Constitution of independent India made all forms of discrimination on grounds of religion, race, caste, gender or place of birth punishable by law. In fact the independent Indian state went a step further and instituted certain legal and institutional measures, albeit temporarily, to enable the historically disadvantaged groups and communities of people, to participate in the game of democratic politics on equal terms. These included reservations for the Scheduled Castes and Scheduled tribes in jobs, education and elected bodies in proportions to their population.

What has happened to the caste system during the last five or six decades? The dominant tendency in sociological literature on caste has been to view it from a cultural perspective or an ideological system, a system of values and ideas, which was peculiarly Indian, and an essential part of classical Hinduism. Such perspectives tend to also look at caste in unitary terms, a pan Indian reality, and without any significant variations in its structure or ideology across different regions or sub-regions of India/south Asia. Its association with Hinduism, where it supposedly had the sanction from some scriptural sources, further reinforces such a stance. The fact that caste differences exist among non-Hindu Indians is invariably seen only as an evidence of their Hindu ancestry (Jodhka 2004). Such perspectives also ignored the elements of power and domination that were so central to the everyday working of caste.

However, despite its pan Indian presence, the actual frâmes of reference of caste are regional in character, which ought to be looked at historically. As is widely known, there are different sets of caste 16 groups in different regions. The specific historical trajectory, the patterns of politico-economic changes experienced during the colonial and post-independence period and the composition of different ethnic communities determine the actual working of caste relations in a given region. Overlooking these obvious facts about caste also makes it appear like an unchanging reality.

## DEMOCRACY AND THE INDIAN STATE

Democracies everywhere, but perhaps nowhere more so than in India, present a complex scenario of tensions between constraints and liberty, unfreedom and freedom, the imperatives of the modern national security state and the aspirations of a free citizenry. The very fact that India has repeatedly been able to mount general elections since it gained its freedom from British rule in 1947, and on a scale never before witnessed in history, is adduced as evidence of the strength of Indian democracy — an accomplishment that seems all the more remarkable given the precarious state of democracy in most of the world. Indeed, assumptions about the robustness of democracy in India always take as their implied referent the contrast that comes to mind with Pakistan and many other states in the global South. Pakistan has been under military rulers for 32 of its sixty years of its existence, and even its civilian rulers have always governed with the apprehension that a coup might summarily remove them from office – as the constant tussle between Benazir Bhutto and Nawaz Sharif, each removed from office more than once to pave the way for the other, amply suggests. In Africa, democratic states have had at least as fragile an existence, and military dictatorships, despotisms, and authoritarian democracies have indisputably been the norm.

So just what is it that accounts for the resilience and endurance of Indian democracy? Why has it flourished in India when it has failed in other states? And why has it done so even though India's mass poverty, widespread illiteracy, slow economic growth, a large bureaucracy clearly indifferent to norms of efficiency, a culture of permissive corruption, and unrivaled heterogeneity were all, according to classical accounts, supposed to militate against the growth of democracy? The rhetoric of the state was redistributive, but in practice substantial redistribution was abandoned. Some considerations quickly come to mind, and are offered here as an aid to rumination, and with the hope that researchers will find these suggestions of sufficient intellectual interest to pursue them at greater length:

1. The Congress, for all its authoritarian tendencies and its close identification with the Nehru-Gandhi family, furnished a considerable element of stability. In 1985, the Congress completed 100 years of its existence, and only a few Western democracies have had political parties which have similarly stood the test of time. To be sure, the Congress of Indira Gandhi, and even more so of contemporary times, may not bear much of a resemblance with the Indian National Congress during the time of Beasant, Tilak, Gandhi and later, but nonetheless the very presence of the Congress signifies certain continuities.
2. India had, from the colonial period, a relatively centralized state – and, at the same time, some machinery for local elections and political representation. Though center-state relations have not been without deep difficulties, India has achieved a not insignificant balance between Federal/center and the states. The creation of linguistic states was in itself an important accommodation in this regard. It is important to issue a caveat here about supposing that the colonial legacy was all-important: the British in India, for example, resisted universal franchise, and only after independence did this become a reality.
3. India inherited and retained a well-oiled civil service. India had what is called "a bourgeois revolution"; the demand for Pakistan, by contrast, was led by landed aristocrats. This might also explain why land reforms have been less far-reaching in Pakistan and why that country is still said to be governed more by feudal norms.

4. Notwithstanding full adult franchise from the outset, participation has been gradual and more easily assimilable without disturbing the center excessively. Linguistic communities; mobilization of low caste communities and of OBCs; the emergence of regional parties (which counted more on the 'backward castes' to whom the Congress had paid insufficient attention); and the advent even of Hindu nationalists: all this happened incrementally, as it were, and allowed absorption of these various constituencies into the national mainstream. Reservations allowed middling and lower castes a political voice.
5. India retained civil society & state institutions that have provided stability. Two that come to mind are the Supreme Court and the Electoral Commission. The same Supreme Court that sentenced Mohammed Afzal to death, notwithstanding the failure of the state to produce decisive evidence against the condemned man, also acquitted other men for want of evidence.
6. Strong people's and grassroots movements – dalit, ecological, women's movements, among others – have persisted and flourished.
7. A strong and, on the whole, independent press has characterized the history of independent India, though doubtless there are many stories to be told about the capitulation and subservience of the press to the state and more recently to corporate interests. Even if the press has often been a bulwark of support to élites, the vigilance of the English-language press during the anti-Muslim pogrom in Gujarat in 2002, to take one example, cannot be denied.
8. One should not understate important legislative gains for ordinary people, including the passage of the National Rural Employment Guarantee Act, the Forest People's Land Rights Bill, the Right to Information Act, and the Protection of Women from Domestic Violence Act. One can argue this even while conceding that progressive legislation, for example on the practice of dowry, can coexist alongside a resolute determination to prevent its implementation. The law can obfuscate problems as much as it can help to relieve them, an outcome all but assured when the state has no substantive commitment to the idea of an open society and distributive

equality. One can also identify other problems with such legislation: it has been said that something like 90 percent of the requests filed under the Right to Information Act emanate from institutions and employees of the state, and more often than not such interests stem from nothing more substantial than the attempt of an employee to find out the salaries of other employees. Ultimately, however, arguments against legislation that in principle is progressive are not easily sustained.

9. In the wisdom of the Indian people is the first source of India's renewal. Time after time the illiterate electorates of India have shown better judgment than the educated. The poor are more committed to the ballot box in India than the elites; in the modern West, such as the US, it is the other way around. The ruling party was thrown out in 1977, 1980, and in several elections since then, including the election of 2004.
10. The Constitution of India remains, despite attempts to subvert its emancipatory provisions, a document and a vision that continues to hold out the promise of equality, justice, and opportunity. It has survived the wreckage of an authoritarian executive and will outlive the Supreme Court's present disposition to allow massive land grabs in the name of progress and development.
11. Though Mohandas Gandhi's assassins never seem to rest, the spectre of Gandhi remains to haunt, guide, and inspire Indians who are resistant to everything that passes for "normal politics" and have not entirely succumbed to the oppressions of modernity. As I have elsewhere written, Gandhi took great risks and was not in the least cowed down by history, the sanctity of traditions, or scriptural authority. There is something ineffable in all this; the place of Gandhi's long shadowy presence in politics is hard to document.
12. The relationship of Sanskritization to democracy needs much further thought. The middle class phenomenon is less important as a phenomenon in absolute numbers than it is as a sign to the poor that their aspirations to enter into the mainstream of democratic life might yet bear fruit.
13. The intellectual class in India – comprised not merely of academics, but of writers, filmmakers, public intellectuals, and others — survived the onslaught of colonialism better

than did intellectual classes in most other colonized societies. It may have to do, in part, with the insularity, secretiveness, and esotericism of Brahmin life and networks.

14. Hinduism itself, I suspect, has facilitated the pluralist nature of the Indian polity. The attempt has been to turn Hindus into the proper religious subjects of a proper nation-state, but the fundamental anarchy of Hinduism resists such attempt. On the other hand, one can argue that the caste system is intrinsically hierarchical and oppressive. This subject needs much further inquiry.
15. The cultural and intellectual project of achieving the nation-state was taken rather seriously in India from the outset of independence, taking a leaf here from colonialism's epistemological projects. Let us think of state institutions such as the Akademis (Sahitya, Lalit Kala, Sangeet Natak), the ICHR, the state-sponsored histories, and so on; on the other hand, let us not forget the place of Hindi-language cinema. (This is also quite clearly seen in the Indian diaspora.)

In thinking about Indian democracy and its future prospects, commentators have lavished far too much attention on "politics" in the narrowest conception of the term. There is much speculation, for example, on whether India might move towards a two-party system or some variation of it, with the Congress and the left parties constituting one bloc and the other bloc being constituted by BJP and its allies.

But this kind of scenario has little room for parties such as the Bahujan Samaj Party (BSP) and the Samajwadi Party (SP), which together dominate politics in Uttar Pradesh, where efforts by the Congress to reinvent itself do not hold much promise of success. In the General Elections of 2004, the Left Front won 60 seats and came to hold the decisive swing vote. While so far the left has show little inclination to revolt, and West Bengal is rapidly retooling itself to become attractive to the corporate world and foreign investors, the possibility of genuine and irreconcilable differences developing between the Congress and the Left Front can never be entirely ignored.

Certainly, if the persistent invocations of the "new India", the roaring economy, and the entrepreneurial and aggressively capitalist spirit of India are any guide, at least the Indian middle classes have signified their assent to the idea that an economic rather than a political conception of democracy will drive the Indian future.

## Role of Political Parties

As with any other democracy, political parties represent different sections among the Indian society and regions, and their core values play a major role in the politics of India. Both the executive branch and the legislative branch of the government are run by the representatives of the political parties who have been elected through the elections. Through the electoral process, the people of India choose which representative and which political party should run the government. Through the elections any party may gain simple majority in the lower house. Coalitions are formed by the political parties, in case no single party gains a simple majority in the lower house. Unless a party or a coalition have a majority in the lower house, a government cannot be formed by that party or the coalition.

India has a multi-party system, where there are a number of national as well as regional parties. A regional party may gain a majority and rule a particular state. If a party is represented in more than 4 states, it would be labelled a national party. Out of the 66 years of India's independence, India has been ruled by the Indian National Congress (INC) for 53 of those years.

The party enjoyed a parliamentary majority save for two brief periods during the 1970s and late 1980s. This rule was interrupted between 1977 to 1980, when the Janata Party coalition won the election owing to public discontent with the controversial state of emergency declared by the then Prime Minister Indira Gandhi. The Janata Dal won elections in 1989, but its government managed to hold on to power for only two years.

Between 1996 and 1998, there was a period of political flux with the government being formed first by the nationalist Bharatiya Janata Party (BJP) followed by a left-leaning United Front coalition. In 1998, the BJP formed the National Democratic Alliance with smaller regional parties, and became the first non-INC and coalition government to complete a full five-year term. The 2004 Indian elections saw the INC winning the largest number of seats to form a government leading the United Progressive Alliance, and supported by left-parties and those opposed to the BJP.

On 22 May 2004, Manmohan Singh was appointed the Prime Minister of India following the victory of the INC & the left front in the 2004 Lok Sabha election. The UPA ruled India without the support of the left front. Previously, Atal Bihari Vajpayee had taken office in October 1999 after a general election in which a BJP-led coalition of

13 parties called the National Democratic Allianceemerged with a majority. In May 2014, Narendra Modi of BJP was elected as Prime Minister of India.

Formation of coalition governments reflects the transition in Indian politics away from the national parties toward smaller, more narrowly based regional parties. Some regional parties, especially in South India, are deeply aligned to the ideologies of the region unlike the national parties and thus the relationship between the central government and the state government in various states has not always been free of rancor. Disparity between the ideologies of the political parties ruling the centre and the state leads to severely skewed allocation of resources between the states.

## MAJOR CHALLENGES BEFORE INDIAN DEMOCRACY

The lack of homogeneity in the Indian population causes division between different sections of the people based on religion, region, language, caste and race. This has led to the rise of political parties with agendas catering to one or a mix of these groups.

Some parties openly profess their focus on a particular group; for example, the Dravida Munnetra Kazhagam's and the All India Anna Dravida Munnetra Kazhagam's focus on the Dravidian population, and the Shiv Sena's pro-Marathi agenda. Some other parties claim to be universal in nature, but tend to draw support from particular sections of the population. For example, the Rashtriya Janata Dal(translated as National People's Party) has a vote bank among the Yadav and Muslim population of Bihar and the All India Trinamool Congress does not have any significant support outside West Bengal.

The narrow focus and votebank politics of most parties, even in the central government and central legislature, sidelines national issues such as economic welfare and national security. Moreover, internal security is also threatened as incidences of political parties instigating and leading violence between two opposing groups of people is a frequent occurrence.

Economic issues like poverty, unemployment, development are main issues that influence politics. *Garibi hatao* (eradicate poverty) has been a slogan of the Indian National Congress for a long time. The well known Bharatiya Janata Party encourages a free market economy. The Communist Party of India (Marxist) vehemently supports leftwingpolitics like land-for-all, right to work and strongly opposes neo-liberal policies such as globalization, capitalism and privatization.

Terrorism, Naxalism, religious violence and caste-related violence are important issues that affect the political environment of the Indian nation. Stringent anti-terror legislation such as TADA, POTA and MCOCA have received much political attention, both in favour and opposed.

Terrorism had effected politics India since its conception, be it the terrorism supported from Pakistan or the internal guerrilla groups such as Naxalites. In 1991 the former prime minister Rajiv Gandhi was assassinated during an election campaign. The suicide bomber was later linked to the Sri Lankan terrorist group Liberation Tigers of Tamil Eelam, as it was later revealed the killing was an act of vengeance for Rajiv Gandhi sending troops in Sri Lanka against them in 1987.

The Babri Masjid demolition on December 6, 1992 by Hindu Karsevaks resulted in nation-wide communal riots in two months, with worst occurring in Mumbai with at least 900 dead. The riots were followed by 1993 Mumbai Bomb Blasts, which resulted in more deaths.

Law and order issues, such as action against organised crime are issues which do not affect the outcomes of elections. On the other hand, there is a criminal–politician nexus. Many elected legislators have criminal cases against them. In July 2008, the *Washington Post* reported that nearly a fourth of the 540 Indian Parliament members faced criminal charges, "including human trafficking, immigration rackets, embezzlement, rape and even murder".

## ECONOMY AND DEMOCRACY

As the new government is formed, there will be a burst of competing prescriptions about the best way forward to intensify reform with a primary focus on gross domestic product growth that is somehow 'inclusive'.

Instead, what is needed is a reflection, and introspection, on the first principles of economic democracy as outlined above.

An explosion of material aspirations is posing new challenges to Indian democracy.

Beneath all the outrage about crony capitalism, inept governance and absent jobs is an unrest that arises from a fundamental mismatch between the economic and political sphere.

While the Indian government can blame the euro crisis for contributing to the slowdown, the current mess is largely self-inflicted. The first wave of privatisation and deregulation, begun nearly twenty years ago, has largely run its course. But the coalition government, pulled by conflicting interests and lacking clear leadership, has not pushed significant new reforms to liberalise the economy. Even in instances where it manages to reach a decision, pressure from smaller allies often causes it to rollback policies. The U-turn on opening the country's retail sector to international competition is a case in point.

Beyond the policy paralysis, the country has another problem: a growing debt burden. The Indian government's debt stands at nearly 70% of GDP and its fiscal deficit is 5.9% of GDP, up from 4.8% a year ago. Public debt in itself isn't bad, especially when private investment is low and growth is faltering. The numbers also seem manageable when compared to those in the euro zone. But in the context of India's economy it raises some questions.

First, increases in government spending aren't driven by investments needed for long-term growth. Instead, a third of the government's expenditure is spent on interest payments and subsidies. A poor country like India needs social programmes to provide basic necessities to a large number of its citizens. But there is very little evidence that subsidies on fuel and electricity actually benefit the poor. Controlled fuel prices seem largely driven by political considerations.

The continued support of loss-making state-owned enterprises (SOEs) is also hard to justify. Consider Air India, the poster-child for this policy. The state-run airline has floundered for years due to mismanagement and labour troubles. Yet the government continues to pump billions of dollars to bail out the carrier. It recently announced plans to inject $5.8 billion into Air India over the next eight years. A similar story repeats in other sectors of the economy: inefficient SOEs continue to devour public funds, at the expense of private competitors. Protection of public-sector jobs trumps any economic rationale.

This spending binge is not only misallocating resources, but also crowding-out private-sector credit. Over the coming year, the government will borrow around $110 billion to fund its revenue shortfall; it plans to front load most of the borrowing in the first six months. Since Indian banks are required to hold government notes, the success of the bond sale is guaranteed. But India's financial system isn't deep enough to absorb demand from this huge borrowing programme. Consequently, borrowing rates for the private sector may increase. Companies may also look overseas to fund their operations, exposing them to currency risk with a volatile rupee.

Unfortunately, the situation isn't likely to improve anytime soon. In the parliament no single party has a clear mandate and the largest party, Congress, is beholden to smaller regional allies for majority. Welfare programmes and populist policies that appeal to their base guarantee the support of these parties. As the government is more concerned with short-term survival, any difficult decisions are put on the back burner.

That is a shame. Continued growth promises to lift millions of Indians out of poverty. But this requires the country's leaders to take a long view and think beyond the next election cycle. Under the current electoral arithmetic, that seems unlikely.

## References

Athreya, Venkatesh B.; Lindberg D.S. (1990) Barriers Broken: Production Relations and Agrarian Change in Tamil Nadu. New Delhi: Sage.

Ahmad, Imtiaz. *State and Foreign Policy: India's Role in South Asia*. New Delhi: Vikas, 1993.

Ali, Tariq. *An Indian Dynasty: The Story of the Nehru-Gandhi Family*. New York: Putnam, 1985.

Ashton, S.R. *British Policy Towards the Indian States, 1905-1939*. London Studies on South Asia, No. 2. London: Curzon, 1982.

Austin, Granville. *The Indian Constitution: Cornerstone of a Nation*. Oxford: Clarendon Press, 1966.

Baird, Robert. *Religion in Modern India*. New Delhi: Manohar, 1981.

Baker, Christopher J. *An Indian Rural Economy: The Tamiland Countryside*. Oxford: Clarendon Press, 1984.

Baker, Christopher J. *The Politics of South India, 1920-1937*. Cambridge: Cambridge University Press, 1976.

Brecher, Michael. *Nehru: A Political Biography*. London: Oxford University Press, 1959.

Brecher, Michael. *The Politics of Succession in India*. Westport, Connecticut: Greenwood, 1976.

Brown, Judith M. *Gandhi and Civil Disobedience*. London: Cambridge University Press, 1977.

Brown, Judith M. *Modern India: The Origins of an Asian Democracy*. New Delhi: Oxford University Press, 1985.

15

# A Historical Analysis of the Making of the Indian Constitution

**DR MANBIR SINGH**
*Associate Professor, Department of History, M.B( PG) College, Dadri, Gautam Budha, Nagar, Uttar Pradesh.*

The East India Company had established its control over almost all parts of India by the middle of the 19th century. There were numerous risings in the first hundred years of British rule in India. They were, however, local and isolated in character. Some of them were led by the nobility who were refusing to accept the changing patterns of the time and wanted the past to be restored. But the risings developed a tradition of resistance offoreign rule, culminating in the 1857 revolt.

The Revolt of 1857, which was called a Sepoy Mutiny by British historians and their imitators in India but described as "the First War of Indian Independence" by many Indian historians, shook the British authority in India from its very foundations.

The Revolt of 1857, an unsuccessful but heroic effort to eliminate foreign rule, had begun. The capture of Delhi and the proclamation of Bahadurshah as the Emperor of Hindustan are a positive meaning to the Revolt and provided a rallying point for the rebels by recalling the past glory of the imperial city.

On May 10, 1857, soldiers at Meerut refused to touch the new Enfield rifle cartridges. The soldiers along with other group of civilians, went on a rampage shouting 'Maro Firangi Ko'. They broke open jails, murdered European men and women, burnt their houses and marched to Delhi. The appearance of the marching soldiers next morning in Delhi was a'signal to the local soldiers, who in turn revolted, seized the city and proclaimed the 80-year old Bahadurshah Zafar, as Emperor of India. Within a month of the capture of Delhi, the Revolt spread to the different parts of the country. Kanpur, Lucknow, Benaras, Allahabad, Bareilly, Jagdishpur and Jhansi. In the absence of any leader from their own ranks, the insurgents turned to the traditional leaders of Indian society. At Kanpur, NanaSaheb, the adopted son of last Peshwa, Baji Rao II, led the forces. Rani Lakshmi Bai in Jhansi, Begum Hazrat Mahal in Lucknow and. Khan Bahadur in Bareilly were in command. However, apart from a commonly shared hatred for alien rule, the rebels had no political perspective or a definite vision of the future. They were all prisoners of their own past, fighting primarily to regain their lost privileges. Unsurprisingly, they proved incapable of ushering in a new political order.

## FORMATION OF INDIAN NATIONAL CONGRESS

The Indian National Congress was founded in the year 1885. The first session of Congress was presided over by Womesh Chandra Banerjee who was also elected as the first president of Indian National Congress party. Around seventy reputed delegates that included educationalists, lawyers, journalists etc. attended the first session of the congress when it was established. The Indian national congress was considered to be a royal party when it was established. Read on about the history of Indian National Congress.

The Indian National Congress had the following aims and objectives when it was established:

- Inculcate a feeling of national unity and try to eradicate the notion of race, creed and provincial prejudices.
- Seek the cooperation of all the Indians in its efforts and allow them to take part in the administrative affairs of the country.
- Find a solution to the social problems of the country.

The Indian National Congress had a royal air about it which faded as time passed by.

Though the Congress was made to improve India, the Muslims were opposed to the party. Muslim leaders like Sir Syed Ahmed Khan and Syed Ameer Ali got invitation to attend the conference when congress party was established but they refused. They also told other Muslims to abstain from joining the party. He predicted that Congress would become a party dominated by the Hindus. The Congress party was broadly divided among two types of members-the conservatives and the leftists. The former had a cautious approach towards the policies while the latter were more into socialism. During the moderate phase of the congress they were extremely loyal to the British but with time the party entered the extremist phase and expressed its displeasure in the policies of the British.

## INDIAN NATIONAL MOVEMENT (1917–1947)

The third and final phase of the Nationalist Movement [1917-1947] is known as the Gandhian era. During this period Mahatma Gandhi became the undisputed leader of the National Movement. His principles of nonviolence and Satyagraha were employed against the British Government.

Gandhi made the nationalist movement a mass movement. Mohandas Karamchand Gandhi was born at Porbandar in Gujarat on 2 October 1869. He studied law in England. He returned to India in 1891. In April 1893 he went to South Africa and involved himself in the struggle against apartheid (Racial discrimination against the Blacks) for twenty years.

Finally, he came to India in 1915. Thereafter, he fully involved himself in the Indian National Movement. Mahatma Gandhi began his experiments with Satyagraha against the oppressive European indigo planters at Champaran in Bihar in 1917.

In the next year he launched another Satyagraha at Kheda in Gujarat in support of the peasants who were not able to pay the land tax due to failure of crops. During this struggle, Sardar Vallabhai Patel emerged as one of the trusted followers of Gandhi.

In 1918, Gandhi undertook a fast unto death for the cause of Ahmedabad Mill Workers and finally the mill owners conceded the just demands of the workers. On the whole, the local movements at Champaran, Kheda and Ahmedabad brought Mahatma Gandhi closer to the life of the people and their problems at the grass roots level. Consequently, he became the leader of the masses.

### The Non Co-operation Movement

This movement lasted from September 1920 to February 1922.The Non Cooperation Movement in India was the first of the three major movements carried out by Gandhi. The movement was started with the thought in mind that the British rule had lasted in India only because of the cooperation by Indians. If Indians refused to cooperate then India would gain Independence. The Movement soon caught national attention and millions joined the movement. People left their offices, jobs, factories or any other business which cooperated the

British. People forced their children out of the government schools and colleges. The failure of these movements made many people poor, uneducated and illiterate due to withdrawal from government offices, schools, factories and services. The name of Mahatma Gandhi began spreading around. People started following him in all parts of the country. However, the movement could not continue as anticipated by Mahatma because of the incident of Chauri Chaurah. He had hoped for a nationwide peaceful and non-violent movement.

## The Chauri Chaurah incident

In 1922, there was a mob violence at Chauri Chaurah, Uttar Pradesh in which the people burned a police station and killed 22 policemen. It happened because when a group of people were demonstrating peacefully the police had fired upon them which stirred the people to attack. Because of this violent incident Mahatma Gandhi had to stop the Non Cooperation Movement.

## Swaraj Party And Simon Commission (1927)

The suspension of the Non-Cooperation Movement led to a split within Congress in the Gaya session of the Congress in December 1922. Leaders like Motilal Nehru and Chittranjan Das formed a separate group within the Congress known as the Swaraj Party on 1 January 1923.

The Swarajists wanted to contest the council elections and wreck the government from within. Elections to Legislative Councils were held in November 1923. In this, the Swaraj Party gained impressive successes. In the Central Legislative Council Motilal Nehru became the leader of the party whereas in Bengal the party was headed by C.R. Das. The Swaraj Party did several significant things in the Legislative Council. It demanded the setting up of responsible government in India with the necessary changes in the Government of India Act of 1919. The party could pass important resolutions against the repressive laws of the government.

When a Committee chaired by the Home Member, Alexander Muddiman considered the system of Dyarchy as proper, a resolution was passed against it in the Central Legislative Council. After the passing away of C.R. Das in June 1925, the Swarj Party started weakening.

The Act of 1919 included a provision for its review after a lapse of ten years. However, the review commission was appointed by the

British Government two years earlier of its schedule in 1927. It came to be known as Simon Commission after the name of its chairman, Sir John Simon.

All its seven members were Englishmen. As there was no Indian member in it, the Commission faced a lot of criticism even before its landing in India. Almost all the political parties including the Congress decided to oppose the Commission.

On the fateful day of 3 February 1928 when the Commission reached Bombay, a general hartal was observed all over the country. Everywhere it was greeted with black flags and the cries of 'Simon go back'. At Lahore, the students took out a large anti-Simon Commission demonstration on 30 October 1928 under the leadership of Lala Lajpat Rai.

In this demonstration, Lala Lajpat Rai was seriously injured in the police lathi charge and he passed away after one month. The report of the Simon Commission was published in May 1930. It was stated that the constitutional experiment with Dyarchy was unsuccessful and in its place the report recommended the establishment of autonomous government.

There is no doubt that the Simon Commission's Report became the basis for enacting the Government of India Act of 1935.

## THE DANDI MARCH OR THE SALT SATYAGRAHA

The Salt Satyagraha was started by Mahatma Gandhi on 12 March 1930 from Sabarmati Ashram to 5 April till Dandi, Gujarat where he manufactured Salt, broke the Salt Law and started a nationwide Civil disobedience. The Salt March, also known as the Salt Satyagraha, began on 12 March 1930 and was an important part of the Indian independence movement. It was a direct action campaign of tax resistance and non violent protest against the British salt monopoly in colonial India, and triggered the wider Civil Disobedience Movement. This was the most significant organised challenge to British authority since the Non-cooperation movement of 1920–22, and directly followed the Purna Swaraj declaration of independence by the Indian National Congress on 26 January 1930.

Mohandas Karamchand Gandhi (commonly called Mahatma Gandhi) led the march from his base, Sabarmati Ashram near Ahmedabad, to the coastal village of Dandi, located at a small town called Navsari, in the state of Gujarat. As he continued on his 24-day, 240-mile (390 km) march to Dandi to produce salt without paying the tax, growing number of Indians joined him along the way; Initially with 78 volunteers it ended up in thousands. When Gandhi broke the salt laws at 6:30 am on 5 April 1930, it sparked large scale acts of civil disobedience against the British Raj salt laws by millions of Indians. The campaign had a significant effect on changing the world and British attitude towards Indian independence and caused large numbers of Indians to join the fight for independece for the first time.

After making salt at Dandi, Gandhi continued southward along the coast, producing salt and addressing meetings on the way. The Congress Party planned to stage a satyagraha at the Dharasana Salt Works, 25 miles south of Dandi. However, Gandhi was arrested on the midnight of 4–5 May 1930, just days before the planned action at Dharasana. The Dandi March and the ensuing Dharasana Satyagraha drew worldwide attention to the Indian independence movement through extensive newspaper and newsreel coverage. The satyagraha against the salt tax continued for almost a year, ending with Gandhi's release from jail and negotiations with Viceroy Lord Irwin at the Second Round Table Conference. Over 80,000 Indians were jailed as a result of the Salt Satyagraha. However, it failed to result in major concessions from the British.

The Salt Satyagraha campaign was based upon Gandhi's principles of nonviolent protest called satyagraha, which he loosely translated as "truth-force." Literally, it is formed from the Sanskrit words satya, "truth", and agraha, "force." In early 1930 the Indian National Congress chose satyagraha as their main tactic for winning Indian independence from British rule and appointed Gandhi to organise the campaign. Gandhi chose the 1882 British Salt Act as the first target of satyagraha. The Salt March to Dandi, and the beating by British police of hundreds of nonviolent protesters in Dharasana, which received worldwide news coverage, demonstrated the effective use of civil disobedience as a technique for fighting social and political injustice. The satyagraha teachings of Gandhi and the March to Dandi had a significant influence on American activists Martin Luther King, Jr., James Bevel, and others during the movement for civil rights for blacks and other minority groups in the 1960s.

## The Poona Act, The Second World War And National Movement

By 1930, Dr Ambedkar had become a leader of national stature championing the cause of the depressed people of the country. While presenting a real picture of the condition of these people in the First

Round Table Conference, he had demanded separate electorates for them. On 16 August 1932 the British Prime Minister Ramsay MacDonald made an announcement, which came to be as the Communal Award. According to this award, the depressed classes were considered as a separate community and as such provisions were made for separate electorates for them.

Mahatma Gandhi protested against the Communal Award and went on a fast unto death in the Yeravada jail on 20 September 1932. Finally, an agreement was reached between Dr Ambedkar and Gandhi. This agreement came to be called as the Poona Pact. The British Government also approved of it. Accordingly, 148 seats in different Provincial Legislatures were reserved for the Depressed Classes in place of 71 as provided in the Communal Award. The third Round Table Conference came to an end in 1932. The Congress once more did not take part in it. Nonetheless, in March 1933, the British Government issued a White Paper, which became the basis for the enactment of the Government of India Act, 1935.

### The Second World War And National Movement

In 1937 elections were held under the provisions of the Government of India Act of 1935. Congress Ministries were formed in seven states of India. On 1 September 1939 the Second World War broke out. The British Government without consulting the people of India involved the country in the war.

The Congress vehemently opposed it and as a mark of protest the Congress Ministries in the Provinces resigned on 12 December 1939. The Muslim League celebrated that day as the Deliverance Day. In March 1940 the Muslim League demanded the creation of Pakistan.

## THE QUIT INDIA MOVEMENT

The Quit India movement was the final of the three major nationalist movements in India. It was started in August, 1942 by M.K. Gandhi. Though the Quit India Movement collapsed within a very short time it will be a mistake to suppose that the movement was a total failure. Firstly, the movement revealed the determination of the people to undergo any amount of suffering for the cause of the country. Secondly, the popular character of the August Rebellion was revealed through the participation of students, working class and peasants. In the opinion of Sumit Sarkar, it was the participation of the peasant community that turned the movement into a mass upsurge. Thirdly, the 1942 Movement marked the end of Indias struggle for freedom and may be regarded as an apex of the freedom struggle. Fourthly, the violent mass upsurge of 1942 convinced the British ruler that their hold was sure to collapse in India sooner or later...

The nationalist movements failed in their primary objective, achieving independence for India, as they were often called off before they naturally concluded. However they sparked nationalist sentiment with the Indian populace, figures like MK Gandhi united a nation behind his non-violent philosophy and undoubtedly put crucial pressure on the British occupation.

While in the later years of the Raj economic factors like the reversing trade fortunes between Britain and India and the cost of fielding the Indian armed forces abroad lumped on the British tax payer by the 1935 Government of India act, had mounting implication for British administration, united resistance further drew light on the growing disparity of the British failures to achieve solidarity over India. Indeed Nationalist Movements in India were merely another notch on Britain's ever scarred grip over its Raj, faced with a magnitude of issues, Nationalist Movements attributed to but were not solely responsible for India's independence in 1947.

## Constitution

- Constitution is a legally sanctified document, considering of the basic governing principles of the State and sets out the framework and the principal functions of the organs of the Government of a State.
- There are various forms of Government prevalent across the world. Constitution of a country gives idea about the basic structure of the political system under which its people are to be governed.
- The idea of Constitutionalism suggests way and means to work out a governmental form, which exercises power and ensures, at the same time, individual freedom and liberty.
- Constitutionalism suggests a way for reconciling the power of the State with individual liberty, by prescribing the principles of organizing the State
- It defines the powers of the main organ of the State, demarcates their responsibilities and regular their relationships with each other and with the people.
- Constitution serves as the "Fundamental Law" of a country; any other laws made must be in conformity with it, in order to be legally endorsed.

## Significance of the Constitution

- The philosophy embodied in a nation's Constitution determines the kind of Government present there
- A Constitution outlines the vision of the State and is its most important document
- A Constitution ensure certain rights to its citizens as well as defines their duties.
- A Constitution is an expression of faith and hopes, that people have from the State, and the promises that they wish to make for the future.

### *Is the Constitution static?*

- A Constitution is an extension of the philosophical and organizational frameworks into the future.
- But a State has to face the challenges of changing social, economic and political conditions in the society
- All living constitutions provide for procedures for introducing changes in the them by means of amendments. So, the constitution is not static.

### *Written and Unwritten Constitutions*

- Constitutions of most countries came into existence as a result of a conscious decision to have such a document. These are the 'written' Constitution, which provide institutional arrangements and procedures.
- But, the laws and institutions of British Constitution have gradually evolved over the centuries. The British Constitution is an 'unwritten' Constitution. It comprises the constitutional conventions that act as precedents for the working of institutions and other documents such as the statutes and Acts of Parliament. Here the Parliament is supreme, unlike the 'written' Constitution where, the Constitution is supreme.
- In Britain, any change in the Constitution is possible by means of laws passed by the Parliament. There is no distinction between an ordinary law and a constitutional law. This is an example of the most flexible form of Constitution.

## Constitutional Developments

The Indian administrative structure is largely a legacy of the British rule. The various functional aspects such as public services, education system, political set-up, recruitment, training, office procedures, districts administration, local administration, police system, revenue administration, budgeting, auditing, and so on, have their roots in the British rule.

The British rule in India can be divided into two phases- the Company rule till 1858 and the Crown's rule from 1858 to 1947.

## Landmarks

The landmarks in the development of the Constitution are:
Milestones:

- 1687: The first Municipal Corporation in India was set up in Madras
- 1772: Lord Warren Hastings created the office of District Collector.
- 1829: The office of the Divisional Commissioner was created by Lord William Bentick.
- 1859: The portfolio system was introduced by Lord Canning.
- 1860: A system of Budget was introduced.
- 1870: Lord Mayo's resolution on financial decentralization visualized the development of local self-government institutions in India.
- 1872: First census in India was conducted during Lord Mayo's period.
- 1881: First regular census was conducted during the period of Lord Ripon.
- 1882: Lord Ripon's resolution was hailed as the 'Magna Carta' of local self government. He is regarded as the 'Father of local self-government in India'.
- 1905: The tenure system was introduced by Lord Curzen.
- 1905: The Railway Board was set up by a resolution of the Government of India.
- 1921: Public Accounts Committee was created at the Centre
- 1921: Railway Budget was separated from the General Budget.
- 1935: Reserve Bank of India was established by an Act of the Central Legislature.

## Regulating Act of 1773

This was the first step taken by the British Government to control and regulate the affairs of the East India Company in India.

- It designated the Governor of Bengal as the Governor-General of Bengal

- The first Governor-General was Lord Warren Hastings
- It subordinated the Governors of Bombay and Madras to the Governor-General of Bengal
- The Supreme Court was established at Fort William (Calcutta) as the Apex Court in 1774.

## Pitt's India Act of 1784

- It was introduced to remove the drawbacks of the Regulating Act.
- Was named after the then British Prime Minister.
- Placed the Indian affairs under the direct control of the British Government
- Established a Board of Control over the Court of Directors.

## Charter Act of 1833

- It made the Governor-General of Bengal as the Governor-General of India.
- First Governor-General of India was Lord William Bentick
- All civil and military powers were vested in him
- Governments of Bombay and Madras were deprived of their legislative powers
- This was the final step towards centralization in the British India.
- The Act ended the activities of the East India Company as a commercial body.

## Charter Act of 1853

- The legislative and executive functions of the Governor-General's Council were separated.
- It introduced a system of open competition as the basis for the recruitment of civil servants of the Company.

Government of India Act of 1858

- This Act transferred the Government, territories and revenues of India from the East India Company to the British Crown.
- In other words, the rule of Company was replaced by the rule of the Crown in India.
- The powers of the British Crown were to be exercised by the Secretary of State for India
- The Secretary of State was a member of the British Cabinet
- He was assisted by the Council of India, having 15 members

- He was vested with complete authority and control over the Indian administration through the Governor-General as his agent
- He was responsible ultimately to the British Parliament.
- The Governor-General was made the Viceroy of India.
- Lord Canning was the first Viceroy of India.

## Indian Council Act of 1861

- It introduced for the first time the repetitive institutions of India
- It provided that the Governor-General's Executive Council should have some Indians as the non-official members while transacting the legislative businesses.
- Initiated the process of decentralisation by restoring the legislative powers to the Bombay and the Madras President
- It accorded statutory recognition to the portfolio system.

## India Council Act of 1892

- Introduced the principle of elections but in an indirect manner
- Enlarge the functions of the Legislative Councils and gave them the power of discussing the Budget and addressing questions to the Executive.

## Indian Councils Act of 1909

- This Act is also known as the Morley- Minto Reforms (Lord Morley was the then Secretary of State for India and Lord Minto was the then Governor-General of India).
- It changed the name of the Central Legislative Council to the Imperial Legislative Council
- Introduced a system of communal representation for Muslims by accepting the concept of 'separate electorate'.
- Lord Minto came to be known as the 'Father of Communal Electorate'.

## Government of India Act of 1909

- This Act is also known as the Montague- Chelmsford Reforms.
- Montague was the then Secretary of State and lord Chelmsford was the then Governor-General of India.
- The Central subjects were demarcated and separated from those of the Provincial subjects

- The scheme of dual governance, 'Dyarchy', was introduced in the Provincial subjects
- The Act introduced, for the first time, bicameralism and direct elections in the country
- The Act also required that the three of the six members of the Governor-General's Council (other than Commander-in-Chief) were to be Indians.

## Government of India Act of 1935

- The Act provided for the establishment of an All-India Federation consisting of the Provinces and the Princely States as units
- The Act divided the powers between the Centre and the units in items of three lists, namely the Federal List, the Provincial List and the Concurrent List.
- The Federal List for the Centre consisted of 59 items, the Provincial List for the provinces consisted of 54 items and the Concurrent List for both consisted of 36 items
- The residuary powers were vested with the Governor-General.
- The Act abolished the Dyarchy in the Provinces and introduced 'Provincial Autonomy'.
- It provided for the adoption of Dyarchy at the Centre.
- Introduced bicameralism in 6 out of 11 Provinces.
- These six Provinces were Assam, Bengal, Bombay, Bihar, Madras and the United Province.

## Indian Independence Act of 1947

- Till 1947, the Government of India functioned under the provinces of the 1919 Act only. The provisions of 1935 Act relating to Federation and Dyarchy were never implemented.
- The Executive Council provided by the 1919 Act continued to advice the Governor-General till 1947.
- It declared India as an Independent and Sovereign State.
- Established responsible Governments at both the Centre and the Provinces.
- Designated the Governor-General of India and the provincial Governors as the Constitutional Heads(normal heads).
- It assigned dual functions (Constituent and Legislative) to the Constituent Assembly and declared this dominion legislature as a sovereign body.

## AMENDMENT OF THE CONSTITUTION OF INDIA

Amendment of the Constitution of India is the process of making changes to the Indian constitution. Such changes are made by the Parliament of India. They must be approved by a super-majority in each house of Parliament, and certain amendments must also be ratified by the states. The procedure is laid out in Part XX, Article 368 of the constitution.

Despite these rules there have been over ninety amendments to the constitution since it was enacted in 1950. The Indian Supreme Court has ruled, controversially, that not every constitutional amendment is permissible. An amendment must respect the "basic structure" of the constitution, which is immutable.

### Procedure

A proposed amendment begins in Parliament where it is introduced as a bill. It must then be approved by each House of Parliament. In each house it must be supported by (1) a two-thirds majority of those present and voting, and (2) a simple majority of all members (present or not). Certain amendments must then also be ratified by the legislatures of at least one-half of the states. Once all other stages have been completed an amendment receives the assent of the President of India, but this final stage is a formality.

Despite the super-majority requirement in the constitution it is one of the most frequently amended governing documents in the world; amendments have averaged about two a year. This partly because of length and detail of the constitution. It is the longest of any sovereign nation in the world, consisting of over 390 articles and 117,000 words. The document is very specific in spelling out government powers and so amendments are often required to deal with matters that could be addressed by ordinary statutes in other countries.

Another reason is that the Parliament of India is elected by means of single seat districts, under the plurality (or "first past the post") system used in the United Kingdom and the U.S. This means that it is possible for a group of MPs to win two-thirds of the seats in Parliament without securing two-thirds of the vote.

For example in the first two elections held under the constitution the Indian National Congress party won less than one half of the national vote but roughly two-thirds of seats in the Lok Sabha (lower house). In India every constitutional amendment is formulated as a statute.

The first amendment is called the "Constitution (First Amendment) Act", the second, the "Constitution (Second Amendment) Act", and so forth. Each usually has the long title "An Act further to amend the Constitution of India".

## SUBJECT OF AMENDMENTS

### Fundamental Rights

The most important and frequent reason for amendments to the Constitution is the curtailment of the Fundamental Rights charter. This is achieved by inserting laws contrary to the fundamental rights provisions into Schedule 9 of the Constitution. Schedule 9 protects such laws by making them open only to limited judicial review.

The typical areas of restriction include laws relating to property rights, affirmative action in favour of minority groups such as "scheduled castes", "scheduled tribes" and other "backward classes". In a landmark ruling in January 2007 the Supreme Court of India confirmed that all laws (including those in Schedule 9) would be open to judicial review if they violate the basic structure of the constitution. Chief Justice Yogesh Kumar Sabharwal noted "If laws put in the Ninth Schedule abridge or abrogate fundamental rights resulting in violation of the basic structure of the constitution, such laws need to be invalidated".

### Territorial Changes

Constitutional amendments have been made to facilitate changes in the territory of India due to incorporation of the former French Colony of Pondicherry, the former Portugese Colony of Goa and a minor exchange of territories with Pakistan. Amendments are also necessary with regard to littoral rights over the exclusive economic zone of 200 miles and the formation of new states and union territories by the reorganization of existing states.

### Transitional Provisions

The constitution includes transitional provisions intended only to remain in force for a limited period. These need to be renewed periodically. Amendments to continue reservation in parliamentary seats for scheduled castes and tribes is extended every ten years. The President of India's rule was imposed in Punjab for an extended period of time in blocks of six months until the Khalistan Movement and insurgency subsided.

## Democratic Reform

Amendments have been made with the intent of reform the system of government and incorporating new "checks and balances" in the constitution. These have included the:

- Creation of the National Commission for Scheduled Castes.
- Creation of the National Commission for Scheduled Tribes.
- Creation of mechanisms for *Panchayati Raj* (local self governance).
- Disqualification of members from changing party allegiance.
- Restrictions on the size of the cabinet.
- Restrictions on imposition of an internal emergency.

## Text of Article 368

*The following is the full text of Part XX or Article 368 of the constitution, which governs constitutional amendments. The provisions in* italics *were inserted by the Forty-second Amendment Act but have been declared invalid by the Supreme Court in the* Minerva Mills *case. The text is up-to-date as of July 2008.*

(1) Notwithstanding anything in this Constitution, Parliament may in exercise of its constituent power amend by way of addition, variation or repeal any provision of this Constitution in accordance with the procedure laid down in this article.

(2) An amendment of this Constitution may be initiated only by the introduction of a Bill for the purpose in either House of Parliament, and when the Bill is passed in each House by a majority of the total membership of that House and by a majority of not less than two-thirds of the members of that House present and voting, it shall be presented to the President who shall give his assent to the Bill and thereupon the Constitution shall stand amended in accordance with the terms of the Bill: Provided that if such amendment seeks to make any change in –

(a) article 54, article 55, article 73, article 162 or article 241, or

(b) Chapter IV of Part V, Chapter V of Part VI, or Chapter I of Part XI, or

(c) any of the Lists in the Seventh Schedule, or

(d) the representation of States in Parliament, or

(e) the provisions of this article, the amendment shall also require to be ratified by the Legislatures of not less than one-half of the States by resolutions to that effect passed by those Legislatures before the Bill making provision for such amendment is presented to the President for assent.

(3) Nothing in article 13 shall apply to any amendment made under this article.

(4) *No amendment of this Constitution (including the provisions of Part III) made or purporting to have been made under this article whether before or after the commencement of section 55 of the Constitution (Fortysecond Amendment) Act, 1976 shall be called in question in any court on any ground.*

(5) *For the removal of doubts, it is hereby declared that there shall be no limitation whatever on the constituent power of Parliament to amend by way of addition, variation or repeal the provisions of this Constitution under this article.*

The wording of Section (1) resembles Article 46 of the Constitution of Ireland, enacted in 1937, which states "Any provision of this Constitution may be amended, whether by way of variation, addition, or repeal, in the manner provided by this Article".

## References

Austin, Granville: *The Indian Constitution: Cornerstone of a Nation*, Oxford, Clarendon Press, 1966.

Charles Howard McIlwain: *Constitutionalism: Ancient and Modern,* N.Y., Cornell University Press, 1958.

Francis, E.: *Bureaucratic Power in National Politics,* Boston, Little Brown and Company, 1978.

Friedrich, J.: *Constitutional Government and Democracy,* Boston, Ginn, 1950.

Kenneth C. Wheare: *Modern Constitutions*, New York, Oxford University Press, 1951.

Morris, W.H.: *The Government and Politics of India,* London, Hutchinson, 1971.

Rourke, E.: *Bureaucratic Power in National Politics,* Boston, Little Brown and Company, 1978.

Uphoff, N.: *Local Organizations: Intermediaries in Rural Development,* Ithaca, Cornell University Press, 1984.

# 16

# The Salient Features and the Core Philosophy of the Indian Constitution

**DR. ALKA TOMAR**
*Associate Professor, Department of Political Science, B.S.M. (PG) College, Roorkee, Uttarakhand*

## ATTITUDE OF THE CONSTITUENT ASSEMBLY

Divergent views and attitudes were seen in the framing of Indian Constitution. The members of the Constituent Assembly had a variety of perceptions about the future Indian polity. Their divergent views on the major issue of the political system Were quite interesting.

### Adult Franchise

Should adult franchise be introduced, involving an increase in the electorate from 35 million to 170 million? Maulana Azad advocated its deferment for 15 years. Prasad and Nehru plumped for adult franchise as an act of faith. The vote favouring it was carried amidst acclamation.

### Jammu and Kashmir

Nehru favoured incorporation of a section establishing a special relatioI;lship with the state of Jammu and Kashmir, thus inferentially recognising the state's right to frame its own constitution within the Indian Union. Patel wanted the state to be fully integrated with the Union.

The "Cabinet was divided on the issue and the trend in the Constituent Assembly favoured Sardar's stand. But when the matter came before the Assembly, Patelput the unity and solidarity of the, Government before everything else and backed the Nehru formula.

## Reservation for Minorities

The most delicate issue related to safeguards for minorities. Azad wanted reservation of seats for the Muslims and other minorities within the framework of general electorates. Patel opposed such safeguards. Nehru left it to Patel to jump the hurdle as Chairman of the Advisory Committee on Minorities. Two women members played a key role in this high-strung drama. Amrit Kaur, speaking for the Indian Christians, said that reservation of seats and weightage based on religion or sect would lead to fragmentation of the Indian Union. The Sikhs demanded the same treatment as given to the Muslims..

After the Committee had-wrestled with the problem for weeks, Patel decided to clinch the issue at its final meeting. He called on Begum Aizaz Rasul of Lucknow to state the Muslim view. She was a zealous leader of Muslim League before partition and had even gone to the length of giving up Saree and adopting the costume worn by the Begums of Oudh. The Muslims left behind. in India, she said nervously, were an integral part of the nation and needed no safeguards.. Patel seized this crucial movement to declare that the Muslims-were unanimously in favour of joint electorates and adjourned the meeting.

## Office of the President and Governors

Much heat was generated on whether the President of the Republic and Governors of the Constituent States should be elected by popular vote and whether they should have discretionary powers. Legal luminaries and constitutional experts had a field day, but Nehru and Patel brought a practical approach to bear on the issue. They opposed popularly elected heads. Indeed, Nehru as Prime Minister took steps to see that; the Union President even though chosen by an electoral college consisting of all the members of the Central and State Legislatures, would be a constitutional figure head. Patel as Home Minister made sure that Governor of a State was the nominee of the Union Government and had enough discretionary powers to act as the executive agent of the Centre in an emergency.

## Link Language

The question of a national link language posed the most difficult hurdle. Swami Dayanand and Mahatma Gandhi, both from Gujarat and Tilak and Savarkar, from Maharashtra had zealously pleaded for Hindi as the symbol of nationhood. Prasad and Patel strongly supported Hindi, while Nehru left it to the Hindi lobby to work out a formula acceptable to the non-Hindi regions, especially Madras and Bengal. Finally, the formula providing for replacement of English by Hindi in fifteen years was embodied in the Constitution, along with each side did it with mental reservation.

## Fundamental Rights

A great deal of excitement caused over the issue; should the Fundamental Right to be embodied in the Constitution guarantee fair payment for private property acquired by the state and should the right be made justiciable? Nehru was against making the right justiciable. Patel stood rocklike for the Fundamental Rights adopted by the Congress Party under his Presidentship in 1931 in Karachi. After a prolonged tug-of-war Patel won because he had the backing of the distinguished lawyers, who were fashioning the Constitution, and of the overwhelming majority of members of the Constituent Assembly.

## Secular State

Another issue which the Assembly faced was about secular or non-secular character of the Constitution. There was a strong view point that after the partition of country secularism had no meaning. If the Muslims all over the world can have theocratic state, where they could preach and propagate their own faith, then why the Hindus of India cannot have their own Hindu State. On the other hand, there was predominantly Congress section in the Assembly which firmly believed that India should be a secular state.

## Socialism

It was principally Patel's conservative influence that kept the Constitution from having a greater socialist content than it has; perhaps it was in deference to his wishes that Nehru omitted the world 'socialism' from the Objective Resolutions.

## Village Panchayat

The word Panchayat did not once appear in the Draft Constitution. Within a few months a reaction to this omission set in as Assembly members had time to consider the Draft. President Prasad was the most prominent among the critics. On 10 May, 1948, Prasad wrote to B. N. Rau that "I like the idea of making the Constitution begin with the village and go up to the Centre. The village has been and will ever continue to be our unit in this country." Prasad believed that the necessary articles could be redrafted, making the village Panchayats the electoral college for electing representatives to the Provinces and the Centre. But Rau rejected Prasad's suggestion. In his reply Rau said that the Assembly had already decided on direct election of Lower Houses both at the Centre and the Provinces and that he was doubtful. If the vote could be reversed a remark that indicated the general popularity of a Parliamentary constitution.

## The Constituent Assembly (Legislative)

When the Assembly met for purposes of ordinary law-making it was called the Legislative wing of the Constituent Assembly or the Constituent Assembly (Legislative), Presided over by the Speaker, it functioned as the Legislature of the country with the secretariat of the pre-independence Legislative Assembly as its Secretariat. The first meeting of the first session of the Constituent Assembly (Legislative) was held in the Assembly Chamber of the Council House (now called the Lok Sabha-Chamber of the Parliament House) on November 17,1947 at-!1 a.m. with the I president of the. Constituent Assembly in the chair. G. V Mavalankar was declared duly elected for the office of the Speaker. Dr. Rajendra Prasad vacated the chair which was then occupied by Speaker Mavalankar.

The Constituent Assembly in its capacity as Dominion Legislature was in existence for nearly two years and one month. Between November 17, 1947 and December 24, 1949 it had in all six sessions consisting of 226 days.

The Constituent Assembly was able to conclude its labours within a period of less than three years-2 years, 11 months and 17 days, to be exact. On the 46th November, 1949, it could proudly declare on behalf of the people of India that "'We do hereby adopt, enact and give to ourselves this Constitution." It embodied all the objectives of democracy, secularism and economic and social justice. In a sense, the Indian Constituent Assembly occupied a peculiar position.

## Salient Features

The Constitution of a country, in simple terms, is a collection of the legal rules providing the framework for the government of the country. It reflects the dominant beliefs and interests or some compromise between conflicting beliefs and interests, which are characteristic of the society at the time it was framed and adopted.

No Constitution is perfect and the Constitution of India is no exception to this general rule. But It goes to the credit of India that the urge for constitutional government was so deep-seated in her that she devised a Constitution of her own within three years after achieving, political independence. The Constitution she adopted was intended to be not merely a means of establishing a governmental machinery but also an effective instrument for orderly social change.

The strength and stability of a constitution depends largely on Its ability to sustain a healthy and peaceful social system and when occasion demands, facilitate the peaceful transformation of its economic and social order. From this point of view the Constitution has set an ideal which not even its severest critic would characterise as outmoded or reactionary. Its basic objective is to establish a. democratic, socialist, secular republic with a view to securing justice, liberty, equality and fraternity to all its citizens. It aims to translate into practice the noble concept of à co-operative commonwealth, a blending of political democracy with economic and social democracy. It embodies the most comprehensive policy directions to the state and its agencies to ensure the establishment of a welfare state.

The Constitution of India is among the longest in the world. It continued the constitutional development that took place under the British, retaining the basic precepts of the Government of India Act of 1935 and taking from it approximately 250 articles, verbatim or with minor changes.

When India gained independence, the Constituent Assembly, functioning under a modified Government of India Act of 1935, became the Provisional Parliament. Its fundamental task, however, remained that of framing the Constitution. Dr. Ambedkar chaired the Drafting Committee and steered the document through nearly a year of debate over its various provisions. Four leaders, Nehru, Patel, Prasad and Maulana Azad, through their commanding grip on the Congress Assembly Party and the Assembly's eight committees, constituted a virtual oligarchy within the Assembly. Issues were openly debated, but the influence of the Congress leaders was nearly irresistible. Although they themselves were by no means always of one mind, they sought to promote consensus and in the end, the Constitution was adopted by acclamation on January 26, 1950, Republic Day, the new Constitution went into effect. The new India was to be a parliamentary democracy, federal, republican and secular. There were some members of the Assembly who pushed for a Gandhian

Constitution, one that would provide for a decentralised state with the Village Panchayats as its nucleus. The vast majority, however, were, committed from the beginning to a centralised parliamentary government.

## OUTSTANDING FEATURES OF THE INDIAN CONSTITUTION

Dr. Subhash Kashyap observes, "The Constitution of India is a most comprehensive document. It is unique in many ways. It cannot be fitted in any particular mould or model. It is a blend of the rigid and the flexible, federal and unitary and presidential and parliamentary. It attempts a balance between the fundamental rights of the individual on the one hand and the socio-economic interests of the people and security of the state on the other. Also, it presents a via-media between the principles of parliamentary sovereignty and judicial supremacy." The following are the outstanding features of the Indian Constitution:

1. *A Written Constitution*: The Republic of India has a written and enacted Constitution, it contains 395 Articles (divided into 22 parts) twelve Schedules and three Appendices. In its present form it covers 319 octavo pages. "Like the Constitution of the United States of America, Canada and France, India too has a written Constitution, though it differs from those documents in many: respects."
2. *The longest known Constitution*: The Constitution of India has the' distinction of being the most lengthy and detailed constitutional document the world has so far produced. The original Constitution contained as many as 395 Articles and 8 Schedules (to which additions were made by subsequent amendments). Even after the repeal of several provisions it still contains 395 Articles and 12 Schedules.

   It has been the endeavour of the framers of the Constitution to provide the solution of all the problems of administration and governance of the country. Even those matters that are subject of conventions in other countries have been put down in black and white. Thus, while the U.S. Constitution originally comprises only 7 Articles, the Australian 128 Articles, the Canadian 141-' Articles, the Constitution of India in original form consists of 395 Articles divided into 22 parts and 8 Schedules. As a result of some amendments made since then, some new Articles have been added and some old ones repealed. The number of Schedules has also risen. The bulk of the Constitution continues to be still increasing.

This extraordinary bulk of the Constitution is due to several reasons:

(a) The Constituent Assembly wanted to incorporate in the Constitution the accumulated experience gathered from the working of all the constitutions of the world and to avoid all possible defects and loopholes thereof.

(b) In addition to the Union, it includes the Constitutions of the States also. The American Federal Constitution covers only the organisation, of national government leaving state constitutions to be framed by the states themselves.

(c) It has detailed distribution of legislative, administrative and financial powers between the Union and the States.

(d) The vastness of the country and the peculiar problems to be solved have also contributed towards the bulk of the Constitution. Thus, there is one entire part (Part XVI) relating to the scheduled castes and tribes and other backward classes; one part (Part XVIII) relating to official language and another (Part XVIII) relating to Emergency provisions.

(e) Since all the units of the Indian Union are not of the same type, the Constitution had to make provisions for all these distinct types. Special provisions have been inserted to meet the regional problems and demands in certain states, such as Nagalnd, Assam, Manipur, Sikkim and Mizoram.

(f) The Constitution carries an elaborate chapter on Fundamental Rights, each right being accompanied by a detailed statement of restrictions imposed thereon.

(g) It also includes a chapter on Fundamental Duties.

(h) Besides, a complete chapter of the Constitution deals with non-justicable Directive Principles of State Policy.

It is sometimes asked why the framers of the Indian Constitution deemed it necessary to draw up such a ponderous constitutional document and ignored what Sir Ivor Jennings has described as the golden rule for all constitution makers,viz., "never to put anything that can be safely left out." The answer, as Sir Ivor has himself pointed out, is that the great volume of the Indian constitution is largely a legacy of the past. The British Government had set 'fashion by framing lengthy and detailed constitutions for India in enacting government of India Acts of 1919 and 1935. The 1935 Act was, in fact the longest measure ever passed by the British Parliament. The new Constitution lo India is like the Act of 1935, "not merely a constitution but also a detailed legal code dealing with all important aspects of the constitutional and administrative system of the country."

3. *Popular Sovereignty*: The Constitution proclaims the sovereignty of the people m its opening words. The Preamble begins with the words, 'we the I people of India, having solemnly resolved to constitute India into a Sovereign socialist Secular Democratic Republic." The idea is reaffirmed in several places the Constitution, particularly in the chapter dealing with elections. Article 326 declares, "The elections to the House of People and to the Legislative assembly of every state shall be on the basis of adult suffrage." As a result, the governments at the Centre and in the States derive their authority from the people who choose their representatives for Parliament and the State Legislatures at regular intervals. Further, those who wield the executive power of the government are responsible to the legislature and through them to the people. Thus, in the affairs of the state, it is the will of the people that prevails ultimately and this is the principle of popular sovereignty.
4. *Sovereign Democratic Republic*: The Preamble of the Constitution 'declares India to be a Sovereign Democratic Republic. It is sovereign since India has emerged as a completely independent state. The Dominion Status of India established under the Independence Act of 1947 has been terminated and India is now a full-fledged state with all the characteristics of sovereignty. The word

   Democratic' signifies that the real power emanates from the people. The Constitution introduces universal adult franchise and confers on the adult Population of the country the right to elect their representatives for the Union Parliament and State Legislatures at the time of periodical elections to be held every five years. The word 'Republic' is used to denote that the state is headed not by a permanent head like the Queen of Britain but by a President indirectly elected by the people.

5. *Both Rigid and Flexible*: The Indian Constitution is partly rigid and partly flexible. The procedure laid down by the Constitution for its amendment is neither very easy, as in England, nor very rigid as in the United States. In England which has no written Constitution, there is no difference between a constitutional law and an ordinary one. The constitutional law can be amended exactly in the same manner in which ordinary legislation is passed or amended. In the United States, however, the method of constitutional amendment is highly rigid. It can be carried out only with the agreement of the two-thirds majority of the Congress and its subsequent ratification by at least three-fourths of the states. The Constitution of India strikes a golden mean, thereby avoiding the extreme flexibility of the English Constitution and the extreme rigidity of the American Constitution..

   It is only the amendment of few of the provisions of the Constitution that' requires ratification by the State Legislatures and even then ratification by only 1/2 of them would suffice (while the American Constitution requires ratification' by 3/4 of the states). The rest of the Constitution may be amended by a special majority of the Union Parliament, i.e., a majority of not less than 2/3 of the members of each House present and voting, which, again, must be a majority of the total membership of the House.

   On the other hand, Parliament has been given the power to alter or modify many of the provisions of the Constitution by a simple majority as it required for general legislation, by laying down in the Constitution that such change "shall not be deemed to be 'amendments' of the Constitution."

   The very fact that within a period of 54 years the Constitution had been amended 86 times proves that the Constitution is flexible. It should, however, be noted that the basic structure of the Constitution cannot be amended.

6. *Cabinet Government*: The Constitution establishes Cabinet type of Government both at the Centre and in the Units. The most distinctive feature of a cabinet system of Government is the complete and continuous responsibility of the executive to the legislature. The Cabinet is composed of the Prime Minister,

who is the Chief of the executive and his senior colleagues who share y. the responsibility with him for the formulation and execution of the policies of;' the government.

Under the Cabinet system, the Head of the state occupies a position of great dignity, but the Cabinet or the Ministry, which assumes full responsibility for acts performed in his name, exercises practically all authority, nominally vested in him. The unity and collective responsibility of the Cabinet are achieved through the Prime Minister, who is the key-stone of the Cabinet arch. The real merit of a cabinet system is that the executive being responsible o the legislature is always being watched. The moment it proves unequal to the task or it goes off the track or flouts the will of the legislature, it can be removed from office by a successful vote of no-confidence.

7. *Secular State*: By adding the word 'secular' to the existing description of the country as a 'Sovereign Democratic Republic', in the Preamble, the commitment to the goal of secularism has been spelled out in clear terms. A secular state has negative and positive aspects. Negatively, it is the antithesis of a communal or theocratic state, which officially identified itself with a particular religion. Pakistan, for instance, has proclaimed itself an Islamic state. In a secular state, on the other hand, there is no official or state religion. In its positive aspect, secular states treat all its citizens alike and give them equal opportunities. According to Prof. Alexandrowicz, "India as a secular state guarantees, constitutionally, freedom of religion all persons, and does not assign a special position to any particular religion.,,4 The state has no official religion. No discrimination can be made on the basis of religion, faith, caste, colour and sex. Every citizen is equal before law. It guarantees to religious "minorities the right to maintain their own language and to establish educational institutions of their choice. An important manifestation of secularism in India is the abolition of communal electorates and the adoption of the provision that elections are to be held on the basis of universal franchise and joint-electorates.

8 *A Federal System with Unitary Bias*: "Perhaps the most remarkable achievement of the Indian Constitution is to confer upon a federal system the strength of a unitary government. Though normally the system of government is federal, the

Constitution enables the federation to transform into a unitary state."

The Constitution of India establishes a federal polity, which has been created by dividing the country into states, and allocating them functions as specified in the Constitution. Like all other federations India has a written constitution, which is rigid to a large extent. There is a dual polity and division powers between the Centre and States. There is also a provision for Supreme court which is the guardian of our Constitution and decides all disputes which might arise between the Centre and the States.

These characteristics of the federal set-up notwithstanding, the Indian constitution has a unitary bias. For instance, after distributing the legislative powers three lists, residual subjects are left with the Union. Even in matters in the concurrent list, the Union government has the final say. Unlike other federations Parliament in India has a right to change the boundaries of then states. The heads of the States, i.e., the Governors are appointed by the president and are his agents in the States. The Centre can, at any time, declare emergency in the States and with that declaration can take over the administration of that State in its own control.

The choice of federalism as a constitutional form and as the basis of a national government in India was not a sudden development upon the transfer of-power on August 15, 1947. It was there for many years and, in a limited form, it was already in operation in British India. For the solution of the constitutional problem of a multi-social, multi-lingual and multi-communal country like India with a vast area and huge 'population, federalism was only a natural choice. Nevertheless, the framers were cautious to ensure that the unity they sought to establish through federalism was of an abiding nature, and in case of a future conflict between that unity and the diversity preserved under the Constitution, the former should prevail over the latter. In other words, it was their intention to create an indestructible Union and the supremacy of the Union over the States in a number of matters vitally affecting the interests of the nation.

9. *Universal Franchise without Communal Representation*: The adoption universal adult suffrage (Article 326), without any

qualification either of sex, property, taxation or the like, is a 'bold experiment' in India, having regard to the vast extent of the country and its population, with an overwhelming illiteracy. The suffrage in India, it should be noted, is wider than that in England or the United States. The concept of popular sovereignty, which underlies the declaration in the Preamble that the Constitution is adopted and given by the people of India' upto themselves, would indeed have been hollow unless the franchise-the only effective medium of popular sovereignty in a modern democracy, were extended to the entire population which was capable of exercising the right and independent electoral machinery (under the control of the Election Commission) was set up to ensure the free exercise of it.

No less creditable for the framers of the Constitution is the abolition of communal representation, which in its trail had brought in the bloody and lamentable partition of India. In the Constitution there was no reservation of seats except for the scheduled castes and tribes and for the Anglo-Indians and that only for a temporary period.

10. *Compromise between Judicial Review and Parliamentary Supremacy*: "Parliament in India is not as supreme as the British Parliament. At the same time judiciary in India is not as supreme as in the United States of America which recognises no limit on the scope of judicial review.

The Indian Constitution wonderfully adopts the via-media between the American system of judicial supremacy and the English principle of parliamentary supremacy, by endowing the judiciary with the power of declaring a law as unconstitutional if it is beyond the competence of the legislature according to the distribution of powers provided by the Constitution, or if it is in contravention of the fundamental rights guaranteed by the Constitution, but at the same time, depriving the judiciary of any power of ' Judicial review' of the, wisdom of legislative policy. Thus, it has avoided expressions like 'due process' and made fundamental rights such as that of liberty and property subject to regulation by the legislature. Further, the major portion of the Constitution is' liable to be amended by the Union Parliament by a special majority, if in any case the judiciary proves too obtrusive. The theory underlying the Indian Constitution in this respect can hardly be better expressed than in the word of Jawaharlal Nehru: "No Supreme Court, no judiciary, can stand in judgment: over the sovereign will of Parliament, representing the will of the entire community. It can pull up that sovereign will if it goes wrong, but, in the ultimate analysis, where the future of the community is concerned, no judiciary can come in the way Ultimately, the fact remains that the Legislature must be supreme and must not be interfered with by the Courts of Law in such measures as social reform."

11. *Single Citizenship*: Although India has a federal government yet double citizenship, as provided for in the U. S. Constitution, has not been provided for All the Indians irrespective of their domicile, enjoy a single citizenship of India j whereas in United States all the citizens enjoy the right of double citizenship.

    Since Americans are considered to be the citizens of the State where they are domiciled and then they are the citizens of the U.S.A. as a whole. In both these capacities, they enjoy different rights and owe different obligations. The principle of single citizenship was provided for in the Indian Constitution in order to foster strong bond of social and political unity among the people of India, who are hitherto divided on account of racial discrimination, variety of languages and multiplicity of religious and cultural background.

12. *Independence of Judiciary*: The framers of the Constitution were aware that democratic freedoms were meaningless in the, absence of an independent machinery to safeguard them. No subordinate or agent of the Government could' be trusted to be just and impartial in judging the merits of a conflict in which the Government itself was a party. Similarly, a judiciary subordinate either to the Centre or the States could not be trusted as an impartial arbiter of conflicts and controversies between the Centre and the States. These were the compelling reasons for the creation of an independent judiciary as an integral part of the Constitution and for the adoption of judicial independence as a basic principle of the Constitution. In its bid to establish complete independence of the judiciary, the

Constitution has first erected a wall of separation between the executive and the judiciary. After effecting such separation, it has created conditions that are conducive to making the judiciary independent. Thus, rigid qualifications are laid down for the appointment of judges and provision has been made for compulsory consultation of the Chief Justice of India in the appointment of every judge of the Supreme Court and the High Courts. They are given high salaries, their conditions of service cannot be altered to their disadvantage and their conduct is made a subject beyond the scope of discussion in the legislature. They can be removed from office only for proved misbehavior. For this purpose, both the Houses of Parliament will have to pass resolutions against a judge supported by a two-thirds majority of those who sit and vote and at least an absolute majority of the total membership of the House.

13. *Fundamental Rights*: Like the Constitution of the United States of America, the Constitution of India also includes a separate chapter guaranteeing fundamental rights to all the citizens. These rights are justiciable and inviolable. They are binding ()n the legislature as well as on the executive. If any of the rights is violated, a citizen has the right to seek the protection of the judiciary. Any act of the Legislature or order of the Executive can be declared null and void if it violates any of the Fundamental Rights guaranteed to the citizens by the Constitution.
14. *Fundamental Duties*: Another feature, which was not in the original constitution, has been introduced by the 42nd Amendment, 1976, by introducing Article 51A as Part IVA of the Constitution. The 42nd Amendment Act introduced' 'Fundamental Duties' to circumscribe the fundamental rights, even though the duties, as such, cannot be judicially enforced. The incorporation of fundamental duties in the Constitution was, thus, an attempt to balance the individual's civic 'freedoms' with his civic obligations and thus, to fill a serious gap in the Constitution.
15. *Directive Principles of State Policy*: The Directive Principles of State Policy is another distinctive feature of the Indian Constitution. This feature has been taken from the Irish Constitution. The philosophy behind the Directive Principles

is that the state and every one of its agencies are commanded to follow certain fundamental principles while they frame their policies regarding the various fields of state activity. These principles, on the one hand, are assurances to the people as to what they can expect from the state and on the other, are directives to the Government, Central and State, to establish and maintain a new "social order in which justice, social, economic and political, shall inform all the institutions of national life."

The precepts of the Directive Principles are not justiciable-that is, they are not enforceable by a court as are the Fundamental Rights. They are designed rather to serve as a guide for the Union Parliament and the State Assemblies in framing new legislation. Taken together, they inscribe the objectives of a modern welfare state and as distinguished from a merely regulatory Or negative state. They lay down the social and economic principles that the framers of the Constitution wanted free India to follow and "constitute a very comprehensive political, social and economic programme for a modern democratic state." If the Fundamental Rights of citizens declared in Chapter III of the Constitution lay the foundations of political democracy in India, the Directive Principles spell out the norms of social and economic democracy in the country.

## References

Austin, Granville: *The Indian Constitution: Cornerstone of a Nation*, Oxford, Clarendon Press, 1966.

Carl J. Friedrich: *Constitutional Government and Democracy,* Boston, Ginn, 1950.

Derrett, J. : *Religion, Law, and Constitution Law in India,* London, Faber, 1968.

Friedrich, J.: *Constitutional Government and Democracy,* Boston, Ginn, 1950.

Howard McIlwain: *Constitutionalism: Ancient and Modern,* N.Y., Cornell University Press, 1958.

Kenneth C. Wheare: *Modern Constitutions*, New York, Oxford University Press, 1951.

17

# The Role of Ambedkar in the Dalit Movement of India

**Dr M. S. Ranawat**
*Director, Shri Nat Nagar Shodh Sansthan*
*Sitamao (Malwa), Madhya Pradesh*

**Abstract:** *Babasaheb Ambedkar has undoubtedly been the central figure in the epistemology of the dalit universe. It is difficult to imagine anything serious or important in their collective life that is totally untouched by Ambedkar. For the dalit masses he is everything together; a scholar par excellence in the realm of scholarship, a Moses or messiah who led his people out of bondage and ignominy on to the path of pride, and a Bodhisatva in the pantheon of Buddhism. He is always bedecked with superlatives, quite like God, whatever may be the context in dalit circles. Dalits, a modern term for untouchables in India, are underprivileged people in all social, economic, cultural and political fronts of our society which led to their misery, discrimination, exploitation and oppression by the caste dominated social stratification of India. The Constitution of India classifies Dalits as Scheduled Castes (SCs). They are the people who cultivate the land, mend the shoes, wash the clothes, clean the toilets, scavenge the dead animals or unknown human bodies and do all types of menial works, but share the stigmas of untouchability and are frequently denied the chance to eat, smoke and even seat with the members of upper castes. They often use separate wells and tube wells from those maintained for others. These pitiable conditions of Dalits were seen and addressed by some eminent social and political philosophers like Jyotiba Phule, Mahatma Gandhi, Dr. Bhim Rao Ambedkar and others. Dr. Ambedkar, borne in a poor Dalit family became the first Law Minister of India after independence and the chief architect of Indian Constitution.*

## DALIT MOVEMENT: AN OVERVIEW

The Dalit question is one of the most important questions in today's political and academic debates in India. The term Dalit has been derived from the Sanskrit root dal which means broken, burst, downtrodden, split, ground-down. It is an expression of the existing contradiction, inequality and exploitation in the Indian hierarchy. The Dalits are considered outcastes falling outside the traditional four-fold Hindu Caste System consisting of the hereditary Brahman, Kshatriya, Vaishya and Shudra classes. Unfortunately they are usually supposed to be impure and polluting and are therefore physically and socially excluded and isolated from rest of the society. Previously they were referred to with different nomenclatures like Chandals, Avarnas, Achhuts, Adidravidia, Depressed classes, Utouchables, Oppressed Hindus, Harijans etc. at different point of time. The Constitution of India classified Dalits as Scheduled Castes (Government of India Act 1935). However after the emergence of the Dalit Panther Movement in 1973 they themselves preferred to be called as Dalits in India. Recently the Govt. of Bihar under the leadership of CM Sri Nitish Kumar included 19 castes of Dalits into Mahadalits. Mahadalits are extremely weaker and poorest amongst Dalits. A Dalit is usually a Hindu but it may also be a Buddhist, Sikh, Muslim or Christian. The Caste and analogous systems of social hierarchy also operate across the world particularly in Asia (Nepal, Pakistan, Sri Lanka, Bangladesh, Malaysia and Japan), East South Africa (Kenya, Nigeria, Rwanda, Senegal, Somalia, Mauritius, Fiji, Surinam, the Carribean), UK and North America. Asia remains the continent with the longest share of Dalits

The Scheduled Castes are known as harijnas i.e children of God – a term coined by Mahatma Gandhi in 1933.There are many studies on the Dalit or SC socio-political condition but there are only a few systematic empirically sound studies on their movements. The Mahar movement of Maharashtra has been seen as all India movement.Dr Ambedkar was an all India leader. While bargaining with the British and the caste – Hindus he represented all the dalit of the country but his role in mobilizing the SCs outside Maharashtra is not documented.

There is no full fledged study or even an anthology giving information about various SC movements in different parts of the country in colonial and post colonial period. Two papers – one by Gail Omvedt and Bharat Patankar and the other by Ghanshyam Shah give an overview of the dalit liberation in India. The former deals with the colonial period whereas the latter looks at both the colonial and the post colonial periods. The study by Verba, Ahmad and Bhatt (1972) on the Blacks and the harijnas gives a comparative picture of the movements of these communities in the USA and India.

The main issues around which most of the Dalit movements have been centered in the colonial and post colonial periods are confined to the problem of untouchability.They launched movements for maintaining or increasing reservations in political offices, government jobs and welfare programmes.

Ghanshyam Shah classifies the Dalit movements into reformative and alternative movements. The former tries to reform the caste system to solve the problem of untouchability.The alternative movement attempts to create an alternative socio-cultural structure by conversion to some other religion or by acquiring education, economic status and political power. Both types of movements use political means to attain their objectives. The reformative movements are further divided into Bhakti movements, neo-Vedantik movements and Sanskritisation movements.

The alternative movements are divided into the conversion movement and the religious or secular movement. The latter includes the movement related to economic issues. In the context of dalit identity and ideology Shah has classified dalit movements into movements within cultural consensus, competing ideology and non Hindu identity, Buddhist dalits and counter ideology and dalit identity. The first three are based around religious ideologies whereas the last is based on class.Patankar and Omvedt classify the dalit movement into caste based and class based movements.

In the 1990s with the increased political participation in elections and success of Bahujan Samaj Party in Uttar Pradesh some scholars consider their mobilization as a new political movement of the dalits.

Bhakti movement in 15th century developed two traditions of saguna and nirguna.The former believes in the form of God mostly Vishnu or Shiv relating to the Vaishnavite or Shaivaite traditions. It preaches equality among all the castes though it subscribes to the varnashram dharma and the caste social order. The devotees of Nirguna believe in formless universal God.Ravidas and Kabir are the major figures of this tradition. It became more popular among the dalits in urban areas in the early 20th century as it provided the possibility of salvation for all. It promised social equality. Through these movements Fuller argues devotionalist ethic come to be widely reinterpreted as a charter of egalitarianism.

Neo-vedantik movement was initiated by Hindu religious and social reformers. These movements attempted to remove untouchability by taking them into the fold of the caste system.Dayanand Sarawati the founder of Arya Samaj believed that the caste system was a political institution created by the rulers for the common good of society and not a natural or religious distinction. Satish Kumar Sharma's book Social Movements and Social Change is the only full-fledged study which examines the relationship between the Arya Samaj and the untouchables. The study is confined to Punjab only but some of the observations are relevant for other part of the country as well.Arya Samaj was against the political movements of the untouchables. It went against any move initiated by the untouchables for their solidarity and integration.

The neo-Vedantic movements and non-Brahmin movements played an important catalytic role in developing anti-caste or anti Hinduism dalit movements in some parts of the country. The Satyashodhak Samaj and the self-respect movements in Maharashtra and the Tamil Nadu,the Adhi Dharma and Adi Andhra movement in Bengal and Adi-Hindu movement in Uttar Pradesh are important anti-untouchability movements which were launched in the last quarter of the 19th and the early part of 20th century.

There are scattered references to the Adi-Andhra, the Adi-Hindu and the Namashudra movements. Mark Juergensmeyer's book Religion as Social Vision deals with the Adi Dharma movement against untouchability in 20th century Punjab. The main plea of the movement was that the untouchables constituted a quam a distinct religious community similar to those of Sikhs, Hindus and Muslim communities. Nandini Gooptu in her study on UP in the early 20th century briefly analyses the emergence of the Adi-Hindu movement in the urban areas of the region. Like Adi-Dharma, the leaders of the Adi-Hindu movement believed that the present form of Hinduism was imposed on them by the Aryan invaders. The movement did not pose a direct threat to the caste system. It was in essence, conceived as and remained a protest against the attribution of low roles and functions to the untouchable by means of a claim not to be Aryan Hindus; it was not developed into a full blown, direct attack on the caste system.

A section of untouchables who could improve their economic condition either by abandoning or continuing their traditional occupations launched struggles for higher status in the caste hierarchy. They followed Sanskritic norms and rituals. They tried to justify their claim to a higher social status in the caste hierarchy by inventing suitable mythologies. The Shanars or Nadars of Tamil Nadu however have crossed the boundary of untouchability.The Iravas of Kerala have also blurred if not completely destroyed, the line of untouchability.The Nadars organized movements in the late 19th century against the civic disabilities they suffered. They formed their caste organization in 1903 called SNDP Yogam.According to it the low social status of the Iravas is due to their low social and religious practices. The association launched activities for Sanskritising the norms and customs of the Iravas.They launched a Satyagraha for temple entry in the 1920s.They bargained with a government for economic opportunities and political positions.

A major anti-touchability movement was launched by Dr Ambedkar in the 1920s in Maharashtra. He saw the opportunity and possibility of a advancement for the untouchables through the use of political means to achieve social and economic equality with the highest classes in modern society. He organized the independent labour party on secular lines for protecting the interests of the laboring classes. It was dominated by Mahars.

The Dalits demanded a separate electorate in the 1930s which led to a conflict between Ambedkar and Gandhi. In the early 1930s Ambedkar concluded that the only way of improving the status of the untouchables was to renounce the Hindu religion. He found that Buddhism was appropriate as an alternative religion for the untouchables. He preferred Buddhism because it was an indigenous Indian religion of equality; a religion which was anti-caste and Anti Brahmin. Ambedkar and his followers were converted to Buddhism in 1956.The movement for conversion to Buddhism has spread dalit consciousness irrespective of whether dalits became Buddhist or not. The Dalits of Maharashtra launched the Dalit Panther Movement in the early 1970s.Initially it was confined to the urban areas of Maharashtra not it spread to Gujarat, Karnataka, AndhraPradesh, Uttar Pradesh and other states.

Assertion for dalit identity has almost become a central issue of dalit movement. This involves local level collective action against discrimination and atrocities. Statues of Dr Ambedkar are found not only in urban dalit localities but also in many villages where their number is fairly large. Dalits contribute to installing Ambedkar statues in their neighbourhood.They struggle to get a piece of land from local authorities to install the statue. The statues and photos of Dr Ambedkar are an expression of dalit consciousness and their assertion for identity.

There are several local movements in which Dalits en mass migrate from their villages protesting against discrimination and atrocities. In the 1980s there were five such incidents.Desai and Maheria document one of the micro-level movements. In protest against torture and beating the dalits of the village Sambarda undertook hijarat en mass migration like refugees from their native village and camped in the open before the district collector office for 131 days in 1989.Their demand was for alternative settlement where their life and dignity will be secured. They wanted a concrete solution: alternative land to protect their dignity. They succeeded in their mission against all odds and collusion between the ruling elite and vested interests. The village level movements succeeded in mobilizing dalits of different parts of Gujarat.

The Dalit movements are dominated by their middle class raising issues related to identity and reservations of government jobs and political positions. There is widespread local level assertion against the practice of untouchability and discrimination. Their struggles have brought dalits on the agenda of mainstream politics. In academic circles the movements have forced a section of intellectuals to critically review not only Indian traditions and culture but also the paradigms of modernity and Marxism. They have exploded number of myths created by Brahminical ideology. The Dalit movements have also successfully built up a good deal of pressure on the ruling classes. However several scholars and activists feel that dalits have been reduced to a pressure group within the mainstream politics. Gail Omvedt observes that the post-Ambedkar Dalit movement was ironically only that in the end- a movement of dalits, challenging some of the deepest aspects of oppression and exploitation but failing to show the way to transformation.

## THE LIFE AND PHILOSOPHY OF AMBEDKAR

Fifty nine years back on 6 December 1956 Dr. Bhimrao Ramji Ambedkar attained 'Mahaparinirvan'. Born on 14th April 1891, in the military town Mhow, he was the fourteenth child of his parents. Parents from untouchable community viz. Mahar, his father was a retired army officer and headmaster in a military school, and his mother an illiterate woman.

Since he was born in an untouchable caste, he was made to sit separate from other students in a corner of the classroom. Despite all kinds of humiliations, he passed his high school in 1908 with flying colours. This was such an exceptional achievement for an untouchable, that he was felicitated in a public meeting.

Four years later he graduated in Political Science and Economics from Bombay University. After his graduation he went to the USA to study economics at the Columbia University with a scholarship form the Maharaja of Baroda. Bhimrao remained abroad from 1913 to 1917 and again from 1920 to 1923. In the meantime he had established himself as an eminent intellect. Columbia University had awarded him the PhD for his thesis, which was later published in a book form under the title "The Evolution of Provincial Finance in British India". But his first published article was "Castes in India – Their Mechanism, Genesis and Development". In 1920 he went to London where he got his Bar-at-Law at Gray's Inn for Law. During his sojourn in London from 1920 to 1923, he also completed his thesis titled "The Problem of the Rupee" for which he was awarded the degree of DSc.

During the brief stay in India from 1917 to 1920 he first got a job as Military Secretary in Baroda Raja's office. Here he was ill treated again by the upper caste employees. Even drinking water was not given to him and files were kept at a distance from him. He couldn't continue in Baroda and later taught at Sydnom College in Bombay and also brought out Marathi weekly whose title was 'Mook Nayak' (meaning 'Dumb Hero'). He had to face similar experience of untouchability and dishonour even in Bombay.

It is also interesting to note and which not many Ambedarkites have ventured, that Dr Ambedkar was a socialist to the core of his heart. The disappointing relation with the communist movement stands as the single most unfortunate paradox of contemporary Indian history. It didn't come out of much of ideological differences, which certainly existed in the form of certain unclear theoretical constructs in the mind of Ambedkar – as from the attitudes of the communist leaders towards the Dalit movement. These leaders in the Trade Unions of Bombay dogmatically regarded the caste question as an unimportant super-structural issue, which would automatically disappear when the revolution takes place. Their orthodox outlook regarding untouchability, caste disparity, discrimination was the basics on which Ambedkar's entire thesis on Communism was formed. For historical reasons the leadership of this communist movement however came from the middle class educated youth who had to come from upper castes communities, the majority being the Brahmin itself.

Ambedkar's writing on Marxism is heavily reflects his frustration with the Bombay-Communists. This legacy to identify Marxism with its self-appointed practitioners still appears to be followed by Dalits.

They cite examples of the parliamentary communist parties to show the lacuna or inapplicability of Marxism. It is necessary for them to understand that Marxism intrinsically solicits criticism but it presupposes its careful study.

As Anand Teltumde puts it, although Ambedkar could not discuss the philosophy of communism in the manner it deserved, he was never antagonistically disposed towards it. Rather, he acknowledged the beauty of communist philosophy and said that it was closer to his own. Preoccupied with the mission of liberating the Dalits, he insisted, quite like Marx, that the test of the philosophy was in practice, and opined that if communists worked from that perspective, to win success in India would be far easier than in Russia (Janata, 15 January, 1938). He always regarded communism as the ultimate benchmark to assess his highest ideal – Buddhism. With unpleasant experience with communist dogma and vulgarity of his times, he did sound polemically against Communism and appeared at times even professing its doom but it all underscored his wrath against the dogma that occupied the communist practice.

Despite all these aspects of Ambedkar's disagreements with Communism it is cannot be ruled out that Ambedkar was not a Socialist. He was a socialist of a different kind. One of his prime conflicts with Marx was 'dictatorship of the proletariats', which he condemned saying that dictatorship of any kind is unethical. His stood for greater democracy of, by, for and among the oppressed ones in every field. At one stage he was clearly of the opinion that the historical conflict is between the exploited and exploiters and that all.

It is with this idea that Dr. Ambedkar, formed the Independent Labour Party, participated in the provincial elections and was elected to the Bombay Legislative Assembly. During these days he stressed the need for abolition of the 'Jagirdari' system, pleaded for workers' Fight to strike and addressed a large number of meetings and conferences in Bombay Presidency. In 1939, during the Second World War, he called upon Indians to join the Army in large numbers to defeat Nazism, which he said, was another name for Fascism.

He stood for the nationalisation of property like land, banks etc. Ambedkar was also an advocate of women's rights. He struggled for women's liberation from the caste-entrenched patriarchal system. At the conference of the Depressed Classes Women in Nagpur in 1942, he stated: 'let every girl who marries stand by her husband, claim to be her husband's friend and equal, and refuse to be his slave'. He resigned from the Nehru's cabinet as Law Minister only when the cabinet refused to pass the Women's Rights Bill. This strongly proves that his idea of Socialism was embedded in his core agenda of freedom for all from all forms of bondage.

## AMBEDKAR AND DALIT MOVEMENT

While coming back to India in 1923, Ambedkar again experienced humiliation. The upper caste lawyers would not even have tea at his desk. But his greatest consolation was his clients, whom he treated with liberal mind. His reputation and fame among the Depressed Classes began to grow. He visualised and struggled for a casteless and equal India.

By the time he returned to India, Bhimrao had equipped himself fully to wage war against the practice of untouchability. In 1924 he started the organisation 'Bahiskrit Hitakarini Sabha' (Outcastes Welfare Association), for the upliftment of the untouchables. Ambedkar adopted a two-pronged strategy. First, the eradication of illiteracy and economic uplift of the downtrodden and second, initiating non-violent struggle against visible symbols of casteism, like denial of entry into temples and drawing water from public wells and tanks.

The problems of the downtrodden were centuries old and difficult to overcome. Their entry into temples was forbidden. They could not draw water from public wells and ponds. Their admission in schools was prohibited. Ambedkar won two major victories when the High Court of Bombay gave a verdict in favour of the untouchables. On 25th December 1927, he led the Mahad March at the Chowdar Tank at Colaba, near Bombay, to ensure the untouchables right to draw water from the public tank. The marchers were met with the brutality of caste Hindus. He then burnt copies of the 'Manusmriti' publicly terming it a document of discrimination with a number of his supporters. It was an act of great courage to do so in the den of violent Chitpawan Brahmins in Maharastra. The two struggles shook the religious foundation on which the caste system is built. This marked the beginning of the anti-caste and ant-priest movement in Maharastra. The temple entry movement launched by Dr. Ambedkar in 1930 at Kalaram temple, Nasik is another landmark in the struggle for human rights and social justice.

He was fully convinced that nothing could emancipate the Dalits except through a complete destruction of the caste system. He continued his movement to attack the base of caste system in every possible way. In the meantime, the Simon Commission visited India and Dr. Ambedkar met the commission in Pune in which Ambedkar presented his position on depressed classes.

He then followed it up during the round table conference after which Ramsay McDonald? announced 'Communal Award' as a result of which several communities including the 'depressed classes' were given the right to have separate electorates. Gandhiji wanted to defeat this design and went on a fast unto death to oppose it. On 24th September 1932, Ambedkar and Gandhiji reached an understanding, which became the famous Poona Pact. According to this Pact, in addition to the agreement on electoral constituencies, reservations were provided for untouchables in Government jobs and legislative assemblies. The Pact carved out a clear and definite position for the downtrodden on the political scene of the country. For the first time in Indian history it opened up opportunities of education and government service for them and also gave them a right to vote.

Dr. Ambedkar attended all the three Round Table Conferences in London and each time, forcefully projected his views in the interest of the 'untouchable'. He exhorted the downtrodden sections to raise their living standards and to acquire as much political power as possible. He was of the view that there was no future for untouchables in the Hindu religion and they should change their religion if need be. In 1935, he publicly proclaimed," I was born a Hindu because I had no control over this but I shall not die a Hindu".

## POST-AMBEDKAR DALIT MOVEMENT

The post Ambedkar Dalit movement had witnessed several ups and downs. On one side a categorical awakening among the Dalits had grown beyond all levels of history and on the other it has somewhere stagnant after Ambedkar mainly due to ideological disposition of stagnation. It would be opportune to look at the post Ambedar Dalit movement and do a stock taking of the changes within the Dalit politics to understand the phenomenon. Subash Gatade says that the ups and downs through which the Dalit politics passed through after the death of Dr. Babasaheb Ambedkar can be broadly divided into three phases – Rise and Fall of the Republican Party, emergence of the Dalit Panthers and thirdly the growing assertion of Dalits for political power and their consequent refusal to remain satisfied merely with education and job opportunities arising out of the policy of reservation.

There is no need to underline the immense potentialities in the phenomenon of Dalit assertion in today's caste ridden polity. There is no denying the fact that it is a step ahead in the real democratisation of the Indian society and the polity dominated by Brahminical values and traditions despite nearly six decade experiment in electoral democracy. The impressive intervention of BSP under Kanshiram in the national politics underlines this third stage. It is noteworthy that while in the earlier two stages in the post Ambedkar Dalit movement the unfolding Dalit politics in Maharashtra guided its orientation, its role has been increasingly marginalised in the third stage. The success achieved by BSP has certainly encouraged emergence of similar experiments in different parts of the country.

At this stage there is another factor that developed among Dalit castes too. These are organising themselves under the banners of their respective caste and sub-caste for achieving their rights. Consequently their guns are trained besides the Varna system also on the so-called rich Dalit castes or the creamy layer in them, which they feel, have monopolised a large part of the reserved posts. The Mahar/neo-Buddhists vs. Matang and Charmakar debate in Maharashtra, Mala vs. Madiga in Andhra Pradesh are symptomatic of this rising trend. This propensity is similar in most states where the marginalized Dalits are organising themselves into a movement for castewise categorisation of reserved seats in educational institutions and jobs etc, which could not avail of the quota for historical reasons, could avail of it.

It is indeed ironical that at a time when the issue of Dalit assertion has got acceptance even in the mainstream polity in the 90s a counter tendency has emerged which seem to fracture the new found identity. One could also perceive the whole process as an explosion of identities hitherto suppressed by the hegemonic caste and class structure. In the beginning of the 70s the term Dalit denoted a broad, homogenous fraternity. This is no more the case. If you just say Dalit you are making an incomplete statement. It would be necessary to also specify whether he is a Mala or a Madiga or a Matang or a Charmakar. This process has thrown up new 'icons' from among the different castes and the sub–castes as well. This clearly gives a broader picture of the fact that how much the individual caste identity had become more important than the collective one of the 70s.

Another aspect that the Dalit movement in the post-Ambedkar era failed to address is that of the direct challenges of communal fascism. Communal-fascism is exploring its way to elaborate its base, activities and action. It appears that building of philanthropic and religious institutions like Saraswati Sishu Mandir, Vanvasi Kalyan Ashram, Sanghs, Deen Dayal Shodh Sansthan, Sanskriti Bihar, Vikas Bharit, Gayatri Pariwar, Brahmakumari Samaj, etc. are some of the strategies adopted to create inroads among the Dalits & Adivasis. Another strategy applied is the steady and systematic capturing of the community panchayats and organisations. The best example of this is Gujarat where the communal fascists have got their stranglehold and successfully executed the carnage against the Muslims by communalising Dalits and Adivasis.

Resultant is the perpetual assurance of control over these communities plus a bonus of sustaining casteism. Expansion of caste fascism has so far and is disintegrating the Dalit ideology, theology, and identity and intimidated their very existence. Apparently this ruptures the community, deteriorates the noble notions of sharing, caring and co-operation, expansion of patriarchy and battered the inkling of community ownership over resources. Let us not forget Ambedkar was the greatest fighter against religious fascism and historical caste fascism.

Thirdly Dalit movement neither understand the politics of imperialist globalisation not address it in any form. Rather than entering the debate in a critical way from the subaltern perspective, it remained passive to the process of globalisation, and many times joined the sustaining party. Globalisation in India marked through Economic Reforms launched in July 1991 in India were in nature of a crisis management response to the economic and political crises that erupted in early 90s. The blue print for the Reforms was provided by the combination of macro-economic stabilisation and structural adjustment programme of International Monetary Fund (IMF) and World Bank respectively, which had been adopted by many countries before in similar situations.

This had quantitative and qualitative adversities on food security, employment, inflation, poverty alleviation schemes as well as social security. For example reservation in the educational institutions and the financial assistance in the form of scholarships and freeships had gone out of context, with the advent of education as an industry. Without education, all constitutional safeguards including the reservation in services would be futile. The Reforms have already resulted in freezing the grants to many institutions and in stagnating, if not lowering, the expenditure on education. The free market ethos has entered the educational sphere in a big way. Commercialisation of education is no more a mere rhetoric; it is now the established fact. Commercial institutions offering specialised education signifying the essential input from utilitarian viewpoint have come up in a big way from cities to small towns.

It is the same way that the employment sector had its impact due to the thus called 'economic reforms'. Howsoever, unsatisfactory the results of the implementation of reservation in employment may be, its importance from the Dalit viewpoint cannot be under emphasised. As could be evidenced by the organised private sector, where it would be difficult to find a Dalit employee (save of course in scavenging and lowliest jobs), without reservations Dalits would have been totally doomed. The importance of reservations thus could only be assessed in relation to situations where they do not exist. Whatever be their defects and deficiencies, they have given certain economic means of livelihood and some social prestige to the sons and daughters of over 1.5 million landless labourers. Whether they get real power or not, over 50,000 Dalits could enter the sphere of bureaucratic authority with the help of reservations. Besides these tangible benefits promised by the policy, it has instilled a hope in Dalit community. This hope predominantly manifests in the form of spread of education among them. Their emotional bond with the nation and its Constitution despite heaps of injustice and ignominy they bear every moment of their life may also be significantly attributable to the Reservation Policy.

The selling out the PSU, the disinvestment of PSUs, promotion of privatisation, the letting off of land to the corporates, etc. had crafted formulae of neo-colonisation. This is high time that Dalit leadership across the country enters this debate in a big way, which it had until now failed to do.

Coming back to Ambedkar, he was not dogmatic but pragmatic. He had rightly confronted the forces of fascism, communalism and capitalism. He believed that any system that promotes unequal human relationships should not thrive. Unfortunately, his socio-economical writings were kept aside while his writings on religion and caste system of 30s were used more by the representatives of the movement, thus clearly alienating a vast masses of the unorganised labour away from the mainstream Ambedkarite movement. That is why today, despite globalisation resulting in wars and multiple conflicts, yet we

Dalits simply remain as silent spectators, just waiting for our turn of reservation. Dalits are confined to use the Dalit card for just reservation in education and employment, nothing else.

The forth barrier of the post Ambedkar Dalit movement is the emergence of a new sect of Dalit elite. This Dalit elite whom Baba Saheb had opposed tooth and nail in his lifetime had become the Sarkari Babu Sahab clan, who not only take the benefits of reservations but also conveniently forget the community once they get there. It is also observed that while this sect functions throughout with the brand 'Dalit', also engage in all the corrupt practices that was once the cornerstone of Brahministic culture and ethics. It is interesting that Ambedkar fought for the rights of Dalits and had a broader vision, which couldn't be inculcated by post–Ambedkar Ambedkarites. He wanted to give his people an identity so that they get out of Varna System, but here what we see is the stimulation of the culture of varna and caste within the Dalit communities.

Despite the leaps and bounds, the Dalit movement made in Indian context, the failure of Ambedkarite movement to address the questions of fascism, communalism, globalisation, imperialism and the most importantly patriarchy in relation with casteism has altogether dragged the Dalit movement to the crossroad in the present context.

## DALIT MOVEMENT AT A CROSSROAD

Any pragmatic and progressive movement cannot stand on the selective criticism of a few religious texts or political ideologies and conveniently keeping quiet on other questions. A movement cannot be built on superfluous philosophy of negativism. It has to provide its own alternative to the people. To quote V.B. Rawat, Dalits have their own distinct identity and culture and those claiming to provide them an alternative God really misquote Ambedkar and kill their revolutionary spirit as suggested by many Dalit activists.

Ambedkar's popularity among the Dalits is not due to the corrupt Dalits who use all tactics to grab money and power but the poor Dalits who consider him as the liberator. There are many reasons for the same. Ambedkar is a uniting factor for Dalits. No doubt that he has become an icon of Dalits from North to South from Hindi heartland to the southern Tamilnadu. However he himself was against 'hero worship' of any time. He believed in the exploration of knowledge on historical and scientific basis. This has to be a regular, rather ongoing, process which is only possible by addressing the problems of the oppressed and exploited masses. The undeniable fact is the Ambedkar is mainly known among the working class Dalits. The only way to salute Bhimrao is by truly standing against oppressive structure, for equality and justice.

## References:

Aggarwal, L. B.: *The Harijans in Rebellion*, Taraporewala and Sons, Bombay, 1934.

Ainapur, L. S.: *Dynamics of Caste Relations in Rural India*, Rawat Publications, Jaipur, 1986.

Anand, J. H.: *Dalit Literature is the Literature of Protest*, Dalit Solidarity, Delhi, 1995.

Bose, N. K.: *The Scheduled Castes and Tribes and Their Present Conditions*, University of Calcutta, Calcutta, 1969.

Engineer, Asghar Ali.: *Mandal Commission Controversy*, Ajanta Publications, Delhi, 1991.

Fisher, F.B.: *Touching the Untouchables, India's Silent Revolution*, MacMillan, New York, 1920.

Kakade, S. R.: *Scheduled Castes and National Integration: A Study of Marathwada*, Radiant Pub., New Delhi, 1990.

Khare, R. S.: *The Untouchable as Himself: Ideology, Identity and Pragmatism Among the Lucknow Chamars*, Cambridge University Press, London, 1984.

Kshirsagar, R. K.: *Dalit Movement in India and Its Leaders (1857-1956)*, MD Pub. Pvt. Ltd., New Delhi, 1994.

Mallik, Suneila: *Social Integration of the Scheduled Castes*. Abhinav, New Delhi, 1979.

Punalekar, S. P.: *Dalit Women in India: Issues and Perspectives*, Gyan Publishing House, New Delhi, 1995.

Rajshekar, V. T. : *Dalit Movement in Karnataka*, Christian Literature Society, Madras, 1978.

Webster, John: *The Christian Dalits: A History*, Indian Society for Promoting Christian Knowledge (ISPCK), Delhi, 1994.

18

# Gandhi and Practice of Untouchability in India

**DR. AJAY PARMAR**

*Assistant Professor, Department of History, M.P.G. College, Mussoorie, Uttarakhand.*

**Abstract:** *The issue of untouchability assumed a truly national dimension after Gandhi offered unqualified support to the Vykom Satya-graha launched by some local leaders of Travancore in modern day Kerala, who were trying to remove the ban on the entry of untouchables on the roads surrounding the Vykom temples. Through Young India, Gandhi informed the country about the sufferings of the satyagrahis and, soon after that, the cause was taken up by the national press. In the twenties and early thirties of twentieth century Gandhi was not the undisputed leader of the masses. There were many who did not have faith in his non-violent non-cooperation movement. But his social reforms like eradication of untouchability and picketing toddy shops and sarvodaya ideals received the attention of one and all.*

## MOVEMENT AGAINST UNTOUCHABILITY

A new twist to the civil disobedience movement came in September 1932 when Gandhi, who was in Yeravda Jail, went on a fast as a protest against the segregation of the so-called "untouchables" in the electoral arrangement planned for the new Indian constitution. Uncharitable critics described the fast as a form of coercion, a political blackmail. Gandhi was aware that his fast did exercise a moral pressure, but the pressure was directed not against those who disagreed with him, but against those who loved him and believed in him. He did not expect his critics to react in the same way as his friends and co-workers, but if his self-crucifixion could demonstrate his sincerity to them, the battle would be more than half-won. He sought to prick the conscience of the people and to convey to them something of his own inner anguish at a monstrous social tyranny. The fast dramatized the issues at stake; ostensibly it suppressed reason, but in fact it was designed to free reason from that mixture of inertia and prejudice which had permitted the evil of untouchability, which condemned millions of Hindus to humiliation, discrimination and hardship.

The news that Gandhi was about to fast shook India from one end to the other. September 20, 1932, when the fast began, was observed as a day of fasting and prayer. At Shantiniketan, poet Tagore, dressed in black, spoke to a large gathering on the significance of the fast and the urgency of fighting an age-old evil. There was a spontaneous upsurge of feeling; temples, wells and public places were thrown open to the "untouchables". A number of Hindu leaders met the representatives of the untouchables; an alternative electoral arrangement was agreed upon, and received the approval of the British Government before Gandhi broke his fast.

More important than the new electoral arrangement was the emotional catharsis through which the Hindu community had passed. The fast was intended by Gandhi "to sting the conscience of the Hindu community into right religious action". The scrapping of separate electorates was only the beginning of the end of untouchability. Under Gandhi's inspiration, while he was still in prison, a new organization, Harijan Sevak Sangh was founded to combat untouchability and a new weekly paper, the Harijan, was started. Harijan means "children of God"; it was Gandhi's name for the "untouchables" After his release Gandhi devoted himself almost wholly to the campaign against untouchability. On November 7, 1933, he embarked on a country-wide tour which covered 12,500 miles and lasted for nine months. The tour evoked great enthusiasm for the breaking down of the barriers which divided the untouchables from the rest of the Hindu community, but it also provoked the militancy of the orthodox Hindus. On June 25, while Gandhi was on his way to the municipal hall in Poona, a bomb was thrown at his party. Seven persons were injured, but Gandhi was unhurt. He expressed his "deep pity" for the unknown thrower of the bomb. "I am not aching for martyrdom," he said, "but if it comes in my way in the prosecution of what I consider to be the supreme duty in defence of the faith I hold in common with millions of Hindus, I shall have well earned it." Gandhi's fast had aroused public enthusiasm, but diverted it from political to social issues. In May 1933, he suspended civil disobedience for six weeks. He revived it later, but confined it to himself. A year later he discontinued it: this was a recognition of the fact that the country was fatigued and in no mood to continue a campaign of defiance. These decisions disconcerted many of his adherents, who did not relish his moral and religious approach to political issues, and chafed at his self-imposed restraints. Gandhi sensed the critical mood in the Congress party and in October 1934, announced his retirement from it. For the next three years, not politics but village economics was his dominant interest.

## THE CURSE OF UNTOUCHABILITY

I DO NOT want to be reborn. But if I have to be reborn, I should be born an untouchable, so that I may share their sorrows, sufferings, and the affronts leveled at them, in order that I may endeavour to free myself and them from that miserable condition. I, therefore, prayed that, if I should be born again, I should do so not as a Brahmin, Kshatriya, Vaishya or Shudra, but as an Atishudra. (YI, 4-5-1921, p144)

I was wedded to the work for the extinction of 'untouchability' long before I was wedded to my wife. There were two occasions in our joint life when there was choice between working for the untouchables and remaining with my wife and I would have preferred the first. But thanks to my good wife, the crisis was averted. In my Ashram, which is my family, I have several untouchables and a sweet but naughty girl living as my own daughter. (YI, 5-11-1931, p341)

Love of the people brought the problem of untouchability early into my life. My mother said. 'You must not touch this boy, he is an untouchable.' 'Why not?' I questioned back, and from that day my revolt began. (H, 24-12-1938, p393)

Swaraj is a meaningless term, if we desire to keep a fifth of India under perpetual subjection, and deliberately deny to them the fruits of national culture. We are seeking the aid of God in this great purifying movement, but we deny to the most deserving among his creatures the rights of humanity. Inhuman ourselves we may not plead before the Throne for deliverance from the inhumanity of others. (YI, 25-5-1921, p165)

It is simple fanatical obstinacy to persist in persecuting man in the sacred name of religion. (YI, 11-3-1926, p95)

For reforms of Hinduism and for its real protection, removal of untouchability is the greatest thing...Removal of untouchability is....a spiritual process. (YI, 6-1-1927, p2)

If untouchability lives, Hinduism must die. (H, 28-9-1947, p349)

I would far rather that Hinduism died than that untouchability lived.190

In battling against untouchability and in dedicating myself to that battle, I have no less an ambition than to see a complete regeneration of humanity. It may be a mere dream, as unreal as the silver in the sea-shell. It is not so to me while the dream lasts, and in the words of Romain Rolland, 'Victory lies not in realization of the goal, but in a relentless pursuit after it. (YI, 26-11-1931, p372)

## UNTOUCHABILITY: ITS SOURCE

It is usual to hear all those who feel moved by the deplorable condition of the Untouchables unburden themselves by uttering the cry "We must do something for the Untouchables". One seldom hears any of the persons interested in the problem saying 'Let us do something to change the Touchable Hindu'. It is invariably assumed that the object to be reclaimed is the Untouchables. If there is to be a Mission, it must be to the Untouchables and if the Untouchables can be cured, untouchability will vanish. Nothing requires to be done to the Touchable. He is sound in mind, manners and morals. He is whole, there is nothing wrong with him. Is this assumption correct? Whether correct or not, the Hindus like to cling to it. The assumption has the supreme merit of satisfying themselves that they are not responsible for the problem of the Untouchables.

*How Natural is such an Attitude is Illustrated by the Attitude of the Gentile towards the Jews:* Like the Hindus the Gentiles also do not admit that the Jewish problem is in essence a Gentile problem. The observations of Louis Goulding on the subject are therefore very illuminating. In order to show how the Jewish problem is in its essence a Gentile problem, he says:

"I beg leave to give a very homely instance of the sense in which I consider the Jewish Problem in essence a Gentile Problem. A close acquaintance of mine is a certain Irish terrier of mixed pedigree, the dog Paddy, who is to my friend John Smith as the apple of both his eyes. Paddy dislikes Scotch terriers; it is enough for one to pass within twenty yards of Paddy to deafen the neighbourhood with challenges and insults. It is a practice which John Smith deplores, which, therefore, he does his best to check—all the more as the objects of Paddy's detestation are often inoffensive creatures, who seldom speak first. Despite all his affection for Paddy, he considers, as I do, that Paddy's unmannerly behaviour is due to some measure of original sin in Paddy. It has not yet been suggested to us that what is here involved is a Scotch Terrier Problem and that when Paddy attacks a neighbour who is peacefully engaged in inspecting the evening smells it is the neighbour who should be arraigned for inciting to attack by the fact of his existence."

There is here a complete analogy between the Jewish Problem and the problem of the Untouchables. What Paddy is to the Scotch Terrier, the Gentile is to the Jews, and the Hindu is to the Untouchables. But there is one aspect in which the Jewish Problem stands in contrast to the Gentile Problem. The Jews and the Gentiles are separated by an antagonism of the creeds. The Jewish creed is opposed to that of the Gentile creed. The Hindus and the Untouchables are not separated by any such antagonism. They have a common creed and observe the same cults. The second explanation is that the Jews wish to remain separate from the Gentiles. While the first explanation is chauvinistic the second seems to be founded on historical truth. Many attempts have been made in the past by the Gentiles to assimilate the Jews. But the Jews have always resisted them. Two instances of this may be referred.

The first instance relates to the Napoleonic regime. After the National Assembly of France had agreed to the declaration of the 'Rights of man' to the Jews, the Jewish question was again reopened by the guild merchants and religious reactionaries of Alsace. Napoleon resolved to submit the question to the consideration of the Jews themselves. He convened an Assembly of Jewish Notables of France, Germany and Italy in order to ascertain whether the principles of Judaism were compatible with the requirements of citizenship as he wished to fuse the Jewish element with the dominant population. The Assembly consisting of III deputies, met in the Town Hall of Paris on the 25th of July 1806, and was required to frame replies to twelve questions relating mainly to the possibility of Jewish patriotism, the permissibility of inter-marriage between Jew and Non-Jew, and the legality of usury.

So pleased was Napoleon with the pronouncements of the Assembly that he summoned a Sanhedrin after the model of the ancient council of Jerusalem to convert them into the decree of a Legislative body. The Sanhedrin, comprising of 71 deputies from France, Germany, Holland and Italy met under the presidency of Rabbi Sinzheim, of Strassburg on 9th February 1807, and adopted a sort of Charter which exhorted the Jews to look upon France as their fatherland, to regard its citizens as their brethren, and to speak its language, and which also pressed toleration of marriages between Jews and Christians while declaring that they could not be sanctioned by the synagogue. It will be noted that the Jews refused to sanction intermarriages between Jews and non-Jews. They only agreed to tolerate them.

The second instance relates to what happened when the Batavian Republic was established in 1795. The more energetic members of the Jewish community pressed for a removal of the many disabilities under which they laboured. But the demand for the fuller rights of citizenship made by the progressive Jews was at first, strangely enough, opposed by the leaders of the Amsterdam community, who feared that civil equality would militate against the conservation of Judaism and declared that their co-religionists renounced their rights of citizenship in obedience to the dictates of their faith. This shows that the Jews preferred to live-as strangers rather than as members of the community.

Whatever the value of their explanations the Gentiles have at least realized that there rests upon them a responsibility to show cause for their unnatural attitude towards the Jews. The Hindu has never realised this responsibility of justifying his treatment of the Untouchables.

The responsibility of the Hindus is much greater because there is no plausible explanation he can offer in justification of untouchability. He cannot say that the Untouchable is a leper or a mortal wretch who must be shunned. He cannot say that between him and the Untouchables, there is a gulf due to religious antagonism which is not possible to bridge. Nor can he plead that it is the Untouchable who does not wish to assimilate with the Hindus.

But that is not the case with the Untouchables. They too are in a different sense an eternal people who are separate from the rest. But this separateness, their segregation is not the result of their wish. They are punished not because they do not want to mix. They are punished because they want to be one with the Hindus. In other words, though the problem of the Jews and of the Untouchables is similar in nature—inasmuch as the problem is created by others—it is essentially different. The Jew's case is one of the voluntary isolation. The case of the Untouchables is that of compulsory segregation. Untouchability is an infliction and not a choice.

## UNTOUCHABILITY AND CASTE

It is a wrong to destroy caste because of the outcaste, as it would be to destroy a body because of an ugly growth in it or of a crop because of the weeds.

The outcasteness, in the sense we understand it, has therefore to be destroyed altogether. It is an excess to be removed, if the whole system is not to perish. Untouchability is the product, therefore, not of the caste system, but of the distinction of high and low that has crept into Hinduism and is corroding it.

The attack on untouchability is thus an attack upon this 'high-and-low'-ness. The moment untouchability goes, the caste system itself will be purified, that is to say, according to my dream, it will resolve itself into the true Varnadharma, the four division of society, each complementary of the other and none inferior or superior to any other, each as necessary for the whole body of Hinduism as any other. (H, 11-2-1933, p3)

### Varnashrama Dharma

Varnashrama Dharma defines man's mission on this earth. He is not born day after day to explore avenues for amassing riches and to explore different means of livelihood; on the contrary, man is born in order that he may utilize every atom of his energy for the purpose of knowing his Maker. It restricts him, therefore, for the purpose of holding body and soul together, to the occupation of his forefathers. That and nothing more or nothing less is Varnashrama Dharma. (YI, 27-10-1927, p357)

I do, however, believe in varna which is based on hereditary occupations. Varnas are four to mark four universal occupations,- imparting knowledge, defending the defenseless, carrying on agriculture and commerce, and performing service through physical labour. These occupations are common to all mankind, but Hinduism, having recognized them as the law of our being, has made use of it in regulating social relations and conduct. Gravitation affects us all, whether one knows its existence or not. But scientists who knew the law have made it yield results that have startled the world. Even so has Hinduism startled the world by its discovery and application of the law of varna. When Hindus were seized with inertia, abuse of varna resulted in innumerable castes, with unnecessary and harmful restrictions as to inter-marriage and inter-dine. These restrictions may be necessary in the interest of chastity and hygiene. But a Brahmana who marries a Shudra girl, or vice versa, commits no offence against the law of varnas. (YI, 4-6-1931, p129)

Today Brahmins and Kshatriyas, Vaishyas and Shudras are mere labels. There is utter confusion of varna as I understand it and I wish that all the Hindus will voluntarily call themselves Shudras. That is the only way to demonstrate the truth of Brahminism and to revive Varnadharma in its true state. (H, 25-3-1933, p3) I believe that every man is born in the world with certain natural tendencies. Every person is born with certain definit limitations which he cannot overcome. From a careful observation of those limitations the law of varna was deduced. It established certain spheres of actions for certain people with certain tendencies. This avoided all unworthy competition. Whilst recognizing limitations, the law of varna admitted of no distinctions of high and low; on the one hand, it guaranteed to each the fruits of his labours, and one the other, it prevented him from pressing upon his neighbours. This great law has been degraded and fallen into disrepute. But my conviction is that an ideal social order will only be evolved when the implications of this law are fully understood and given effect to. (MR, Oct. 1935, p413)

## Inter-marriage and Inter-dining

Though there is in Varnashrama no prohibition against inter-marriage and inter-dining, there can be no compulsion. It must be left to the unfettered choice of the individual as to where he or she will marry or dine. (H, 16-11-1935, p316)

## Caste

......I consider the four divisions alone to be fundamental, natural and essential. The innumerable sub castes are sometimes a convenience, often a hindrance. The sooner there is fusion the better. (YI, 8-12-1920, p3)

From the economic point of view, its value was once very great. It ensured hereditary skill; it limited competition. It was the best remedy against pauperism. And it had all the advantages of trade guilds. Although it did not foster adventure or invention there, it is not known to have come in the way either... Historically speaking, caste may regarded as man's experiment or social adjustment in the laboratory of Indian society. If we can prove it to be a success, it can be offered to the world as a leaven and as the best remedy against heartless competition and social disintegration born of avarice and greed. (YI, 5-1-1921, p2)

## Caste and Varna

...I have frequently said that I do not believe in caste in the modern sense. It is an excrescence and a handicap on progress. Nor do I believe in inequalities between human beings. We are all absolutely equal. But equality is of souls and not bodies. Hence, it is a mental state. We need to thing of, and to assert, equality because we see great inequalities in the physical world. We have to realize equality in the midst of this apparent external inequality. Assumption of superiority by any person over any other is a sin against God and man. Thus caste, in so far as it 0connots distinctions in status, is an evil. (YI, 4-6-1931, p129)

Caste distinctions have taken such deep root amongst us that they have also infected the Muslims, Christians and followers of other religions in India. It is true that class barriers are also to be found in more or less degree in other parts of the world. This means that it is a distemper common to the human race. It can be eliminated only by the inculcation of religion in its true sense. I have not found sanction for such barriers and distinctions in the scriptures of any religion.

In the eye of religion all men are equal. Learning, intellect or riches do not entitle one to claim superiority over those who are lacking in these. If any person is suffused and sanctified with the purifying essence and discipline of true religion, he regards himself under the obligation to share his advantages with those who have fewer. That being so, in our present fallen state, true religion requires us all to become Atishudras by choice.

We must regard ourselves not as owners, but as trustees of our wealth, and use it for the service of society, taking for ourselves no more than a fair return for service rendered. Under this system there would be none poor, none rich. All religions would be held equal. All quarrels arising out of religion, caste or economic grievance would cease to disturb peace on earth. (Hu, 19-9-1945)

## ROLE OF MAHATMA GANDHI IN UPLIFTING THE UNTOUCHABLES

According to Gandhiji, the practice of untouch-ability is "a leper wound in the whole-body of Hindu politic". He even regarded it as "the hate fullest expression of caste". He made it his life's mission to wipe out untouchability and to uplift the de-pressed and the downtrodden people. As a servant of mankind, he preached that all human beings are equal and hence the Harijans too have a right for social life along with other caste groups.

## Gandhiji's Appeal to the Conscience of the People

Gandhiji believed in the four-fold division of the Hindu society into four varnas. He regarded untouchables as. Shudras and not as the Panchamas or fifth Varna or Avarna.

Hence he sincerely felt the need for bringing about a basic change in the caste structure by uplifting the untouchables and not by abolishing the caste as such. He appealed to the conscience of the people to realise the historical necessity of accommodating the "Harijans" by providing them a rightful place in the society.

Gandhiji had much compassion for the Harijans. He said: "I do not want to be reborn. But if I am to be born, I would like to be born an untouchable, so that I may share their sorrows and sufferings."

He was of the opinion that the practice of untouchability was a moral crime. He said that "if untouchability is not wrong, then nothing in the world is wrong." He believed that a change of heart on the part of the Hindus was essential to enable the social and cultural assimilation of Harijans. He was very much moved by their social distress and started a nationwide movement to remove their disabilities.

## Gandhiji's Campaign against Untouchability

Gandhiji who regarded untouchability as a blot on Hinduism wanted to do away with it com-pletely. He wrote in 1920 "… Without the removal of the taint [of untouchability], "Swaraj" is a meaningless term." He even felt that the foreign domination of our country was the result of our exploitation of almost one-sixth of our own people in the name of religion.

He advocated positive means for the uplift of Harijans. He addressed various public meetings reposing doctrines of Harijan welfare. He led several processions of Harijans with other upper caste people and made them participate in "poojas, bhajans, keerthans and puranas".

He believed that opportunities of education and temple entry would reduce social inequalities be-tween Harijans and caste Hindus. He launched movements for cleaning Harijan residential areas, for digging wells for them and for similar other beneficial things. Gandhiji wrote in "Young India" in April 1925. "Temples, public wells ana public schools must be open to the untouchables equally with caste Hindus." He started two journals, 'Harijan' and 'Young India' through which he advocated his ideas. He started an ashram where people of all castes and creeds could come and stay without any differences.

Gandhiji served the "Harijan Sevak Sangha" started by the social reformer Takkar Bapa in the year 1932 for working out the religious and social welfare of the Harijans. The organisation opened schools and dispensaries in various places and arranged for free educational facilities and scholar-ships for Harijan children.

## Political Role of Gandhiji

As a much respected political leader of the masses, Gandhiji could never ignore the tasks of the removal of untouchability and upliftment of Harijans. Gandhiji entered the Indian freedom struggle in 1919.

From 1920 onwards, under the leadership of Gandhiji the Indian National Congress became committed to get the independence on the one hand and to the removal of untouchability on the other. In 1920 itself, he declared that "Untouchability cannot be given a secondary place in the programme" of Congress.

## Gandhiji's Protest against the Proposal of Separate Electorate for Harijans

Gandhiji was very much against the British policy of "divide and rule". He condemned the British policy of separating the Harijans from the rest of the Hindu Hence he protested against the proposal of creating separate electorate for the Harijans. He said to Ambedkar who was in favour of the pro-posal, that "the political separation of the untouchables from the Hindus would be suicidal to the nation."

Gandhiji declared at the Minorities Committee of the Second Round Table Conference in Lon-don [1932] that "we do not want the untouchables to be classified as a separate class. Sikhs may remain such in perpetuity, so many Muslims and Christians. Will the untouchables remain untouch-ables in perpetuity? I would rather feel that Hinduism died than that untouchability lived. I will resist it with my life."

## Impact of Gandhiji's "fast-Unto-Death" Satyagraha

In spite of Gandhiji's protest, the British Prime Minister decided to grant separate seats for the depressed classes and the right of double vote in which they could elect their own representatives and also vote in which they could elect their own representatives and also vote in general elections. In protest against this "communal award" Gandhiji decided to stage the fast unto death satyagraha. This declaration of Gandhiji opened the eyes of the whole country towards the problem of untouchables.

In 1932 the Harijan Sevak Sangh was formed and its Conference at Bombay pledged that the right to use the public roads, wells etc. would be given statutory recognition when the Swaraj Parlia-ment met.

This pledge was stressed by Gandhiji in 1932 when he said, "There could be no rest…until untouchability becomes a thing of the past." The Harijan movement gained strength throughout the country. Gandhi went on an all-India tour to collect huge sums of money for this programme.

## GANDHIJI COMMITS CONGRESS FOR THE REMOVAL OF UNTOUCHABILITY

At the behest of Gandhiji and the Congress, all the Congress candidates who contested elections in 1937 had pledged them-selves to the removal of untouchability. An early as in 1931 itself at the Karachi Session of the

Congress at the behest of Gandhiji, a resolution was adopted. It declared, "all the citizens are equal before law irrespective of caste, creed or sex." In 1938, the Removal of the Civil Disabilities Act was passed by the Madras Legislature which provided that no Harijan shall be disabled from any social or public amenity. In the same year, it also passed the Malabar Temple Entry Act which threw open the temples in Malabar.

In 1939, the temple of Madurai was opened to the Harijans. Thus Gandhiji's fast and his Harijan movement released tremendous forces throughout the country, which led to the removal of some of the disabilities of the Harijans.

### Gandhiji's personal involvement in the Harijan welfare activities

Gandhiji was not just a preacher. He practised what he preached. He could win the hearts of millions of Harijans because of his sincere approach to solve their problems. Gandhiji lived with the Harijans and shared their dis-tress by indicating in them the ideas of better social adjustment with the rest of the Indian community. He advocated equal opportunities of education and intermingling of Harijan students with those of the upper castes. He fought for various legal protections against several kinds of injustices done to them. He adopted a Harijan child and set an example for others to emulate.

As a result of his sincere efforts and strong recommendations, untouchability was declared illegal under the Indian Constitu-tion. At his behest an opportunity was given to Dr. B.R. Ambedkar, leader of the depressed classes, to join the Central Cabinet and to be the chief architect of the Indian Constitution.

## Gandhiji's Proposals for Harijan Welfare

Gandhiji's proposals for Harijan welfare include the following:

1. Those who claim themselves to be the servants of Harijan must serve the Harijans with all the dedication.
2. Awareness must be created among the Harijans regarding cleanliness, sanitation and health.
3. The practice of carrying human waste on head must be stopped.
4. They should be persuaded to drop their habit of eating carrion and dead animals.
5. Practice of untouchability must be immediately stopped by all.
6. Harijans must be provided with drinking water facility.
7. Good houses at low cost but with enough provision for lighting and ventilation must be built for Harijans.
8. Harijan children must be made to go to school and even adult education programme should be introduced.
9. Harijans must be persuaded to drop their habit of drinking alcohol.
10. Harijans must be allowed to enter all the public places and to draw water from the wells.
11. There should be no bar for the entry of Harijans to temples.
12. "Harijan Day" should be observed by all at least one day in a year.

Ambedkar and Gandhiji who fought against the problem of untouchability and served to promote the welfare of "untouchables" are not alive today. Their followers are, however, continuing their work. Untouchability has not yet become "the thing of the past".

The removal of untouchability requires a basic transformation in the general attitude towards it. Gandhiji was right when he wrote in his letter to Thakkar Bapa: "The salvation of the depressed class will come only when the caste Hindu is made to think and is forced to feel that he must alter his ways. I want a revolution in the mentality of the caste Hindus." The country is awaiting such a revolution.

## References

Biswas, C.C. : *Bengal's Response to Gandhi*, Kolkata, Minerva Associates, 2004.

Chavan, Sheshrao : *Mahatma Gandhi : Man of the Millennium*, Delhi, Authors Press, 2001.

George, Davis : *Dynamics of Power : The Gandhian Perspective*, New Delhi, Frank Bros. & Co., 2000.

Kachappilly, Joy : *Gandhi and Truth : An Approach to the Theology of Religions*, New Delhi, Akansha, 2005.

Kripalani, Krishna : *All Men are Brothers*, Navjivan Publishing House, 1937.

Kumar, Ravindra : *Gandhian Thoughts : An Overview*, New Delhi, Gyan, 2006.

Pandey, Janardan : *Gandhi and 21st Century*, 1998.

Parihar, A.K.S. : *Mahatma Gandhi : His Thoughts, Life and Ideas*, New Delhi, Swastik Pub., 2007.

Parikh, Nilam : *Gandhiji's Lost Jewel: Harilal Gandhi*, New Delhi, National Gandhi Museum, 2001.

Singh, Ramjee : *Gandhi and The New Millennium*, Delhi, Commonwealth, 2000.

Vettickal, Thomas : *Gandhian Sarvodaya : Realizing a Realistic Utopia*, New Delhi, Gyan Publishing House, 2002.

Weber, Thomas : *Gandhi, Gandhism and the Gandhians*, New Delhi, Roli Books, 2006.

19

# Caste System in Indian Society with Reference to the Women

**DR. NISHA CHAUDHARY**

*Assistant Professor, Department of Sociology, Amar Singh (P.G.) College, Lakhoti, Bulandshehar, Uttar Pradesh.*

Assessments of human development at the aggregate level hide gender differences. Women belonging to marginalised groups suffer triple deprivations arising out of lack of access to economic resources, caste and gender discrimination. SC and ST women constitute perhaps the most economically deprived section of Indian society. Most of them don't own agricultural land and work as wage labourers.

In 2001, about 57% of SC and 37% of ST women respectively were agricultural wage labour in rural areas, as compared with 29% for non-SC/STs. In urban areas, 16% SC and 14% ST women were daily wage labourers as compared with only 6% from non-SC/STs. Only 21% of SC women were cultivators compared with 51% for STs and 45% for non-SC/STs. SC/ST women also faced differential treatment in wage-earning, particularly in urban areas. In 2000, SC and ST women casual labourers received daily wages of Rs 37 and Rs 34 respectively, compared with Rs 56 for non-SC/ST women; the national average was Rs 42.

Besides this, a large number of SC women are engaged in so-called 'unclean' occupations, like scavenging. Because of their association with these occupations, the women face discrimination in the social and economic spheres.

Lack of educational development is another important problem. In 2000, the literacy rate among SC and ST rural females (aged 15 and above) was 24% and 23% respectively, compared with 41% for non-SC/ST women. The literacy rate among SC women in urban areas was

48%, compared with 54% and 70% for ST and non-SC/ST women respectively. The dropout rate among SC and ST women is also relatively high at every stage of education. The high dependence on casual labour, with relatively low earnings, among SC and ST women induced a high degree of deprivation and poverty among them.

The gender break-up of poverty is not available. However, the high degree of deprivation is reflected in other indicators of wellbeing — under-nutrition and health. About 65% and 56% of ST and SC women respectively suffered from anaemia compared to 47.6% of non-SC/ST women. In 1998-99, 21.2% of SC and 26% of ST children under four years of age suffered from malnutrition (based on weight-for-age). Of these underweight children, 54% of SCs and 56% of STs were severely undernourished. There is a significant difference between SC and ST children and non-SC/ST children, 13.80% and 41.1% of whom are malnourished and undernourished respectively.

While the Government of India has adopted the national goal of reducing the present infant mortality rate (IMR) to 60 by 2000, the SC's IMR, child mortality and under-5 mortality is 83.00, 39.50 and 119.3, respectively. Compare this with 61.8, 22.2 and 82.6 for non-SC/STs, respectively. Similarly, IMR, child mortality and under-5 mortality are 84, 46.3 and 126 among STs.

About 72% of births to SC women and 81% of births to ST women took place at home; the corresponding figure for others is 59%.

Because of their lower social status, sexual exploitation of SC/ST women is also high. There are some caste-related social customs and religious practices in Hindu society that exploit only women from dalit communities. One of these customs is devdasi or jogini, involving religious prostitution imposed on unfortunate girls who are married to a village god and then become the subject of sexual exploitation by upper caste men in a village. A primary survey estimates the number of joginis in six districts of Andhra Pradesh at 21,421. There are similar practices in states like Tamil Nadu, Karnataka and Maharashtra where dalit women are designated devdasis or devotees of god.

## THE ECONOMIC EXCLUSION OF THE DALITS IN INDIA

In much of South Asia and India in particular, caste has become coterminous with race in the definition and exclusion of distinct population groups because of their descent. For one hundred and sixty million Dalits or 'untouchables' at the bottom of India's caste system – a population on par with that of Russia or Brazil – the exclusion extends to the economic realms of wages, jobs, education, and land. Despite formal protections in law, discriminatory treatment remains endemic and discriminatory societal norms continue to be reinforced by government and private structures, often through violent means.

Dalits are denied access to land, forced to work in degrading conditions, and routinely abused at the hands of the police and of higher-caste groups that enjoy the state's protection. In what has been called India's "hidden apartheid," entire villages in many Indian states remain completely segregated by caste. Untouchability endures as a cover for exploitative economic relationships and the caste system survives a cruel and efficient economic order.

Under constitutional provisions and various laws, the state grants Dalits a certain number of privileges, including reservations (quotas) in education, government jobs, and government bodies. National and state legislation also outlaw the practice of bonded labour and manual scavenging, set ceilings on a single landowner's holdings, allocate surplus government lands to Dalit and tribal populations, and criminalise the practice of 'untouchability' and other atrocities against low-caste communities.

The government has also attempted to increase the self-sufficiency of the scheduled-caste1 population through financial assistance for self-employment activities and through development programs designed to increase education and skills. Protective measures are monitored by the National Commission for Scheduled Castes and Scheduled Tribes. Development measures for the educational, social, and economic uplifting of scheduled castes are administered by the Department of Welfare. Despite this large body of legislation and administrative agency mandates assigned exclusively to deal with the plight of scheduled castes, the laws have benefited few and, due to a lack of political will, development programs and welfare projects designed to improve economic conditions for Dalits have generally had little effect.

Although the constitutional abolition of 'untouchability' in 1950 meant that upper-caste Hindus could no longer segregate Dalits or force them to perform any 'polluting' occupation, caste prejudice and corruption within the police and judiciary have effectively ensured that atrocities against Dalits go unpunished, that land reforms remain unimplemented, and that prohibitions on bonded labour and manual scavenging remain unenforced. Upper-caste threats of physical abuse and social boycotts for refusing to perform demeaning tasks also ensure preservation of the economic status quo.

Any strategy to combat racial discrimination against Dalits must begin with a meaningful understanding of the economics of exclusion. This paper sets out to describe the links between racial and economic discrimination against Dalits in India, and the violent and degrading mechanisms by which each is sustained and institutionalised.

It argues that the government's longstanding failure to enforce its own protective legislation or implement strategies to narrow the socio-economic gap between Dalits and the rest of the population has only been exacerbated by India's economic reforms. The paper ends with possible strategies at the national and global level to break the cycle of economic dependency and physical vulnerability.

## CASTE AND EMPLOYMENT DISCRIMINATION

Allocation of labour on the basis of caste is one of the fundamental tenets of the caste system. In traditional Indian society, Hinduism's fourfold varna theory describes a broad functional division of labour. For those within the four principal caste categories, caste has not proved to be a completely rigid system. Just as the higher ritual status of Brahmins does not necessarily translate into economic or political supremacy, those lower in the ranks are able to move up in the local hierarchy through the capture of political power, the acquisition of land, and migration to other regions.

For Dalits, however, who occupy the fifth and lowest caste category, caste remains a determinative factor for the attainment of social, political, civil, and economic rights. Migration and the anonymity of the urban environment have in some cases resulted in upward occupational mobility, but the majority continues to perform their traditional or 'polluting' functions. A lack of training and education, as well as discrimination in seeking other forms of employment, have kept these traditions and their hereditary nature alive. Many 'untouchable' community members, for example, continue to work as leather workers, disposers of dead animals, and manual scavengers. As part of village custom, Dalits are made to render free services in times of death, marriage, or any village function. The cleaning of the whole village, the digging of graves, the carrying of firewood, and the disposal of dead animals are also tasks that Dalits are made to perform. A majority of the Dalit rural workforce subsists on the menial wages of landless agricultural labourers, earning less than US$1 a day. Those in urban areas, work mostly in the unorganised sector. India's much touted system of affirmative action or reservations for scheduled castes assists less than 1 percent of the Dalit population. In all forms of labour, women are consistently paid less than men, compounding the dual discrimination of caste and gender.

## Manual Scavenging

According to government statistics, an estimated one million Dalits are manual scavengers (a majority of them women) who clear faeces from public and private latrines and dispose of dead animals; unofficial estimates are much higher. Manual scavenging is a caste-based occupation, deemed too polluting and filthy for anyone but Dalits. Manual scavengers exist under different caste names throughout the country, such as the Bhangis in Gujarat, the Pakhis in Andhra Pradesh, and the Sikkaliars in Tamil Nadu.

Members of these communities are invariably placed at the very bottom of the caste hierarchy, and even the hierarchy of Dalit sub-castes. Using little more than a broom, a tin plate, and a basket, they are made to clear faeces from public and private latrines and carry them to dumping grounds and disposal sites. Though long outlawed, the practice of manual scavenging continues in most states.

An activist in the southern state of Andhra Pradesh, who has been working for the rehabilitation of cleaning workers for the past sixteen years, describes the pay scale in his state: Private cleaners receive Rs.5 to ten a month for each house they clean [US$0.11 to $0.21].

They clean up to ten to fifteen houses a day, many of which have six or more family members. Those employed by urban municipalities are paid Rs.2,000 to Rs.2,500 [US$43-$53] a month but are only paid once every four to six months. Some are permanent, and some are casual. There are no health benefits, no gloves, no masks, and no utensils. The majority is made up of women. Social discrimination against scavengers is rampant.

Most scavengers live in segregated rural colonies and are unable to make use of common resources. According to the activist: In one toilet there can be as many as four hundred seats which all have to be manually cleaned. This is the lowest occupation in the world, and it is done by the community that occupies the lowest status in the caste system. Even other scheduled-caste people won't touch the safai karamcharis [cleaning workers]. It is 'untouchability' within the 'untouchables,' yet nobody questions it. Poverty among Bhangis is so acute, that some have even been known to separate non-digested wheat from buffalo dung to make chappatis (flat bread). When interviewed in early 1998, thirty-year-old Parsotambhai, a mother of three in Ahmedabad district, Gujarat, earned Rs.10 (US$0.21) a month for each house she cleaned. She also received small amounts of food once a day and complained that there was too much work. Others voiced similar complaints:

They give one person too much work so they have to take their family members, even their children, at night to finish the work; otherwise, they would be fired. It takes four people to do the work that they give one person. None of the children are really studying. Girls sometimes study up to fifth standard, boys up to seventh.

The Employment of Manual Scavengers and Construction of Dry Latrines (Prohibition) Act, 1993 prohibits the employment of scavengers or the construction of dry (non-flush) latrines with imprisonment for up to one year and/or a fine as high as Rs.2,000 (US$43). Offenders are also liable for prosecution under the Scheduled Castes and Scheduled Tribes (Prevention of Atrocities) Act, 1989. In 1992, the government launched a national scheme that called for the identification, training, and rehabilitation of safai karamcharis (cleaning workers) throughout the country. Yet when confronted with the existence of manual scavenging and dry latrines within their jurisdiction, state governments often deny their existence altogether or claim that a lack of water supply prevents states from constructing flush latrines. This despite the fact that a sum of Rs.4,640,000,000 (US$992.3 million) was allocated to the scheme under the government's Eighth Five-Year Plan. Activists claim that the resources, including government funds, exist for construction and for the rehabilitation of scavengers; what is lacking is the political will to do so.

## References

Bisht B.S. : *Ethnography of a Tribe : Study of Anwals of Uttarakhand Himalaya*, Rawat, Delhi, 2001.

Blunt, E. A. H.: *Caste System of Northern India*, Oxford University Press, London, 1931.

Karma Oraon : *Dimension of Religion, Magic and Festivals of Indian Tribe: The Munda*, Kanishka, 2002.

Karve, Irawati: *Hindu Society: An Interpretation*, Sangam Press, Poona, 1961.

Murugkar, Lata. *Dalit Panther Movement in Maharashtra: A Sociological Appraisal*, Popular Prakashan, Bombay, 1991.

Naidu, A. Nagaraja: *Caste and Land in Colonial South India*, Rawat Publications, New Delhi, 1994.

Omprakash, S.: *Development of the Weaker Section: Problems, Policies and Issues*, Uppal Publishing House, New Delhi, 1989.

Paranjpe, A. C.: *Caste, Prejudice and the Individual*, Lalvani Publishing House, New Delhi, 1970.

Sharma, B. D.: *Dalits Betrayed*, Har-Anand Publications, New Delhi, 1994.

Sharma, K. L.: *Caste, Class and Social Movements*, Rawat Publications, Jaipur, 1986.

20

# The Impact of Population Growth on the Development Process in India

**DR. PANKAJ KUMAR**
*Assistant Professor, Department of Geography, J.V.Jain (P.G.) College, Saharanpur, Uttar Pradesh.*

Distribution of population refers to general distribution of population of a region or a country. But density of population refers to average number of persons per sq km. The table given on the next page shows the distribution of population and density of population in the states and *Union Territories of India* according to the census of 2001. The table shows that the highest population is found in the state of *Uttar Pradesh (16,6052,859)* and the highest density is recorded in the state of *West Bengal (904)*. The lowest population is found in the state of *Sikkim* and the lowest of population is recorded in the state of *Arunachal Pradesh*. According the *Union Territories*, the highest population and highest density of population occur in *Delhi*. The lowest population is found in *Lakshadweep*; but the lowest density of population prevails in the *Andaman and Nicobar Islands*. The over-all picture (*States and the Union territories together*) shows the following facts: (1) the highest population in *U.P.*, (2) the highest density of population in *Delhi*, (3) the lowest population in *Lakshadweep* and (4) the lowest density of population in *Arunachal Pradesh*.

## POPULATION SIZE, DISTRIBUTION AND GROWTH

Populations are dynamic entities. Over time they grow or decline, they become younger or older and their geographic distribution changes. Such changes are the cumulative effects of the events that people undergo during their lives, namely births, deaths and migrations. One of the concerns in demography is to trace out the consequence of changes in individual-level behaviour for aggregate processes. The combination of these individual events shapes the population of each country, and, though partially predictable, the outcome is sometimes surprising. While no other century has witnessed such rapid and accelerating population growth as did the twentieth, population declines have been observed in several countries during the past decade or so. Such declines are foreseen to become the rule rather than the exception in some regions of the world, while in other regions the population will continue to grow, albeit at a more moderate pace.

## POPULATION SIZE AND DISTRIBUTION

In the year 2005, the world population is estimated to have reached 6.5 billion, more than two and a half times the level in 1950; according to the medium-variant projection of the 2004 Revision, it is expected to reach 9.1 billion in 2050. The less developed regions, with 5.3 billion people in 2005, account for the vast majority of the world population (81.3 per cent). The more developed regions have an estimated population of 1.2 billion, or 18.7 per cent of the world population.

More and more of the world's inhabitants are coming to reside in the less developed regions, increasing from 67.7 per cent in 1950 to a projected 86.4 per cent in 2050. Within the less developed regions in 2005, the least developed countries account for about 0.8 billion and other less developed countries for 4.5 billion. The share of the least developed countries is projected to grow from 8.0 per cent in 1950 to 19.1 per cent in 2050. Asia, with a population of 3.9 billion in 2005, is by far the most populous major area; its share of the world population stays fairly stable over time, rising and falling slightly in the neighbourhood of 55-60 per cent between 1950 and 2050.

The population shares of two other major areas,however, have shifted considerably since 1950, and this shifting is expected to continue. Europe's population represented 21.7 per cent of the world population in 1950, a figure that was reduced by almost half by 2005, to 11.3 per cent. Europe's share of the world population is projected to decline furthermore, to 7.2 per cent in 2050. At the same time, Africa's share of the world population has been increasing, from 8.9 per cent in 1950 to 14.0 per cent in 2005, and is projected to reach 21.3 per cent in 2050, close to Europe's share in 1950. The social and economic disadvantages afflicting least developed countries are often vividly expressed in basic demographic indicators. In assessing the challenges to international development that are presented by these countries, it should be remembered that they account for a relatively small share of the world population: 11.7 per cent in 2005. The other less developed countries, which include China and India, the two most populous countries collectively account for 69.5 per cent of the world population. Most of the world's population is found in a small set of very populous countries. A mere 4.8 per cent of all countries, that is, the 11 largest countries, each with an estimated population of 100 million or more in the year 2005, lay claim to 60.9 per cent of the world population. The vast majority of the world's countries are actually relatively small in terms of their population size—of all countries, 77.2 per cent have populations under 20 million (with almost one third of all countries having fewer than 1 million). Taken as a group, these small countries account for only 11.6 per cent of the world population, while countries with populations from 20 million to 100 million include 18.0 per cent of all countries and 27.5 per cent of all population. Taken together, the 11 largest countries are home to more than 3.9 billion people.

Jointly, China and India account for more than 37 per cent of the world population in 2005, with estimated populations of 1.3 billion and 1.1 billion, respectively. A further 9 countries account for almost a quarter of the earth's population, namely, the United States of America, Indonesia, Brazil, Pakistan, the Russian Federation, Bangladesh, Nigeria, Japan and Mexico. Eight of the 11 most populous countries are considered to be less developed, leaving only 3 in the more developed regions (the United States of America, with a population of 298 million; the Russian Federation, with 143 million; and Japan, with 128 million). These large, more-developed countries account for almost 9 per cent of the world population, a considerable share but far below that of China and India. The concentration of world population in large countries has been lessening, and this trend is projected to continue. In 1950, the combined populations of some 21 countries accounted for three-quarters of the population of the globe, a number that increased to 24 countries in 2005. By 2050, according to the mediumvariant projection, 28 countries will be needed to reach that same share. Inevitably, several countries are projected to change ranks over thenext 45 years. India and China will likely trade places at the very top of the population rankings , Nigeria is expected to rise from 9th to 6th in rank, and the Russian Federation will likely fall from 7th to 17th.

In addition, three least developed countries—Bangladesh, the Democratic Republic of the Congo and Ethiopia—will be among the ten most populous countries. Population growth would be substantially greater in the absence of fertility decline. If fertility were to be held constant at its current level for every country, the world population would reach a total of 11.7 billion persons by the year 2050, almost doubling its present size. The extent of growth is all the more impressive when one considers that an assumed constant fertility fixes a number of countries at below-replacement fertility levels.

Alternatively, if total fertility were to adhere to the high-fertility variant , usually half a child above what is assumed in the medium-variant projection but generally declining over time, the world total would reach 10.6 billion in 2050. Under the low-fertility assumption, by contrast, with total fertility rates usually set at half a child below the medium variant, world population would reach 7.7 billion, far lower but still representing an addition of 1.2 billion persons to the world's current total. Evidently, the pace and depth of fertility decline will continue to have an important impact on world population levels and trends. Anticipated mortality trends will also influence the overall population.

The basic projection variants assume a single course of mortality change, usually a continuous decline, for each country. If mortality rates were held constant at their current levels, however, under the medium fertility variant world population would rise to 8.1 billion persons in 2050, about 1 billion less than the projected levels. Although there are important differences across these projection variants, in one respect they all agree: an era of substantial world population growth lies ahead. The estimated and projected world population levels are the product of divergent trends across the more developed and less developed regions. For the more developed regions, it seems that an era of population decline may not be too far into the future. According to the medium-variant projection, the aggregate population of this region will rise from the year 2005 estimate of 1.21 billion persons to a peak of 1.25 billion around 2030, and will then fall to 1.24 billion by the end of the projection period, yielding a net addition of only about 25 million.

Only the high fertility variant suggests continued growth in the populations of the more developed regions. Note that if current levels of fertility were to be maintained, as assumed in the constant fertility variant, the populations of the more developed regions would fall below the medium-variant projection. Likewise, the path of fertility decline will make an important difference to the futures of the other less developed countries, a group that includes China, India, Indonesia, Brazil, Pakistan and other populous nations. The medium-variant projection for these countries indicates continued population growth, with their total rising from 4.5 billion persons in 2005 to 6.1 billion in 2050. Continuation of current fertility rates would add an expected 1.6 billion persons to the total population of these countries (relative to the medium variant), whereas the expected total would be only 632 million above the current population if the low fertility variant were to prevail. To sum up, for all less developed regions combined, constant fertility would imply total populations of 10.5 billion in 2050, well above the 7.8 billion produced by the medium variant.

Under most projection scenarios, population decline will occur in the more developed regions at some point in the projection period The anticipated trend at the aggregate level, however, masks differences at the national and regional level. Some developed countries are expected to continue to grow, but others may experience population declines. Overall, among all countries with a population of at least 100,000 in the year 2000, according to the results of the medium variant, 44 countries are expected to experience a reduction in population between 2005 and 2050, the majority of them located in the more developed regions.

The prospects for population decline in selected countries and regions of the more developed world are quite striking The most substantial population decline relative to present levels is likely to occur in Eastern Europe, which is projected to lose about 25 per cent of its current total population by 2050. The Russian Federation, which constitutes approximately 48 per cent of Eastern Europe's population in 2005, is projected to decline by some 22 per cent. Other Eastern European countries, such as Ukraine, Belarus and Bulgaria, are also expected to experience a substantial decline in their population size. The least developed countries comprise 50 countries that are located mainly in Africa and Asia, plus small island developing States1 from Oceania and the Caribbean.

Jointly, these countries have recorded relatively higher fertility and mortality levels than the more developed regions and the other less developed countries, a trend that is expected to continue in the coming decades. Since the 1970s, the least developed countries have experienced, on average, the highest population growth rates in the world. Even though they represent a relatively small share of the world population, just under 12 per cent in 2005, it is expected that the overall population increment in those countries will account for 37 per cent of all world population growth during the period 2005-2050.

Though fertility has been declining in most countries of this group, averaging on the whole about 5 children per woman in 2000-

2005, mortality trends have not shown encouraging signs since the late 1980s. Continued population growth in already fragile economies will exacerbate problems of resource allocation for education and health care. Southern Europe and Japan will likely see declines of about 7 and 12 per cent, respectively, by 2050. Little change is anticipated in the total populations of Western Europe, while an increase in the order of 10 per cent is projected for Northern Europe, even though some countries within that region will experience substantial declines (e.g., Latvia, Lithuania and Estonia). In both Northern and Western Europe, immigration is likely to play an important role in maintaining or slightly increasing the population size. Population declines or only slight increases are also projected between 2005 and 2050 in some less developed countries, for example, those in the Southern Africa region, which are among the countries most highly affected by the HIV/AIDS epidemic. Among these countries, only Namibia is thought likely to experience substantial continued population growth, mainly because of its relatively high fertility.

During the period 2000-2005, the estimates show that 16 countries across the world experienced a reduction in population of more than 5,000 persons, ranging from 37 thousand in Estonia to close to more than 3 million in the Russian Federation. Except for Serbia and Montenegro, all countries included in this group are located in Eastern and Northern Europe or are successor States of the former USSR. Losses will be greater and more widespread by 2045-2050. During the last five years of the projection period, 31 countries are expected to experience population declines of 100,000 persons or more (up from 9 countries in 2000-2005), with an additional 15 countries losing more than 25,000 persons or more. Comparing 2000-2005 with 2045-2050, countries newly experiencing declines in 2045-2050 are located in Asia, Southern and Western Europe and also include Cuba and Mexico. Among the five countries that are expected to lose the largest absolute amount of population in 2045-2050, three are from Eastern Asia: China, Japan and the Republic of Korea. As in 2000-2005, the Russian Federation and Ukraine are expected to be among the countries with the biggest declines.

## POPULATION GROWTH RATES

Throughout the course of human history, and partially as a consequence of high mortality levels, population growth rates were on average quite low. It was probably not until the Seventeenth and eighteenth centuries that annual growth rates as high as 0.5 per cent were being sustained. From then until the dawn of the twentieth century, annual population growth at the rate of half a percentage point was the norm. But improvements in sanitary measures as well as access to antibiotics during the twentieth century, among other factors, led to a reduction in mortality levels. Consequently, population growth accelerated to historically unprecedented rates , reaching levels of around 2 per cent annually in 1965–1970. Since that historic peak, world population growth has greatly decelerated, and if the medium projections made in the 2004 Revision come to pass, the world will be returning to the 0.5 per cent rate of growth. The rapid growth of the twentieth century may come to be seen as an extraordinary but historically isolated

Phenomenon. The annual population growth rate2 of the world is now estimated at 1.21 per cent. At present, the growth rate of the more developed regions 'stands at 0.30 per cent per annum—about half of the norm in the eighteenth and nineteenth centuries—whereas the growth rate for the least developed countries is 2.40 per cent, far above the historical norm. The other less developed countries have an intermediate position with a growth rate of 1.27 per cent.

Growth rates in all three regions are projected to decline over time under the medium-variant projection, but only the more developed regions are thought likely to enter an era of population decline during the projection period. By 2050, the combined population of the more developed regions will have been declining in absolute terms for 20 years, whereas the least developed countries will still be growing at a rate of 1.30 per cent annually. An inspection of growth rate trajectories for the major areas of the world shows that two will be sharply distinguishable from the others.

Population growth rates in Africa are expected to be the highest throughout the projection period, falling to 1.21 per cent in 2045–2050, while those for Europe are projected to be the lowest, reaching -0.37 per cent by the end of the projection period. Growth rates of the other major areas—Asia, Latin America and the Caribbean, Northern America and Oceania—are expected to converge to between 0.19 and 0.45 per cent in 2 045-2050. Noticeably, most of the convergence in terms of growth rates between these major areas actually occurred between 1950 and 2005, while growth rates from Africa and Europe actually diverged from those of the rest of the world.

At the country level, among the ten countries with the highest population growth rates in 2000- 2005, five are from Africa and five from Asia, with values ranging from around 3.40 per cent in Niger,

Uganda and Chad to 6.51 per cent in the United Arab Emirates. Most countries included in the list have relatively high fertility levels, the main cause of such growth, but the soaring growth rates in the countries from the Arabic Peninsula (United Arab Emirates, Qatar and Kuwait) are largely due to international migration. By 2045-2050, all countries with the highest projected growth rates are in Africa, except for Afghanistan. Nevertheless, the anticipated growth rates are much lower than current ones, ranging from 1.75 per cent in Burkina Faso to 2.39 per cent in Uganda.

At the other end of the spectrum, the countries with the lowest rates of population change in 2000-2005 (*i.e.,* fastest rates of decline) are all from Eastern and Northern Europe or are successor States of the former USSR. Estimates of growth rates range from about -0.4 per cent in Romania, Lithuania and Armenia to about -1.10 per cent in Georgia and Ukraine. A few of these countries will continue to have some of the lowest rates of change in the world by 2045-2050, joined mainly by members of the small island developing States1.

## THE DISTRIBUTION OF POPULATION

Division According to Density of Population: The distribution of population in India shows the following density pattern according to census 2001.

Regions of Shows population Density (density below 100 per sq. km.): In includes *Jammu and Kashmir, Sikkim, Arunachal Pradesh, Mizoram states and Union Territories Andaman and Nicobar*. In the low population density due to ragged is topography and forested land with the severity of climate.

Regions of Medium Population Density (between 101 and 250 per sq. km.): It includes *Himachal Pradesh, Madhya Pradesh, Manipur, Meghalaya, Nagaland, Orissa, Rajasthan, Chhattisgarh and Uttaranchal states.* These regions are hilly, mountainous or forested, and some are deserted. Hence population is medium.

Regions of Considerably High Population Density (between 251 and 500 per sq. km.): This region includes *Andhra Pradesh, Assam, Gujrat, Haryana, Karnataka, Maharashtra, Punjab, Tamil Nadu, Tripura, Goa, Jharkhand states and Union Territories of Darda & Nagar Haveli.* Fairly high population of this region is due to the advancement of agriculture, mining and industry. Economic progress and job opportunities contribute much for this population.

Regions of High Population Density (between 501 and 1000 per sq. km.): *Bihar, Kerala, Uttar Pradesh and West Bengal* are included in this population zone. This high population is due to very fertile soil, advancemant of agriculture, minings, industries, trade and commerce and opportunities for subsistence.

Regions of Very High Population Density (above 1001 per sq. km.): It includes the *Union Terrtories of Delhi, Chandigarh, Pandicherry, Lakshadweep and Daman & Diu.* The high density of this region is due to high economic and administrative activites.

## THE CAUSES FOR THE UNEVEN DISTRIBUTION OF POPULATION

The distribution of population in India is not uniform. Some areas have high density of population, while others have medium or low density. The following physical and cultural factors are responsible for the uneven distribution of population in the country. The physical factors are gifts of nature; they influence much for the distribution of population.

Difference in Relief: The relief of the country exerts immense influence in the population distribution of a country. Extremely ragged topography associated with thick forest-cover do not encourage settlement as in the Himalayas and in the north-eastern hilly states of India. But the river valleys with alluvial plaints provide easy livings for which the population is high. The population of the Ganga-brahmaputra plain is distinctively high.

Variation in Vlimate: Climate exerts a great influence on human settlement. The *Marausthali of western Rajasthan* is sparsely populated; it is the hottest place in India and it has the extreme type of climate with little rainfall. Due to the adverse climate condition, the *Marusthali* is sparsely populated. On the other hand, the mild and equitable climate of the *Ganga plain* encourages settlements.

Influence of Soil: Agriculture depends on soil condition. The fertility of soil determines the cultivation of crops. Thus the livings and subsistence of the people depend on soil and low on rocky waste or infertile soil.

The great northern plains of India have fertile soil and on these plains density of population is remarkably high.

Influence of River: Rivers provide water to agriculture and other indispensable needs (drinking water and others) of the people. They also provide avenues for trade and commerce. That is why it is frequently said; the river valleys are the cradles of civilization. All the river valleys, which have fertile soil and tolerable climate, are thickly populated.

Presence of Minerals: Mineral deposits attract population. The discovery of enormous mineral deposits in the *Chhotanagpur plateau* region has contributed much to the growth of high concentration of population to this region.

The cultural factors are also responsible for the uneven distribution of population. These factors are man-made and popularly known as non-physical factors or cultural factors.

Development of Industries: Development of industries also attracts population. A few decades ago, there was very low population in Durgapur region; but with the development of industries in the Durgapur belt, the population has steadily increased.

Historical & Political Factors: After the partition of Bengal, when the Indian indepence was achieved, the population of *West Bengal* grew up rapidly due to the influx of the people from the other side of *Bengal*.

Religious Influence: *Varanasi, Mathura, Haridwar, Nabadweep, Puri* are the sacred religious centres of the *Hindus, Agra* of the *Muslims and Amritsar of the Sikhs*. They are densely populated due to religious factors.

## Bibliography

Berry, J.K. : *Beyond Mapping, Concepts, Algorithms and Issues in GIS*, Fort Collins, CO: GIS World Books, 1993.

Cronon, William: *Changes in the Land: Indians, Colonists, and the Ecology of New England.* New York: Hill and Wang, 1983.

Goodwin, Mark: *Envisioning Human Geographies*. London: Arnold, 2004.

Harvey, Francis : *A Primer of GIS, Fundamental Geographic and Cartographic Concepts,* The Guilford Press, 2008.

Johnston, R.J: *Geographies of Global Change: Remapping the World*. Blackwell Publishers, London, 2002.

Lewis, Peirce. *New Orleans: The Making of an Urban Landscape*. Cambridge, MA: Ballinger Publishing Co., 1976. Annotation

Michael, H.: *City Form and Natural Process: Towards a New Urban Vernacular.* London: Croom Helm, 1984.

Peet, Richard: *Modern Geographical Thought*. Oxford: Wiley-Blackwell, 1998.

Soja, Edward: *Postmodern Geographies: The Reassertion of Space in Critical Social Theory*. Verso, London, 1989.

21

# Human Rights: Concept, Issues and Emerging Problems

**DR IMRAN KHAN**

*Post Doctoral Fellow, Indian Institute of Social Science Research (I.C.S.S.R.), New Delhi.*

**Abstract:** Human rights are rights inherent to all human beings, whatever our nationality, place of residence, sex, national or ethnic origin, colour, religion, language, or any other status. We are all equally entitled to our human rights without discrimination. These rights are all interrelated, interdependent and indivisible. Universal human rights are often expressed and guaranteed by law, in the forms of treaties, customary international law , general principles and other sources of international law. International human rights law lays down obligations of Governments to act in certain ways or to refrain from certain acts, in order to promote and protect human rights and fundamental freedoms of individuals or groups.

## CONCEPT

Although ideas of rights and liberty have existed in some form for much of human history, there is agreement that the earlier conceptions do not closely resemble the modern conceptions of human rights. According to Jack Donnelly, in the ancient world, "traditional societies typically have had elaborate systems of duties... conceptions of justice, political legitimacy, and human flourishing that sought to realize human dignity, flourishing, or well-being entirely independent of human rights. These institutions and practices are alternative to, rather than different formulations of, human rights". The history of human rights can be traced to past documents, particularly Constitution of Medina (622), Al-Risalah al-Huquq (659-713), Magna

Carta (1215), the English Bill of Rights (1689), the French Declaration of the Rights of Man and of the Citizen (1789), and the Bill of Rights in the United States Constitution (1791). The modern sense of human rights can be traced to Renaissance Europe and the Protestant Reformation, alongside the disappearance of the feudal authoritarianism and religious conservativism that dominated the Middle Ages. One theory is that human rights were developed during the early Modern period, alongside the European secularization of Judeo-Christian ethics. The most commonly held view is that the concept of human rights evolved in the West, and that while earlier cultures had important ethical concepts, they generally lacked a concept of human rights. For example, McIntyre argues there is no word for "right" in any language before 1400. Medieval charters of liberty such as the English Magna Carta were not charters of human rights, rather they were the foundation and constituted a form of limited political and legal agreement to address specific political circumstances, in the case of Magna Carta later being recognised in the course of early modern debates about rights. One of the oldest records of human rights is the statute of Kalisz (1264), giving privileges to the Jewish minority in the Kingdom of Poland such as protection from discrimination and hate speech. Samuel Moynsuggests that the concept of human rights is intertwined with the modern sense of citizenship, which did not emerge until the past few hundred years.Human rights are commonly understood as inalienable fundamental rights to which a person is inherently entitled simply because she or he is a human being. This chapter examines the concept of human rights and its origins, explaining the different terms and classifications.

## Historical Antecedents

The origins of human rights may be found both in Greek philosophy and the various world religions. In the Age of Enlightenment (18th century) the concept of human rights emerged as an explicit category. Man/woman came to be seen as an autonomous individual, endowed by nature with certain inalienable fundamental rights that could be invoked against a government and should be safeguarded by it. Human rights were henceforth seen as elementary preconditions for an existence worthy of human dignity.

Before this period, several charters codifying rights and freedoms had been drawn up constituting important steps towards the idea of human rights. During the 6th Century, the Achaemenid Persian Empire of ancient Iran established unprecedented principles of human rights.

Cyrus the Great (576 or 590 BC - 530 BC) issued the Cyrus cylinder which declared that citizens of the empire would be allowed to practice their religious beliefs freely and also abolished slavery. The next generation of human rights documents were the *Magna Charta Libertatum* of 1215, the Golden Bull of Hungary (1222), the Danish Erik Klipping's *Håndfaestning* of 1282, the *Joyeuse Entrée* of 1356 in Brabant (Brussels), the*Union of Utrecht* of 1579 (The Netherlands) and the English *Bill of Rights* of 1689. These documents specified rights which could be claimed in the light of particular circumstances (*e.g.*, threats to the freedom of religion), but they did not yet contain an all-embracing philosophical concept of individual liberty. Freedoms were often seen as rights conferred upon individuals or groups by virtue of their rank or status.

In the centuries after the Middle Ages, the concept of liberty became gradually separated from status and came to be seen not as a privilege but as a right of all human beings. Spanish theologists and jurists played a prominent role in this context. Among the former, the work of Francisco de Vitoria (1486-1546) and Bartolomé de las Casas (1474-1566) should be highlighted. These two men laid the (doctrinal) foundation for the recognition of freedom and dignity of all humans by defending the personal rights of the indigenous peoples inhabiting the territories colonised by the Spanish Crown.

The Enlightenment was decisive in the development of human rights concepts. The ideas of Hugo Grotius (1583-1645), one of the fathers of modern international law, of Samuel von Pufendorf (1632-1694), and of John Locke (1632-1704) attracted much interest in Europe in the 18th century. Locke, for instance, developed a comprehensive concept of natural rights; his list of rights consisting of life, liberty and property. Jean-Jacques Rousseau (1712-1778) elaborated the concept under which the sovereign derived his powers and the citizens their rights from a social contract. The term human rights appeared for the first time in the French *Déclaration des Droits de l'Homme et du Citoyen*(1789).

The people of the British colonies in North America took the human rights theories to heart. The American Declaration of Independence of 4 July 1776 was based on the assumption that all human beings are equal. It also referred to certain inalienable rights, such as the right to life, liberty and the pursuit of happiness. These ideas were also reflected in the Bill of Rights which was promulgated by the state of Virginia in the same year. The provisions of the

Declaration of Independence were adopted by other American states, but they also found their way into the Bill of Rights of the American Constitution. The French *Déclaration des Droits de l'Homme et du Citoyen* of 1789, as well as the French Constitution of 1793, reflected the emerging international theory of universal rights. Both the American and French Declarations were intended as systematic enumerations of these rights.

The classic rights of the 18th and 19th centuries related to the freedom of the individual. Even at that time, however, some people believed that citizens had a right to demand that the government endeavour to improve their living conditions. Taking into account the principle of equality as contained in the French Declaration of 1789, several constitutions drafted in Europe around 1800 contained classic rights, but also included articles which assigned responsibilities to the government in the fields of employment, welfare, public health, and education. Social rights of this kind were also expressly included in the Mexican Constitution of 1917, the Constitution of the Soviet Union of 1918 and the German Constitution of 1919.

In the 19th century, there were frequent inter-state disputes relating to the protection of the rights of minorities in Europe. These conflicts led to several humanitarian interventions and calls for international protection arrangements. One of the first such arrangements was the Treaty of Berlin of 1878, which accorded special legal status to some religious groups. It also served as a model for the Minorities System that was subsequently established within the League of Nations.

The need for international standards on human rights was first felt at the end of the 19th century, when the industrial countries began to introduce labour legislation. This legislation - which raised the cost of labour - had the effect of worsening their competitive position in relation to countries that had no labour laws. Economic necessity forced the states to consult each other. It was as a result of this that the first conventions were formulated in which states committed themselves *vis-à-vis* other states in regard to their own citizens. The Bern Convention of 1906 prohibiting night-shift work by women can be seen as the first multilateral convention meant to safeguard social rights. Many more labour conventions were later to be drawn up by the International Labour Organisation (ILO), founded in 1919. Remarkable as it may seem, therefore, while the classic human rights had been acknowledged long before social rights, the latter were first embodied in international regulations.

The atrocities of World War II put an end to the traditional view that states have full liberty to decide the treatment of their own citizens. The signing of the Charter of the United Nations (UN) on 26 June 1945 brought human rights within the sphere of international law. In particular, all UN members agreed to take measures to protect human rights. The Charter contains a number of articles specifically referring to human rights. Less than two years later, the UN Commission on Human Rights (UNCHR), established early in 1946, submitted a draft Universal Declaration of Human Rights (UDHR) to the UN General Assembly (UNGA). The Assembly adopted the Declaration in Paris on 10 December 1948. This day was later designated Human Rights Day.

During the 1950s and 1960s, more and more countries joined the UN. Upon joining they formally accepted the obligations contained in the UN Charter, and in doing so subscribed to the principles and ideals laid down in the UDHR. This commitment was made explicit in the Proclamation of Teheran (1968), which was adopted during the first World Conference on Human Rights, and repeated in the Vienna Declaration and Programme of Action, which was adopted during the second World Conference on Human Rights (1993).

Since the 1950s, the UDHR has been backed up by a large number of international conventions. The most significant of these conventions are the International Covenant on Civil and Political Rights (ICCPR) and the International Covenant on Economic, Social and Cultural Rights (ICESCR). These two Covenants together with the UDHR form the International Bill of Human Rights. At the same time, many supervisory mechanisms have been created, including those responsible for monitoring compliance with the two Covenants.

Human rights have also been receiving more and more attention at the regional level. In the European, the Inter-American and the African context, standards and supervisory mechanisms have been developed that have already had a significant impact on human rights compliance in the respective continents, and promise to contribute to compliance in the future. These standards and mechanisms will be discussed in more detail throughout this book.

## DEFINING HUMAN RIGHTS

Human rights are commonly understood as being those rights which are inherent in the mere fact of being human. The concept of human rights is based on the belief that every human being is entitled to enjoy her/his rights without discrimination. Human rights differ from other rights in two respects. Firstly, they are characterised by being:

- Inherent in all human beings by virtue of their humanity alone (they do not have,*e.g.*, to be purchased or to be granted);
- Inalienable (within qualified legal boundaries); and
- Equally applicable to all.

Secondly, the main duties deriving from human rights fall on states and their authorities or agents, not on individuals.

One important implication of these characteristics is that human rights must themselves be protected by law ('the rule of law'). Furthermore, any disputes about these rights should be submitted for adjudication through a competent, impartial and independent tribunal, applying procedures which ensure full equality and fairness to all the parties, and determining the question in accordance with clear, specific and pre-existing laws, known to the public and openly declared.

The idea of basic rights originated from the need to protect the individual against the (arbitrary) use of state power. Attention was therefore initially focused on those rights which oblige governments to refrain from certain actions. Human rights in this category are generally referred to as 'fundamental freedoms'. As human rights are viewed as a precondition for leading a dignified human existence, they serve as a guide and touchstone for legislation.

The specific nature of human rights, as an essential precondition for human development, implies that they can have a bearing on relations both between the individual and the state, and between individuals themselves. The individual-state relationship is known as the 'vertical effect' of human rights. While the primary purpose of human rights is to establish rules for relations between the individual and the state, several of these rights can also have implications for relations among individuals. This socalled 'horizontal effect' implies, among other things, that a government not only has an obligation to refrain from violating human rights, but also has a duty to protect the individual from infringements by other individuals. The right to life thus means that the government must strive to protect people against homicide by their fellow human beings. Similarly, Article 17(1) and (2) of the ICCPR obliges governments to protect individuals against unlawful interference with their privacy. Another typical example is the Convention of the Elimination of All Forms of Racial Discrimination (CERD), which obliges states to prevent racial discrimination between human beings. State obligations regarding human rights may involve desisting from certain activities (*e.g.*,torture) or acting in certain ways (*e.g.*, organising free elections).

## HUMAN RIGHTS ISSUES

### Abolition of Bonded Labour

The Commission has been involved in the monitoring of the implementation of the Bonded Labour System (Abolition) Act as per the directions of the Supreme Court in WP (Civil) No. 3922 of 1985 (PUCL v State of Tamil Nadu & Others).

The Commission is presently monitoring the BLS (Abolition) Act by calling for information from the States on a quarterly basis on identification, release and rehabilitation of bonded labour.

In September 2000, the NHRC constituted a Group of Experts to closely examine the matter and to prepare a report on the status, suggest methods of improving the existing schemes and make recommendations to effectively implement the laws for abolition of bonded labour system and other connected matters.

The Report of the Expert Group was submitted to the Supreme Court. The Report contained a status of the work relating to the abolition of the bonded labour system in the various States. It detailed the position of the various existing schemes and made several recommendations to amend the Act so as to make it more effective.

The NHRC through its Special Rapporteurs has been interacting with the State Governments and with the Ministry of Labour to evolve suitable measures to eradicate the problem of bonded labour.

The Commission is involved in sensitizing the District Magistrates, Deputy Commissioners, Deputy Development Commissioner and other Senior Officers of the State Government by holding Sensitization Workshops. These workshops are presided over by the Chairperson and Members of the Commission. During 2003-04 sensitization workshops for the District Magistrates were held in Punjab, Uttar Pradesh, Bihar and Karnataka. During 2004-05, four additional workshops are proposed to be held.

### Functioning of the Mental Hospitals at Ranchi, Agra and Gwalior

The Management of the mental hospitals at Ranchi, Agra and Gwalior came under the scrutiny of the Supreme Court through Writ

Petitions (C) No.339/96, No.901/93, No.80/94 and No.448/94 in the matter of Rakesh Chandra Narain etc. v. State of Bihar etc.. The Supreme Court in its Order dated 11 November, 1997 requested the National Human Rights Commission to be involved in the supervision of the functioning of these three hospitals. In pursuance of the Order of the Supreme Court, the Commission remains deeply involved in overseeing the functioning of the Ranchi Institute of Neuro Psychiatry and Allied Sciences (RINPAS), Institute of Mental Health and Hospital (IMHH), Agra and the Gwalior Mansik Arogyashala (GMA), Gwalior. The Commission continues to monitor the implementation of the tasks assigned to these Institutions by the Supreme Court while granting them autonomous status in September 1994.

A Member and Special Rapporteur of the Commission visit these Institutions periodically and submit detailed reports on the working of various services and facilities, treatment and care of patients, training and research activities and community health services as specified by the Supreme Court.

As a result of the monitoring by the Commission, improvements have since been noticed in the working of these Institutions. Admissions and discharge have been streamlined in accordance with the provisions of the Mental Health Act, 1987. A clear shift from custodial to treatment and care concerns is noticeable in the functioning of these institutions. Cell admissions have been totally stopped. Switch over from close to open system of custody of patients is being steadily improved. Incidence of death of patients has come down as a result of close scrutiny of every case by the Commission. Library facilities, training activities and research works have shown appreciable improvement at RINPAS, Ranchi and the IMH&H, Agra. The aspect of Community Mental Healthcare is receiving greater attention than before.

A Core Group headed by a Member of the Commission has been set up for rehabilitation of mentally ill cured patients languishing in the three mental hospitals.

## Functioning of the Government Protective Home (Women), Agra

As per the directions of the Supreme Court of India in the Writ Petition No.1900/81 - Dr. Upendra Bakshi & Others v State of Uttar Pradesh vide Order dated 11-11-1997, the Commission has been supervising the functioning of the Government Protective Home (Women), Agra. The District Judge of Agra has been entrusted with the responsibility of conducting monthly inspections and submitting a visit report to the Commission. The Reports are scrutinized by the Commission and appropriate directions given to the State Government for overall improvement of the functioning of the Home.

A Member of the Commission as well as a Special Rapporteur of the Commission frequently visit the Home to make a broad assessment of the functioning of the Institution. The Home was last visited on 5th May, 2003 and certain discrepancies were noticed during the visit. The Commission has taken up the matter with the State Government.

The Commission called the Director (Women's Welfare), Govt. of Uttar Pradesh for a discussion alongwith the Superintendent of the Home and the District Probation Officer, Agra to review the functioning of the Home on 20-01-2004. The Director (Women's Welfare) was directed to take pro-active steps in Agra and elsewhere in the State for effective cooperation between the concerned wings of the administration for effective implementation of the Immoral Trafficking Prevention Act. The Director (Women's Welfare) was asked to draw up an action plan within a given time frame for implementation of the Act in law and spirit.

## Right to Food

On 3rd December, 1996, the Commission took cognizance of a letter from Shri Chaturanan Mishra, the then Union Minister for Agriculture regarding starvation deaths due to the drought in Bolangir district of Orissa. On 23rd December, 1996, the Indian Council of Legal Aid and Advice and others filed a Writ Petition (Civil) No.42/97 before the Supreme Court of India under Article 32 of the Constitution, alleging that deaths by starvation continued to occur in certain districts of Orissa.

When the Writ Petition came up before the Supreme Court of India on 26th July, 1997, the Court directed as under:-

"In view of the fact that the NHRC is seized of the matter and is expected to give its report after an enquiry made at the spot, it would be appropriate to await the report.Learned Counsel for the petitioner submitted that some interim directions are required to be given in the meantime. If that be so, the petitioner is permitted to approach the National Human Rights Commission with its suggestion." Pursuant to the Orders of the Supreme Court, the Indian Council of Legal Aid and Advice filed a petition before the Commission on 1st September, 1997 making a number of suggestions in regard to interim relief to the affected population.

After due consideration of the matter, the Commission, on 17-02-1998, arrived at the view that some interim measures should be undertaken for an overall period of two years. The Commission also requested the Orissa State Government to constitute a Committee to examine all aspects of the Land Reform question in the KBK Districts. Further the Commission with the assistance of one of its Special Rapporteur has been regularly monitoring the progress of implementation of its directions.

The Commission observed that as starvation deaths reported from some pockets of the country are invariably the consequence of mis-governance resulting from acts of omission and commission on the part of the public servant, they are of direct concern to the Commission under the provisions of the Protection of Human Rights Act, 1993. The Commission holds the view that to be free from hunger is a Fundamental Right of the people of the country. Starvation, hence, constitutes a gross denial and violation of this right.

Following this, the Commission felt the need to formulate a programme of action for making Right to Food a reality in the country. With this in view, a meeting was organized, with leading experts on the subject, in January, 2004 to discuss issues relating to 'Right to Food'.

The Commission has approved the constitution of a Core Group on Right to Food, that can advise on issues referred to it and also suggest appropriate programmes, which can be undertaken by the Commission.

## Preventing Employment of Children by Government Servants: Amendment of Service Rules

With a view to preventing employment of children below 14 years of age by Government servants, the Commission recommended that the relevant Service Rules governing the conduct of Central and State Government employees be amended to achieve this objective. The Union Ministry of Personnel and Public Grievances and Pensions (Department of Personnel & Training), has informed the Commission that the Central Government has amended the All India Services (Conduct) Rules, 1968 as well as the Central Civil Services (Conduct) Rules, 1964. Except for the State of Manipur, all the States/UTs have also brought out the required amendments to the Conduct Rules of their employees. The Commission intends to monitor the issue and see whether the Central and State Governments actually take action against those public servants who continue to employ children as domestic servants.

## Abolition of Child Labour

The NHRC has been deeply concerned about the employment of child labour in the country as it leads to denial of the basic human rights of children guaranteed by the Constitution and the International Covenants.

The Commission on 'child labour has observed that – "No economic or social issue has been of such compelling concern to the Commission as the persistence, fifty years after Independence, of widespread child labour in our country. It prevails, despite articles 23,24,39(e) & (f), 41, 45 and 47 of the Constitution and despite the passing of various legislations on the subject between 1948 and 1986. It has defied the terms of six Conventions of the International Labour Organization to which India is a party and the Convention on the Rights of the Child, in addition. Despite the announcement of a National Child Labour Policy in 1987, the subsequent constitution of a National Authority for the Elimination of Child Labour (NAECL) and the undertaking of National Child Labour Projects (NCLP) in an increasing number of areas of our country, the goal of ending child labour remains elusive, even in respect of the estimated two million children working in hazardous industries who were to be freed from such tyranny by the year 2000". The Commission focusing its attention on the following industries where from rampant reports of child labour were received. These interalia include the :-

- Bangle/glass industry
- Silk industry
- Lock industry
- Stone-Quarries
- Brick Kiln
- Diamond cutting
- Ship-breaking
- Construction-work
- Carpet-weaving.

The Commission monitors the child labour situation in the country through its Special Rapporteurs, visits by members, sensitization programmes and workshops, launching projects, interaction with the industry associations and other concerned agencies, coordination with the State Governments and NGOs to ensure that adequate steps are taken to eradicate child labour.

The Commission believes that unless and until the reality of free and compulsory education for all upto the completion of the age of 14 years is realized, the problem of child labour shall continue. The Commission has involved the NGO sector in the non-formal education of child labourers and a number of such schools/training centres are functioning in the districts of the carpet belt. There has also been a distinct improvement in the level of awareness among the general public about child labour issues.

## REHABILITATION OF MARGINALIZED AND DESTITUTE WOMEN IN VRINDAVAN

The Commission, since 2000, has been monitoring the implementation of its recommendations for the rehabilitation of marginalized and destitute women residing in Vrindavan. In this context, it had also directed the concerned officials of the Government of Uttar Pradesh to regularly apprise the Commission about the overall progress made towards improving the condition of destitute and marginalized women. In order to have first hand information about the status of marginalized and destitute women in Vrindavan, Members and senior officials of the Commission, have been visiting Vrindavan from time to time and reiterating Commission's directions regarding grant of pension, accommodation, LPG connections, ration cards, health care & sanitation, cremation fund, vocational training, social security cards and recreational facilities to the concerned officials so that expeditious action is taken on the matter.

### Combating Sexual Harassment of Women at the Work Place

The Commission has taken a keen interest with regard to the implementation of the guidelines and norms prescribed by the Supreme Court on preventing and combating sexual harassment at the workplace (1997 VII AD S.C. 53), popularly known as the Vishaka guidelines. Due to its persistent perseverance and supervision, all the States and Union Territories have forwarded their compliance reports confirming thereby the constitution of complaints mechanism and the required amendments in the Conduct Rules for their employees.

## Harassment of Women Passengers in Trains.

The Commission has been deeply concerned about harassment of women passengers in trains. In order to find a solution, it held several meetings with the officials of the Ministry of Railways, Railway Protection Force, Government Railway Police and representatives of NGOs. In pursuance of the decisions taken in those meetings, the Ministry of Railways have made available FIR forms in Hindi, English and a few regional languages in trains. It has also incorporated a module on gender sensitisation in the training programmes for the Probationers of the Traffic and Security Department of the Railways. The Commission also recommended to the Ministry of Railways the following – (i) availability of FIR forms in all other regional languages, (ii) preparation and display of messages in the railway coaches, (iii) preparation and display of graphics and other publicity materials at the railway platforms, (iv) printing of the message on the back of the ticket saying that sexual harassment of women in trains is a crime, and (v) preparation of power point presentation that could be made in software for the television showing briefly the issue and its implications.

## Abolition of Manual Scavenging

The Commission has been vigorously pursuing the need to end the degrading practice of manual scavenging in the country. It has taken up this matter at the highest echelons of the Central and State Governments through a series of interventions.

The Commission held a number of meetings with the State Governments. On the eve of Independence Day, 2002, the Chairperson, NHRC wrote a letter to the Prime Minister of India drawing his attention towards the problem. As a result, the Prime Minister in his Independence Day speech stressed the need to end the practice of Manual Scavenging. As a follow up of the Prime Minister's announcement, the Planning Commission has prepared a 'National Action Plan' for the Total Eradication of Manual Scavenging by 2007. Emphasis in this Action Plan is on -

i) Proper identification of those engaged in manual scavenging
ii) Enforcement of the prohibition law
iii) Involvement of NGOs.
iv) Better coordination at Central and State levels.

According to information available with the Commission the following States have adopted the Central Act:-

Andhra Pradesh, Assam, Chhattisgarh, Gujarat , Haryana, Karnataka, Kerala, Madhya Pradesh, Maharashtra, Orissa, Tamil Nadu, Tripura, Uttar Pradesh and Uttaranchal. The State of Punjab has adopted their own similar Act.

States who claim themselves to be "Manual Scavenging Free" are :

Arunachal Pradesh, Delhi, Goa, Himachal Pradesh, Meghalaya, Mizoram, Nagaland and Sikkim; and States who have not yet adopted the Central Act are :

Bihar, Jammu & Kashmir, Jharkhand, Manipur, Rajasthan, West Bengal.

The Union Territories of Andaman & Nicobar Islands, Chandigarh, Dadra & Nagar Haveli, Daman & Diu,Lakshadweep and Pondicherry have not furnished the information.

## Dalits issues including atrocities perpetrated on them

Deeply concerned by the discrimination and other human rights violations faced by the Scheduled Castes, the NHRC has taken several initiatives to ameliorate their situation and protect their rights. They include the redressing of individual complaints; constitution of a Dalit Cell in 2003 headed by a Member of the Commission with the aim to monitor implementation of programmes; research studies on the socio-economic conditions of the Musahars, and the political and cultural status of dalit women in Haryana; and the preparation of a handbook on discrimination in order to sensitize teachers. The Commission requested Shri KB Saxena, IAS (Retd.), to conduct a study on the atrocities against the Scheduled Castes, which has been completed. The Commission proposes to mount an appropriate campaign in this regard.

## Problems faced by Denotified and Nomadic Tribes

The communities designated as Denotified Tribes (DNT) and Nomadic Tribes (NT) of India were identified as "Criminal Tribes" (which included both castes as well as tribes) in pre-independence India. Though the Criminal Tribes Act, 1871 was annulled soon after independence, the police, as well as members of the public, frequently and most regrettably continue to treat persons belonging to these communities as "born criminals" and "habitual criminals". They, therefore, remain amongst the most discriminated and disadvantaged groups in the country.

Acting on a petition filed by eminent activist and author, Smt. Mahasvetadevi, President, Denotified & Nomadic Tribals Rights Action Group in May, 1998, the Commission convened a meeting of the Chief Secretaries and senior officers of the concerned States on 15 February, 2000 to deal the matter.

The recommendations included that a retired senior police officer of high reputation may be appointed in every state to watch the cases of atrocities against DNTs. The National Police Academy and other institutions imparting training to police officers be advised to reorient their syllabi and Habitual Offenders Act be repealed. The States were asked to report the action taken on the recommendations made. These included proper enumeration providing education, employment and other infrastructural facilities to them, and work out action plans for DNTs.

The matter has been taken up with the State Governments, and is being pursued by the Commission.

## RIGHTS OF THE DISABLED

The NHRC is deeply concerned about the fact that people with disabilities face various forms of discrimination, social exclusion and marginalization. The Commission has therefore taken several initiatives to protect the rights of the disabled. Notably, the NHRC has been redressing individual complaints from NGOs and others; the Commission reviewed relevant legislations and made recommendations for improvements thereon; it has successfully championed the need to enumerate the disabled in Census 2001. It has made recommendations to both Union Ministers and Chief Ministers of all States and Union territories requesting them to evolve a State Disability Policy and Plan of Action, to provide social security, employment opportunities, rehabilitation, and barrier-free infrastructure to benefit the disabled. In addition, the Commission has been taking steps to spread awareness of the rights of the disabled through publications, besides undertaking research studies. The Commission has been advocating the need for a Comprehensive and Integral International Convention on the Protection and Promotion of the Rights of Persons with Disabilities.

## RIGHT TO HEALTH

For the Commission it has been important to link the issue of health to that of human rights. When linked together, more can be done to advance human well-being than when health, and human rights, are considered in isolation. The Commission constituted a Core Advisory Group on Health, comprising of eminent medical experts with a request to prepare a plan of action for systemic improvements in the health delivery systems of the country. The Commission organized three major national consultations on maternal anemia, human rights and HIV/AIDS, and access to healthcare. Based on these consultations, detailed recommendations have been

sent to the concerned authorities. Furthermore, the Commission has also been working on issues like sub-standard drugs and medical devices, illegal trade in human organs, emergency medical care, and fluorosis. In partnership with Jan Swasthya Abhiyan, between July to December 2004, the Commission is organizing five regional and one national public hearing on access to healthcare.

## HIV/AIDS

Deeply concerned about the need to protect the human rights of those affected/infected by HIV/AIDS, the Commission has been redressing individual cases relating to discrimination faced by them. It has organized a national consultation on this issue and made recommendations to concerned authorities on issues like consent, testing, respect for confidentiality, protectionof vulnerable groups, prevention of mother-to-child transmission, etc. It has also launched a multi-media campaign to disseminate information on human rights and HIV/AIDS to various target groups. A Member of the Commission has been designated to serve as the Focal Point on HIV/AIDS related maters.

## Relief work for the Victims of 1999 Orissa Cyclone

The Commission has been observing the system of providing relief by various Governmental and non-Governmental Organisations to the affected people of Orissa to ensure that relief reaches the deprived ones on a uniform basis. In the beginning, the Special Rapporteurs of NHRC were directed to keep a watch on the system of dispensation of the relief measures to the affected people and send reports to the Commission on daily basis. The Commission considered the reports submitted by the Secretary General and the Special Rapporteurs on 08.12.1999 and issued several directions/ recommendations for implementation by the State Government. The directions/recommendations were also brought to the notice of concerned authorities of the State Government as well as in the Ministry of Agriculture. Chairperson, NHRC carried out a review of the Cyclone Relief and Reconstruction work in a meeting taken at Bhubaneswar on 29.1.2002. The Chief Secretary, Orissa was asked to send quarterly reports of the progress. Quarterly reports are being monitored by the Commission on a regular basis.

## Monitoring of relief measures undertaken after Gujarat Earthquake 2001

The Commission took suo-motu cognizance of the calamity that arose from the devastating earthquake, which hit large areas in the State of Gujarat on 26th January, 2001. The Commissionobtained a report from one of its Special Rapporteurs on the relief and rehabilitation measures being under taken so as to enable the Commission to take steps for issuing appropriate directions/guidelines to the concerned authorities. The Secretary General, NHRC also visited the affected areas and submitted a report. The reports submitted by the Secretary General and the Special Rapporteur were considered by the Commission on 29.5.2001 and it gave certain directions and made recommendations for immediate attention and action by the concerned authorities in Gujarat and the Central Government.

In order to monitor closely the follow-up action taken by the State Governments to impact its directions, the Commission set up a Group consisting of Shri PGJ Nampoothiri, Special Rapporteur, NHRC; Shri Gagan Sethi, Managing Trustee of Jan Vikas Trust; Smt. Annie Prasad, President of Kutch Mahila Sangathan and Prof. Anil Gupta, IIM, Ahmedabad. The Commission considers the reports sent by the Committee in its meetings held from time to time.

## District Complaints Authority

The Commission had mooted the idea of setting up of a district level setup to promote Police-Community relations and suggestions were invited from a number of Senior Police Officers. Shri Rajbir Deswal, then Superintendent of Police, Fatehbad informed the Commission that they had established an organization called "Fateh Dwaj", a registered organization to promote police-public relations with a membership of about 80 persons drawn from different walks of life. The Commission discussed the issue and the Kerala pattern of District Human Rights Authority, and recommended two measures to promote public confidence and means of redressal of the members of the public against increasing police incivility and high-handedness.

The composition of the "District Police Complaints Authority" was as under :-

1. The Principal Judge of the District concerned – Chairman
2. The Collector of the District – Member
3. The Senior Superintendent of Police - Member

## In-charge of the District

The District Superintendent of Police shall be the ex-officio Member Secretary of the Committee.

The functions of the Authority are to examine grievances of the public in the matter of rude and uncivil behaviour towards the public, abuse of authority, misuse of power, wrongful arrests and detentions, custodial violence and to make appropriate recommendations to Government or the State or National Human Rights Commission. This system is in existence and is working in the State of Kerala.

As the approval of the High Courts of the concerned State Governments was required for the implementation of the proposal, Chief Justices of all High Courts and Chief Ministers/Administrators of States/UTs were addressed by the Commission to constitute a District Complaints Authority in each District.

Arunachal Pradesh, Kerala, Meghalaya, Orissa and UT of Lakshadweep reported to have constituted the District Complaints Authority.

The matter is being pursued with the State Judiciaries and State Governments/Union Territory Administrations.

## POPULATION POLICY – DEVELOPMENT AND HUMAN RIGHTS

In order to initiate a dialogue from the perspective of both development and human rights with regard to the implementation of effective population policies at the Centre and State levels as well as deliberate on the mechanisms to achieve this objective, the Commission in collaboration with the Department of Family Welfare, Ministry of Health and Family Welfare and the United Nations Population Fund organised a two-day

Colloquium on 'Population Policy – Development and Human Rights'. The Recommendations and Declaration that emerged from this Colloquium was adopted by the Commission and the same were sent to all the State Governments/Union Territories for compliance.

## Emerging Problems

Gross human rights violations — such as forced displacement, forced labor, genocide and torture — have long made international headlines and been on the political agenda of the international community. In a changing and globalized world, human rights violations are no longer associated solely with governments, but also with multinational corporations ("MNCs").

The Business and Human Rights Resource Center — widely acknowledged as providing the broadest array of "balanced information of business and human rights" — has documented abuses ranging from health and safety violations in the workplace, to murder, torture, and forced displacement at the hands of military and security forces protecting company facilities. Indeed, attention to corporate human rights responsibility, the issue's significance for contemporary business practice, and the need for regulative outreach to non-state actors have increased tremendously.

Often the human rights performance of corporations and their host governments overseas are intertwined and complicate the allocation of responsibility.

The latest case to feature extensively in international headlines, that is emblematic of interdependencies between states and corporation, concerns the oil operations of the France-based Total S.A. ("Total") in Myanmar (formerly Burma). The activities of Total in conjunction with the U.S.-based Unocal Corp. ("Unocal") in Burma resulted in prominent litigation against the respective corporations in European and North-American jurisdictions. Major cases against MNCs for human rights violations committed abroad have been brought in both U.S courts under the U.S. Alien Tort Statute ("ATS") and European domestic courts.

Like its joint venture partner Unocal, Total was alleged to have used forced labor provided by the Burmese government to build a pipeline.

The case against Total on charges of complicity in crimes against humanity has just been reopened in Belgian courts, after cases against Unocal in U.S. courts and against Total in French courts had been settled on similar charges. The case of Total shows that out-of-court settlements will not protect MNCs in the long-run from liability; rather, corporations themselves, NGOs with human rights agendas, academics, and policymakers must recognize and address the significance of corporate human rights issues.

## References

Agosín, Marjorie, ed. *Women, Gender, and Human Rights: A Global Perspective.* New Brunswick, NJ: Rutgers University Press, 2001.

Allen, Robin and Rachel Crasnow. *Employment Law and Human Rights.* New York: Oxford University Press, 2002.

Alston, Philip. *The United Nations and Human Rights: A Critical Appraisal.* Oxford, UK: Clarendon Press, 1992.

Beitz, Charles R. *The Idea of Human Rights.* Oxford: Oxford University Press, 2009.

Donnelly, Jack. *International Human Rights.* 3d ed. Dilemmas in World Politics. Boulder, CO: Westview, 2006.

Forsythe, David P. *Human Rights in International Relations.* 2d ed. Themes in International Relations. Cambridge, UK: Cambridge University Press, 2006.

Freeman, Michael. *Human Rights: An Interdisciplinary Approach.* 2d ed. Key Concepts. Cambridge, UK: Polity, 2011.

Kamminga, Menno T., and Martin Scheinin, eds. *The Impact of Human Rights Law on General International Law.* Oxford: Oxford University Press, 2009.

Meron, Theodor. *The Humanization of International Law.* Hague Academy of International Law Monographs 3. Leiden, The Netherlands: Martinus Nijhoff, 2006.

Vincent, Andrew. *The Politics of Human Rights.* Oxford: Oxford University Press, 2010.

Vincent, R. J., ed. *Foreign Policy and Human Rights: Issues and Responses.* Cambridge, UK: Cambridge University Press, 2009.

22

# The Role of Political Parties and the Participation of Women in Indian Politics

**AMITABH BHATT**
*Assistant Professor, Department of Political Science, M.P.G. College, Mussoorie, Uttarakhand*

## THE INDIAN POLITICAL SYSTEM

### Party System and Women's Representation

India is a bicameral parliamentary democracy, with a strong multi-party political system. The lower house is called the Lok Sabha (Peoples' Assembly) and has 545 members. The upper house is called the Rajya Sabha (States' Assembly) with 250 members. In 1991, women constituted 5.2 per cent of the membership of the Lok Sabha and 9.8 per cent of the membership of the Rajya Sabha. This was lower than the preceding 1989 parliament. The election results in 1996 showed a further decline in women's representation. This trend is worrying given the recent state-led initiatives to ensure women's representation in political institutions.

One of the reasons for this decline may be the strength of the party system itself, which can lead to the marginalization of issue-based politics, or to an expropriation of movements that are based on single issues. The women's movement in India has had to confront this issue. Indian political parties are, however, organizationally weak and dependant on local elites. This might be a second factor for the resistance to implementation of gender-sensitive political initiatives.

### Women's Movement and the Issue of Representation

The demand for greater representation of women in political institutions in India was not taken up in a systematic way until the setting up of the Committee on the Status of Women in India (CSWI) which published its report in 1976. Before this the focus of the growing women's movement had been on improving women's socio-economic position. The CSWI report suggested that women's representation in political institutions, especially at the grass-roots level, needed to be increased through a policy of reservation of seats for women. In 1988, the National Perspective Plan for Women suggested that a 30 per cent quota for women be introduced at all levels of elective bodies. Women's groups insisted that reservation be restricted to the panchayat (village council) level to encourage grass-roots participation in politics. The consensus around this demand resulted in the adoption of the 73rd and 74th amendments to the Indian Constitution in 1993.

In 1995, the question of quotas was raised again, but this time the focus was women in parliament. Initially, most political parties agreed to this proposition. But soon doubts surfaced. When the bill addressing this issue was introduced in the Eleventh Parliament in 1997, several parties and groups raised objections.

The objections focused around two main issues: first, the issue of overlapping quotas for women in general and those for women of the lower castes; second, the issue of elitism. Most women's groups felt that the caste issue was a divisive one for women. Also, many felt uneasy about giving special privileges to elite women by ensuring seats for them in the parliament, while they had previously supported quotas for women at the grassroots level of the panchayats. To date, the amendment has not been passed by parliament. However, the current government of the Hindu nationalist BJP has committed itself to introducing another quota bill for women in parliament.

## PROFILE OF WOMEN IN THE INDIAN PARLIAMENT

The 39 women representatives in the 1991-1996 Indian Parliament were mostly middle-class, professional women, with little or no links to the women's movement. A significant number of them accessed politics through their families, some through student and civil rights movements, and some as a result of state initiatives aimed at increasing representation from the lower castes.

### Gender and Caste in Parliament

Caste has been an important feature of Indian public and political life. Most of the women MPs in the Tenth Parliament were members of the higher castes. For example, there were six women from the Brahmin caste. This represents a sizeable 17.14 per cent of the women MPs, while Brahmins comprise only 5.52 per cent of the population.

However, it is important to guard against making an easy correlation between caste and political representation. For example, of the six women who are Brahmins, two are MPs from the Communist Party of India. In both cases the caste factor is less important than their privileged class backgrounds. Further, both were products of political movements, the nationalist struggle and the anti-emergency movement.

The number of women who are able to avail of India's caste-based reservation system remains small. While 22 per cent of the parliamentary seats were reserved for the Scheduled Castes, women occupied only 4.1 per cent of the reserved seats. Two women MPs were from what are called the Scheduled Tribes. However, out of 39 women MPs in the Tenth Lok Sabha (representing seven per cent of the total), 14 per cent were from the Scheduled Castes. Two women MPs belonged to the "backward" castes and represented open constituencies. Caste, therefore, affects the profile, loyalties, and work of representatives in the Indian Parliament.

## Class, Social Position and Gender in Public Life

Out of the 39 women MPs in the 1991-1996 Lok Sabha, 32 had postgraduate qualifications; in the Rajya Sabha 14 out of the 17 women were graduates. The class position of these women is obviously more important to their educational levels than caste. Only one out of the seven lower caste women MPs was not a graduate, and the one Scheduled Caste woman MP in the Rajya Sabha had postgraduate education. The levels of education are also reflected in the professional profiles of these women. Thirty per cent of women MPs in the Rajya Sabha for example were lawyers, and 25 per cent in the Lok Sabha were either teachers or lecturers.

Most of the women MPs (about 65 per cent) were between their late 30s and 60s, and therefore did not have the responsibility of bringing up a young family. Given the almost universal marriage pattern that exists in India, the figure for unmarried MPs is extraordinarily high, and indicates the social pressures on women who join public life. For those who are married, the pressures of public life are eased a bit by their class situation. Most MPs are able to afford paid help in the home. In many cases the joint family system, or at least strong family support also helps. However, the constraints of family life continue to be real concerns even for privileged women.

Women have different strategies to cope with these constraints. If the family has accepted a woman's career in politics, she can negotiate with her family. This is more likely if the family is an elite political family with more than one member participating in politics. If the woman was already active in political life before she married, she can face tremendous pressures from her husband's family to conform to a traditional role that allows little scope for pursuing an active political career.

A woman politician's options in this case are either to conform to the expectations of the family and retreat from public life, or to leave the family in pursuit of an uncertain future in party politics. In the latter case, the lack of family support and the stigma of divorce are a clear disadvantage for a woman in politics.

Class also mediates the influence of religion. With only one woman Muslim MP in the Rajya Sabha and one in the Lok Sabha, Muslim women are significantly under-represented. Dr. Najma Heptullah, who was also the Deputy Speaker of the Rajya Sabha, is from an elite class and educational background, and enjoys support for her work from both her natal and marital family. Margaret Alva, a Christian, and then Minister of State, and Founder Chair of the National Commission for Women of India, is from a similar background. In both cases the families were involved in the national movement, were influenced by liberal ideology, and were highly educated.

Thus, the majority of women in the Indian Parliament are elite women. While their public role challenges some stereotypes, their class position often allows them far greater range of options than are available to poorer women.

## ACCESSING THE SYSTEM

Surprisingly, active participation in the women's movement has not been one of the entry routes into formal party politics for women MPs.

### Kinship or more?

"Male equivalence" has been a dominant explanation for how women access political life. The assumption here is that women access political life with the support, backing and contacts of the family, in particular that of the husband. In the sample of 15 women surveyed, 1/3 of the women MPs, for example, have "family support" in the background. However, in a well-argued critique of this theory, Carol Wolkowitz points out that "male equivalence" is an inadequate conceptual framework. First, because it is the public sphere (e.g. state institutions, press, and political discourse) that has to be negotiated if the family decision to put forward a woman in politics is to succeed;

it is not a private, but a public matter. Second, in many cases the husbands do not support the candidature of the wife at all. It is the pressure of party political bosses that forces the issue in many cases. The centralized system of distribution of seats in mass political parties helps in this context. A party's concern with levels of representation of certain groups within its ranks, and consequences for legitimacy of the party among the under-represented groups might be the motive for including women.

## Social and Political Movements

Together with "kinship link" and state initiatives, an important factor impacting on women's access to political life seems to be social and political movements. These movements have created windows of opportunity and some women have been able to take advantage of these opportunities to access political life. For example, the national movement was an important mobilizer of women. Gandhi's contribution to bringing women into politics is well-documented; the left movement also mobilized women. Women's organizations were constituted under the umbrella and control of the party - the Mahila Congress and the All India Women's Federation (CPI). However, none of the women interviewed in this survey had strong links with the women's wing of their party prior to their entry into parliamentary politics.

The civil rights and anti-emergency movement led by Jaiprakash Narayan (JP) in 1975-1977 was an important political movement that brought students to the forefront of national politics. Many women, both on the right and on the left wing, joined this movement and continued on in politics. Finally, in the context of current politics in India, fundamentalist and communal parties are mobilizing women. One of the most charismatic woman MP's is Uma Bharti, the product of the rise of Hindu militancy in Indian politics. She is the member of the Vishwa Hindu Parishad, a mobilizational wing of the BJP and a "preacher" of Hindu texts by profession. She was in the forefront of the movement that brought down the Babri Mosque in Ayodhyaya.

## Political Leadership and Quotas

The influence of individual national leaders is also an important factor that militates against the "male equivalence" theory. While Indira Gandhi, for example, did little to promote women's representation in politics, Rajiv Gandhi accepted the principle of reservation of seats for women. He initiated measures that had a direct impact on the inclusion of women in politics, e.g., the 1993 provision for reservation of 33 per cent of elected seats on village panchayats for women. As we have mentioned, who is able to take advantage of such reservations is mediated by class, ethnicity and caste. However, the support of the state and state/political leaders can be important to women who want to access the political system. Quotas for women as a strategy for accessing the political arena has growing support among women MPs, despite the fact that very few have accessed the system through that route, and are firm believers in the meritocratic argument. Most women MPs have supported the 81st Amendment, which would ensure a 33 per cent quota for women in parliament, even though party discipline has not allowed them to vote for this. This issue highlights the constraints that the party system poses for women politicians.

## GENDER AND PUBLIC POWER

### What do Women MPs do ?

Out of the 20 Congress women MPs in the 1991-1996 Lok Sabha, none was a Cabinet minister; two were Ministers of State; and two were Deputy Ministers of State. In the Rajya Sabha, out of seven Congress women MPs, one is a Minister of State. The portfolios of these Ministers included, Human Resource Development, Civil Aviation and Tourism, Health and Family Welfare, and Personnel and Public Grievances. All these are generally regarded as "soft portfolios"; this does not, however, take away from the responsibility that these women ministers have. One Congress woman MP is the Deputy Chairperson of the Rajya Sabha. At the level of the party, one MP was on the disciplinary committee of the party, and one was the President of the Mahila Congress. Among BJP women, the one Rajya Sabha member was the spokesperson on the economy and general political line of the party. Of the 10 members of the Lok Sabha, one was one of the vice-presidents of the party, and two were on the National Executive Committee of their party. The system of institutional incentives and disincentives at the level of the party and parliament impact on the issues that women espouse in parliament. Most women MPs interviewed did not have women's issues high on their list of interests. Rather, they wanted to be on committees relating to economy, international relations, and trade. As ambitious women these MPs want to be where power and influence converge.

### The Accountability Question

One of the important issues for any discussion on gender and representation has to deal with the constituency that women represent. As there are no "women's only" constituencies, women MPs are not accountable to women as women. And yet, when issues regarding women are raised in the parliament, these women are expected to, and do participate in the debates. Issues such as the welfare of women and violence against women are particularly important in uniting women MPs. These issues are discussed in the "ladies room" in the parliament. However, as all the MPs questioned made clear, they are "party women first"; party whip is rarely flouted. Some women MPs are also asked by the party leadership to get involved in the women's wing of the party. While the women MPs do not necessarily see this role as an enhancement of their status within the party, some have made a success of this role and as a result gained influence with the leadership of the party.

As "party women" with political ambitions, women MPs respond to the institutional incentives and disincentives that are placed on them. All these factors limit the potential of these women MPs representing the interests of Indian women across a range of issues. As a result there seems to be little regular contact between women's groups and women MPs. The exception here is of course the women's wing of political parties that do liaise with women MPs. This does allow the possibility of women MPs becoming conduits between the party's leadership and its women members. They are also consulted from time to time by the party leadership on issues regarding the family, and women's rights. But non-party women's groups do not seem to approach women MPs.

## References

Benjamin, J.: *Socio-religious Status of Panchayati Raj in India*, New Delhi, Ashish Publishing, 1991.

Bilquis, A: 1981, *Women Members of Union Parishad, A Few Statistics*, NILG, Dhaka.

Charles, Heinsath: *Indian Nationalism and Hindu Social Reform*, Princeton, Princeton University Press, 1964.

Dak, T.M.: *Women and Work in Panchayati Raj*, Delhi, Discovery, 1988.

Hasan, Mushirul: *India's Partition: Process, Strategy and Mobilization*, New Delhi, Oxford UP, 1993.

Marilee, Karl : *Women and Empowerment in Panchayati Raj System in India*, Zed Books Limited, London, 1995.

Nanda, B.R.: *Indian Women: From Purdah to Modernity*, New Delhi, Vikas, 1976.

Sharma, A : *Women in Panchayati Raj*, New York Press, New York, 1990.

23

# The Role and Functions of Panchayati Raj Institutions in India with Special Reference to Assam

**DR. UPENDRA ADHIKARI**
*Assisatant Professor, Department of Political Science, Kurseong College, District- Darjeeling, West Bengal, India*

Panchayati Raj Institutions – the grassroots units of self-government – have been proclaimed as the vehicles of socio-economic transformation in rural India. Effective and meaningful functioning of these bodies would depend on active involvement, contribution and participation of its citizens both male and female. Gandhiji's dream of every village being a republic and Panchayats having powers has been translated into reality with the introduction of the three-tier Panchayati Raj system to enlist people's participation in rural reconstruction. April 24, 1993 is a landmark day in the history of Panchayati Raj in India as on this day the Constitution (73rd Amendment) Act, 1992 came into force to provide constitutional status to the Panchayati Raj institutions.

## EVOLUTION OF PANCHAYATIRAJ IN INDIA

India has a chequered history of panchayati raj starting from a self-sufficient and self-governing village communities that survived the rise and fall of empires in the past to the modern legalized institutions of governance at the third tier provided with Constitutional support.

### Early History

During the time of the Rig-Veda (1200 BC), evidences suggest that self-governing village bodies called 'sabhas' existed. With the passage of time, these bodies became panchayats (council of five persons). Panchayats were functional institutions of grassroots governance in almost every village. The Village Panchayat or elected council had large powers, both executive and judicial. Land was distributed by this panchayat which also collected taxes out of the produce and paid the government's share on behalf of the village. Above a number of these village councils there was a larger panchayat or council to supervise and interfere if necessary. Casteism and feudalistic system of governance under Mughal rule in the medieval period slowly eroded the self-government in villages. A new class of feudal chiefs and revenue collectors (zamindars) emerged between the ruler and the people. And, so began the stagnation and decline of self-government in villages. During the British rule, the autonomy of panchayats gradually declined with the establishment of local civil and criminal courts, revenue and police organisations, the increase in communications, the growth of individualism and the operation of the individual Ryotwari '(landholder-wise) system as against the Mahalwari or village tenure system.

## During British Rule

The panchayat had never been the priority of the British rulers. The rulers were interested in the creation of 'controlled' local bodies, which could help them in their trading interests by collecting taxes for them. When the colonial administration came under severe financial pressure after the 1857 uprising, the remedy sought was decentralisation in terms of transferring responsibility for road and public works to local bodies. However, the thrust of this 'compelled' decentralisation was with respect to municipal administration.

From 1870 that Viceroy Lord Mayo's Resolution (for decentralisation of power to bring about administrative efficiency in meeting people's demand and to add to the finances of colonial regime) gave the needed impetus to the development of local institutions. It was a landmark in the evolution of colonial policy towards local government. The real benchmarking of the government policy on decentralisation can, however, be attributed to Lord Ripon who, in his famous resolution on local self-government on May 18, 1882, recognised the twin considerations of local government: (i) administrative efficiency and (ii) political education. The '''Ripon Resolution''', which focused on towns, provided for local bodies consisting of a large majority of elected non-official members and presided over by a non-official chairperson. This resolution met with resistance from colonial administrators. The progress of local self-government was tardy with only half-hearted steps taken in setting up municipal bodies. Rural decentralisation remained a neglected area of administrative reform.

The Royal Commission on Decentralisation (1907) under the chairmanship of C.E.H. Hobhouse recognised the importance of panchayats at the village level. The commission recommended that "it is most desirable, alike in the interests of decentralisation and in order to associate the people with the local tasks of administration, that an attempt should be made to constitute and develop village panchayats for the administration of local village affairs".

But, the Montague-Chemsford reforms (1919) brought local self-government as a provincial transferred subject, under the domain of Indian ministers in the provinces. Due to organisational and fiscal constraints, the reform was unable to make panchayat institutions truly democratic and vibrant. However, the most significant development of this period was the 'establishment of village panchayats in a number of provinces, that were no longer mere ad hoc judicial tribunal, but representative institutions symbolising the corporate character of the village and having a wide jurisdiction in respect of civic matters'. By 1925, eight provinces had passed panchayat acts and by 1926, six native states had also passed panchayat laws.

The provincial autonomy under the Government of India Act, 1935, marked the evolution of panchayats in India. Popularly elected governments in provinces enacted legislations to further democratise institutions of local self-government. But the system of responsible government at the grassroots level was least responsible. D.P. Mishra, the then minister for local self-government under the Government of India Act of 1935 in Central Provinces was of the view that 'the working of our local bodies... in our province and perhaps in the whole country presents a tragic picture... 'Inefficiency' and 'local body' have become synonymous terms....'.

In spite of various committees such as the Royal Commission on Decentralization (1907), the report of Montague and Chemsford on constitutional reform (1919), the Government of India Resolution (1918), etc., a hierarchical administrative structure based on supervision and control evolved. The administrator became the focal point of rural governance. The British were not concerned with decentralised democracy but were aiming for colonial objectives.

The Indian National Congress from the 1920s to 1947, emphasized the issue of all-India Swaraj, and organized movements for Independence under the leadership of Mahatma Gandhi. The task of preparing any sort of blueprint for the local level was neglected as a result. There was no consensus among the top leaders regarding the status and role to be assigned to the institution of rural local self-government; rather there were divergent views on the subject. On the one end Gandhi favoured Village Swaraj and strengthening the village panchayat to the fullest extent and on the other end, Dr. B.R. Ambedkar opposed this idea. He believed that the village represented regressive India, a source of oppression. The model state hence had to build safeguards against such social oppression and the only way it could be done was through the adoption of the parliamentary model of politics During the drafting of the Constitution of India, Panchayati Raj Institutions were placed in the non-justiciable part of the Constitution, the Directive Principles of State Policy, as Article 40. The Article read 'the State shall take steps to organise village panchayats and endow them with such powers and authority as may be necessary to enable them to function as units of self-government'. However, no worthwhile legislation was enacted either at the national or state level to implement it. In the four decades since the adoption of the Constitution, panchayat raj institutions have travelled from the non-justiciable part of the Constitution to one where, through a separate amendment, a whole new status has been added to their history

## Post-independence Period

Panchayat raj had to go through various stages. The First Five Year Plan failed to bring about active participation and involvement of the people in the Plan processes, which included Plan formulation implementation and monitoring. The Second Five Year Plan attempted to cover the entire countryside with National Extensive Service Blocks through the institutions of Block Development Officers, Assistant Development Officers, Village Level Workers, in addition to nominated representatives of village panchayats of that area and some other popular organisations like cooperative societies. But the plan failed to satisfactorily accomplish decentralisation. Hence, committees were constituted by various authorities to advise the Centre on different aspects of decentralisation.Panchayati Raj in Indian Villages

Panchayats have been the backbone of the Indian villages since the beginning of recorded history. Gandhiji, the father of the nation, in 1946 had aptly remarked that the Indian Independence must begin at the bottom and every village ought to be a Republic or Panchayat having powers. Gandhiji.s dream has been translated into reality with the introduction of the three-tier Panchayati Raj system to ensure people.s participation in rural reconstruction.

## The 73rd Amendment Act, 1993

The passage of the Constitution Act, 1992 marks a new era in the federal democratic set up of the country and provides constitutional status to the Panchayati Raj Institutions. Consequent upon the enactment of the Act, almost all the States/UTs, except J&K, NCT Delhi and Uttaranchal have enacted their legislation. Moreover all the States/UTs except Arunachal Pradesh, NCT Delhi and Pondicherry, all other States/UTs have held elections.

As a result, 2,32,278 Panchayats at village level; 6,022 Panchayats at intermediate level and 535 Panchayats at district level have been constituted in the country. These Panchayats are being manned by about 29.2 lakh elected representatives of Panchayats at all levels. This is the broadest representative base that exists in any country of the world. developed or underdeveloped. The main features of the Act are. a 3-tier system of Panchayati Raj for all States having population of over 20 lakh; Panchayat elections regularly every 5 years; reservation of seats for Scheduled Castes, Scheduled Tribes and women; appointment of State Finance Commission to make recommendations as regards the financial powers of the Panchayats and constitution of District Planning Committees to prepare development plans for the district as a whole. As per the Constitution Act, the Panchayati Raj Institutions have been endowed with such powers and authority as may be necessary to function as institutions of selfgovernment and contains provisions of devolution of powers and responsibilities upon Panchayats at the appropriate level with reference to the preparation of plans for economic development and social justice; and the implementation of such schemes for economic development and social justice as may be entrusted to them.

## FINANCIAL POWERS OF PANCHAYATI RAJ INSTITUTIONS

Article 243-G of the Constitution of India provides that the States/ UTs may, by law, endow the Panchayats with such powers and authority as may be necessary to enable them to function as institutions of self-government and to prepare plans for economic development and social justice and their implementation including those in relation to the matters listed in the Eleventh Schedule. As per Article 243-H of the Constitution, State Legislatures have been empowered to enact laws;

- To authorise a Panchayat to levy, collect and appropriate some taxes, duties, tolls and fees;
- To assign to the Panchayat, some taxes, duties, tolls levied and collected by the State Government;
- To provide for making grants-in-aid to the Panchayats from the Consolidated Fund of the State; and
- To provide for constitution of such funds for Panchayats for crediting all money received by or on behalf of Panchayats and also the withdrawal of such money therefrom.

## State Finance Commissions and PRIs

Article 243-I of the Constitution provides for constitution of a State Finance Commission to review the financial position of Panchayats and to make recommendations to the Governor regarding the principles governing the major issues mentioned in Article 243-H. All the States/UTs barring Arunachal Pradesh constituted State Finance Commissions and all the SFCs except Bihar have submitted their Reports to the respective State Governments.

The States of Assam, Karnataka, Kerala, Madhya Pradesh, Punjab, Rajasthan, Tamil Nadu, Tripura and West Bengal have accepted most of the recommendations of the SFCs. Andaman and Nicobar Islands, Dadra and Nagar Haveli, Daman and Diu and Lakshadweep Islands have received Reports of the Finance Commission which will be placed on the table of Houses by the Ministry of Home Affairs being the nodal Ministry.

States such as Andhra Pradesh, Himachal Pradesh, Haryana, Karnataka, Kerala, Madhya Pradesh, Maharashtra, Rajasthan, Sikkim, Tamil Nadu, Tripura, Uttar Pradesh, Assam, Punjab, Orissa and West Bengal have constituted second generation of State Finance Commissions. The Finance Commission for the four UTs has also been constituted by the Central Government. Constitution of State Finance Commission is now due in Goa, Manipur and Gujarat.

## Eleventh Finance Commission

The Eleventh Finance Commission recommended '1600 crores per annum for rural local bodies. Out of total grants, an amount of

'197.06 crores was earmarked for development of data base on the finance of the Panchayats and an amount of '98.61 crores for maintenance of accounts of Panchayats as the first charge on these grants. The Commission also recommended that in cases where elected local bodies are not in place, the Central Government should hold the grants for local bodies in trust on a non-lapsable basis during 2000-05 and that the Central Government would withhold a part of the recommended grants in case of such bodies to whom functions and responsibilities have not been devolved. Besides, the Commission recommended that Audit of accounts of the local bodies should be entrusted to the C&AG who may get it done through his own staff or by engaging outside agencies on payment of remuneration fixed by him and an amount of halfa-per cent of the total expenditure incurred by the local bodies should be placed with the C&AG for this purpose, and the report of the C&AG relating to audit of accounts of the Panchayats should be placed before a Committee of the State Legislature constituted on the same lines as the Public Accounts Committee.

The Ministry of Finance releases Grants recommended by the Eleventh Finance Commission to the States. For the year 2000-2001 ad-hoc grants of '57,186 lakhs were released to the States on.on Accounts. basis to the extent of 50% of allocated grants. EFC Grants were not released during 2000-2001 to the States of Andhra Pradesh, Assam, Bihar, Gujarat, Jharkhand and Punjab as elections were due. During the year 2001-02, funds were released to the tune of '2,06,944 lakhs. However, these grants were withheld for the States of Arunachal Pradesh, Jharkhand, Jammu and Kashmir and Punjab due to pending Panchayat elections. During the current year, an amount of '3,56,822 lakhs has been released as on 4.12.2002.

## FUNCTIONING OF TRADITIONAL PANCHAYAT

Lack of democracy in the functioning of traditional Panchayat is obvious. There are no women in Traditional Panchayat council. In many Panchayats the traditional Panchayats kept changing the leadership just to attract more money from the INGOs. Within a month after tsunami struck, the traditional Panchayat leaders came to know about INGOs and they started demanding more funds. There was no systematic interface between traditional panchayats and constitutional panchayats due to the domination of traditional panchayat leaders. NGOs directly dealt with the traditional Panchayats in spite of the lack of faith in equity and gender insensitivity. There was no proper sensitization among the officials, NGOs and INGOs on Panchayati Raj Institutions. Several Panchayat Presidents did not realize their role and responsibilities in disaster management. Sensitized Panchayat Presidents joined together with the traditional Panchayats and successfully carried out relief and rehabilitation activities.

They ensured the coordination among the government functionaries and departments, and sensitized the Village Panchayat Presidents and responded quickly by establishing contacts with the affected persons, and helped them to move to safe places. They made initial arrangements for the affected people food, drinking water, clothing and other basic needs. According to the president of Kameshwaram Panchayat, the Panchayat area is sandy so the sand suck the water quickly hence the village was affected by the flood miserably: the structure of the village is that it is surrounded by sand dunes and trees on both the sides.

Only one side is low laying area, so the sand dunes and trees safeguarded the people from the sea water. Further, if at all the sea water entered the village, the water rushed out to the low lying area so the water did not stagnate in that village. The deaths occurred not only due to sea water, but also because of the trees that fell on the people.

During the cyclone and heavy rainy seasons –the thatched houses because of their light weight which did not fall down easily. So loss of life was meager; but, the tiles made up of mud got moistened and broke into pieces and fell. Each piece was like a stone and caused more injuries.

To be safe from earthquake, some village people in Gujarat, preferred to have the traditional type of houses made up of light roof materials and thin round shape walls pasted with cow dung and camel dung. The study found that the training to the Gram Panchayat President is important, in relief and rehabilitation activities.

Relief activities started by the government only after three days of the occurrence. The food packets provided by the government were not eatable. Instead of providing food packets, government could have made arrangements to prepare food on the spot with the help of community and Panchayats. Linkages with block and district committees have not yet been initiated. The process of building up of disaster preparedness among the local body institutions has been initiated by the Government of Tamil Nadu and UNDP. Generally

NGOs are not yet coming forward in building up disaster preparedness. They concentrated more on relief instead of involving community and empowering them. It has been noticed that there is no culture of working together and through a system. The role of women and Dalits in relief and rehabilitation activities did not get attention of the relief agencies. They were side lined and due representation was not given to them. The impact of tsunami on Dalit habitation and livelihood was not immediately realized. In respect of relief and rehabilitation activities there was no relief code and management policy from the perspective of grassroots institutions.

Traditional knowledge, wisdom and practices are not given recognition which resulted in wastages of resources, duplication and delay in the execution of relief and rehabilitation activities. All activities were supply-driven not on demand-driven. Even after the bitter experiences, lessons were not learnt from the past. In the 1977 Vedaranyam Flood, the Government forecast made the people stay inside the houses. This reduced human loss. Committees which were constituted did not work properly. No training was given to the committee members. Plans for preparedness have not yet been drafted in Tamil Nadu.

## Role of PRIs in Disaster Management

The past experience shows that Government, INGOs and NGOs have taken number of measures for relief, rehabilitation and reconstruction activities regarding disaster. Based on experience an array of reports has been prepared for dissemination. Very useful recommendations have been made. But there is no proper initiative to make use of all those suggestions.

Government structure in Orissa is very weak but bureaucrats in Tamil Nadu are efficient and they are delivering goods. When tsunami struck, decision making powers were decentralized and respective affected District Collectors were given powers to take decisions based on the ground realities. Apart from the District Collectors many officials efficiently worked. In that situation, the local body institutions were sidelined both by Government and NGOs. Not only in Tamil Nadu, had the same situation prevailed in Andhra Pradesh and Gujarat also. People and their assets were damaged due to flood, cyclone, tsunami and earthquake and they are still in the process of rehabilitation and reconstruction.

It is to be noted that assistance could be extended to the affected at any amount. And people must be made to work for their development. The external agencies can work with people in the system created for them. If any institution or organization or group works for them, community's pride and self respect will be eroded.

People should have a feeling that they can manage on their own with support from others. Despite huge loss of lives and livelihoods in the recent disaster, generous support from the donor agencies and Government enabled the communities to overcome the shock and they started rebuilding. They spent huge amounts on relief, rehabilitation and reconstruction process. But this study found that it had not produced the results to the level of investment.

The study found that the relief activities were not gender sensitive and equity oriented. It was supply driven and not demand driven. In this situation, the 73rd and 74th Constitutional Amendment envisages the panchayats should strive for the welfare, safety and the prosperity of the villages. According to the 74th Constitutional Amendment Act the panchayats should prepare the plan for the socio economic development of the people. While preparing the socio economic development plans the panchayats could include disaster management as one of its components. As there was no system, structure and procedures at the grassroots level, the resources dumped at that level had not met the felt needs of the community.

In this situation, reconstruction could be done by preparing micro plan at the panchayat level. While preparing micro plan, panchayat could make reliable assessments on the nature and the extent of damages caused by the disaster. The environmental norms such as distance from the sea, identification of safe locations, designs, technologies and materials for construction of safe disaster resistance buildings should be considered. It could ensure that all the vulnerable are identified and included so that they get what is due to them from the reconstruction activities. Panchayats could make use of this opportunity to meet long felt needs.

For instance, they could develop new connecting roads that didn't exist earlier. With regard to damage assessment, the Panchayat could identify number of houses damaged and its magnitude. Public buildings (Anganwadi schools, health centres, community halls, Panchayat building, PDS shop, vocational training centres or any other government structures can be used very effectively). Basic services (including drinking water supply, access roads, sewage disposal, drainage, electricity and communication) apart from the physical damages Panchayats should be aware of the damages.

Panchayats should take responsibility to assess the damages and accordingly the relief has to be given.

To ensure the rehabilitation for a long-term development the Panchayats must be made to concentrate on the following activities:

- Rebuilding livelihoods,
- Opportunity for adopting innovative approaches,
- Build their sustainable network of village-based economies,
- Use the opportunity to strengthen and improve the among the people of the village.

Through pro active and well-planned rehabilitation work, we can reduce gender based, caste-based, religion-based, class-based divisions in relief and rehabilitation activities. A few well trained, well oriented gram panchayat presidents took effects in relief rehabilitation and reconstruction activities. This yielded good results. Based on the field experience, this study suggested the following recommendations to strengthen the community and Panchayats. At every gram panchayat Disaster Management Committee headed by gram Panchayat presidents is to be formed.

Government should form disaster management committees as statutory committees. In such disaster management committee SHGs, Youth and Elders should be integrated and they have to be oriented. At every ward, a sub committee at village level headed by ward member has to be constituted. Integrating Disaster Management Training with Panchayat Raj Capacity building exercise should be carried out regularly. In every committee women and Dalit representatives should be incorporated.

Allocation of separate Contingency fund for Disaster Management for every gram panchayat is an imperative. Government should allocate Rs.1 lakh as untied fund every year to each Gram Panchayat for disaster preparedness and management activities. There should be synergy between the constitutional panchayats and traditional panchayats. For all relief activities, the government departments have to rely on the committees constituted at the grassroots. A new culture has to be created at the ground to involve people. It requires a special training at all levels from Gram Sabha members to higher officials at district and state level. At every gram panchayat a contingency plan has to be developed. At every block and at every district, plan has to be prepared and implemented with the active participation of the stakeholders. Panchayats have to take responsibility from the stage of assessment of the loss to reconstruction.

Panchayats should have contingency fund. In the same way, every gram panchayat should have food stock through every ration shop. The entire physical infrastructure created through various government departments have to be handed over to the panchayats during the period of disaster. Every state should have a Disaster Management Act, policy and clear cut guidelines to carry out relief, rehabilitation and reconstruction works. Role clarity has to be ensured. Clear cut guidelines have to be prepared for disaster management at the gram panchayat level.

Since drought, flood and other disasters are now frequently occurring, each state should have a department meant for disaster relief with sufficient authority. In the regular development activities preparedness component has to be incorporated consciously. A well-maintained communication system has to be developed. With regard to data on the loss and compensation, the panchayat should be held responsible. Gram Panchayat should be made responsible for collecting vital statistics. It has to update the data regularly. This data should be validated by the Gram Sabha.

The data have to be confirmed in the Gram Sabha meeting. All relief and rehabilitation activities will be carried out only based on the data already confirmed. Currently, we need people-centred approach. It should be community-based intervention. Involvement of Constitutional local bodies is more important. All reconstruction activities should be carried out with the support of Village micro plan. Building confidence among people to organize and respond to disaster is also essential.

Based on the 73rd Constitutional Amendment, Panchayats are established as institutionalized structure both in urban and rural areas. But, people are in the periphery. Empowering the people is the process if we include local bodies in the disaster management. This could be a much more profitable system. Usually context decides. As already seen in this study, the empowered and sensitized Panchayat leaders delivered services even during disasters. So Panchayats are the best deliverable institutions where they are not target oriented. They are working in a demand driven way. If we empower Panchayats and the reverse the supply driven process by way of demand driven process, the whole system and society will change for better. Institutionalized, efficient, well coordinated, participatory inclusive, gender sensitive, disaster management initiatives are the basic ingredients of good governance.

## PANCHAYATI RAJ SYSTEM IN ASSAM

Under the Rural Panchayat Act 1948, there were two tiers of Panchayats – Primary Panchayats at village level and Rural Panchayats at Mouza level.

However Assam Panchayati Raj Act 1959 introduced a three-tier system and they are; Gaon Panchayat, Anchalik Panchayat and Mohokuma Parishad. Assam Panchayati Raj Act 1972 again changed it to a two-tier system and they are Gaon Panchayat and Mohokuma Parishad. Assam Panchayati Raj Act 1986 again introduced a three-tier system – Gaon Panchayat, Anchalik Panchayat & Mohokuma Parishad.

Finally Assam Panchayat Act 1994 following the 73rd Constitutional Amendment settled with a three-tier system structured as Gaon Panchayat, Anchalik Panchayat and Zilla Parishad.

### The 73rd Amendment Act, 1993

The Salient Features of the Act are :

a. To provide 3-tier system of Panchayati Raj for all the States having population of over 20 Lakhs.
b. To hold Panchayat Elections regularly every 5 years.
c. To provide reservation of seats for Scheduled Castes, Scheduled Tribes and Women (not less than 33%)
d. To appoint State Finance Commission to make recommendations as regards the financial powers of the Panchayats.
e. To constitute District Planning Committee to prepare draft development plan for the district as a whole.

### Powers and Responsibilities

According to the Constitution, Panchayats shall be given powers and authority to function as institutions of self-government.

The following powers and responsibilities are to be delegated to Panchayats at the appropriate level :-

a. Preparation of Plan for economic development and social justice.
b. Implementation of schemes for economic development and social justice in relation to 29 subjects given in Eleventh Schedule of the Constitution.
c. To levy, collect and appropriate taxes, duties, tolls and fees.

## Structure of the Panchayati Raj System in Assam

***Gaon Panchayats:***

a. President – directly elected by people.
b. One Vice President – to be elected from among the members of Gaon Panchayat.
c. Ten members – directly elected by people.

***Zilla Parishad:***

a. President – elected from among the directly elected members of Zilla Parishad.
b. Vice President-elected from among the directly elected members of Zilla Parishad.
c. Members –
    1. Members directly elected from the Zilla Parishad constituencies of the district.
    2. Presidents of the Anchalik Panchayats.
    3. Members of House of people & member of Legislative Assembly.

***Anchalik Panchayats:***

a. President – to be elected by the elected members of the Anchalik Panchayats.
b. Vice President-to be elected by the elected members of the Anchalik Panchayats.
c. Members –
    1. One member from each Gaon Panchayat area to be directly elected by people.
    2. President of the Gaon Panchayats falling within the jurisdiction of the Anchalik Panchayat.
    3. Members of Parliament and Legislative Assembly.

## Functions of the Panchayati Raj Bodies:

***Gaon Panchayat:***

1. Preparation of Annual Plans for the development of the Gaon Panchayat area.
2. Preparation Annual Budget of Gaon Panchayat.
3. Mobilisation of reliefs in natural calamities.
4. Removal of encroachments on public properties.

5. Organising voluntary labours and contribution for community works.
6. Maintenance of essential statistics of villages.
7. Such other development works as may be entrusted.

### *Zilla Parishad:*

It should be the function of a Zilla Parishad to prepare plans for economic development and social justice of the district and ensure the coordinated implementation of such plan.

### *Anchalik Panchayat:*

a. Preparation of Annual Plan in respect of the schemes entrusted to it by virtue of the Act and those assigned to it by the Government or the Zilla Parishad and submission thereof to the Zilla Parishad within the prescribed time for integration with the District Plan;
b. Consideration and consolidation of the Annual Plans of all Gaon Panchayats under the Anchalik Panchayat and submission of consolidated plan to the Zilla Parishad;
c. Preparation of Annual Budget of the Anchalik Panchayat and submission to Zilla Parishad for approval within the prescribed time;
d. Performing such functions and executing such works as may be entrusted to it by government or the Zilla Parishad;
e. To assist the government in relief operation in natural calamities;
f. Such other development works as may be entrusted.

## References

Alam, Bilquis: 1981, *Women Members of Union Parishad, A Few Statistics*, NILG, Dhaka.

Arvind, Sharma : *Women in World Religion*, New York Press, New York, 1990.

Mathur, B.B.: *Women and Depressed Class Population in India*, Allahabad, Chugh, 1994.

Nair, Janaki: *Women and Law in Colonial India*, New Delhi, Kali, 1996.

Tinker, I.: *Persistent Inequalities: Women and World Development*, New York, OUP, 1990.

24

# Panchayati Raj System after 73rd Constitutional Amendment

**DR. PRAKASH DAHIYA**
*Department of Political Science ,
Satyawati College (Evening), University of Delhi, Delhi.*

Panchayati Raj Institutions – the grassroots units of self-government – have been proclaimed as the vehicles of socio-economic transformation in rural India. Effective and meaningful functioning of these bodies would depend on active involvement, contribution and participation of its citizens both male and female. Gandhiji's dream of every village being a republic and Panchayats having powers has been translated into reality with the introduction of the three-tier Panchayati Raj system to enlist people's participation in rural reconstruction. April 24, 1993 is a landmark day in the history of Panchayati Raj in India as on this day the Constitution (73rd Amendment) Act, 1992 came into force to provide constitutional status to the Panchayati Raj institutions.

Panchayats have been the backbone of the Indian villages since the beginning of recorded history. In 1946, Gandhi had aptly remarked that the Indian independence must begin at the bottom and every village ought to be a Republic or a Panchayat with powers. His dream got translated into reality with the introduction of the three-tier Panchayati Raj system to ensure people's participation in rural reconstruction.

The passage of the Constitution (73rdAmendment) Act, 1992 (or simply the Panchayati Raj Act) marks a new era in the federal democratic set up of the country. It provided the much needed constitutional sanction to the Panchayati Raj Institutions (PRIs) for functioning as an organic and integral part of the nation's democratic process. It came into force with effect from April 24, 1993 and did not apply to the Schedule V areas of the nine states, Schedule VI Areas of the North-East and the District of Darjeeling in West Bengal as well as J&K. The Panchayati Raj Act was needed in order to streamline the functioning of the PRIs, which were marked by long delays in holding of Panchayat elections, frequent suspension / super session / dissolution of the Panchayat bodies, lack of functional and financial autonomy, inadequate representation of marginalized and weaker sections and meager, occasional and tied Government grants. This crippled the functioning of Panchayats and did not allow them to function as institutions of local Self-Government as had been envisaged in the Constitution.

## WHY PANCHAYATI RAJ INSTITUTIONS?

Panchayati Raj means democratic decentralisation. It falls within the great tradition of our country. We often talk about Punch Parmeshwar. It means that the god speaks through the Panch. Panch Parmeshwar can never be prejudicial to anybody. It is how we under-stand about the Gram Panchayats. Our tradition of Gram Panchayat is elaborately manifested in our languages. Besides, we also have tradi-tion of Caste Panchayat. The Caste Panchayat looked after the problems at local level. Sometimes, it also functioned as inter-village panchayat. Among tribals, even today, the role of traditional panchayat is so much important that the member of the tribe makes his first approach to it. If he is dissatisfied at this level, then he goes to the court of law. In some villages, the Caste Panchayat is also impor-tant. A large number of decisions pertaining to social and marital conflicts and disputes are solved by the Caste Panchayat.

The role of Panchayati Raj has to be analysed with reference to this great Indian tradition. Gandhiji had a conviction that Gram Panchayat should be made all-powerful so that it could take all deci-sions pertaining to its administration and development.

Gandhiji often talked about and actually stood for Gram Swaraj. Literally, it means autonomy of village. The village as a collectivity should rule over itself. The theory of Gram Swaraj as given by Gandhiji runs as below:

My idea of village swaraj is that it is a complete republic, independent of its neighbours for its own vital wants and yet interdependent for many others in which dependence is a necessity. Thus every village's first concern will be to grow its own food crops and cotton for its cloth. It should have a reserve for its cattle, recreation and play-ground for adults and children... The government of the village will be conducted by a panchayat of five persons annually elected by the adult villagers, male and female, possessing minimum prescribed qualification. These will have all the authority and jurisdiction re-quired. Since there will be no system of punishment in the accepted sense, this panchayat will be the legislature, judiciary and executive combined to operate for its year of office... here there is perfect de-mocracy based upon individual freedom.

The individual is the architect of his own government. The law of non-violence rules him and his government. He and his village are able to defy the might of a world. For the law, governing every villager is that he will suffer death in the defence of his and his village's honour.

## A Constitutional Obligation

The constitution of Panchayati Raj is not the sweet will of the state government. It is the result of the provisions made in Indian Constitu-tion. The Directive Principles of State Policy lies down that the state shall take steps to organise village panchayats ...to enable them to function as units of self-government. The objective of the constitution of Panchayati Raj was mainly two-fold:

(i) decentralisation of power, and

(ii) development of vil-lages.

Yet anther reason for the creation of Panchayati Raj was to seek the cooperation and participation of masses of people in the na-tional reconstruction and development. Initially, in 1952, the Panchayati Raj bodies were entrusted with the implementation of Community Development Projects (CDPs).

The institution of shram- dan, voluntary labour, was created to involve the people in the development of their own village. The Panchayati Raj, however, did not make any headway in the development of village. The CDPs were considered as projects of development from the above, that is, the gov-ernment. It was essential for development that the initiative should have come from the below, the masses of people and in fact, from the grassroots.

To overcome this difficulty a committee headed by Bal- want Rai Mehta was constituted. This committee made initial experiment in Andhra Pradesh and Rajasthan. The Mehta Committee was the watershed in the development of Panchayati Raj.

## Balwant Rai Mehta Committee

The Balwant Rai Mehta Committee found that the CDPs when came at the Gram Panchayat level were considered as programmes of the government and not programmes of the village people. The village self-sufficiency could not be attained without the active partnership of the village people. The Mehta Committee, therefore, suggested that the villagers should be given power to decide about their own felt needs and implement the programmes accordingly. Bidyut Mohanty, while explaining the recommendations of the Mehta Committee, ob-serves:

In 1959, the Balwant Rai Mehta Committee suggested that an agency should be set up at the village level which would not only represent the interests of the village community but also take up the develop-ment programmes of the government at its level. The Gram Panchayat which was to constitute this agency was, therefore, per-ceived as an implementing agency of the government in a specific, namely, developmental sphere.

## 73RD AMENDMENT ACT, 1992

The Salient Features of the Act are :

a. To provide 3-tier system of Panchayati Raj for all the States having population of over 20 Lakhs.
b. To hold Panchayat Elections regularly every 5 years.
c. To provide reservation of seats for Scheduled Castes, Scheduled Tribes and Women (not less than 33%)
d. To appoint State Finance Commission to make recommendations as regards the financial powers of the Panchayats.
e. To constitute District Planning Committee to prepare draft development plan for the district as a whole.

## Powers and Responsibilities of PRIs

According to the Constitution, Panchayats shall be given powers and authority to function as institutions of self-government. The following powers and responsibilities are to be delegated to Panchayats at the appropriate level :-

a. Preparation of Plan for economic development and social justice.
b. Implementation of schemes for economic development and social justice in relation to 29 subjects given in Eleventh Schedule of the Constitution.

c. To levy, collect and appropriate taxes, duties, tolls and fees.

Some important features of the Act are given below:

(1) Panchayats will be considered political institutions in a truly de-centralised structure.

(2) The Gram Sabha shall be recognised as the life-line of the Panchayati Raj. The voters of the village of clusters of villages will constitute its membership.

(3) There will be direct elections in all the three tiers of governance:
   (i) Gram Panchayat at the village level,
   (ii) Panchayat Samiti at the intermediate level; and
   (iii) Zila Parishad at the district level.

(4) So far as the empowerment of women is concerned, the Act has provided that at least one-third of the total seats at all levels shall be reserved for women of whom, one-third shall be from the scheduled castes and scheduled tribes. In this context it is impor-tant to note that at least one-third of the total posts of the office bearers at all levels will also be reserved for the women.

(5) Each PRI will have tenure of five years and in case it is dissolved by the state government fresh election will be held within a pe-riod of six months.

(6) The election to local bodies has to be conducted regularly.

(7) There will be a separate Election Commission and also a Finance Commission for PRIs in every state.

(8) It is obligatory on the part of centre as well as the state to provide adequate funds for the PRIs to enable them to function properly. In addition, the PRIs will have their own fund raising capacity on the basis of the local resources.

(9) Some states like Rajasthan, Haryana and Orissa have debarred the candidates, having more than two children, from contesting in the election with a view to controlling population growth, given the low average age of marriage of girls (19); they would have crossed the two children norm by the time they contest for elec-tions. Hence, it will be difficult for the states to get suitable women candidates for the Panchayati Raj elections.

(10) Some states like Bihar, Himachal Pradesh, Uttar Pradesh, Hary-ana and Karnataka have provision of Nyaya Panchayat to settle the disputes at all the three levels.

However, the 73 rd Amendment Act does not make it obligatory for states to provide for Nyaya Panchayats to solve local disputes. Sec-ondly, although the objective of the Act is to build the Panchayati Raj as an effective decentralised political institution at the grassroot level, the division of functions in its XI Schedule makes it in reality, essen-tially an implementing agency for developmental activities.

## Functions of Panchayati Raj

The structure of Panchayati Raj is designed in such a way that the 73rd Constitution Amendment Act gives certain powers and func-tions to the three-tier structure of the Panchayati Raj. The idea is to decentralise the power of rural administration to the elected repre-sentatives. The Act enables the elected representatives to take their own decisions within the framework of Act. Some of the important functions of the Panchayati Raj are enumerated below:

1. Agricultural development and irrigation facilities;
2. Land reforms;
3. Eradication of poverty;
4. Dairy farming, poultry, piggery and fish rearing;
5. Rural housing;
6. Safe drinking water;
7. Social forestry, fodder and fuel;
8. Primary education, adult education and informal training;
9. Roads and buildings;
10. Markets and fairs;
11. Child and women development;
12. Welfare of weaker sections, scheduled castes and scheduled tribes.

Some Special Provisions:

1. Enforcement of prohibition;
2. Protection of land;
3. Minor forest produce;
4. Water resources;
5. Village markets;
6. Development.

If we analyse the functions of Panchayati Raj, it is found that the Act is highly elaborate. The functions of Panchayati Raj in terms of Gram Sabha, Panchayat Samiti, and Zila Parishad are spelt out sepa-rately. Quite like functions the administrative powers are also ascribed to each tier. On the whole, the Panchayati Raj system em-powers the total functioning of the village system. It stresses on the limited autonomy of the village but also encourages it for interde-pendence with other clusters of villages.

## ISSUES IN IMPLEMENTATION OF THE PANCHAYATI RAJ ACT

Despite the positives like enactment of State Panchayati Raj Acts, Setting up of State Election Commission and State Finance Commissions, and holding of regular Panchayat elections providing reservation for SCs/STs/Women in Panchayats, the results of implementation of the Constitution (73rd Amendment) Act, 1992 at the ground level have fallen far short of expectations. Stating specifically,

1. Although the political decentralization can be clearly seen in the regular Panchayat elections with good participation of people, the administrative and fiscal decentralization have remained rather limited. The State Governments have failed to give up their control on matters of local administration and finance.
2. Panchayats have not been granted enough powers for revenue generation. As a result, they only have limited functional autonomy.
3. Recommendations of State Finance Commissions (SFCs) are generally not taken seriously.
4. Powers given to the State Election Commissions also vary from State to State. They should have been given powers to deal with all matter relating to Panchayat elections namely, delimitation of constituencies, rotation of reserved seats in Panchayats, finalization of electoral rolls, etc.

### Panchayats (Extension to the Scheduled Areas) Act, 1996 (or PESA Act, 1996)

The PESA Act, 1996 is regarded as a corrective legal measure to the 73rd amendment (Panchayati Raj Act) in order to extend the provisions of the Panchayat Raj to the Scheduled and Tribal areas falling under the Schedule Five areas of the nine States, namely Andhra Pradesh, Chhattisgarh, Jharkhand, Gujarat, Himachal Pradesh, Maharashtra, Madhya Pradesh, Orissa and Rajasthan.

The PESA Act, 1996 which came into force on 24thDecember, 1996. It gave radical governance powers to the tribal community and recognizes its traditional community rights over local natural resources.

It not only accepts the validity of "customary law, social and religious practices, and traditional management practices of community resources", but also directs the state governments not to make any law which is inconsistent with these.

Accepting a clear cut role of the community, it gives wide ranging powers to *Gram Sabhas*, which had hitherto been denied to them by the lawmakers of the country. The State Governments were required to enact their legislation in accordance with the Provisions of Act before the expiry of one year i.e. 23rd December, 1997.

## POOR IMPLEMENTATION OF THE PESA ACT, 1996

It also needs to be pointed out that tribal areas represent the last sumps of natural resources on this planet, simply because tribal lifestyle and culture have inherent respect for the forests and natural resources and tribal religions and outlook ensures survival of all living beings, through holistic and ecologically sound belief system. PESA offers a wonderful way to strengthen their hands in the larger interest of social justice as well as deepen grass-root democracy.

Implementing the following suggestions will achieve both the goals.

- Even after a decade and a half after the PESA Act, there is very little awareness about the Gram Sabha being designated as a self governing body or having legal jurisdiction over the natural resources and forests. Neither is there any support mechanism for the Gram Sabhas to play any significant role.
- It is a clear indication that sincere implementation of PESA has not been seriously attempted by the state governments. They still want to govern the PESA areas through the centralized administration and laws that actually weaken what PESA provisions offer the tribal community. There is hardly any willingness on the part of the officials of various departments to relinquish control on resources and functions that are given to the Gram Sabhas by PESA. Nor do they have any respect for tribal lifestyle and culture. What is needed is the empowerment and capacity building of the tribal community through a sustained awareness campaign so they can take charge of their lives as envisioned in the PESA provisions.
- There is an urgent need to amend the Indian Forest Act, Land Acquisition Act, and other related Acts so that the ownership

on minor forest produce, water bodies and land resources are explicitly handed over to the Gram Sabhas of the PESA areas.

- No State Government officer should have the power to over-rule any recommendation of a Gram Sabha. This legacy of British Raj is anti-democratic and must be abolished immediately.
- The current system of governance is still largely colonial in nature and the bureaucracy conditioned on centralized authority has been unable to accept the radical change envisioned in the PESA Act. Therefore, in order to sensitize them an immediate extensive training-cum-awareness campaign for all relevant officials of various ministries should be initiated.
- There is a need that Gram Sabha institutions should be developed as institutions ofself-governance and not treated merely as institutions of local governance. The required administrative structure and machinery should be provided for making the Gram Sabha an effective body of district administration. It is also imperative that the Gram Sabhas have direct access to funds so that they can exercise their power rather independently.
- Physical infrastructure in interior areas should be strengthened in order to protect the life and property of tribals. Special attention should be paid to the construction of culverts, bridges, check dams, compound walls for schools, etc.
- The concept of community ownership of resources in PESA areas should be integrated into the provisions of the Centrally Sponsored Schemes. All community resource based schemes should involve Gram Sabhas in planning and implementation.

## References

Calman, J.: *Women and Politics in India,* Colorado, Westview Press, 1992.

Erikson, E. H.: *Panchayati Raj and Society,* New York, W. W. Norton, 1993.

Mohiuddin Khan: 1988, *Development Strategies for Panchayati Raj,* Dhaka, Bangladesh.

Panini, M.N.: *Accounts of Women Fieldworkers Studying their Own Communities,* Delhi, Hindustan, 1991.

25

# Participation of Women in Panchayati Raj Institutions

**DR NALIN SINGH PANWAR**
*Assistant Professor, Schools of Studies in Political Science and Public Administration, Vikram University, Ujjain, Madhya Pradesh*

**Abstract:** *In modern era of the participation and administrative state many writers have voiced their concern over the problem of responsiveness of the administrative state to the norms of democratic procedures. To safeguard individual rights and liberties against bureaucratic or arbitrary abuse an increase in women's vigilance and participation in politics is necessary. Modern state should show "concern for individual people in the criteria used in making decisions; as an effort to assign each women's need equal weight in policy deliberations and as an effort to make as broad as feasible the opportunities for women to participate in the decisions that affect them." The term 'political participation' refers to those voluntary activities by which members share in the selection of rulers and, directly or indirectly, in the formation of public policy. These activities are like casting vote, seeking information, holding discussions, attending meetings, making financial contributions to political parties, staging strikes and demonstrations, communicating with the legislators and other leading figures and the like. It follows that political participation "is the involvement of the individual at various level in the political system. Political activity may range from non-involvement to office-holding. It is also important to stress that participation "may result in the motivation for increased participation, including the highest level – that of holding various types of offices - which involves the process of political recruitment. The idea of political justice and equality is explained in article 1 of the Universal Declaration of 1948 in these words, "All human beings are born free and equal in dignity and rights. They are endowed with reason and conscience and should act towards one another in spirit of brotherhood".*

## PANCHAYAT RAJ SYSTEM IN INDIA

Panchayats have been the backbone of the Indian villages since the beginning of recorded history. In 1946, Gandhi had aptly remarked that the Indian independence must begin at the bottom and every village ought to be a Republic or a Panchayat with powers. His dream got translated into reality with the introduction of the three-tier Panchayati Raj system to ensure people's participation in rural reconstruction.

The passage of the Constitution (73rd Amendment) Act, 1992 (or simply the Panchayati Raj Act) marks a new era in the federal democratic set up of the country. It provided the much needed constitutional sanction to the Panchayati Raj Institutions (PRIs) for functioning as an organic and integral part of the nation's democratic process. It came into force with effect from April 24, 1993 and did not apply to the Schedule V areas of the nine states, Schedule VI Areas of the North-East and the District of Darjeeling in West Bengal as well as J&K.

The Panchayati Raj Act was needed in order to streamline the functioning of the PRIs, which were marked by long delays in holding of Panchayat elections, frequent suspension / super session / dissolution of the Panchayat bodies, lack of functional and financial autonomy, inadequate representation of marginalized and weaker sections and meager, occasional and tied Government grants. This crippled the functioning of Panchayats and did not allow them to function as institutions of local Self-Government as had been envisaged in the Constitution.

## PRIMARY FEATURES PRIS ACT, 1993

The Act has five main features: (a) a 3-tier system of Panchayati Raj for all States having population of over 20 lakh; (b) Panchayat elections regularly every 5 years; (c) reservation of seats for Scheduled Castes, Scheduled Tribes and women (not less than one-third of seats); (d) appointment of State Finance Commission to make recommendations as regards the financial powers of the Panchayats, and (e) constitution of District Planning Committees to prepare development plans for the district as a whole.

Thus, the Panchayats have been endowed with such powers and authority as may be necessary to function as institutions of self-government and social justice. Providing real functional autonomy at the village level is at the core of the amendment Act.

### Achievements

As a result of the enactment of the Act, 2,32,278 Panchayats at village level; 6,022 Panchayats at intermediate level and 535 Panchayats at district level have been constituted in the country. These Panchayats are being manned by about 29.2 lakh elected representatives of Panchayats at all levels. This is the broadest representative base that exists in any country of the world – developed or under-developed.

## ISSUES IN IMPLEMENTATION OF THE PANCHAYATI RAJ ACT

Despite the positives like enactment of State Panchayati Raj Acts, Setting up of State Election Commission and State Finance Commissions, and holding of regular Panchayat elections providing reservation for SCs/STs/Women in Panchayats, the results of implementation of the Constitution (73rd Amendment) Act, 1992 at the ground level have fallen far short of expectations. Stating specifically,

1. Although the political decentralization can be clearly seen in the regular Panchayat elections with good participation of people, the administrative and fiscal decentralization have remained rather limited. The State Governments have failed to give up their control on matters of local administration and finance.
2. Panchayats have not been granted enough powers for revenue generation. As a result, they only have limited functional autonomy.
3. Recommendations of State Finance Commissions (SFCs) are generally not taken seriously.
4. Powers given to the State Election Commissions also vary from State to State. They should have been given powers to deal with all matter relating to Panchayat elections namely, delimitation of constituencies, rotation of reserved seats in Panchayats, finalization of electoral rolls, etc.
5. Gram Sabhas have not been empowered and strengthened to ensure greater people's participation and transparency in functioning of Panchayats as envisaged in the Panchayat Act.

### Panchayats (Extension to the Scheduled Areas) Act, 1996 (or PESA Act, 1996)

The PESA Act, 1996 is regarded as a corrective legal measure to the 73rd amendment (Panchayati Raj Act) in order to extend the provisions of the Panchayat Raj to the Scheduled and Tribal areas falling under the Schedule Five areas of the nine States, namely Andhra Pradesh, Chhattisgarh, Jharkhand, Gujarat, Himachal Pradesh, Maharashtra, Madhya Pradesh, Orissa and Rajasthan. The PESA Act, 1996 which came into force on 24th December, 1996. It gave radical governance powers to the tribal community and recognizes its traditional community rights over local natural resources.

It not only accepts the validity of "customary law, social and religious practices, and traditional management practices of community resources", but also directs the state governments not to make any law which is inconsistent with these. Accepting a clear cut role of the community, it gives wide ranging powers to *Gram Sabhas*, which had hitherto been denied to them by the lawmakers of the country. The State Governments were required to enact their legislation in accordance with the Provisions of Act before the expiry of one year i.e. 23rd December, 1997.

## PESA: A POTENT WEAPON AGAINST THE NAXAL VIOLENCE

### Poor Implementation of the PESA Act, 1996

It also needs to be pointed out that tribal areas represent the last sumps of natural resources on this planet, simply because tribal lifestyle and culture have inherent respect for the forests and natural resources and tribal religions and outlook ensures survival of all living beings, through holistic and ecologically sound belief system. PESA offers a wonderful way to strengthen their hands in the larger interest of social justice as well as deepen grass-root democracy. Implementing the following suggestions will achieve both the goals.

- Even after a decade and a half after the PESA Act, there is very little awareness about the Gram Sabha being designated as a self governing body or having legal jurisdiction over the natural resources and forests. Neither is there any support mechanism for the Gram Sabhas to play any significant role.
- It is a clear indication that sincere implementation of PESA has not been seriously attempted by the state governments. They still want to govern the PESA areas through the centralized administration and laws that actually weaken what PESA provisions offer the tribal community. There is

hardly any willingness on the part of the officials of various departments to relinquish control on resources and functions that are given to the Gram Sabhas by PESA. Nor do they have any respect for tribal lifestyle and culture. What is needed is the empowerment and capacity building of the tribal community through a sustained awareness campaign so they can take charge of their lives as envisioned in the PESA provisions.

- There is an urgent need to amend the Indian Forest Act, Land Acquisition Act, and other related Acts so that the ownership on minor forest produce, water bodies and land resources are explicitly handed over to the Gram Sabhas of the PESA areas.
- No State Government officer should have the power to over-rule any recommendation of a Gram Sabha. This legacy of British Raj is anti-democratic and must be abolished immediately.
- The current system of governance is still largely colonial in nature and the bureaucracy conditioned on centralized authority has been unable to accept the radical change envisioned in the PESA Act. Therefore, in order to sensitize them an immediate extensive training-cum-awareness campaign for all relevant officials of various ministries should be initiated.
- There is a need that Gram Sabha institutions should be developed as institutions ofself-governance and not treated merely as institutions of local governance. The required administrative structure and machinery should be provided for making the Gram Sabha an effective body of district administration. It is also imperative that the Gram Sabhas have direct access to funds so that they can exercise their power rather independently.
- Physical infrastructure in interior areas should be strengthened in order to protect the life and property of tribals. Special attention should be paid to the construction of culverts, bridges, check dams, compound walls for schools, etc.
- The concept of community ownership of resources in PESA areas should be integrated into the provisions of the Centrally Sponsored Schemes. All community resource based schemes should involve Gram Sabhas in planning and implementation.

## PARTICIPATION OF WOMEN IN PRIS

For sustainable economic and social development to take place in any country, it is necessary that people participate in the political process. Panchayati Raj is not a new phenomenon in India. Its illustration in history goes back to more than 1000 years. The British almost destroyed these ancient republics, as well as the involvement of women in politics. From 2 October 1959 when the first Panchayati Raj Institution (PRI) was inaugurated in 24 April, 1993 when the 73rd Amendment Act came into force, it has been an uncertain and undulating journey for Panchayats (Sahni, S. and Kaul, S., 2009).

In a country like India, where social orientation is based on class, caste and gender, the picture of deprivation and inequality is appalling. The women are not considered as a social group. They are either included with men or totally ignored. In post-independent India, the Sarada Act provided an impetus to the battle for the rights of Women. The passing of the Hindu Code Bill, 1955 and the provision of equal rights for women in the Constitution of India improved the status of the women. In June 1954, the first post-war all-India organisation of Women, the National Federation of Indian Women (NFIW) was formed in view of impending socio-political issues. Later, the 73rd constitutional Amendment Act (1992) created space for women in political participation and decision-making at the grass root level by providing that 1/3rd of the seats would be reserved for women all over the country. The 73rd Constitutional Amendment Act (CAA), 1992 says- "It provides reservations for women in PRIs set up in two ways; for the office of the members and for that of the chairpersons". As per the clause (2) and (3) of article 243(d), not less than one third of the seats meant for direct election of members at each tier of the Panchayats are to be reserved for the women.

### Gandhi on Women's Participation

In his scheme of the democratic government, Gandhi wanted a humble or as he put it, rural president as the ceremonial head of the Indian state, so that even the humblest and lowliest could feel that Swaraj (self rule) had come to them.

Commenting on the Indian Independence Bill of 1947, Gandhi indicated his choice as follows: (*Harijan,* 15.6.1947 and also *Ibid. 18.1.1948)*

"If I have my way, I would put a suitable Harijan girl in the presidential chair. In a free India, Knowledge of English won't be necessary for the President. She need not have knowledge of high politics. All the learned statesmen of the country would help her to carry on the government...I would rejoice to think that we had a Mehtar (scheduled caste) girl of stout heart, incorruptible and of crystal like purity to be our first President. It is no vain dream."

The head of the state of Gandhi's conception would, thus, be the symbol of the neglected sections of the society, including the untouchable, the minority religionist and the women. Good performance by the elected representatives delivers positive results, benefiting both the providers (representatives) and the beneficiaries (the community). The process of getting elected to institutions of local governance enhances one's self-esteem and steels the confidence, leading to heightened effectiveness. Greater participation of women in politics was viewed as dependent not just on fulfilling the law, but on assuring principles, democratic and meaningful administration of government. Women needed to know where and how to direct their concerns so that solutions were found to the problems women faced.

## The Emperical Study

The article has been organised in two sections. Section I would throw light in the current status of the women in Panchayati Raj Institution (PRI) System. Section II would deal with the challenges involved in women participation in PRI system.

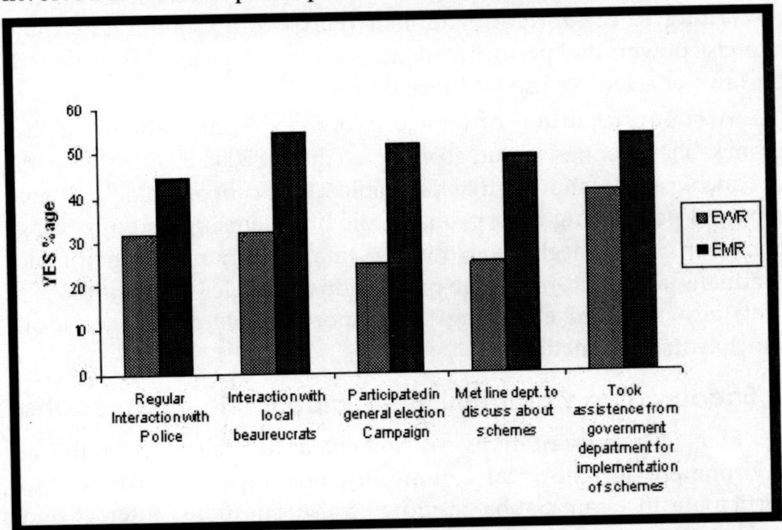


***Figure: Interactive Role of Elected Representatives (Yes %)***

## STATUS AND QUALITY OF WOMEN PARTICIPATION IN PANCHAYATI RAJ SYSTEM

According to the Ministry of Panchayati Raj's mid-term appraisal of the 'State of the Panchayats 2006-07', "No less than 10 lakh women are in our Panchayati Raj institutions, comprising 37 per cent of all those elected and rising to as high as 54 per cent in Bihar, which has 50 per cent reservation for women."

Increased political accountability to women comes out only from increasing their numbers amongst decision-makers, although this is necessary and important. It must also be linked to improved democratic governance overall, understood as inclusive, responsive and accountable management of public affairs.

The benchmark generally selected for evaluating women's participation in politics is their representation in term of numbers or percentages. This does not facilitate adequate understanding, because representation does not, in itself, constitute evidence of participation. Thus, several indicators have been identified for determining the status and quality of women participation in the local political process.

### 1. Participation in the Gram Sabha

Participation has been taken as a vital index for the women members to assess their empowerment in Panchayati Raj Institutions. According to the 73rd Amendment (Part IX), a Gram Sabha may exercise powers and perform functions at the village level as provided by laws enacted by its state legislature.

A large proportion of female is organising and attending the gram sabha meetings. A study conducted during 2008-2009 by Ministry of Panchayati Raj showed that a sizeable 93 per cent of male Pradhans reported performing their primary role of organising and attending the Gram Sabha meetings. However, smaller in numbers than male Pradhans, a significantly large proportion of female Pradhans (86 per cent) also reported executing this important role of being a local Panchayati Raj functionary.

### 2. Encouraging Community Participation in Gram Sabha

Elected representatives are expected to create an enabling environment for the local community, and especially women, to participate in Gram Sabha meetings, raise questions, interact and present their opinions. In a study, conducted by the Ministry of Panchayati Raj, showed the attendance in Gram Sabha meetings, which is an important indicator of the quality of women representatives' participation. The study showed a low participation of women citizens in Gram Sabha meetings, suggesting low levels of mobilisation by elected women representatives. About 63 per cent of elected representatives themselves indicated that less than 25 per cent of women participate in the Gram Sabha meetings. This participation was particularly low in Orissa, Chhattisgarh, Madhya Pradesh and Goa, but high in Kerala, West Bengal, Karnataka, Assam and Tripura. The latter category of states has higher levels of political mobilisation.

### 3. Interaction with Government Officials

According to the statistics and data (Ministry of Panchayati Raj) the womenfolk participate in the gram sabha meetings; however, there persists hesitation when it comes to interaction with the officials about there problems or developmental works. Sometimes gender disparity becomes a hindrance towards putting forward their view point. The all-India figure shows that more than half the total Pradhans maintained good relations with the local police. By contrast, only 31 per cent of Ward Members reported interaction with the local police. Among the elected women representatives, nearly 32 per cent reported regular interaction with the police, in comparison to 45 per cent of the men (study conducted by Ministry of Panchayati Raj).

### 4. Participation in Community Mobilisation

Effective participation is not adequately reflected in statistics on meeting attendance, but may also be tested by evaluating the elected representatives in terms of their articulation, openness to discussions, adopting issues and generally solving problems of the community. They are more effective when they succeed in mobilising the community about various developmental issues and thus, create awareness among the people. A study on the all-India level on community mobilisation on health-related issues showed that the total of 43 per cent of women representatives and about 47 per cent of men reported taking part in health-related campaigns.

#### *Challenges Involved*

- Non-cooperation of the male members that they primarily face on the basis of gender discrimination
- Often, the men of the village do not accord them the respect and regard that is their due. Officials take advantage of their inexperience and poor education.

- Effective devolution is so uneven and inadequate that oftentimes, even the most able women are crippled for want of the rightful allocation of functions, finances and functionaries without which effective Panchayati Raj is rendered impossible.
- Elected women members are sometimes used as dolls behind their husbands or men in the family. In many parts of India, especially in northern states the husband performs the duties of the women pradhans and gram sabha members in lieu of the women themselves.

## Conclusion

The 73rd Constitution Amendment Act in India focused on political structures and processes of rural India and vulnerable populations. Earlier, participation of women in Panchayati Raj Institutions was questioned in terms of the substance and effectiveness of representation. Local committees insufficiently represented women. Women were rarely heads of Panchayats and needed the lower positions to advance within the system. Thus, the act has been passed to assure women's representation in Indian Panchayati Raj System. However, women members of Panchayats needed to be educated and informed about politics: their rights, the nature of Indian democracy, policies and programmes for women and the underprivileged and voting rights. Women's centres and other organisations can serve as catalysts to mobilise women and help solve political dilemmas.

There are several challenges still that the women are facing in the local governance system. Rural women were particularly vulnerable as a group because of strong traditional values maintained in rural areas, patriarchal families, lack of women's education and access to information, poor exposure to the "outside" world and lack of power.

A combination of constitutional provisions, government policies, social action and self awareness among rural women will eventually result in Indian women becoming part of the mainstream political power sharing and decision-making.

## References:

Ministry of Panchayati Raj, 2009.Study on EWRs in Panchayati Raj Institution [PDF]. New Delhi: Ministry of Panchayati Raj.

Kaul, Shashi and Sahni, Shradha,2009. Study on the Participation of Women in Panchayati Raj Institution.

Aziz, Abdul, et. al., Decentralized Governance and Planning: a Competitive Study in Three Southern Indian States, New Delhi, Macmillan, 2002.

D'lima, Hezel, Women in Local Government in Maharashtra, New Delhi, Concept Publishing Company, 1983.

Desai and Krishnaraj, Women and Society in India, New Delhi, Ajanta Pablications, 1990.

Jain, Devaki (ed), Indian Women, Publication Division of Ministry of Information and Broadcasting, Government of India, 1996.

Joshi, R. P. (ed), Constitutionalisation of Panchayati Raj. A Reassessment, Jaipur, Rawat Publications, 1998.

Mandal, Amal, Women in Panchayati Raj Institutions, New Delhi, Kanishka Publishers, 1998.

Manikyamba, P., Women in Panchayati Raj Structure, New Delhi, Gyan Publishers, 1989.

Mathew, George, Panchayati Raj: From Legislature to Movement, New Delhi, concept Publishing Company, 2002.

# 26

# E-Governance and Rural Development

**DR VED PRAKASH JOSHI**
*Assistant Professor, Department of Commerce,*
*M.P.G. College, Mussoorie, Uttarakhand.*

**Abstract:** *Rural e-Governance applications in the recent past have demonstrated the important role the Information and Communication Technologies (ICT) play in the realm of rural development. Several e-Governance projects have attempted to improve the reach, enhance the base, minimize the processing costs, increase transparency, and reduce the cycle times. The use of Information and Communication Technology in governance processes and by governments has been mostly centered in the deployment of ICT applications and solutions to streamline government's operations reduce transactional costs, and increase transparency and accountability of public institutions. E-government or online government has indeed taken off since the end of the millennium. 'Modernization' of public state institutions complemented by the delivery of specific government services has thus been the cornerstone of this approach. As a matter of fact, many developing countries have complemented existing national ICT strategies with e-government policies and/or ad hoc deployment of solutions for specific national sectors. The latest trend on e-government, in response in part to the many failures of many of related initiatives, suggests a more citizen-centric approach in which egovernment priorities are much more responsive to citizens needs and development agendas. Rural e-Governance applications in the recent past have demonstrated the important role the Information and Communication Technologies (ICT) play in the realm of rural development. Several e-Governance projects have attempted to improve the reach, enhance the base, minimize the processing costs, increase transparency, and reduce the cycle times.*

## RURAL DEVELOPMENT

India is a nation of villages. The rural mass in the nation comprises the core of Indian society and also represents the real India. According to the Census Data 2001, there are 638,387 villages in India that represent more than 72 per cent of the total population. So development of these rural mass is one of the key areas of consideration in the government policy formulation. Rural Development (External website that opens in a new window)which is concerned with economic growth and social justice, improvement in the living standard of the rural people by providing adequate and quality social services and minimum basic needs becomes essential. The present strategy of rural development mainly focuses on poverty alleviation, better livelihood opportunities, provision of basic amenities and infrastructure facilities through innovative programmes of wage and self-employment etc.

The government of India has started many programmes aimed at improving the standard of living in villages or rural areas. To build rural infrastructure, the government launched a time-bound business plan for action called Bharat Nirman (External website that opens in a new window)in 2005. Under Bharat Nirman, action is proposed in the areas of Water Supply, Housing, Telecommunication and Information Technology, Roads, Electrification and Irrigation.

In view of the sheer size and diversity of our country, delivery of governance to the remote corners in a meaningful and locally relevant manner is a huge challenge. The administrative setup has evolved by incorporating our age old institutions with the modern democratic organs to meet this challenge. To make this challenge easy Panchayati Raj (External website that opens in a new window)came into existence. Panchayats have historically been an integral part of rural life in India, and the Constitution (73rd Amendment) Act, 1992 has institutionalised the Panchayati Raj at the Village, Intermediate and the District levels, as the third tier of governance. In May 2004, the Ministry of Panchayati Raj was formed as the Nodal agency looking after the empowerment of Panchayati Raj Institutions in the country. The use of information - communication technology has made this challenge more convenient.

## ROLE OF ICT IN E-GOVERNANCE AND RURAL DEVELOPMENT

Information and Communication Technologies (ICTs) play a key role in development & Economic growth of Rural India. Political,

Cultural, Socio-economic Developmental & Behavioral decisions today rests on the ability to access, gather, analyze and utilize Information and Knowledge. ICT is the conduits that transmit information and knowledge to individual to widen their choices for Economic and social empowerment. In near future people will be carrying a handheld computer connected to the Web to get the information about the World at their fingertips. Government of India is having an ambitious objective of transforming the citizen-government interaction at all levels to by the electronic mode (e-Governance) by 2020.

A successful ICT application in e-Governance giving one-stop solutions for rural community is the need of the hour. ICT is crafted to enable the Electronic Governance through wireless communication, thus it's integrally interlinked and knitted.

India is a country of villages and to improve and sustain the overall prosperity, growth and development in the global competitive regime, National E-governance plan (NEGP) seeks to lay the foundation with various projects, starting from the grass-root levels, and provide impetus for long-term e-governance within the country. In this direction rural e-Governance applications implemented in the recent few years have been demonstrating the importance of Information and Communication Technologies (ICT) in the concerned areas of rural development. Indeed, some of the schemes introduced in rural India have improved the government services immensely.

Instances like Mahatma Gandhi National Rural Employment Guarantee Act (MGNREGA), Warana Project in Maharashtra, Online Income Tax, Online Central Excise, Unique ID and E-office has accelerated growth of respective areas and contributing to country's economic development. Similarly, at state level the various rural E-governance projects such as SETU Project in Maharashtra etc, projects that have been providing excellent services and saving time and money of people as well as of government and are contributing their might to the socio-economic development of rural India. Being ICT a significant instrument in E-Governance and Rural Development, appropriate infrastructure/design is mandatory for proper functioning as follows:-

- As designed of citizen centric services, and dependable service delivery mechanisms.
- Selection of appropriate (dependable, maintainable, cost effective) technologies for rural connectivity, and information processing solutions.

- As designed of cost effective delivery stations (kiosks) to build new services.
- Demonstration of transparency and efficiency to remove distrust and build confidence among the citizens on functioning of service delivery mechanisms.
- Invite private participation to reduce the burden on the central servicing agency, bring in the expertise, enhance the speed of implementation, and offer better value proposition to the citizens.

The term e-governance focuses on the use of new ICTs by governments as applied to the full range of government functions. Thus e-governance is the application of information and communication technology for delivering government services, exchange of information, communication, transactions, integration, various stand-alone systems, and services between government and citizens, government and business as well as back office processes and interactions within the entire government frame work.

The government being the service provider it is important to motivate the employees for delivering the services through ICT. E-governance seek to achieve Efficiency, Transparency, and Citizen's Participation. Enabling E-governance through ICT contributes to Good Governance, Trust and Accountability, Citizen's Awareness, and empowerment, Citizen's Welfare, Democracy, Nation's Economic growth. ICT is the biggest enabler of change and process reforms fade in face of what ICT has achieved in few years.

E-governance services through ICT refer to transactional services that involve local, state or national government. ICTs acts in speeding up the flow of information and knowledge between government and citizens and transforming the way in which governments and citizens interact.

According to the United Nations Development Program (UNDP) the challenge for all countries is to create and develop a system of governance that promotes supports and sustains human development. Governments in many parts of the world have made huge ICT investments aimed at improving governance processes.

In the present century, the advancements in Information and Communication Technologies (ICTs) are changing the various components of human life. The changes in the ICTs have brought a positive impact in the process of public service delivery and socio-economic structure of communities.

In India, e-Governance applications in the recent past have demonstrated their positive impact in minimizing the processing costs, increase transparency and support economic development by income generating ventures, increase in agricultural production, and improvements in health and education sectors, all of which promote the overall quality of life of rural people. ICT contributes in providing the transactional services for the rural people with the benefit of time and cost savings in obtaining the public services with efficiency and effectiveness and it also examines changes in agricultural productivity and improved quality of life due to the ICT services. In addition to the above AEPS, GPS etc. are pivotal in ICT services.

The rural ICT applications attempt to offer the services of central agencies (like district administration, cooperative union, and state and central government departments) to the citizens at their village door steps. These applications utilize the ICT in offering improved and affordable connectivity and processing solutions. Several Government-Citizen (G-C) e-Government pilot projects have attempted to adopt these technologies to improve the reach, enhance the base, minimize the processing costs, increase transparency, and reduce the cycle times to half.

A large number of rural E-Government applications, developed as pilot projects, were aimed at offering easy access to citizen services and improved processing of government-to-citizen transactions. The idea that the primary and the sheer object of ICT in e-governance and rural development is individual's motivation to collective mobilization for an integrated rural development.

## ICT AVAILABILITY FOR RURAL APPLICATIONS

Computers have become more powerful, user friendly and less expensive. The PC revolution has brought them closer to the users to the extent that in number cases users have designed and developed their own applications. However, till recently, it has not become easy to create local content and regional language interfaces, to facilitate their use in villages. In addition, although the hardware costs are coming down, the total cost of ownership for rural applications is quite high. The costs of the minimum required gadgets like PC, Modem, Power stabilizer, and Printer along with the license costs of software (OS, Database, and Application as applicable) does not justify their use for offering government related information services, just on the basis of return-on-investment criterion. These equipments become obsolete too soon, and have high maintenance costs in the rural areas. At the current cost levels, to breakeven, the kiosk operators will have to find alternative revenue generation activities utilizing these equipments. We notice that in many cases such business potential does not exist and even if it existed, the kiosk owners / operators are not trained to develop new solutions.

Several entrepreneurs are attempting to offer inexpensive hardware and software solutions for rural applications. The CorDECT technology by nLogue Communications and the Simputer by PicoPeta Simputers Pvt.Ltd. are good examples of such initiatives. These organizations developed the computer and wireless connectivity solutions with indigenous components, software, and open source systems. It is hoped that large scale production of these systems would bring in appropriate cost effective technologies for rural applications. MSSRF based at Chennai is doing pioneering work in designing appropriate technologies for the rural poor.

## Application Design and Reengineering of Backend Processes

Rural applications will have to give utmost importance to their offerings to the socially and economically backward communities. These citizens must find the services relevant and beneficial to them. The user interfaces must be in regional language and the services should be designed to offer good responses to their applications and aim at minimizing the need for citizen's trips to district / taluka head-quarters. The applications must record the progress of user transactions and retrieve them on user's query. They must offer privacy and security to the user data. This becomes more important when the service delivery agents are private partners. All these call for significant reengineering and mechanization of backend processes.

Many successful urban ICT applications and rural projects like Bhoomi15 have exploited the developments in the server, network, and software technologies, to improve the processing of back-end processing applications. Application design must start with good understanding and documentation of process flows and bottlenecks in the existing system. Application maintenance requires good quality documentation of application and database design at both system and user levels. Ideally they should belong to the central services agency and must be made available to the maintenance and training agencies.

## E-GOVERNMENT WEB OF INTERRELATIONSHIPS

The target of eGovernment encompasses four main groups: citizens, businesses, governments (other governments and public agencies) and employees. The electronic transactio ns and interactions between government and each group constitute the eGovernment web of relationships and the respective four main blocks of eGovernment, that are: 1. Government to Citizens (G2C) 2. Government to Business (G2B) 3. Government to Government (G2G) 4. Government to Employees (G2E) Most researchers and academics refer only to the first three blocks, without considering the fourth or simply including it as part of 'government to government' block. The relationships, interactions and transactions between government and employees in fact constitute another large eGovernment block, which requires a separate and very careful handling. Many people today refer to employees as internal customers and as a result, in order for an eGovernment initiative to be customer oriented and centric, it has to take into account needs and requirements of this group as well. More specifically, these eGovernment blocks can be characterised as follows:

1. Government to Citizen: deals with the relationship between government and citizens. EGovernment allows government agencies to talk, listen, relate and continuously communicate with its citizens, supporting, in this way, accountability, democracy and improvements to public services. A broad array of interactions can be developed ranging from the delivery of services and the provision of welfare and health benefits to regulatory and compliance oriented licensing (Riley, 2001). G2C allows customers to access government information and services instantly, conveniently, from everywhere, by use of multiple channels (PC, Web TV, mobile phone or wireless device). It also enables and reinforces their participation in local community life (send an email or contribute to an online discussion forum)
2. Government to Business: consists of the electronic interactions between government agencies and private businesses. It allows e-transaction initiatives such as eprocurement and the development of an electronic marketplace for government (Fang, 2002). Companies everywhere are conducting business-to-business e-commerce in order to lower their costs and improve inventory control. The opportunity to conduct online transactions with government reduces red tape and simplifies

regulatory processes, therefore helping businesses to become more competitive. The delivery of integrated, single-source public services creates opportunities for businesses and government to partner together for establishing a web presence faster and cheaper.

3. Government to Government: refers to the relationship between governmental organizations, as for example national, regional and local governmental organizations, or with other foreign government organizations. Governments depend on other levels of government within the state to effectively deliver services and allocate respons ibilities (Riley, 2001). In order to realize a single access point, collaboration and cooperation among different governmental departments and agencies is compulsory. Online communication and cooperation allows government agencies and departments to share databases, resources, pool skills and capabilities, enhancing the efficiency and effectivity of processes.
4. Government to Employees: refers to the relationship between government and its employees. G2E is an effective way to provide e-learning, bring employees together and to promote knowledge sharing among them. It gives employees the possibility of accessing relevant information regarding: compensation and benefit policies, training and learning opportunities, civil rights laws, etc. G2E refers also to strategic and tactical mechanisms for encouraging the implementation of government goals and programs as well as human resource management, budgeting and accounting (Riley, 2001).

## LEGAL FRAMEWORK FOR E-GOVERNANCE IN INDIALEGAL FRAMEWORK FOR E-GOVERNANCE IN INDIA

Legal enablement of ICT systems in India and legal framework for information society of India are still missing in India. For instance, we have no legal framework for e-courts in India, online dispute resolution in India, mandatory e-governance services in India, etc. Further, we have no dedicated legal framework for cloud computing in India as on date. Although electronic delivery (e-delivery) of services in India is needed yet in the absence of suitable policies and legal frameworks in this regard, e-delivery of services in India is still a dream.

Electronic governance in India (e-governance in India) is still at its infancy stage. Most of the e-governance projects of India under the national e-governance plan (NEGP) are still in the pipeline despite the deadline being passed long before. This is despite the fact that thousand of crores of public money has already been utilised for e-governance projects of India but without any constructive and practical results.

Meanwhile, the World Bank has once again issued $ 150 million loan to India. It has been issued under the category of e-delivery of public services development policy loan of India. The purpose of the loan is to ensure e-services delivery policy in India that is presently missing. However, what is more alarming is the fact that in India we have no legal framework for e-governance that can ensure mandatory e-governance services in India. Although the information technology act 2000 carries provisions pertaining to e-governance services in India yet they are "non mandatory" in nature. This has resulted in a poor e-governance services delivery in India. Till now we have no legal framework that mandates that citizens and organisations can claim e-governance as a matter of right.

Further, the scope of NEGP is very wide covering almost all aspects of governance – right from delivery of services and provision of information to business process re-engineering within the different levels of government and its institutions. It is essential that NGP is implemented, monitored and regulated through a legal framework so that it is no more just a plan but reality.

In fact, while implementing the NEGP, various structural and institutional issues have already arisen which clearly call for a statutory mandate for their resolution. The purpose would be to give statutory mandate to the institutional entities, setting up of a separate fund, defining responsibilities and providing for time frames and oversight mechanisms. Thus, this legislation may, inter alia, contain provisions regarding the following:

(a) Definition of e-governance in the Indian context, its objectives and role,

(b) Coordination and oversight mechanisms, support structures at various levels, their functions and responsibilities,

(c) Role, functions and responsibilities of government organisations at various levels,

(d) Mechanism for financial arrangements including public-private partnership,

(e) Specifying the requirements of a strategic control framework for e-government projects dealing with statutory and sovereign functions of the government,

(f) Responsibility for selection and adoption of standards and inter-operability framework,

(g) Framework for cyber security, privacy protection, data security and data protection etc,

(h) Parliamentary oversight mechanism, and

(i) Mechanism for co-ordination between government organisations at Union and State levels.

## FRAMEWORK FOR E-GOVERNANCE FRAMEWORK FOR E-GOVERNANCE

As described below, the E-Governance framework would include Back-ends (databases of the different government agencies, service providers, state governments etc.), Middleware and the Front-end delivery channels (home PCs, mobile phones, kiosks, integrated citizen service centres etc.) for citizens and businesses. The Middleware comprises of communication and security infrastructure, gateways and integrated services facilitating integration of inter-departmental services.

Adopting a proactive strategy, and acting to bring the Internet to rural and agricultural communities in developing countries will help enable rural people to face the unprecedented challenges brought on by the changing global economy, political changes, environmental degradation. To deal with these challenges, and to make critical decisions, people at all levels of society, must be able to access critical information and communicate.

All the organisations discussed in the paper face common issues of implementation, but differ in scale, connectivity technologies, services offered, revenue models and organisational structures. In the long run, bringing rich information to the population of rural India, whether in the form of education, market prices, market opportunities, and more, can only have positive impacts on the material well being of rural masses. The time to act to support Internet knowledge and communication systems in developing countries is now. Today we truly live in a global village, but it is a village with elite information "haves" and many information "have-nots." With the new technologies available to us we have an opportunity to change this.

*E-Governance in India:* Technology cannot work in isolation; it has to reach out to one and all. It is vital for citizens to receive the services they need when required at the minimum cost. A government should be able to handle information quickly and efficiently, be it monitoring project status or reaching out to people. The advent of Information Technology as a highly leveraged enabling to for delivery of services in the public and private sector has now been universally recognised. Through the deployment of IT, existing government processes can be re-engineered to transform into government services based on paper less electronic mail for simple transaction. For more complex transaction the provision of fully interactive online services will, give the citizen access to government services with faster response at places and at times that are more convenient. These services include providing information, collecting taxes, granting licenses, paying grants and benefits, collecting and analysing statistics and procuring goods and services. E-Governance is the application of IT to the processes of governments functioning to bring about Simple Moral Accountable Responsive and Transport (SMART) governance that works better, costs less and is capable of fulfilling the citizen's need as never before. E-governance has been identified into four stages. The first stage is called 'E-foundation'. At this stage the basic infrastructure are set in place. Also, primary applications like LAN are implemented and information is created. The second stage is that of E-facilitation, which involves participation of the stakeholders, the government employee and the citizen. The E-business stage has desk-based transactions on the web. The fourth stage being E-commerce. E-governance will therefore be defined as the use of IT for:

- Efficient delivery of government services to citizens and business.
- Better dissemination of government information.
- Improved efficiency of government information.
- Improved revenue collection and budgetary controls.

E-governance means to fundamentally change as to how the government operates and this implies a new set of responsibilities for the executive, legislature and citizenry.

## Benefits of E-Governance

- E-governance provides integrated government services through a single window by re-engineering of government processes.

- E-governance is capable of not only speeding up transactions but also transparent functioning.
- E-governance can reduce the procedural and postal delays involved in current system. This might help control corruption and increase participation of people in policy decision process by improving the degrees of communication between government and public.
- E-governance helps common man getting governed with minimum red tape and zero corruption.

## References:

Artherton, F.C.: *Can Technology Protect Democracy?*, Washington, DC, Roosevelt Centre for American Policy Studies and Sage, 1987.

Beniger J.R.: *The Control Revolution*, Cambridge, Harvard University Press, 1986.

Davies.A.: *Telecommunications and Politics. The decentralised alternative*, London, Pinter, 1994.

Doulton, A.: *Government and Community Information Services*, Oxford, Dragonflair and CDW & Associates, 1994.

Freeman C.: *The Economic of Innovation*, Harmondsworth, Penguin, 1984.

Graham S.: *Best Practice Developing Community Teleservice Centres*, Manchester, University of Manchester, 1991.

Jaeger, C.: *Information Society and Spatial Structure*, London, Belhaven, 1989.

Jarillo, J.C.: *Creating the Borderless Organization*, Oxford, Butterworth-Heinemann, 1993.

Kable: *Civil Service IT Market Profile 1995-6*, London, Kable, 1995.

Lynn P.: *Public Perceptions of Local Government: Its Finances and Services*, London, HMSO, 1992.

Macpherson, C.B.: *Democratic Theory. Essays in Retrieval*, Oxford, Clarendon Press, 1973.

Masuda Y.: *Managing in the Information Society*, Oxford, Basil Blackwell, 1990.

Naisbitt, J.: *Ten New Directions Transforming our Lives*, London, Macdonald, 1984.

Politt. C: *Managerialism and the Public Services*, Oxford, Blackwell, 1993.

Sabel. C: *The Second Industrial Divides. Possibilities for Prosperity*, New York, Basic Books, 1984.

Williams F.: *The Coming of the New Telecommunications Structure for the Information Age*, New York, Free Press, 1991.

27

# Secularism, Caste and Communal Violence in Indian Perspective

**DR NALIN SINGH PANWAR**
*Assistant Professor, Schools of Studies in Political Science and Public Administration, Vikram University, Ujjain, Madhya Pradesh*

India has become the country where caste and communal violence are the most routine, institutionalized order of the day." It is important to note that Van Den Berghe is making an indirect critique of the interventionist practices of secularism in India. He draws a link between the Indian secular practice of recognizing religious identity on the basis of group rights and the escalating levels of religious violence, since „ethnic consciousness is increased and social cleavages deepened" by such policies. He would advocate a policy of non-interference rather than the Indian practice of equal intervention which results in the recognition of collective rights for various religious groups. In that sense, this line of critique would see the policies and practices of secularism as responsible for the increasing politicization of religious identity in India. The second group of critics focuses less on the practice of secularism and more on the values that underlie the doctrine. In some ways, this critique is much more fundamental than Van Den Berghes. The two main protagonists in this camp, T.N Madan and Ashis Nandy, direct their critique towards the consequences of secularization on Indian society. Nandy s critique of secularization can be more aptly characterized as a critique of the effects of modernization on traditional societies. He insists, "Many Indians see the society around them – and often their own children-as l eaving no scope for a compromise between the old and the new, and have to opt for a way of life which fundamentally negates the traditional concepts of a good life. These Indians have now come to sense that it is modernity which rules the world and that religion-as-faith is being pushed to the corner."

Secularization is thus characterized as a process that purges modern life of traditional and religious ways of conceptualizing the world, resulting in the alienation of large parts of the population. Nandy argues that this sense of alienation from modern, secular life is a fertile mindset for intolerance and aggression. He contends, "Much of the fanaticism and violence associated with religion comes today from the sense of defeat of the believers, from their feelings of impotence, and from their free-floating anger and self-hatred while facing a world which is increasingly secular and de-sacralized." Thus, the crux of Nandy s argument is that secularization, as a part of the larger processes of modernization, fuels resentment and anger that then gets channelled into an aggressive politicization of religious identity.

T.N Madan s critique of secularization is also in many ways a critique of modernization; however, Madan is keen to emphasize the specificity of secularism as a Western idea. He claims that "the idea of secularism, a gift of Christianity, has been built into Western social theorists paradigms of modernization, and since these paradigms are believed to have universal applicability, the elements that converged historically to constitute modern life in Europe from the sixteenth century onwards, have come to be presented as the requirements of modernization elsewhere, and this must be questioned."

In fact, he questions the transferability of secularism to societies in South Asia by positing the idea that "once a cultural definition of a phenomenon or of a relationship (say between religion and politics, or society and state) has crystallized, it follows that subsequent formulations of it, whether endogenous or exogenous, can only be re-definitions. In other words, traditions have deep roots in memory." Although, he appears to be making a culturally deterministic argument, he resists the charge by acknowledging the role of creativity and adaptation. Ultimately, however, Madan sees the cultural core of South Asian societies as profoundly religious and a secular framework that cannot acknowledge this character will politicize religious identity in dangerous ways as it becomes a source of resistance to the alien, secular world-view.

Van Den Berghe, Nandy and Madan offer compelling accounts for why religious identity was susceptible to politicization in India. However, there are serious deficiencies in their accounts that need to be addressed before constructing a sound theoretical argument for the politicization of religion in India. The most serious deficiency with Van Den Berghe s account is that he generalizes the extent to which institutionalized identity has resulted in ethnic conflict. For instance, he cannot explain why it is the institutionalization of religious identity, rather than linguistic or caste identities that have resulted in a nationalist movement. It is true that state recognition of special rights to minority groups has politicized these cleavages to some extent, but it is important to note that linguistic conflicts are far less pronounced in India than Hindu-Muslim violence for example. Thus, Van Den Berghe cannot explain why the institutional recognition of some identities has proven to be more dangerous than others situation in India. I chose the Hindu-Muslim example because of the intensity and frequency of violence between these two religious groups. However, it is important to note that conflicts between Hindu Nationalists and other religious minorities also occur on a regular basis.

Nandy and Madan s explanation for the resurgence of religious conflict as related to processes of secularization also reveal some serious problems. Both view secularization as a process that is incompatible with Indian society, which results in the progressive devaluation of religion in public life, and by way of a reaction, the increase in support for fundamentalist and extremist religious organizations and political parties. However, such a position assumes that religiosity is an inherent attribute of Indian society and is problematic in so far as it is significantly ahistorical. Missing from this analysis is a recognition of the significant accommodations and adjustments which were made in India s encounter with modernity. While a critique of the deeply dislocating and disenchanting process of modernization is warranted, it will be shown that the suggestion that India is unable to adapt and accommodate to the demands of modernization due to its inherent religiosity is unsupported by evidence.

Although, there are serious problems with the explanations provided by Van Den Berghe, Nandy and Madan, their arguments cannot be repudiated completely. In fact, aspects of their critique will be retained and modified in light of an insightful and important work on Hindu Nationalism by Thomas Blom Hansen. Hansen s account of the emergence of Hindu Nationalism in his book The Saffron Wave has allowed me to modify and synthesize the critiques of secularism and secularization so as to provide a clearer and more complete account of the politicization of religious identity in India. He locates his explanation for the rise of Hindu Nationalism in "a broader democratic transformation of both the political field and the public culture in post-colonial India." Hansen elaborates on this transformation as an "intensification of political mobilization among the lower castes and the minorities" and "the rise of ambiguous desires of consumerism in everyday life and the exposure to global cultural and economic flows." He argues that these developments in the political field and public culture of contemporary India "fractured social imaginings and notions of order and hierarchy, prompting millions of Hindus to embrace Hindu Nationalist promises of order, discipline, and collective strength"

The strength of Hansen s account lies in its ability to evaluate and synthesize the critiques of secularism and secularization put forth by Van Den Berghe, Nandy and Madan in a more sophisticated manner. Van Den Berghe for instance had critiqued the institutional practices of secularism as responsible for the politicization of religious identity and the intolerance and violence that followed. Hansen does not discard this argument since he also argues that the mobilization of the lower castes and religious minorities through India s policies of official recognition were a deep source of anxiety for the dominant upper-caste Hindu community. However, he is careful to emphasize that the politicization of the Hindu identity was a majoritarian backlash from privileged Hindus who wanted to seek security and recognition under the Hindutva ideology of cultural pride, order, and national strength. This point is crucial because it stresses the ways in which a perceived „threat to the identity of the dominant group often has the most dangerous consequences of persecution, conflict, and violence. Therefore, in trying to understand the conditions under which the politicization of ethnic identity escalates to violent conflict, it would be judicious to keep in mind which groups feel threatened because of their pre-established dominance in society.

Hansen s theory has also proven to be productive in complicating and synthesizing Nandy and Madan s arguments. Both Nandy and Madan are keen to emphasize that secularization, as a part and parcel of the modernization process, is the source of religious conflict in India. They argue that the de-legitimization of religion in public life represses an essential character of South Asian society, which returns in perverted forms of fanaticism and bigotry. In a similar vein, Hansen maintains his focus on modernization as a central category of analysis, but questions the notion that religion has been „repressed in modern society. Instead, he puts forth the argument that religion has become more prominent in modern life because it has shown a remarkable capacity to adapt and adjust to the different dimensions of modernity. For instance, he argues that the Hindu Nationalist movement often "acknowledges the powerful attractions of Western consumerism and modern technology but emphasize that the prerequisite for developing a sovereign national modernity is the cultural unity and purity of the Hindu nation." Thus, modernization has not accelerated the pace of secularization in society as Nandy and Madan contend, rather religion found new ways of existing in modern India by adapting to the technological and consumer revolution.

Two corollaries can be gleaned from this theoretical discussion of the rise of Hindu Nationalism in India. On the one hand, the interventionist and reformist policies of secularism threatened the dominant Hindu community and caused them to react by turning to the ideology of Hindutva for security and recognition. This reaction will be explored in the next section of this paper by looking into the issue of Muslim personal laws and the Mandal Commission s report of 1992. Both issues exemplify how policies of official recognition created anxieties around citizenship for the dominant Hindu community, and also how these anxieties were instrumental in politicizing religious identity in India.

On the other hand, Hindu Nationalism s ability to adapt and adjust to the processes of economic and technological modernization strengthened its appeal to a growing Hindu middle class which envisioned a modern and prosperous India fully integrated into the global economy. The means by which Hindu Nationalism adapted and adjusted to the processes of modernization will be explore in more detail in the forthcoming section on "Modernity and Religion". This part of the paper will seek to show how Hindu Nationalism made itself politically relevant in an era of accelerated modernization.

The preceding theoretical discussion sought to bring together and assess a variety of explanations for the politicization of religion in India. It drew on some important critiques of Indian secularism to understand how religion came to be such a dominant force in Indian politics. However, some of the central assertions made by the critics of secularism were reworked or entirely rejected in light of Thomas Hansen s work on Hindu Nationalism. In what follows I argue that the politicization of religion in India is the result of the simultaneous anxieties and possibilities created by modern life. The anxieties are rooted in the institutional practice of secularism in India which sought to alleviate the inequality between social groups. The possibilities are created by the technological and economic advancements made by modernization. I substantiate the argument with examples from the manipulation of the mass media for religious ends and state policies that heightened ethnic consciousness.

## SECULARISM IN INDIA

Secularism in India has very different meaning and implications. The word secularism has never been used in Indian context in the sense in which it has been used in Western countries i.e. in the sense of atheism or purely this worldly approach, rejecting the other-worldly beliefs.

India is a country where religion is very central to the life of people. India's age-old philosophy as expounded in Hindu scriptures called Upanishad is sarva dharma samabhava, which means equal respect for all religions. The reason behind this approach is the fact that India has never been a mono-religious country. Even before the Aryan invasion India was not a mono-religious country. There existed before Aryan invasion numerous tribal cults from north-western India to Kanya Kumari most of whom happened to be Dravidians. Thus certain languages in North West of Pakistan even today contain some words of Dravidian origin. However, with the invasion of Aryans people of Dravidian origin were driven down south and today we find all Dravidian people in four southern states of India.

Aryans brought new religion based on Vedas and Brahmins dominated intellectual life of north India. But a section of Brahmins also migrated to south and evolved new cults marrying Vedic cults with Dravidian ones. Thus it is said that Hindu Indians worship more than 33 hundred thousand gods and goddesses. Thus even before advent of Christianity and Islam India was multi-religious in nature. Christianity and Islam added more religious traditions to existing Indian traditions. Thus it would be correct to say that India is bewilderingly diverse country in every respect – religious, cultural, ethnic and caste.

India is one country where caste rigidity and concept of untouchability evolved and still plays a major role in religious, social and cultural matters. Caste dynamics in Indian life, even in Christian and Islamic societies, plays larger than life role. Since most of the conversions to Christianity and Islam took place from lower caste Hindus, these two world religions also developed caste structure. There are lower caste churches and mosques in several places.

Under feudal system there was no competition between different religious traditions as authority resided in sword and generally there were no inter-religious tensions among the people of different religions. They co-existed in peace and harmony though at times inter-religious controversies did arise. However, there never took place bloodshed in the name of religion. There was also tradition of tolerance between religions due to state policies of Ashoka and Akbar. Ashoka's edicts clearly spell out policy of religious tolerance and Akbar used to hold inter-religious dialogue among followers of different religions and he also followed the policy of tolerance and even withdrew the jizya tax (poll tax on Hindus which was an irritant. Thus both Ashok and Akbar have place of great significance in religious life of India. No doubt they have been designated as 'great' i.e. they are referred to as Ashoka the Great and Akbar the Great.

Also, India had Sufi and Bhakti traditions in Islam and Hinduism respectively. Both Sufism and Bhakti traditions were based on respect for different religions. The poorer and lower caste Hindus and Muslims were greatly influenced by these traditions. Unlike 'ulama and Brahmans the Sufi and Bhakti saints were highly tolerant and open to the truth in other faiths. They never adopted sectarian attitudes and were never involved in power struggles. They kept away from power structures. Nizamuddin Awliya, a great Sufi saints of 13-14th century saw the times of five Sultans but never paid court to a single one. When the last Sultan of his life sent a message requesting him to come to the court, he refused. Then he sent the message that if Nizamuddin does not come to my court, I (the Sultan) will come to his hospice. He replied that there are two doors to my hospice; if Sultan enters by one, I will leave by the other. Such was the approach of Sufis and Saints to power structure of their time.

Dara Shikoh, was heir apparent to Shajahan, the Moghul Emperor but had sufi bent of mind and was also a great scholar of Islam and Hinduism. He wrote a book Majmau'l Bahrayn (Co-mingling of Two Oceans Islam and Hinduism) and quoting from Hindu and Islamic scriptures showed both religions had similar teachings. The difference was of languages (Arabic and Sanskrit) and not teachings. Thus Dara Shikoh also contributed richly to inter-religious harmony in India.

Most of the conversions to Islam and Christianity took place through Sufis and missionaries with a spirit of devotion. Even today in India most of the Christians and Muslims belong to these lower caste strata. Even centuries after conversion their caste status and economic status has not changed.

## Emergence of Competitive Politics

However, the entire social, economic and political scenario changed after advent of the British rule in 19th century. Differences between Hindu and Muslim elite began to emerge for various reasons – socio-cultural, economic and political. The British rulers adopted the policy of divide and rule, distorted medieval Indian history to make Muslim rulers appear as tyrants to the Hindu elite. This distorted history was taught in new school system, which was established by the British rulers. Also there developed economic and political competition between Hindu and Muslim elite leading to communal tensions. The Hindu elite was quick to adjust to new realities and took to modern education and commerce and industries. The Muslim ruling elite resisted new secular education system and also could not take to commerce and industry. They were thus left far behind in the race for progress.

Sir Syed Ahmad Khan had a perceptive mind. He understood importance of modern education system and founded Mohammedan Anglo Oriental College (MAO College) which became fulcrum of modern education for North Indian Muslim elite. The orthodox Ulama, however, vehemently opposed modern secular education and declared Syed Ahmad Khan as kafir (unbeliever) as he was supporting modern secular education.

Initially Hindu and Muslim elite cooperated with each other and Syed Ahmad Khan always emphasised Hindu-Muslim unity but the competitive nature of political and economic power drove wedge between the two elites and communal tensions began to emerge. When Indian National Congress was formed in 1885, it adopted secularism as its anchor sheet in view of multi-religious nature of Indian society.

India could not head towards Hindu Rashtra (Hindu Nation) as India was not merely a Hindu country. In pre-partition period Muslims were 25% besides Christians, Sikhs, Buddhists and Jains. However, Hindu society was highly fragmented society and far from monolithic. The dalits (low caste people) refused to call themselves as Hindus (subsequently their leader B.R.Ambedkar) adopted Buddhism in protest).

Muslims too, though not monolithic, had semblance of unity and this was used by communal Hindus to try to unite Hindus as one community. However, it is also true that the Hindu elite was more confident than the Muslim elite in the emerging new power-structure and felt more secure. Muslim elite felt less secure and they hitched their wagon with the British rulers. They wanted to share power-sharing arrangement before the British left the country. Thus secularism in India was more a political than philosophical phenomenon. The Indian National Congress adopted secularism, not as this worldly philosophy but more as a political arrangement between different religious communities. As power-sharing arrangement could not be satisfactorily worked out between the Hindu and Muslim elite the country was divided into two independent states of India and Pakistan, Muslim majority areas of North-West going to Pakistan.

After independence and partition a large body of Muslims were left in India and hence the leaders like Gandhi and Nehru preferred to keep India secular in the sense that Indian state will have no religion though people of India will be free both in individual and corporate sense to follow any religion of their birth or adoption. Thus India remained politically secular but otherwise its people continued to be deeply religious. In India right from the British period main contradiction was not between religious and secular but it was between secular and communal. In the western world main struggle was between church and state and church and civil society but in India neither Hinduism nor Islam had any church-like structure and hence there never was any such struggle between secular and religious power structure.

The main struggle was between secularism and communalism. The communal forces from among Hindus and Muslims mainly fought for share in power though they used their respective religions for their struggle for power. Even after partition communal problem did not die. It raised its head again within few years.

The RSS (Rashtriya Swayam Sevak Sangh), which is mainspring of Hindu right remained in existence and at its instance a new political outfit, which was communal in nature came into existence called Jan Sangh. In independent India the Jan Sangh was mainspring of communal problem and it kept on denouncing secularism as western concept alien to the Indian ethos.

Jawahar Lal Nehru, the first Prime Minister of India was great champion of secularism and secular politics. Theoretically speaking the Congress Party was also committed to secularism. However, the Congress Party consisted of several members and leaders whose secularism was in doubt. But it was due to Mahatma Gandhi, Nehru, Maulana Abul Kalam Azad and B.R.Ambedkar that India committed itself to secularism and its Constitution was drafted on secular lines.

Secularism in India, as pointed out before, meant equal respect for all religions and cultures and non-interference of religion in the government affairs. Also, according to the Indian Constitution no discrimination will be made on the basis of caste, creed, gender and class. Similarly all citizens of India irrespective of ones religion, caste or gender have right to vote. According to articles 14 to 21 all will enjoy same rights without any discrimination on any ground. According to Article 25 all those who reside in India are free to confess, practice and propagate religion of one's choice subject of course to social health and law and order. Thus even conversion to any religion of ones choice is a fundamental right. But the BJP (Bhartiya Janta Party) and RSS are opposed to all this. According to them there should be Hindu Rashtra (Hindu Nation) in India and Muslims and Sikhs should be secondary citizens without any political right.

Since the BJP is a political party it cannot say so openly and publicly. It also has to take pledge of secularism for contesting election. But since it is integral part of RSS ideology it is also responsible for RSS beliefs. In fact all secular forces in India consider the BJP as a communal party. It always takes anti-minority stance and accuses the Congress, supposedly a secular party, of 'appeasement' of minorities. It also describes the Congress and other secular parties as indulging in 'pseudo-secularism'.

The RSS and BJP also known as the Sangh Parivar, not only reject secularism but provoke violence against minorities. Since independence several major communal riots have taken pace in India. The first such riot took place in Jabalpur in Central India and last major riot took place in Gujarat in Western India in 2002 in which more than 2000 Muslims were killed and several women were raped. When the Gujarat carnage took place in 2002 BJP was ruling over Gujarat. According to the filed evidence Chief Minister of BJP party Mr. Narendra Modi was involved along with the entire governmental machinery in the carnage and on this basis the US Government denied him visa in early 2005. The BJP was directly involved in high pitch propaganda against the historic mosque called Babri Mosque and ultimately demolished it claiming it to be a birth-place of Lord Ram, a Hindu god.

Mr. Lal Krishna Advani who was then the President of BJP spearheaded the campaign against Babri Mosque and the mosque was demolished right in his presence. He later became Home Minister in the National Democratic Alliance (NDA) ministry. He is known as hardliner Hindu. Shri Vajpayee who became Prime Minister of India in NDA Government, is known as the moderate face of BJP though one can say there is hardly any ideological difference between the two.

## References

Carsten, F. L. : *The Rise of Fascism*, London, Methuen and Co., 1967.

Garg, V.K. : *Caste and Reservation in India*, Alfa Publications, Delhi, 2010.

James M.: *Untouchable : An Indian Life History*, CA, Stanford University Press, 1979.

Lakshmanna, C.: *Caste Dynamics in Village India*, Nachiketa Publications, Bombay, 1973.

Nath, Trilok: *Politics of the Depressed Classes*, Delhi, Deputy Publications, 1987.

Sarkar, J.: *Caste, Occupation and Change*, Delhi, B. R. Publishing Co., 1984.

Sharma, K. L.: *Caste, Class and Social Movements*, Rawat Publications, Jaipur, 1986.

28

# The Role of NGO's in the Implementation of Integrated Rural Development Programme

**SANDEEP KUMAR POSWAL**
*Assistant Professor, Department of Economics, B.S.M. (PG) College, Roorkee, Uttarakhand.*

## INTEGRATED RURAL DEVELOPMENT PROGRAMME (IRDP)

IRDP launched on October 2nd. 1980 all over the Country and accordingly all the 15 Blocks of Boudh- Kandhamal district have been covered under the Scheme.Since then, prior to the above period, IRDP was in operation in 8 blocks of the district since 1978-79. The I.R.D.P. continues to be a major poverty alleviation programme in the field of Rural Development.

The objective of I.R.D.P. is to enable identified rural poor families to cross the poverty line by providing productive assets and inputs to the target groups. The assets which could be in primary, secondary or tertiary sector are provided through financial assistance in the form of subsidy by the Govt.and and term credit advanced by financial institutions. The programme is implemented in all the blocks in the country as a centrally sponsored scheme funded on 50:50 basis by the Centre and State. The Scheme is merged with another Scheme named S.G.S.Y. since 01.04.1999.

TRAINING OF RURAL YOUTH FOR SELF EMPLOYMENT (TRYSEM): The training of Rural Youth for self employment (TRYSEM) is a supporting component of the IRDP, started as a centrally sponsored scheme on 15 th. August,1979. It aims at providing technical and enterpreanual skills to rural un-employed youths in the age group of 18-35 years from the families below the poverty line to enable them to take up income generating schemes. This scheme is no more in operation.It is merged with S.G.S.Y. since 01.04.1999.

SUPPLY OF IMPROVED TOOL-KITS TO RURAL ARTISANS(SITRA):The programme is implemented as a part of IRDP. At the district level, the DRDA is the nodal agency. The scheme is formulated and circulated to all the State Governments on 20 th. July,1992. Under this programme any suitable improved hand tool is to be provided. All the prudential rural artisans will be able to enhance the quality of the product to increase their production and their income and lead a better quality of life. No more in operation, it is merged with S.G.S.Y. since 01.04.1999.

DEVELOPMENT OF WOMEN AND CHILDREN IN RURAL AREAS(DWCRA) : The Development of Women and Children in rural areas(DWCRA) programme was launched as a sub-component of IRDP and a centrally sponsored scheme of the Department of Rural Development with UNICEF cooperation to strengthen the women's component of poverty alleviation programmes.It is directed at raising the income levels of women of poor households so as to enable their organised participation in social develeopoment towards economic self reliance.The DWCRA's primary thrust is on the formation of groups of 15 to 20 women from poor household at the village level for delivery of services like credit and skill training, cash and infrastructural support for self employment.Through the strategy of group formation, the programme aims to improve women's access to basic services of health, education, child care,nutrition and sanitation. It is merged with S.G.S.Y. since 01.04.1999.

GANGA KALYANA YOJANA ( G.K.Y.): It is a centrally sponsored scheme, being launched with effect from 01.02.1997. The objective of the scheme is to provide irrigation through exploitation of ground water( borewells and tubewells) for individual and group of beneficiaries beloning to the target group. This scheme is no more in operation. It is merged with S.G.S.Y. since 01.04.1999.

MILLION WELLS SCHEME( M.W.S.): Million Wells Scheme was taken up as a sub-scheme of N.R.E.P. (National Rural Employment Programme) and Rural Landless Employment Guarantee Programme( R.L.E.G.P.) during the year 1988-89 has continued under J.R.Y. Till 1989-90, the objective of the scheme was to provide open irrigation wells to small and marginal farmers amongst the Scheduled Caste/ Scheduled Tribes and freed Bonded Labourers who are below poverty line, free of cost. From 1990-91 onwards, under Million Wells Scheme, the following works were also included. (a) Construction of open irrigation wellls for the target group; (b) Where wells are not feasible, other scheme of minor irrigation like irrigation tanks, Water Harvesting Structures for the benefit of target group can also be taken up. (c) The provision under M.W.S. can also be utilised for the land development of the target groups. From 01.01.1996, this scheme had been delinked from J.R.Y. and made an independent scheme by itself. Now the scheme is no more in operation and merged with S.G.S.Y. since 01.04.1999.

INDIRA AWAS YOJANA( I.A.Y.): Indira Awas Yojana(I.A.Y.) which was launched during 1985-86 as a sub-scheme of R.L.E.G.P. has continued as part of J.R.Y. since its launch on April,1989. However from 01.01.1996, I.A.Y. has been made a separate scheme. The objective of I.A.Y. then was to provide dwelling units, free of cost to the members of Scheduled Caste / Scheduled Tribes and freed Bonded Labourers living below the poverty line. From 1993-94, the scheme has been extended to non-S.C./S.T. rural poor also. Indira Awas Yojana is a centrally sponsored scheme funded on cost sharing basis between the Government of India and the State Govt. in the ratio of 75:25. The cost of I.A.Y. houses have been enhanced from Rs.14,000/- to Rs.20,000/ - in hilly and difficult areas.

JAWAHAR ROJAGAR YOJANA( J.R.Y.): Alleviation of rural poverty has been one of the main objective of the development programes. Since independence various schemes of employment generation were taken up from time to time in the country. The Eigth plan has also stressed the need for having a larger focus on the programmes aimed at giving self employment and wage employment to the poorer section of the community. During the first four years of the Seventh Five Year Plan, two Wage-employment Programme viz; N.R.E.P.(National Rural Employment Programme) and Rural Landless Employment Guarantee Programme (R.L.E.G.P.) were in operation in the country. From 01.04.1989 i.e. last year of the Seventh Five Year Plan, these programmes were merged in to a single wage employment programme known as Jawahar Rojagar Yojana( J.R.Y.). The primary objectives of J.R.Y. is generation of additional gainful employment for the un-employed and under-employed men and women in rural areas. The secondary objectives of this programme is creation of sustainable employment by strengthening the rural economic infrastructure.

INTENSIFIED J.R.Y. ( I.J.R.Y.):The second stream of JRY called Intensifed J.R.Y. has been introduced from December,1993 in 2 districts of the State. Phulbani district is one of them. The objective of the scheme is to intensify the efforts for rural employment. All employment works resulting in creation of durable productive community assets providing employment on sustained basis may be taken up under the scheme. The basket of schemes may include construction of all weather road, minor irrigation works, soil and water conservation works, water harvesting structures, watershed development, farm forestry etc. Works for strengthening rural infrastructure like primary schools, markets in specially different tribal areas with appropriate supplementary funds from other sources are also taken up. Wage and non-wage ratio under the work should be 60:40.Now it is working in the field of *spice developement*.

OPERATION BLACK BOARD ( O.B.B.) : Universalisation of primary education is the basic input for acquisition of functional skills which are absolutely essential for promoting self reliance of the rural poor and their children. Primary education pre-supposes a basic infrastructure i.e. a school building with a library, facilities for drinking water, toilet etc.A large number of primary schools in the state does not have buildings. To fill up this gap construction of primary school buildings was taken up under O.B.B.programme from the year 1990-91. Sixty percent of funds for the scheme is met by additional JRY grant and 40% from the grant of State School and Mass Education Department.

EMPLOYEMENT ASSURANCE SCHEME ( E.A.S.): The Employment Assurance Scheme( E.A.S.) aims at providing wage employment in unskilled mannual works to the rural poor who are in need of employment and seeking it. The secondary objective is to create economic infrastructure and community assets for sustained employment and development. The Employment Assurance Scheme for generating employment opportunities to the rural poor on an assured basis has been launched from 2nd. October,1993. The scheme is the single wage employment programme implemented at the district/ block level through out the country.The scheme is operative in all the 12 Blocks of this district. A maximum of two adults per family are provided 100 days employment on an assured basis, who need and seek wage employment during the lean agriculture season. The ressources under the scheme would be shared between the Centre and the State in the ratio of 75:25 respectively. Men and women over

18 years of age and below 60 years of age normally residing in the village are covered.

KRUSHAK KALYANA KARJYAKARMA( K.K.K.): Rs.45.00 lakhs was received from Government for the execution of Borewells in this district. Since it is not feasible to construct Borewell as per Geological Survey Report, Government was moved to allow for construction of River Lift Irrigation under the scheme. Subsequently it was decided in the Collecrtor's Conference that un-utilised funds under K.K.K. will be utilised for construction of L.I.Points/Diversion Weirs. Accordingly 2 L.I.Ps for Rs.6.24 lakhs and 21 Diversion Weirs for Rs.39. 60 lakhs making the total of Rs.45.84 lakhs have been taken up by the D.M.,OAIC, and A.S.C.Os respecrtively. The excess amount of Rs.0.84 lakhs sanctioned for execution of Diversion Weirs was adjusted out of EAS funds. This scheme is no more in operation.

RURAL CONNECTIVITY PROGRAMME( R.C.P): The broad objectives of the Rural Connctivity Programme in the State is to provide all weather connectivity as per the prescribed specification from the district to Sub-divisional headquarters,Block headquarters to Tehsil headquarters and from Panchayat Samiti headquarters to Gram Panchayat headquarters in order of priority, in original Guidelines of Rural Connectivity Programme (R.C.P.). RCP funds received for connectivity under 10th. Finance Commission Award(T.F.C.) will be utilised for construction of all weather roads as per action plan approved by the Zilla Parishad.The scheme is implemented since 1996-97.

SWARNAJAYANTI GRAMA SWAROJAGAR YOJANA (S.G.S.Y.): The objective of Swarnajayanti Grama Swarojagar Yojana(S.G.S.Y.) is to provide sustainable income to the rural poor. The programme aims at establishing a large number of Micro-enterprises in the rural areas building upon the potential of the rural poor. It is envisaged that every family assisted under SGSY will be brought above the poverty line in a period of three years. This scheme is launched on 1st April,1999, the programme replaces the earliar Self Employment and allied programmes IRDP,TRYSEM,DWCRA,SITRA,GKY and MWS, which are no longer in operation. The programme covers families under below poverty line in rural areas of the country within this traget group, special safe guard have been provided by reserving 50% of benefits for SC/STs, 40% for women and 3% for physically handicapped persons subject to availability of funds. It is proposed to cover 30% of the rural poor in each block in the next five year.

S.G.S.Y. is a credit cum subsidy programme. It covers all aspects of self employment such as organisation of the poor into self-help groups training, credit technology, infrastructure and marketing. SGSY is a centrally sponsored scheme and funding shared by the Central and State Government in the ratio of 75:25.

JAWAHAR GRAM SAMRIDHI YOJANA( J.G.S.Y.): Jawahar Gram Samridhi Yojana( JGSY) is the restructured streamlined and comprehensive version of erstwhile Jawahar Rojagar Yojana, designed to improve the quality of life of the poor, JGSY has been launched on 1st. April,1999. The primary objectives of the JGSY is creation of demand driven community village infrastructure including durable assets at the village level and assets to enable the rural poor to increase the opportunity for sustained employment. The secondary objective is the generation of supplementary employment for the unemployed poor in the rural areas. The wage employment under the programme shall be given to Below Poverty line ( B.P.L. ) families. JGSY is being implemented entirely at the village Panchayat level. Village Panchayat is the sole authority for preparation of the Annual Action Plan and its implementation. The programme will be implemented entirely as a centrally sponsored scheme on cost sharing basis between the Centre and the State Government in the ratio of 75:25.

DROUGHT PRONE AREA PROGRAMME( D.P.A.P.): The Drought Prone Area Programme(DPAP) aims to mitigate the adverse effect of drought on the production of crops and livestock ,productivity of land, water and human resources.It strives to encourage restoration of ecological balance and seeks to improve the economic and social condition of the poor and the disadvantaged sections of the rural community. Now DPAP is a people's programme with Government assistance. There is a specific arrangement for maintenance of assets and social audit by Panchayati Raj institutions. Development of all catagories of land belonging to Gram Panchayat, Government and individuals fall within the limits of the selected watersheds for development.Allocation is to be shared equally by the Centre and State Government on 50:50 basis Watershed Committees is to contribute for maintenance of the assets created. Utilisation of 50 % of allocation under the Employment Assurance Scheme(EAS) is for the Watershed Development funds are directly released for sanction of projects and release of funds to Watershed Committees and Project Implementing Agencies(PIAs). Village community including self help groups undertake area development by planning and implementation of projects on watershed basis through Watershed Associations and Watershed Committees constituted from among themselves. The Government supplements their work by creating social awareness imparting trainings and providing technical support through the Project Implementation Agencies.

## CAUSES OF THE REGRESSIVE EFFECTS ON THE RURAL LIFE

There have been three causes of this stinging situation. The first was our galloping along the development path instead of travelling along the true locus by creeping walking and running as and when needed.

The second cause refers to the distortion in the concept of rural development which made the formulation of development plans and strategies incompatible to rural economy. The third cause was the rapid population growth which added a lot to make the unemployment situation a mammoth. The first cause relates to our over enthusiasm and the second cause relates to the hereinabove discussed third theme of rural development literature. The third cause relates to the increasing difference of birth rate over death rate and the insignificant performance of'Family Planning Programme'.

On account of extended medical facilities, uplift of living standard due to increased national income, control over epidemics, check on famines, alleviation of starvation, extension of maternity services etc. during the development process in the plan period, the death rate considerably went down (from 27.4 per thousand per year during 1941-50 to 7.6 per thousand per year in 2005) but the birth rate remained slang high (it was 39.9 per thousand per year during 1941-50 and came down only to 23.8 per thousand per year in 2005). Therefore population growth attained an increasingly high rate that was however tried unsuccessfully to be lowered through the'Family Planning Programme'.

## FACTORS RESPONSIBLE FOR CHILD BIRTH

If we go in full detail of why a child is born, we will come across the various factors making a child take birth. The factors making a child take birth can be grouped under four heads namely (i)Biological Factor, (ii)Socio-cultural Factors, (iii)Religious Factors and (iv) Economic Factors.

## Biological Factor

The biological factor refers to the child bearing as a byproduct of sexual gratification. This is one of the most effective factors determining birth rate of the population. A person in the state of aggravated sexual agitation can forgo all social, cultural, religious (spiritual) and economic gains for sexual gratification.

## Socio-cultural and Religious Factors

The socio-cultural and the religious factors refer to the social customs, cultural traditions and religious faiths which play dominant role in the life of people especially in poor and backward communities. The social factors induce a person to have more sons as the sons are believed to be the reliable means of social security and social status for a family. Moreover, they are deemed to care their old, physically wasted and worn-out parents, on one hand, and to provide safety to the family in case of conflicts and death of supportive member/s of the family. The religious factors refer mainly to four beliefs. One states that peace is rendered to the soul after death only if the cremation is performed by a real son. The second speaks of higher spiritual gain or place in Elysium of heaven after death for a person having more sons. The third relates the production of more children to religious service and the fourth specifies child bearing as the pious duty of a woman because she is believed to be sent by God only for increasing progeny.

## Economic Factors

Apart from the socio-cultural and the religious factors, the economic factors are very much effective like the biological factor. A person in acute economic privation leaves even deeply instilled socio-cultural, religious and some times biological allurements too for economic gains. The need of economic support in old age and the poverty are two main economic factors making people tend to produce more children. In old age, when a person becomes generally sick, pulled, worn-out, and non-earning, he becomes dependant to his heirs for food, clothing, medical treatment and other expenses. More the sons or heirs he has, lesser will be the share of burden of supporting him. As regards to poverty, it generates three causes of inducement to the high rate of child-birth.

(a) The prevailing media based fascinating means of entertainment are not only out of the reach of poor man but these have also snatches the old socio-cultural, cheap and some times free entertainment sources from him. Therefore a poverty stricken person has to search the way of entertainment in sex and that too being circumstantially unprotected whereby childbirth goes on taking place one after one successively.

(b) In poor families a child becomes earning hand at the age of seven or eight yrs. On account of the subsistence level of family's living, the expenditure on child's feeding is considerably lower than the wage he earns. Therefore, the surplus of his earning over his consumption adds to family income and thus contributes to the uplift of family's standard of living. The sentiments and feelings regarding education or future welfare of the child droop before the agony of unsatisfied basic needs due to privation. Therefore, a child in a poor family is proved an asset rather than liability, in its stead.

(c) There are some types of family occupations where a number of faithful workmen are required. The required manpower from own family is most desirable there. If a person is owner of a series of units of small scale industries, cottage industries, small business units etc. the hired managing persons generally prove costlier, unfaithful and non-devoted. If a family member is deployed at each such unit the safety and profitability is increased. Similar is the position in a single cottage industry unit where margin of profit is low and hired labour makes the profit uncertain. If family manpower instead of hired one is used the profitability there becomes increased on account of devotedness, faithfulness and per need flexibility in working hours of the working force. Moreover, wage rate of a family labour is generally lower than that of a hired labour because the cost of living of one member of the family is lower than that of the whole family of hired man. Therefore the requirement of man power is tried to meet out by producing more children in the family.

## Performance of Family Planning Programme

As regards to the check on high population growth the prevailing'Family Planning Programme' has been proved insufficient and incomplete. Census figures reveal that the'Family Planning

Programme' in India has fallen short of the goals with which it was implemented. India's family planning program was initiated in 1952 to curb population growth and in due course was given highest priority along with other developmental programs.

All the same, India's population that was below half billion in 1960 crossed the figure of one billion in 2000. It is well proved that the programme failed to instill among the general mass the spirit of'children by choice and not by chance'. Introduction of target free approach in 1996-97, reduced thrust on family planning, poor access to family planning services and inadequate attention on need based methods of sterilization have been the causal factors of the inadequacy and insufficiency of family planning programme in controlling population growth especially in rural areas where it should have been proved but successful.

## RURAL ECONOMIC DIVERSIFICATION -MULTIPLE DIMENSIONS

The term "Economic Diversification" relates to the production of diverse goods and services in a production boundary. In turn, it also relates to pursuance of diverse economic activities by the people of a geographic domain for producing larger range of goods and services. Eventually, the diversity of production and economic activities of the people results into income flows from diverse sources. Such diversification is triggered by the use of resources for production of goods and services from available alternative choices. Often the process of alternative choices also takes into account the efficiency of resource use as well as the opportunity of resource use. Resource allocation itself may get triggered, generally by economic forces, though sometimes there may be non economic reasons, compelling the people to undertake alternative activities. The study domains of economic diversification therefore are certain production boundaries on time and space, and require appropriate observational units and quantitative indicators. Lately, the subject is involving the social scientists to assess its incidence and impact on well being of populace.

As stated above, there is general acknowledgement that not only the economic condition of rural household improves with the blending of non-farm economic activities with farm activities; it has positive impact on efficiency of their farm enterprises. It integrates with the multiti-pronged strategy in the framework of action against poverty, stimulating enhancement of entitlement and access. The opportunities, empowerment and security are the three factors that have complimentary and supplementary role in neutralization of economic deprivation. These three factors are also closely associated with the process of economic diversification. If the opportunity of doing multiple activities enhances returns and exposure and thereby empowers the economic and social wellbeing, the empowerment through literacy, skill, knowledge, awareness, resources and connectivity improves the capacity and scope of harnessing the opportunities. The resultant derivatives are augmented remuneration and returns from diverse sources, contributing to stability of economic condition, security, reduction in vulnerability and risk mitigation. Therefore, studies on different dimensions of diversification of rural economy, improvement in the measurement, factorization and impact and exploration of its indicators are needed for furthering rural livelihood development and well-being.

One of the basic forms of rural economic diversification is the crop diversification. The diversified cropping pattern in a region emerges due to allocation of arable land resources for cultivation of number of alternative crops. The Indian agrarian space is endowed with diversity of agro-climatic conditions and varying degree of augmentation of farming resource through irrigation infrastructure, crop specific farming technologies, diversified demand and post harvest linkages. Such on farm diversification helps in reducing farming risk due to climatic, market and other such aberrations and often improves resource use efficiency (Joshi et. el 2007). However, the crop diversification has been subjected to resource endowment of farmers in terms of land, water, technology, seeds and soil besides externalities such as agro climatic conditions, sustainability and the response to market. The skewed distribution of infrastructure such as road, transportation, market, post harvest handling, irrigation and power are found to be the impediments for both horizontal and vertical diversification. Nevertheless, the crop diversification not only indicates the options and opportunities of cropping, it also harmonises the supply to demand of diverse commodities and in the process diffuses the price volatility in the market.

These studies have assessed the dynamics of crop diversification on aggregate allocation of arable land to different crops in a region as well as diversified value of output and related inferences. One may note that in India, at micro level, the operational holding size is small (Average operational holding is 1.3 Hectares) and individual farmers have limited scope of diversification in his farms.

An extension of the same to more meaningful form of farm sector diversification is through animal husbandry, poultry and fisheries and its measurement in terms of value of outputs. It has been widely acknowledged that in semi arid central and western India having lesser scope of multiple cropping, animal husbandry reduces the vulnerability of farmers. In the regions where forward integration of small cattle holders has been strengthened by institutions such as cooperatives, the economic conditions of farmers have improved. The cooperatives, self help groups and other institutions of marketing etc. have stimulated the process of on-farm and off-farm diversification by putting the opportunity, empowerment and security as the rural development package. The extension of farming activities to certain on farm post harvest operations not only adds to the farm gate value creation it also expands the production entrepreneurship of the farmers to services.

From the point of view of diversification of economy in the production boundary, one may also look into the existence of enterprises in the rural areas and producing non agricultural goods and services. In India, there is a significant presence of small and tiny non agricultural enterprises in the rural areas. There is preponderance of informal and unorganized enterprises in the rural economy, both in terms of their number as well as workforce. Out of total own account enterprises (without hired workers), 11.1 million (92%) non agricultural manufacturing and 9 million (91%) of service sector (excluding domestic trading) enterprises are located in rural sector (NSS 62nd and 63rd Round, reference period 2005-06 and 2006-07 respectively). However, in terms of GDP, these rural enterprises have much smaller share.

The rural non agricultural entrepreneurial diversification may not be simply assessable in terms of their number and GDP share. There are aspects of economy of scale, operating efficiency and technology used in the corresponding large enterprises located in industrial hubs, which are not easily measurable but impinge on efficacy of rural non farm diversification.

The diversification through crops and on and off farm production offers limited perspective of rural economic diversification. It is confined to the production boundary of agriculture and allied sector and producing entrepreneurial units of the farms. Without undermining the significance of such diversification, that eventually strengthens integration of farming with post farming and off-farming activities, the economic gain to its stakeholders will be restricted to the growth potential of farm sector.

For the rural economy to sustain in the long run, the scope of its diversification would necessitate expansion to the wider dimensions of livelihood diversification. The vulnerability of livelihood in rural agrarian segments of developing countries has been acknowledged and the livelihood security is one of the central theme needing attention in the liberalized and market reformed agricultural trade regime. The rural livelihood diversification therefore is an integral dimension of development agenda for strengthening rural livelihood and sustaining livelihood security.

There are two ways to look into livelihood diversification. One, the individuals and/or their groups perform different activities. In other words, the individuals are capable to engage in the alternative choices in the labour market and undertake different forms of rural employment; both farm as well as nonfarm.

From the point of view of rural development, the rural employment diversification is considered to be driving force (UN-Wye Group 2007). Two, the rural income diversification enabling individuals or households to have income sourced from the diversified sources.

There is differentiation in employment diversification and income diversification as both are broadly complementary but may not necessarily be synonymous. The employment diversification is measured in terms of labour force participation in diverse industries and occupation. The wages and remunerations from different employment would add up to income. However, the income diversification is more comprehensive, since it would also account for transfer payments (rents, interests, dividends etc.) to individuals.

As stated above, the crop and farm diversification have potential to augment income and strengthen livelihood. But due to its confinement to labour participation in the farm related activity, it remains diversified in the limited sense. Further, the domain of crop and on farm diversification is the production boundary of primary goods, hence the stability and security of livelihood remains vulnerable despite such diversification. The domain of rural livelihood may extend beyond the rural production boundary. The commutation of rural people to urban neighborhood for their work and jobs as well as income transfers from urban to rural add to the wider dimensions of livelihood diversification.

## INTEGRATED RURAL DEVELOPMENT PROGRAMME

The special programmes to boost the agricultural production in late sixties certainly helped to raise the food production but the benefits were largely reaped by those who had necessary resources. Small and marginal farmers trailed behind, as they were not directly benefited by the Green Revolution. On the contrary, their economic position worsened as the rich farmers declined to offer their lands for shared cropping. Thus to tackle the problems of the rural poor, the Integrated Rural Development Programme (IRDP) was introduced in 1979, with specific focus on the weaker sections of the society, particularly those living in poverty and to involve them in programme implementation. While the earlier programmes emphasized on the delivery systems which suppressed self-reliance, there was good scope for peoples initiatives to build up their economy with dignity.

Heeding to the criticism, further changes were made in the programme during the Seventh and Eighth Plans (1985-1990 and 1992-1997 respectively). These included the linkage between infrastructure and employment schemes, designing of the programme as a credit based self-employment activity, rather than a subsidy distribution and decentralisation of programme implementation through District Rural Development Agency and block authorities. Several sub-schemes such as Development of Women and Children in Rural Areas (DWCRA), Training of Rural Youth for Self-employment (TRYSEM), National Rural Employment Programme (NREP), Jawahar Rojgar Yojana (JRY) were also launched to target the weaker section of the society.

By mid eighties, the Government was able to meet the minimum needs of the poor, which included elementary education, health, water supply, roads, electrification, housing and nutrition. In 1993-94, about 32.37% of the population in India was poor. The percentage of population living in poverty was high by about 17-22% among the Scheduled Castes and Scheduled Tribes, compared to general categories. This was mainly due to small land holdings, landlessness or illiteracy.

## DECENTRALISED PLANNING FOR RURAL DEVELOPMENT

Based on the Sivaraman Committee report, the Planning Commission issued guidelines to all the State Governments in 1987 to consider the block as the unit for planning. The task of planning at the district level was entrusted to the District Planning and Development Council or District Planning Board which had wider representation of the society. This body consisted of elected as well as nominated representatives headed by a Minister or District Collector or a non-official. It was responsible for setting up policy guidelines apart from coordination, monitoring, review, finalization of annual plans and Five Year Plans and collection of data. At the block level, the officers of different departments prepared the plan as per the guidelines received from their district heads.

This process needed further articulation to prepare the plans in consultation with the Gram Panchayats for implementing the development programmes more effectively and economically. Planning at the village level can be very effective as it can address the problems directly and facilitate development at the grassroot level.

## Emphasis on Peoples Participation

In spite of many drawbacks in launching community development programmes, the Panchayati Raj has made significant contribution to the development of the country by creating awareness among the public and by developing political leadership. The system has also helped in reducing the gap between the bureaucracy and the people. Centralisation of power and non-involvement of people in the process of development have been the major concerns ever since the introduction of Panchayati Raj. Although, it was widely acknowledged as the only hope for activating peoples participation which is the soul of a democratic system, the system had generated tension and factions. This necessitated Panchayati Raj reforms through the 73rd Constitutional Amendment in 1992, which empowered the PR institutions to shoulder the responsibility of development and decentralized planning. Till then, all the functions were carried out by the government machinery and there was no scope for participation by the villagers. This had created a dependency syndrome and enabled the government officials to dictate terms to the people (Thapliyal, 1995).

Under this constitutional amendment, 29 items of development were transferred to PRIs. These can be grouped under the following sectors: Agriculture; Forestry and Environment; Industries; Infrastructure, minimum needs; Social welfare; Poverty Alleviation and Maintenance of community assets. Considering the weak status of the Gram Panchayats to facilitate village level micro-planning for development, the District Planning Committee has been strengthened with members representing various government and non-government organisations.

To facilitate the planning at micro-level, it is proposed to strengthen the Gram Sabha (village assembly). The Gram Panchayat can use the Gram Sabha as a forum for discussion and finalization of annual plans. Such a forum can also set the priority for implementing various development programmes. Simultaneously, a suitable mechanism should be developed to sustain the interest of the villagers in Gram Sabha activities. In the absence of adequate participation, vested interests may influence the proceedings for their own benefits. Initiatives from farmers organisations, self help groups, educational institutions and other voluntary organisations to nominate their representatives on the Gram Sabha can ensure their participation in the proceedings and safeguard the interest of the common people (Hegde, 1999).

## References

Basanti Das: *Governmental Programmes for Rural Development*, Discovery, Delhi, 2007.

Bhai, N.: *Harijan Women in Panchayati Raj*, Delhi, BR Publishing 1986

Erikson, E. H.: *Panchayati Raj and Society*, New York, W. W. Norton, 1993.

Granger, Clive W. J.: *Rural Marketing in Economics, Specification and Evaluation*, London, Cambridge University Press, 1999.

Guarti, Luigi, *The Rural Management of Marketing*, Blackwell Publishing, 1994.

Harrigan, K. R.: *Strategies for Declining Businesses*. Lexington, MA: Heath, 1980

James Makens: *Marketing for Hospitality and Tourism*: New Jersey, Prentice-Hall, 1998.

Lock, Dennis: *Rural Marketing Management*, New York, Wiley, 1996.

Madan Mohan: *Impact of Integrated Rural Development Programmes*, Omega Pub, Delhi, 2007.

Meyer, M. W.: *Theory of Organizational Structure in Rural Marketing*, Indianapolis, 1977.

29

# Agricultural Reforms in Indian Economic Sector: Dimensions, Concerns and Reform Process

**SARSHTI GUPTA**

*Research Scholar, Department of Economics, C.C.S. University, Meerut, Uttar Pradesh*

Agrarian reform can refer either, narrowly, to government-initiated or government-backed redistribution of agricultural land or, broadly, to an overall redirection of the agrarian system of the country, which often includes land reform measures. Agrarian reform can include credit measures, training, extension, land consolidations, etc. The World Bank evaluates agrarian reform using five dimensions: (1) price and market liberalization, (2) land reform (including the development of land markets), (3) agro-processing and input supply channels, (4) rural finance, (5) market institutions.

## CONCERNS IN AGRICULTURE

Growth of agriculture decelerated from 3.5% from 1981-82 to 1996-97 to around 2% during 1997-98 to 2004-05 although there are signs of improvement in recent years (more than 3.5% in the last three years). Yield growth has also declined. Farmers' suicides have continued/increased in some states. Farming is becoming a non-viable activity. There are also other problems. Further scope for increase in net sown area is limited. Land degradation in the form of depletion of soil fertility, erosion and, water logging has increased. There has been decline in the surface irrigation expansion rate and reduction in ground water table. exposure of domestic agriculture to international competition, volatility in prices, Increased vulnerability to world commodity prices. Disparities in productivity across regions and crops and between rainfed and irrigated areas increased. Long term factors like steeper decline in per capita land availability and shrinking of farm size are also responsible for the agrarian crisis.

However, there is some dynamism now in agriculture. Agriculture growth in the last three years was nearly 4%. There is some increase in high value agriculture, vertical integration of supply chains and some positive signs on bio technology particularly BT cotton and also some lagging regions like Bihar showing high growth in agriculture.

The Steering Committee report on agriculture for 11$^{th}$ Plan (GOI, 2007a) has identified the possible reasons for deceleration in agriculture since mid-1990s. According to the report, the major sources of agricultural growth are: public and private investment in agriculture and rural infrastructure including irrigation, technological change, diversification of agriculture and fertilizers. It looks like that the progress on all these sources slowed down since mid-1990s.

Because of demographic pressures, there has been significant increase in small and marginal farm holdings. These farmers have to face the challenges of globalization. Risk and uncertainty has also increased as cultivation has spread to marginal lands. The diversification of agriculture also raised concerns on food security.

What are the goals of agricultural development? There are three goals. To achieve 4% growth in agriculture and raise incomes of the farmers. Here challenge is diversification to high value agriculture and rural non-farm by maintaining food security. Foodsecurity does not mean foodgrain security. Second objective is to sharing growth with small and marginal farmers, lagging regions, women etc. Here focus has to be on lagging regions like Eastern India. Third is to maintain sustainability of agriculture by focusing on environmental concerns.

## ECONOMIC REFORMS PROCESS ON INDIAN AGRICULTURAL SECTOR

Agricultural sector is the mainstay of the rural Indian economy around which socioeconomic privileges and deprivations revolve, and any change in its structure is likely to have a corresponding impact on the existing pattern of social equality. No strategy of economic reform can succeed without sustained and broad based agricultural development, which is critical for

- raising living standards,
- alleviating poverty,
- assuring food security,

- generating buoyant market for expansion of industry and services, and
- making substantial contribution to the national economic growth.

Studies also show that the economic liberalization and reforms process have impacted on agricultural and rural sectors very much.

Of the three sectors of economy in India, the tertiary sector has diversified the fastest, the secondary sector the second fastest, while the primary sector, taken as whole, has scarcely diversified at all. Since agriculture continues to be a tradable sector, this economic liberalization and reform policy has far reaching effects on (I) agricultural exports and imports, (ii) investment in new technologies and on rural infrastructure (iii) patterns of agricultural growth, (iv) agriculture income and employment, (v) agricultural prices and (vi) food security. Reduction in Commercial Bank credit to agriculture, in lieu of this reforms process and recommendations of Khusrao Committee and Narasingham Committee, might lead to a fall in farm investment and impaired agricultural growth. Infrastructure development requires public expenditure which is getting affected due to the new policies of fiscal compression. Liberalization of agriculture and open market operations will enhance competition in "resource use" and "marketing of agricultural production", which will force the small and marginal farmers (who constitute 76.3% of total farmers) to resort to "distress sale" and seek for off-farm employment for supplementing income.

## Marginalisation of Small Farmers

A central issue in Agricultural Development is the necessity to increase productivity, employment, and income of poor segments of the agricultural population. Among the rural poor, the small farmers constitute a sizeable portion in the developing countries. Studies by FAO have shown that small farms constitute between 60-70% of total farms in developing countries and contribute around 30-35% to total agricultural output.

Liberalisation era (1990-91) began in India when over 40% of rural households were landless or near landless, and over 96% of the owned holdings and 68.53% (over 2/3rd) of owned land belonged to the size groups (marginal, small and semi-medium). The decade of 1981-82 to 1991-92 seems to have witnessed a marked intensification of the marginalisation process-the percentage of small owners increased from 14.70% to 21.75%. Small farmers emerged as the size group with the largest share of 33.97% in the total land, which is just doubled during this decade. As regards the Large Farmers, they were 1 % of the total owners in 1990-91 but owned nearly 13.83% of the total land. An interesting, but speculative, inference is that the changing position of the large owners represents the other side of the marginalisation process, i.e., the presence, and possibly growing strength, of a small but dominant and influential group in agriculture. Analytical reports reveal that marginalisation process could gather further momentum in the years ahead to become an explosive source of economic and political turbulence, due to the features of prevailing policy-cum-market environment in the country.

Trend towards a greater casualisation (erratic and low-paid work) of the workforce that was witnessed in the 1980s appears to have continued in the 1990s. Low productivity and inability to absorb the growing labour force make the agricultural sector in India witness to a pervasive process of marginalisation of rural people. This process is likely to get intensified in the coming years, raising formidable problems in achieving sustained development of rural areas and rural people.

Both Information Technology, Genetic Engineering and Bio-Technology, which are the "drivers" of globalization with their complementarities of liberalisation, privatisation and tighter Intellectual Properties Rights, are bound to create new risks of marginalisation and vulnerability. Information Technology is able to produce a penetrating and clinical mapping of the land, encompassing the physical, chemical and biological features, and groundwater resources, and forecast of climatic conditions in a focused manner, that even small geographical segments-the small farms-can be benefited through the guidance provided by the ways in which natural and human resources can be optimally combined with appropriate technologies, inputs and options to enhance and diversify agricultural production. Information Technology will facilitate dissemination of information on development, education, extension, husbandry, marketing, production, and research, to agricultural farmers.

## Indian Agricultural Sector

The Indian Agricultural sector provides employment to about 65% of the labour force, accounts for 27% of GDP, contributes 21% of total exports, and raw materials to several industries. The Livestock sector contributes an estimated 8.4 % to the country GDP and 35.85 % of the agricultural output. India is the seventh largest producer of fish in the world and ranks second in the production of inland fish. Fish production has increased from 0.75 million tons in 1950-51 to 5.14 million tons in 1996-97, a cumulative growth rate of 4.2% per annum, which has been the fastest of any item in the food sector, except potatoes, eggs and poultry meat. The future growth in agriculture must come from:

- new technologies which are not only "cost effective" but also "in conformity" with natural climatic regime of the country;
- technologies relevant to rain-fed areas specifically;
- continued genetic improvements for better seeds and yields;
- data improvements for better research, better results, and sustainable planning;
- bridging the gap between knowledge and practice; and
- judicious land use resource surveys, efficient management practices and sustainable use of natural resources.

## REFORMS IN AGRICULTURE SECTOR

Policy reforms in the rural sector are both critical and sensitive in nature as well as in their impact because of heavy concentration of working people in rural areas. At present about 40% of total state expenditure in the rural sector is absorbed by direct subsidies, another 22% by anti-poverty programs and only 38% goes to productivity enhancing expenditure, as opposed to 60% in 1981-82.

During the post-reform period, annual growth rate of agricultural subsidies in real terms has substantially declined. But, it remains as high as 3.6% of GDP per annum.

In real terms, the food subsidy increased from Rs. 10.8 billion in 1989-90 to 14.3 billion in 1995-96 at 1980-81 prices, although food subsidy as a percentage of GDP remained constant at about 0.5%.

The revamped Public Distribution System (PDS) has been introduced since 1992, which is targeted to those poor and backward regions where the Employment Assurance Scheme (EAS) is implemented (Annual Report, Ministry of Rural Areas and Employment, 1996). However, Mr. Yashwant Sinha in his Budget, 2000-01 targeted middle and upper classes. From now on, income-tax payers would not get any commodities under PDS, and the others would not get certain commodities such as sugar.

The fertiliser subsidy as percentage of total agriculture GDP declined from 0.9% in 1990-91 to 0.6% in 1995-96. But in absolute real terms, it has been subjected to high annual variations. The fertiliser subsidy policy affected different fertiliser prices differently.

The prices of phosphoric and potassium fertilisers were decontrolled in 1992, but price control on low analysis nitrogenous fertilisers continued. However, in the current year (2000-01) the subsidy price of urea is fixed at Rs. 4,600 per ton. Same for MOP (Potash) is fixed at Rs. 4,260 per ton and for Di-Ammonium Phosphate (DAP) it is Rs. 8,880 per ton. This means that there would be an increase of 15% in prices of urea and MOP and 7% in the case of DAP.

Power and irrigation subsidies, which are supported by the state governments, accounted for nearly 8% respectively of the total agricultural subsidies (as of 1994-95). During the post-reform period (1990-91 to 1994-95), rural power subsidy grew at the rate of 14% per annum in real terms, while the growth rate of irrigation subsidy remained low at 1.2% per annum (based on the Budget Estimates). But irrigation subsidy was reduced mainly on account of non-wage outlays on operation and maintenance and not because of improvement in cost recovery.

Zonal restrictions on the movement of agricultural commodities have been removed since February, 1993, including the lifting of informal controls on wheat movement by private trade.

The excise duty on coffee has been removed. The role of coffee board has diminished and now there is a trend towards open marketing of coffee. Imports of all agricultural commodities other than cereals, oilseeds and edible oils and all agricultural exports (except onion) have been decannalised.

India has agreed to phase out quantitative restrictions on import of 2700 items, out of which 800 are agricultural commodities by April 2003. An agreement had already been reached with European Union and Australia to remove quantitative restrictions on imports from these countries by April, 2000 (Haque, 1997:12).

Agricultural trade reforms initiated in 1991-92 relaxed quantitative restrictions on a few minor commodities. But by 1994-95, it included rice exports and imports of most edible oils, sugar and cotton. Nevertheless, quantitative restrictions on exports of most agricultural commodities except rice continue.

The share of tradable agricultural production protected by non-tariff barriers on the import side, were reduced from about 96% before

June, 1991 to 77% in July, 1996. With the liberalisation of sugar imports under 0% tariffs, sugar industry has now to compete with imports.

Similarly, the liberalisation of cotton imports at zero percent tariff has been initiated in 1994. Edible oils are now importable at 20% tariff. The tariff on import of pulses has been reduced from 10 percent to 5 percent. In January, 1997 the U.S. and several other developed countries contended that India no longer suffers from balance of payments problems and therefore, the quantitative restrictions on imports by India would have to be removed immediately.

India made an agreement with European Union and Australia to remove quantitative restrictions on many items in three phases of 3 years, 2 years and 1 year, using April, 1997 as the reference year. But the dispute with U.S. has yet to be resolved.

In the livestock sector, state controls and subsidization of dairy co-operatives continue. The Milk and Milk products Order (1992) presents competition in the dairy industry. The poultry feed manufacturing continues to be reserved for the small scale sector.

The commercialization of fishing has been initiated. Agro-industries that export 50% or more of their output, have been allowed to import their inputs duty free and to import capital equipment at concessional import duty rates w.e.f. April, 1993. In 1991, tractors, combine harvesters and rice transplanters were included in the list of products for which there is now automatic approval of foreign equity of up to 51%.

But several other agricultural implements and farm inputs such as plastic piping, sheeting etc. are reserved for production by small-scale firms.

In the area of rural credit, the reforms include:

(i) reducing target group lending from 100 percent to 40 percent in the case of regional rural banks,

(ii) greater freedom to the banks to rationalize their branches,

(iii) deregulation of interest rates of rural cooperative banks,

(iv) permission to urban co-operative banks to lend to borrowers in continguous rural areas and

(v) relaxation of service area restrictions.

Besides, the Reserve Bank of India (RBI) and National Bank for Agriculture and Rural Development (NABARD) have initiated actions for strengthening Regional Rural Banks (RRBs). Further, the 1996-97 budget provides for doubling the paid up share capital of NABARD and establishing agricultural development financial institutions at the state level to promote investment in horticulture, floriculture and agro-processing.

## Agriculture Reforms – The Way Ahead

Sustainable agriculture thus sustains rural livelihoods. This in turn is directly linked to the nation's as well as the household food security. Any development alternative to ensure long-term food security therefore has to be linked to sustainable agriculture.

Let me therefore draw the outline of the sustainable farming systems that the country needs to focus on. This is the overall framework under which location-specific alterations and adaptations need to be tried.

What is needed is a fresh approach that takes the ground realities into consideration before embarking upon any policy imperatives. I am trying to make an attempt, presenting a collection of five of the important rational decisions, which would certainly initiate the revival of Indian agriculture:

*Sustainable farming*: Indian agriculture faces an unprecedented crisis in sustainability. Foodgrain productivity in the food bowl, comprising Punjab, Haryana, and western Uttar Pradesh, is on the decline. The green revolution areas are encountering serious bottlenecks to growth and productivity. The dryland areas (comprising nearly 70 per cent of the cultivable lands) continue to drown in misery and apathy. Excessive mining of soil nutrients and groundwater have already brought in soil sickness. Indiscriminate use of chemical pesticides has done serious harm to environment, human health and ecology. Introducing new Centrally Sponsored Schemes or contract farming to improve production in these areas is going to be counter-productive. Banking upon genetically engineered crops to take care of the second-generation environmental impacts is sure to worsen the existing crisis. Outlays earmarked for genetic engineering in agriculture also need to be diverted to sustainable agricultural practices.

Encouraging sustainable and traditional farming practices therefore is the only way ahead. Agricultural research must reorient itself to meet the new challenges resulting from the collapse of the green revolution technology. Investments and increased outlays for agricultural research that is based on external chemical inputs like fertiliser and pesticides need to be discouraged. Instead, financial allocation should be made for reviving low-input agriculture, which uses cheap and locally available technology and in turn improves production and protects environment. This has been amply demonstrated in several parts of the world (see the accompanying box). Water productivity and efficiency has to be the hallmark of agricultural research based on the local conditions.

## Indian Agriculture Today: A Snapshot

Agriculture employs 60% of the Indian population today, yet it contributes only 20.6% to the GDP. (Isaac, 2005) Agricultural production fell by 12.6% in 2003, one of the sharpest drops in independent India's history. Agricultural growth slowed from 4.69% in 1991 to 2.6% in 1997-1998 and to 1.1% in 2002-2003 (Agricultural Statistics at a Glance, 2006). This slowdown in agriculture is in contrast to the 6% growth rate of the Indian economy for almost the whole of the past decade. Farmer suicides were 12% of the total suicides in the country in 2000, the highest ever in independent India's history. (Unofficial estimates put them as high as 100,000 across the country, while government estimates are much lower at 25,000. This is largely because only those who hold the title of land in their names are considered farmers, and this ignores women farmers who rarely hold land titles, and other family members who run the farms. Agricultural wages even today are $1.5 – $2.0 a day, some of the lowest in the world. (Issac, 2005) Institutional credit (or regulated credit) accounts for only 20% of credit taken among small and marginal farmers in rural areas, with the remaining being provided by private moneylenders who charge interest rates as high as 24% a month. An NSSO2 survey in 2005 found that 66% of all farm households own less than one hectare of land. It also found that 48.6% of all farmer households are in debt. The same year, a report by the Commission of Farmer's welfare concluded that agriculture was in 'an advanced stage of crisis', the most extreme manifestation of which was the rise in suicides among farmers. Given the performance of agriculture and figures of farmer suicides across the country, this can be said to apply to Indian agriculture as a whole.

The biggest problem Indian agriculture faces today and the number one cause of farmer suicides is debt. Forcing farmers into a debt trap are soaring input costs, the plummeting price of produce and a lack of proper credit facilities, which makes farmers turn to private moneylenders who charge exorbitant rates of interest. In order to repay these debts, farmers borrow again and get caught in a debt trap. The researcher will examine each one these 3 causes which led to the crisis in Andhra Pradesh, Kerala and Maharashtra, and analyse the role that liberalisation policies have played.

Andhra Pradesh's experience is particularly relevant in this analysis because of its leadership. Chandra Babu Naidu, Chief Minister of Andhra Pradesh from 1995-2004, was an IT savvy neo-liberal, and believed that the way to lead Andhra Pradesh into the future was through technology and an IT revolution. His zeal led to the first ever state level (as opposed to national level) agreement with the World Bank, which entailed a loan of USD 830 million (AUD 1 billion) in exchange to a series of reforms in AP's industry and government. Naidu envisaged corporate style agriculture in AP, and implemented World Bank liberalisation policies with great enthusiasm and gusto. He drew severe criticism from opponents, saying he was using AP as a laboratory for extreme neo-liberal experiments. Hence, AP's experience with liberalization is critical.

## References

Bhalla : *Articles*

Benghin, John C. : *Global Agriculture Trade and Developing Countries*, Manas, Delhi, 2005.

Bosworth, B.: *Capital Formation and Economic Policy.* Brookings Papers on Economic Activity, 1982

Edwards, C.A. *Sustainable Agricultural Systems.* 1990. Ankeny, Iowa: Soil and Water Conservation Society.

Lakshmi, Narasaiah, M. : *Financing of Agriculture by Regional Rural Banks*, Sonali Pub, Delhi, 2008.

Mellor, J. W.: *The New Economics of Growth*, Ithaca, Cornell University Press, 1976.

Mohanty, A.K. : *Entrepreneurship in Agriculture : Scopes and Opportunities*, Agrotech Pub, Delhi, 2011.

Paul, Sharma, Vijay : *Glimpses of Indian Agriculture : Macro and Micro Aspects*, Academic Foundation, Delhi, 2008.

Samvel, A P V : *Agri-Business Management*, Satish Serial Pub, Delhi, 2008.

Venkateshwara Rao, P. : *Dairy Farm Business Management*, Biotech Books, Delhi, 2008.

30

# Globalization and Its Impact on Tribal's

**DR DUSHYANT KUMAR**
*Assistant Professor, Department Of Political Science, M.B. (P.G.) College, Dadri, G.B. Nagar, Uttar Pradesh*

The tribals are a part of the Indian society and general problems of consciously changing or modernising Indian society are applicable to them. Before independence, tribals enjoyed an almost untrammeled control over forestland and its produce for their survival. Forest offered fodder for their cattle, firewood to warm their hearths, and above all a vital source of day-to-day sustenance. The wonderful equation between man and nature demolished after independence with the encroachment of rapacious contractors on tribal land and the indiscriminate destruction of forest in the name of development.

Tribals in India present a significant degree of cultural and ethnic diversity. They differ in their socio-cultural levels as well as in their behaviour patterns Tribal situation in the country poses peculiar problems of development, not encountered in other areas. The peculiarities can be broadly summed up as geographical, demographic, socio-cultural and exploitative. Tribal development indicates serious challenges to the policy makers, administrators and development activists. The socio-economic forces of modernization and development have no doubt brought some benefits to the people of respective areas, but the benefits accrued to them have been largely outweighted by the harm more to them. Development induced displacement, involuntary migration and resettlement has cause marginalization of tribals and presented enormous problems to them. The new economic regime has led to privatization and marketisation of economy and thus it has been treated as powerful threat to the survival of tribal communities (Singh, 2008).

According to one estimate, irrigation projects, mines, thermal power plants, wildlife sanctuaries, industries, etc., between 1950 and 1990 in India, displaced 213 lakh persons. 85 percent of them are tribals (Fernandes & Paranjpe, 1997). The government is aware of (a) the eroding resources base and socio-cultural heritage of tribal population through a combination of development interventions, commercial interest, and lack of effective legal protection of tribal and (b) the disruption of life and environment of tribal population owing to unimaginative, insensitive package of relief.

## A Tribe Faces Extinction

Several tribal groups spread over the Eastern Ghats across the southern and eastern region of the Indian sub-continent. In Orissa, a tribal group named Dongria Kondh people who inhabit the Niyamgiri Hills now faces extinction. According to the Census, there are only 7,952 surviving members of the Dongria, a sub-sect of the Kondh peoples, who have inhabited the forests of eastern India for thousands of years. On one side sits the state and Central government and the Indian subsidiary of Vedanta Resources Plc, a British mining corporation. They are applying for permission to dig up the Niyamgiris-rich n bauxite, used in the manufacture of aluminium-at the rate of three million tonnes a year and then pour them into a huge alumina refinery, which has already been constructed at the foot of the hills (Foster, 2008, May 18). The Dongria are the next casualities of the headlong rush for industrial development.

## Jarawa Tribes

Jarawa tribals, an ethnic group in Andamans, also faced extinction due to various reasons.

An approximate number of Jarawa tribals were 500. Of these 260 were reported to have survived the devastating tsunami by hanging on to the trees. According to the 2001 census figures, there were around 250 Jarawas inhabiting the middle-south Andaman Islands. These people are still living in primitive stage of the society in isolation.

## Chengara Land Struggle

During the last two years, Chengara in Kerala had become the symbol of a silent war for land. Unlike in Singur or in Nandigram, it was not against eviction. Instead, it was the fight of those who toiled in land, but never possessed any cultivable land, asserting their right to own sustainable land in a society that professes equality and fraternity. The agitation at Chengara in Pathanamthitta district had commenced on August 4, 2007, when 300 families from various parts of the state belonging to Dalits, Adivasis and other landless communities converged on the rubber estate owned by Harrison's Malayalam Plantations Ltd and pitched up thatched sheds and started living there. Their demand was five acres of land for cultivation and Rs 50,000 as financial assistance per family. The demand was later reduced to one acre of land. After 790 days, the struggle has been 'settled' at a discussion convened by the Chief Minister V S Achutanandan with Laha Gopalan and others of the Sadhu Jana Vimochana Samyukta Vedi (SJVSV), which spearheaded the agitation. 1432 families out of the 1738 families who had started living on the rubber plantation of Harrison's will get land and financial assistance to build houses, as part of the settlement.

## Fight for Water

The struggle for water in Plachimada, is another episode in Kerala, where The Coca-Cola Company bottling plant has both drained and contaminated groundwater on which the local farming community depends.

Coca-Cola came to India in 1993, looking for water and markets in a country where one third of all villages are without anything approaching adequate water and shortages are growing every day. Indeed India is facing a gigantic water crisis, even as Coca Cola and other companies haul free water to the cities from the countryside and water parks and golf courses metastasize around cities like Mumbai. The bloom was on neo-liberalism back then when Coca-Cola came in, with central and state authorities falling over themselves to lease, sell or simply hand over India's national assets in the name of economic "reform".

Coca-Cola had sound reasons in zoning in on Plachimada. A rain-shadow region in the heart of Kerala's water belt, it has large underground water deposits. The site Coca-Cola picked was set between two large reservoirs and ten meters south of an irrigation canal. The ground water reserves had apparently showed up on satellite surveys done by the company's prospectors.

The Coke site is surrounded by colonies where several hundred poor people live in crowded conditions, with an average holding of four-tenths of an acre. Virtually the sole source of employment is wage labour, usually for no more than 100 to 120 days in the year.

Within six months, the villager's mostly indigenous adivasis and dalits saw the level of their water drop sharply, even run dry. The water they did draw was awful. It gave some people diarrhoea and bouts of dizziness. To wash in it was to get skin rashes, a burning feel on the skin. It left their hair greasy and sticky. The women found that rice and dal was not cooked but became hard. A thousand families have been directly affected, and well water affected up to a three or four kilometers from the plant. The cruel fact is that water from our underground sources is pumped out free and sold to our people to make millions every day, at the same time destroying our environment and damaging the health of our people. For us rivers, dams and water sources are the property of the nation and her people.

## Narmada People's Struggle

Since 1985, the adivasis of the Narmada valley have been struggling against displacement and destruction resulting from the Sardar Sarovar Project (SSP). Their united fight reveals that not only the political and economic aspects of globalization, but also its intellectual repression must be resisted. The people's knowledge resulting in their land must not be ignored.

Particularly when government information is fraught with consistencies (Aravinda, 2000, November 11). Living in the mountains and plains of the Narmada river valley, stretching for 1,300 km through Madhya Pradesh, Gujarat, and Maharashtra communities including tribal people also known as adivasis have, since 1985, mounted a tenacious struggle against displacement, state repression, and the destruction of natural resources resulting from the Narmada Valley development projects. The projects comprise 30 large dams, 133 medium size dams, and 3,000 small dams, along with 75,000 km of canal networks to direct the waters of the Narmada River to wherever the state decrees (Sangvai, 2000). Sardar Sarovar takes up over 80% of Gujarat's irrigation budget but has only 1.6% of cultivable land in Kutch, 9% of cultivable land in Saurashtra and 20% cultivable land in North Gujarat in its command area. Moreover, these areas are at the tail end of the command and would get water only after all the area along the canal path get their share of the water, and that too after 2020 AD. Culture is defined as patterns of human activity and the symbols that give these activities significance. Globalisation, as a process, has far-reaching cultural potential in India.

Developmental strategies under the New Economic Policies led to a process of conscious and systematic annihilation of culture and identity of the first people-the adivasis-of this country. This process of globalization has invaded India since the introduction of New Liberalisation Policy. The socio-cultural change among the tribal communities has no doubt empowered the tribals; however, their cultural identity is under severe stress. However, it is not too late to rise above the politics of exclusion and marginalization, to unearth and mainstream fast vanishing tribal traditions, whether in India, or in African countries. Perhaps its time to amplify long marginalized voices and awaken contemporary nation States to the realization that only through the establishment of such democratic, reconciliatory, gender friendly grass root tribal traditions could one create a more equitable, more just society and world order. The reality remaining that without rapid action, these native communities may be wiped out, taking with them vast indigenous knowledge, rich culture and traditions, and any hope of preserving the natural world, and a simpler, more holistic way of life for future generations. Globalization does hold out great promise if it managed properly. However, it will only work if the winners share with the losers.

## GLOBALIZATION IN THE FIFTH SCHEDULE AREAS–ALIENATION OF LAND AND RESOURCES

Development carnage under the New Economic Policy and its submission to the powers of globalization have led to a process of conscious and systematic annihilation of the first people – the Adivasis- of this country. The founding fathers of the Indian Constitution, were, with right insight, seriously concerned with the plight of certain deprived and backward sections of the Indian society, and brought into the constitutional framework some special legislations, in order to protect them and their resources.

The Fifth and Sixth Schedules of the Constitution were specifically devoted to the protection of the 80 million adivasis spread across the country. The Indian Constitution thus provided legal safeguards to adivasi communities and all its policies regarding utilisation of resources, whether land, water or forests were based on social equity rather than on market economy. The philosophy of decentralisation, community and customary practices under the system of traditional village panchayats formed the basis for the fiveyear Plans of India. However, fifty years of constitutional safeguards to protect the adivasis from exploitation had not saved them from losing their lands and livelihoods to non adivasis as state inclination to uphold and implement the laws was far from enthusiastic.

Until the nineties the country was guided by the socialistic model of development where the role of the state was clearly welfare and social justice was the fundamental mandate of the state. As strategies of colonialism were defeated and led to revolts in most developing countries, the powerful nations restructured their global agendas through neo-imperial liberalisation philosophies. This process of globalization has invaded India too since the introduction of the New Economic Policy of the Nineties, which is a complete reversal of the welfare and socialistic essence of the Constitution. It has ushered in an era of corporate, especially Trans-national control of resources where the state is handing over the national resources to industries on the pretext that state has failed to deliver. In other words, industry has become the state and has been given the carte blanche to frame the education, health, social, industrial, environment, legal policies-all leading up to the extremely urgent need for privatisation.

Conflicts over rights on land and other natural resources are arising out of swift changes in the New Economic policy of India resulting in a shift in ownership and control over the resources and the means, methods and extent of exploitation. These changes are a direct influence of the industry sector to steer the state away from the socialistic democratic philosophy and to adopt a free market oriented approach. The paradigms of economic development are far removed from community needs and rights, particularly those of dalits, indigenous people and other marginalised poor in the country.

31

# Tokenism to Pro-activism: Decentralisation of Disaster Management and Panchayati Raj Institutions in India

**DR RADHANATH TRIPATHY**
*Associate Professor, Motilal Nehru College (Eve), University of Delhi*

Natural disasters not only take the life of thousands of people, but also deprive millions of their human rights to life, livelihood, food, shelter, health care, education, etc. Further they make the vulnerable and marginalised sections of the society more vulnerable by exasperating the existing socio-economic inequalities and discriminations on the basis of caste, race, gender, age, wealth and disabilities. However the issue of rights in humanitarian crisis borne out of insurgencies and ethnic conflicts in some parts of the world generally receives greater attention of the human rights groups than human rights issue in disaster response and rehabilitation, which affect greater masses of people at fairly regular intervals.

At the time of humanitarian crisis caused by natural hazards, even in the absence of formal rights to humanitarian assistance, humanitarian aid flow from both international and domestic sources to alleviate sufferings of the victims, as if it is a right (Handmer, 2001). A plethora of institutions with scientific and technological knowledge have been working since long in managing natural disaster and mitigating their impact on the life and property of people. In addition to this United Nations, international humanitarian actors (INGOs/NGOs) and nation-states have been constantly engaged in developing and implementing various disaster management policies and programmes. However the issue of human rights of the affected has never been the focal point in the disaster planning, response and recovery till the recent past (AIDMI and Brookings Institute, 2009).

The study of disaster/Disaster management was primarily a subject matter of natural sciences.

Scientists and geographers in the past have resorted to a pure science approach to deal with disaster. Natural hazards and their impacts on the life and property of people were understood in terms of certain natural factors and scientific criteria. However protection from natural disaster is not only about science; it is about legal, political and administrative arrangements that can use the scientific knowledge in the best possible manner. The determining forces of socio-economic, political and administrative factors were not given insignificant importance until the recent past. The efforts of international humanitarian actors and state machineries have failed to promote the participation of community organisations in managing the disaster.

***World's Deadliest Disasters in Recent Past (2004 – 2014)***

| Sl No | Name of Disasters | Year | Country | No of people killed | No of people missing | No of people displaced/ affected |
|---|---|---|---|---|---|---|
| 1 | Typhoon Haiyan | Nov, 2013 | Philippines | 10,000+ | NA | 30,00,000+ |
| 2 | Pakistan Flood | July-Aug. 2010 | Pakistan | 20,000 | NA | 2,00,00,000 |
| 3 | Haiti Earthquake | Jan, 2010 | Haiti | 3,16,000 | NA | 30,00,000 |
| 4 | Sichuan Earthquake | May, 2008 | China | 69,197 | 18,222 | 48,00,000 |
| 5 | Cyclone Nargis | May, 2008 | Myanmar | 1,38,000 | 55,000 | 40,00,000 |
| 6 | Kashmiri Earthquake | Oct, 2005 | Pakistan & India | 1,00,000 | NA | 30,00,000 |
| 7 | Hurricane Katrina | Aug, 2005 | USA | 1836 | 1836 | NA |
| 8 | Indian Ocean Tsunami | Dec, 2004 | Indonesia, Sri Lanka, India, Thailand, etc. | 2,30,000 | 43,000 | 10.69,000 |

*Sources:* Wikipedia, Preventionweb.net & Global Education

This paper makes an effort to analyse the present approach adopted in disaster management to address the issues involved in disasters in India. It is argued here that the holistic and integrated approach that have been officially adopted since 2005 replacing the age old charity-centric approach demands for a decentralisation of disaster management and adoption of community based disaster preparedness (CBDP) besides putting disaster prevention and mitigation in the forefront in disaster management and planning. In this context the rural/local self government that is Panchayati Raj Institutions (PRIs) carries special importance in the management of disasters in India. The role of PRIs is being highlighted in this paper besides discussing various legal and administrative arrangements available in this context at the national, state and district level.

The last few devastating disasters in the world drew our attention to the fact that disaster-affected population face lot of challenges to cope with the situation during and after disaster due to the failure or apathetic attitude of state and non-state actors (INGOs/NGOs). In addition to this various forms of human rights violation in the aftermath of natural disasters (IASC Operational Guidelines, 2011 and Lewis, 2006) and rehabilitation process are frequently reported.

***World Disaster Impacts: 2000 - 2012***

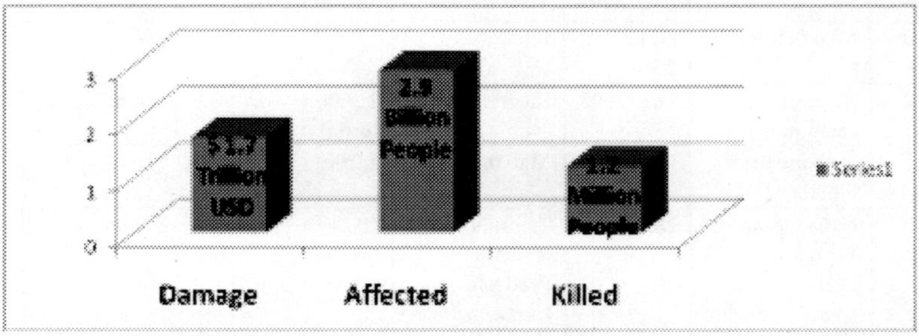

*Sources:* UNISDR (United Nations International Strategy for Disaster Reduction)

## Indian Experience

Brookings-Bern Report (2009) rightly described South Asia as a "theatre of disaster". India, the major component of this region, due to its geo-climatic condition is prone to various kinds of natural disasters. Earthquake, tsunami, cyclone, flood and drought strike India in regular intervals. About 58.6% landmass is prone to earthquakes; 12% land is prone to flood and river erosion; 5700 km of coastline is prone to cyclones and tsunamis; 68% of cultivable land is vulnerable to drought and mountainous and hilly areas have the risk due to landslides.

***The Impacts of Natural Disasters in India***

| *Natural disasters* | *Area affected* | *People exposed* |
|---|---|---|
| Earthquake | 58.6% of the landmass | 3,349,237 |
| Floods | 40 million hectors (12% of the landmass) | 15,859,640 |
| Cyclone/Tsunami | 5,700 KM of coast line | 7,607,821 |
| Drought | 68% of the cultivable area | 58,912,300 |
| Fire incidents, Landslides. Cloud burst, etc. | NA | NA |

*Sources:* Annual Report 2010-11, Union Ministry of Home Affairs, Govt. of India and Preventionweb.net

***India's Deadliest Disasters in the last 2 decades (1993-2014)***

| Sl No | Names of disasters | Year | State/Area | No of people killed | No of people displaced/affected |
|---|---|---|---|---|---|
| 1 | Himalayan Flash Flood | June, 2013 | Uttarakhand | 5,700 | NA |
| 2 | Cyclone Aila | July, 2009 | West Bengal | 149 (in India) | 3 50 000 (in India) |
| 3 | Kosi floods | Aug, 2008 | Bihar | 527 | 3.32 Million |
| 4 | Kashmir earthquake | Oct, 2005 | Kashmir | 1,360(in India) | 3.5 Million(Total) |
| 5 | Maharashtra Floods | July, 2005 | Maharashtra | 1,094 | NA |
| 6 | India Ocean Tsunami | Dec, 2004 | Tamil Nadu, Andhra Pradesh, Kerala & Pondicherry | 10,749 (in India) | 2.79 Million |
| 7 | Bihar flood | July, 2004 | Bihar | 885 | 21.2 Million |
| 8 | Bhuj Earthquakes | Jan, 2001 | Gujarat | 25,000 | 6.3 Million |
| 9 | Odisha Super Cyclone | Oct, 1999 | Odisha | 15,000 | 1.67 Million |
| 10 | Latur Earthquakes | Sept, 1993 | Maharashtra | 9,748 | 30,000 (injured) |

*Sources:* Wikipedia, prevention.net and bostjanbb.hubpages.com/hub/ Worlds-worst-natural-disasters & Ministry of Home Affairs, Government of India.

During the year 2014-15, twenty one states have reported damage due to various kinds of natural disasters such as cyclone, flood, earthquake, etc. Total number of people killed during this period is 1674, cattle perished are 92180, houses damaged are 725390 and 26.72 lakh hectare of cropped areas is affected.

The impacts of natural hazards are more devastating on the life and property of people of India than other parts of the world because of its socio-economic and political conditions and traditional social value system (Asia Pacific Disaster Report, 2010). Unfortunately the past records of disaster management in India demonstrate its failure in many fronts such as relief-centric approach; inadequate early warning system; lack of pre-disaster preparedness; less emphasis on disaster mitigation; inadequate and slow relief; slow rehabilitation; lack of co-ordination; failure to address human rights violation; etc. The measures taken so far by the central and various state governments to deal with disaster and the manner of their execution as brought out in the last few disasters are not in conformity with the international standards and good practices. In addition to the mismanagement in relief distribution and rehabilitation, all too often, human rights abuses have been reported in Indian Ocean Tsunami of 2004, Kashmir earthquake of 2005, Koshi River flood of 2008, Himalayan Flash Flood of 2013 etc. One of the major limitations of disaster management in India is that it is still dominated by the state disaster management machineries and as a result community participation is very poor. The local government (PRIs) at the grass roots level has not been activated to promote community based disaster preparedness (CBDP) and management.

Like other societies, the marginalised, poor, women and lower castes in this part of the world suffer more than the upper class and caste privileged people during and after disaster. The social group most vulnerable to disasters has been identified to be the Dalits-the lower caste people (also known as untouchables or scheduled castes) and women. Humanitarian assistance in past has been provided disproportionately in favor of relatively advantaged groups than the marginalised and poor (Mohan, N and et al, 2005 and Mathai-Luke, 2008). In a number of situations it has been reported that humanitarian actors (both international and domestic) and state agencies were often ignorant of the specific needs of Dalits and other poor and disadvantaged groups (AIDMI and Brookings, 2009, Mohan, Narrayan, Deepu and Rozario, 2005, Narasimhan, 2003 and Batra and Chaudhry, 2005).

## THE DEVELOPMENT OF AN INTEGRATED AND HOLISTIC APPROACH

Only after the widespread devastations witnessed during the Indian Ocean Tsunami of 2004, Indian state has been proactive in developing national policies of disaster management and shifting the emphasis from 'charity and relief-centric approach' to an integrated and holistic approach towards sustainable development. In the present discourse of Disaster Management in India, efforts are being made particularly under the supervision of Government of India to address all necessary elements of the cycle of disaster management such as prevention, mitigation, preparedness, response, relief and rehabilitation. It is a fact to be noted that the institutional and financial arrangements that have evolved till date at national, state and local level under the Disaster Management Act of 2005 are still in the process of consolidation. Ironically, community based disaster management and involvement of local governments (PRIs) are yet to be brought to the mainstream of disaster management. Most importantly the human rights perspective is still missing in the discourse of disaster management in India. The humanitarian actors including state agencies are still guided by the traditional approach and methods because of administrative convenience, unwillingness to take up inherent challenges posed by rights perspective, etc.

As per the provisions of federalism of Indian Constitution is concerned, the primary responsibility of management of disasters (response, relief and rehabilitation) lies with the state government. Every state for this purpose has a Relief Code to regulate distribution of relief and management of rehabilitation process. The Chief Secretary of the state directly supervises the entire process of relief distribution. The relief commissioner at the top and the district collector or district magistrate at the district level used to play the key role in the event of disaster. At the level of Tehsil, the Sub-Divisional Magistrate/officer is responsible to monitor the process of relief distribution. The role of central government is mainly supplementary in nature. It has been playing a great role in providing financial and logistic support such as deployment of para military force, arrangement of relief materials, restoring communication network, etc. However Government of India has been playing a significant role during the last decade in terms of developing disaster management law, policies, guidelines and institutions.

It is unfortunate that India did not have any law and established institutions to address disaster despite being a frequent victim of various natural disasters regularly. The Disaster Management Act was passed and implemented in 2005 only after the divestating Indian Ocean Tsunami of 2004. This Act provides legal, institutional and financial arrangement at national, state and district levels. It aims at promoting disaster management plans and policies and their implementation.

The Disaster Management Act, 2005 established institutions that aim at promoting inclusive and holistic disaster management with greater emphasis on preparedness, prevention and mitigation. Besides addressing all six elements of disaster management, this new approach emphasises on capacity building at all levels; community-based disaster preparedness; consolidation and co-ordination of all initiatives; co-operation with various international and national agencies and multi-sectoral approach. All the institutional mechanisms developed under Disaster Management Act of 2005, work in close harmony and try to achieve the objectives of the new paradigm shift which makes disaster management holistic, integrated and inclusive as against relief-centric.

## Institutionalisation of Disaster Management

The National Disaster Management Authority (NDMA) was set up following the above Act as the apex body in the field of disaster management. The Authority with Prime Minister as its head has the responsibility to formulate policies, plans and guidelines for disaster management and to ensure their implementation throughout the country. The departments of central government and state governments have to formulate their disaster management plans based on these policy and guidelines. A National Executive Committee (NEC) headed by union home secretary has been set up to assist the NDMA and to ensure the compliance of directions issued by central government and guidelines issued by NDMA. Besides preparing national plan for disaster management, the committee co-ordinates all initiatives in the event of disaster.

The state government like the central government has set up State Disaster Management Authority (SDMA) with Chief Minister as its head and State Executive Committee (SEC) with Chief Secretary as its head to assist the above. At the district level, each district has constituted a District Disaster Management Authority (DDMA) with

DM/DC as its head to discharge the responsibility of preparation of disaster plan and its implementation throughout the district. It initiates all necessary measures to meet with the situation of disaster in the line of guidelines of NDMA and SDMA.

National Institute of Disaster Management (NIDM) has been working in collaboration with other research and knowledge-based institutions in the directions of capacity development and creating knowledge regarding disasters and their management. This national level institution since its inception has demonstrated excellence in the field of research on disaster management and creating a national level information base. Above all these, it has been constantly engaged in conducting training programmes for state officials and other stakeholders.

The Disaster Management Act has also instituted National Disaster Response Force (NDRF) for the purpose of providing specialised response at the time of disaster. The Force which consists of 8 battalions works under the control and directions of NDMA. The units of NDRF which are stationed at different strategic locations work in close liaison with the state governments and are always available to them in the event of any disaster situation. In addition to this, these units of NDRF provide training to various stakeholders at different levels. Every state has to develop their State Disaster Response Force (SDRF) in the line of NDRF. Besides these newly developed institutions, the already existing agencies like Armed and para military forces, state police and fire service, civil defence and home guards, NCC, etc are also engaged in the rescue and relief distribution process.

The present paradigm demands an integration of disaster management with finance and planning. Efforts are gradually being taken to mainstream prevention and mitigation measures into central and state level planning and programming. Co-operation from all stakeholders are also being sought in the disaster management process. Planning mechanisms are now giving special attention to disaster risk deduction while formulating plans and programmes. The formulation and implementation of mitigation projects are gradually drawing the attention of central government departments and state governments. The guidelines formulated by NDMA or other research agencies on various type of disasters should form the basis of formation of plans for mitigation projects. These factors are given due weight age by planning bodies while allocating resources. In order to make finance available, National Disaster Response Fund (NDRF) has been set up in 2007 under the control of Home Ministry on the basis of the provisions under section 46 of the Disaster Management Act, 2005. The National Calamity Contingency Fund (NCCF) has been merged with NDRF as per the recommendation of 13th Finance Commission. The Disaster Management Act in its section 47 also contains the provision for a National Disaster Mitigation Fund (NDMF) which is yet to be set up.

## NATIONAL POLICY ON DISASTER MANAGEMENT, 2009

It is for the first time the Government of India on the basis of the provisions of Disaster Management Act, adopted and implemented a National Policy on Disaster in 2009. This policy addresses all aspects of disaster management such as legal, institutional and financial arrangements and gives due importance to prevention, mitigation and preparedness besides rescue, relief and rehabilitation. The vision of this policy is to build a safe and disaster resilient India by developing a holistic, proactive, multi-disaster oriented and technology driven strategy through a culture of prevention, mitigation, preparedness and response. The objectives of the policy are:

- Promoting a culture of prevention, preparedness and resilience at all levels through knowledge, innovation and education.
- Encouraging mitigation measures based on technology, traditional wisdom and environmental sustainability.
- Mainstreaming disaster management into the developmental planning process.
- Establishing institutional and techno-legal framework to create an enabling regulatory environment and a compliance regime.
- Ensuring efficient mechanism for identification, assessment and monitoring of disaster risk.
- Developing contemporary forecasting and early warning systems backed by responsive and failsafe communication with information technology support.
- Promoting a productive partnership with the media to create awareness and contributing towards capacity development.
- Ensuring efficient response and relief with a caring approach towards the needs of the vulnerable sections of the society.
- Undertaking reconstruction as an opportunity to build disaster resilient structures and habitat for ensuring safer living.
- Promoting productive and proactive partnership with media in disaster management.

## Community Based Disaster Management

The responsibility of disaster management in the prevailing discourse primarily lies with central and state government and district administration. But it has been observed in the past disaster situations that these agencies including NGOs have failed (Banerjee & Basu, 2005) to address the problems and needs of disaster-affected people effectively and timely. Due to the lack of timely response, considerable loss of life and property occurs during disaster. However on the contrary it has been witnessed in many disaster situations that the involvement of local communities as well as local government initiatives has made the process of rescue, relief and rehabilitation smooth, effective and human rights friendly. Keeping the above reality and frequent occurrence of various types of disasters in India, in mind it is highly needed to develop Community Based Disaster Preparedness (CBDP) Approach GoI-UNDP, 2009) which operates in the framework of involvement of communities and local governments in the process of disaster management. Therefore the local governments (PRIs and Municipalities) carry special importance in the discourse of disaster management (Pal, 2014). Ironically India still needs to develop an effective community based disaster management through empowering the local governments and increasing their capabilities.

The community based disaster preparedness approaches are increasingly important elements of risk or vulnerability reduction and disaster management strategies. They are associated with a policy trend that values the knowledge and capacities of local people and builds on local resources, including social capital. The CBDP may be instrumental not only in formulating local coping and adaptation strategies, but also in situating them within wider development planning. The primary objective of the concept of community based disaster preparedness (CBDP) is to capacitate communities to prevent, mitigate and cope with disaster effectively. The process of disaster management in the framework of this approach is designed, managed and owned by the community while other state and non-state (INGOs, NGOs and corporate bodies) agencies are just facilitators. The PRIs play significant role in promoting this approach in disaster management. They can establish link through their Gram Sabha and Village Committee on Disaster Management, with the communities and community based organisations (CBOs) and other agencies for facilitating and regulating the activities of Community Based Disaster Preparedness and management.

## PRIs in Disaster Management

It is well established that Indian state in the last decade has been very successful in institutionalising disaster management in terms of developing laws, policies, institutional and financial arrangements dealing with disaster management at different levels. However the role of community (Yudhvir & Sunita, 2013) which is affected and first comes to rescue and relief should not be underestimated. On the contrary the Community Based Disaster Preparedness (CBDP) approach is established to be an effective means in the process of response, mitigation, preparedness, and relief and rehabilitation process.

Participation of people at the bottom level definitely makes disaster management more successful in terms of reducing miseries of disaster-affected people and in promoting and protecting their human rights and dignity. In fact people's participation in disaster management is possible through the grassroots democratic organisations like PRIs and other local government bodies such as municipalities and municipal corporations.

Therefore the most important challenges before the disaster managers are how to effectively involve the PRIs in the disaster management process by developing their capabilities. The PRIs in fact can play a significant role in all stages of disaster management starting from planning to rehabilitation. These institutions have played critical role (Pal, 2014) in the last natural disasters in India. However it is unfortunate that these people's institutions which have got constitutional status and lots of power through 73rd Constitutional Amendment, have not yet got the desired importance (Pal, 2014) in the Disaster Management Act of 2005. Disaster Management following the above discussed paradigm shift needs to be decentralised. In this context, the grassroots democratic institutions like PRIs should be activated and well equipped in the process of management of disasters.

## Why PRIs?

The participation of Panchayti Raj Institutions in disaster management helps in many ways (GOI-UNDP, 2009) in achieving our objective of building a safe and disaster resilient India.

- It is a people's organisation which has a constitutional status. People directly participate through these grassroots democratic institutions in the process of development.

- It makes people involved in the disaster prevention, mitigation, preparedness, and relief and rehabilitation process through social mobilisation.
- The best use of local resources in disaster management is possible through PRIs.
- It can use the traditional wisdom of local communities to complement the modern practices in disaster planning and mitigation.
- It acts as a link between Government, NGOs and Community-based Organisations.
- It makes the implementation of disaster risk reduction programmes more smooth and effective.
- It reduces the practice of depending on government in the event of disasters.
- It brings transparency and accountability in relief distribution and rehabilitation besides making it more effective.
- It promotes the human rights of vulnerable sections (SCs, STs and Women) of the society through their participation in disaster management.

## THE ROLE OF PRI's

The Panchayati Raj Institutions have been playing an active role at the grass roots level in all situation of humanitarian crisis including natural disasters. In fact the representatives of PRIs at all there levels-panchayat, block and district- can play meaningful role in all three stages of disaster management right from the preparatory and planning stage to the stage of long term rehabilitation and reconstruction. They can play leading role (GOI-UNDP, 2009) in all three stages of disaster management – (a) pre-disaster period (b) during the disaster and (c) post-disaster period.

### (a) Pre-disaster Period

The needs of the villagers and local areas in respect to disaster can be better articulated by the people's representatives of the local bodies because of their close proximity to the people (GOI-UNDP, 2009) and their rootedness in the specific local- social-cultural milieu. The PRIs can play a vital role in the disaster-preparedness planning in two ways: Firstly, by making the community involved and by using the local wisdom and Secondly, by integrating measures of disaster risk reduction to the planning of rural development programmes

(Yudhvir and Sunita, 2013). These Panchayati Raj bodies can organise awareness campaign to promote education on the nature of various disasters and preparedness to cope with them among the people who are potentially vulnerable to hazards. The leaders of these local democratic institutions can establish collabration with NGOs and Community Based Organisations (CBOs) while organising pre-disaster preparedness activities. In addition to the above, the identification of resource gaps both manpower and physical and addressing the same through capacity building can also be more accurately done by PRIs. One of the important roles that Gram Panchayat can more effectively play than higher level disaster managers is organising Task Forces and their capacity building. Last but not the least, the leaders of panchayat can better identify the safer places in and around the villages to shift the people, property and livestock in the event of disaster and stock food grains and other necessary items for contingency.

### (b) During Disaster

The role and contribution of PRIs during disaster (GOI-UNDP, 2009) can be seen at different ways. Firstly, at the on-set of disaster, it is the local government and communities that first come to the rescue of the disaster-affected people and to provide them immediate relief before any state agency or non-state humanitarian actors come to the situation. In fact in some remote areas these agencies take days to reach to the help of the people. Secondly, the leaders of the PRIs with the help of the village level workers/volunteers help state administration and humanitarian actors in the rescue and evacuation operation, disposal of dead bodies, distribution of reliefs, constructing temporary shelters, running relief camps, providing medical aid and other assistances, etc. Most importantly, the co-ordination among various agencies, one of the most problematic aspects of disaster management, can be better achieved through the active efforts of local bodies. Thirdly, their involvement makes the relief distribution fair and transparent and thereby prevents violation of any human rights abuses on the basis of caste and gender discrimination.

### (c) Post-disaster Period

The Panchayati Raj bodies also play a crucial role (GOI-UNDP, 2009) in the post disaster management. Assessment of dead persons, livestock and damage to properties, houses and agriculture, etc and identification of victims can be done by the PRIs for the purpose of compensation and rehabilitation. They are in a better position to formulate the rehabilitation and reconstruction programmes for construction of houses, rebuilding of infrastructure and revival of economy, keeping the local conditions and culture in consideration and by using the local resources. In addition to this local government bodies can monitor the implementation of long term rehabilitation and reconstruction projects besides extending help whenever required for their effective and smooth implementation. The participation of people in the post-disaster management process can be encouraged by the leaders of the PRIs. The people's representatives at various levels of Panchyatiraj system can mobilise special funds for the construction of disaster resilient infrastructure. Lastly their involvement makes the rehabilitation just, equitable and friendly to all the sections of the society.

## LINKING DISASTER MANAGEMENT WITH DEVELOPMENT PLANS AND PROCESS

The paradigm shift from relief-centric to a holistic and integrated approach needs linking disaster management with the sustainable development planning (Pal, 2014). In this direction PRIs provide institutional arrangement at a grass roots level by linking the disaster risk reduction activities with the district, block and panchayat level plan. According to Article 243G of the Indian Constitution, Panchayati Raj institutions have been empowered to prepare plans for economic development and social justice in regards to 29 subjects listed in 11$^{th}$ Schedule. Indian constitution for this purpose also provides a provision for planning machineries for all three levels of Panchayati Raj system. The District Planning Committee (DPC) which is responsible to consolidate the plans prepared by the panchayats and municipalities and to prepare the development plan for the district as a whole, consists of representatives (not less than four-fifth of the total members) of panchyats and municipalities. The participation of people's representatives in the plan process ensures the integration of disaster prevention, mitigation, relief and rehabilitation into the development planning (pal, 2014).

### Addressing Vulnerability in Disaster Management

Natural disasters make the vulnerable and marginalised sections of the society more vulnerable by exasperating the existing socio-economic inequalities and discriminations (McEntire, 2011) on the basis of caste, race, religion, gender, age, wealth and disabilities, etc.

Caste-based social exclusion and gender discrimination make Dalits (the untouchable castes) and women the most vulnerable section respectively in the Indian society during and after disaster. The caste and gender based stereotypes and prejudices against Dalits and women are aggravated during and after disaster. Consequently they are subjected to various kinds of human rights abuses (Kent, 2011) in the form of unequal treatment, discrimination, practice of untouchability, physical and sexual violence, etc and are deprived of a just relief and rehabilitation. The World Disaster Report, 2007 observed, "hidden, ignored and simply invisible, the most vulnerable-are those potentially in the greatest need- are rarely, if ever, at the forefront of aid operations".

In the above context, PRIs play a crucial role in terms of protecting their human rights and dignity. It has been widely observed in the past disaster situations in India that the state disaster machineries and other humanitarian actors have not given due importance either intentionally or for practical consideration to the issue of social vulnerability in regards to SCs, STs and Women while planning and executing disaster management programmes. However the 73rd constitutional amendments have ensured participation of these people in the management of local development activities by providing reservation to them in the PRIs. The presence and participation of the representatives of these communities in the decision-making in PRIs help them protect their interest and rights against discrimination and exploitation in the context of disaster (Pal, 2014). The Panchayati Raj institutions can very well address the social vulnerability by providing great scope for these communities in the decision-making process of disaster management.

## Tokenism to Pro-activism

The PRIs as has been argued and established has the potential to help the local communities and particularly the disaster-affected population developing their own plan and strategies of disaster prevention and mitigation and managing the relief distribution and rehabilitation. The panchayat bodies can play a leading role in organising and motivating the communities in building a disaster resilient society through developing their coping capabilities. And most importantly a sustained effort in this direction will not only reduce the dependency of the people on the government and other national and international humanitarian actors but also help mobilise sizeable resources locally to counter disasters and reduce the burden of the government to a great extent. Lastly it promotes transparency and accountability in disaster management and protects the human rights of all including the most vulnerable sections of the society. The discourse of participatory or community based disaster management invites a pro-active role by the panchayati raj institutions and their members.

The capability building of the PRIs needs to be given priority in order to make them discharge their responsibilities effectively and on a sustainable basis. However PRIs have been assigned little importance by the disaster managers both in the Disaster Management Act of 2005 and other disaster policies and programmes. The panchayati raj bodies in order to play a pro-active role in regards to disaster management needs all types of adequate resources -financial, human and technical etc. Therefore the Government of India and state governments should try to decentralise more powers to PRIs regarding disaster management. To make them achieve the objectives of community based disaster preparedness (CBDP), emphasis must be given to the capacity-building of these institutions in terms of financial, infrastructural and man power assistance and proper training of their representatives. The National Disaster Management Authority (NDMA) should pay attention to the above matters and formulate special programmes for the capacity-building of these institutions at all three levels.

The leaders of the PRIs should be trained to evolve a community based disaster preparedness and management plan. It is very important that the local democratic bodies should try to mobilise community to the maximum extent possible to make them participate in the activities relating to disaster management. They also should elicit the support and co-operation of the existing community based organisations (CBOs) and NGOs in the management of disaster planning, relief and rehabilitation. It is also the responsibility of the leaders of the local bodies to develop their own strategies based on specific socio-cultural practices for promoting CBDP rather than excessively depending on the government support and assistance from humanitarian actors. Keeping in view the human rights violation during and after disaster, the PRIs are expected to adopt an inclusive approach as far as gender and caste vulnerability is concerned. Lastly, to make the system work in a transparent and accountable manner, it is highly suggested that PRIs must evolve the Gram Sabha as a powerful institution of people's control and social audit.

## References

All India Disaster Management Institute (AIDMI) & Brooking Institute. (2009). "Protecting and Promoting Rights in Natural Disasters in South Asia: Prevention and Response", Retrieved from www.brookings.edu/n/media/ filestre/reports/2009/ 0701_natural_disasters.pdf.

Asia Pacific Disaster Report, (2010). Retrieved from www.unescap.org/ idd/ pubs/Asia-pacific-Disaster-Report-2010.pdf.

Banarjee, P. & Basu, S. (2005). Indian symposium review tsunami response, Forced Migration Review, special issue, tsunami learning from humanitarian response.

Bosher, L. (2007). *Social and International Elements of Vulnerability*: The case of South India, Bethesda, USA: Academic Press.

Centre for Human Rights and Global Justice and Human Rights Watch, (2007). Caste discrimination against Dalits or so called untouchables in India, report presented in the seventieth session of the committee on the elimination of Social Discrimination.

Cohen, R., & Bradly, M. (2010). Disasters and Displacement: Gaps in Protection. *International Humanitarian Legal Studies.* 1*(1),* 95-142.

Disaster Management Act (2005).

GoI-UNDP Disaster Risk Management Programme 2002-2009.

Handmer, J. (2001). Human Rights and Disasters: Does a rights approach reduce vulnerability? Retrieved from www.radixonline.org.

Hyogo Framework for Action 2005-2015: Building the Resilience of Nations and Communities to Disasters. Retrieved from www.unisdr.org/ 2005/wcdr/.../Hyogo-framework-for-action-english.pdf.

IASC (2006) Operational Guidelines on the Protection of Persons in Situations of Natural Disasters. Retrieved from http:// www.brookings.edu/reports/2006/11.natural disasters_aspx.

Kaelin, W. (2011). A Human Right –Based Approach to Building Resilience to Natural Disasters. Retrieved from www.brookings.edu/papers/ 2011/0606_disasters_human_rights-Kalin.aspx

Kapur Anu. ((2010), Vulnerable India: A Geografical Study of Disasters, Sage Publications, New Delhi, pp 232-33.

Kent, G. (2011). Rights-Based Disaster Planning. Retrieved from www.radixonline.org

Lewis, H. (2006). Human Rights and Natural Disaster: The Indian Ocean Tsunami, *Human Rights,* 33 *(4),* 12-16.

Mathai-Luke, R. (2008). HIV and the Displaced: Deconstructing Policy Implementation in Tsunami in Tamil Nadu, 32 Refugee Watch at 46-47.

McEntire, D.A. (2011). Understanding and Reducing Vulnerability: from the approach of liabilities and capabilities, *Disaster Prevention and Management,* 20 *(3),* 294-313..

Mehta, L. (2001). Reflections on the Kutch earthquake. *Economic and Political Weekly,* 36*(31),* 2931-36.

Ministry of Home Affairs (2009). National Policy on Disaster Management, Government of India.

Ministry of Home Affairs (2014). Annual Report, Government of India.

Mohan, N. Narrain, A., Nitin, R. Deepu & Rozario, C. (2005). Relief and rehabilitation: ensuring inclusion. *Economic and Political Weekly,* 40*(15),* 1493-95.

Naidu, B. R.(1989), Economic Consequences of 1977 Cyclone in Andhra Pradesh, Sri Venkateswara University, Tirupati.

Narasimhan, S. (2003). Lessons from Latur: A Decade after the Earthquake. *Economic and Political Weekly,* 38 *(45),* 4730-32.

Narasimhan, S. (2003). Lessons from Latur: A Decade after the Earthquake. *Economic and Political Weekly,* 38 *(45),* 4730-32.

Pal, M. (2014), Panchayat and Disaster Management: Future Perspective, *Mainstream,* 11*(42),* October 11, 45-53.

Pandey, R. K. (2006), Participation in Practice and Disaster Management: Experience Uttaranchal (India), *Disaster Prevention and Management,* 14*(3),* 67-78.

Praksh L. (2001). Gujarat earthquake and after. *Economic and Political Weekly,* 36*(11),* 908-10.

Pyles, L. (2006). Neoliberalism, INGO practices and sustainable disaster recovery: a post-Katrina case study. *Community Development Journal,* 46*(2),* 168-80.

Smith, K. (1996). Environmental hazards: Assessing risk and reducing disaster, Roultledge.

World Disaster Report (2007). Retrieved from www.ifrc.org/Global/Publications/disasters/WDR/ WDR2007-English.pdf

Yudhvir & Sunita (2013), Role of Panchayati Raj Institutions in Disaster management, *Asian Journal of Multidimensional Research,* 2*(6),* June, 76-85.